The Freedom of the Streets

Gender and American Culture

Coeditors
Thadious M. Davis
Linda K. Kerber

Editorial Advisory Board
Nancy Cott
Cathy N. Davidson
Jane Sherron De Hart
Sara Evans
Mary Kelley
Annette Kolodny
Wendy Martin
Nell Irvin Painter
Janice Radway
Barbara Sicherman

THE FREEDOM OF THE STREETS

WORK, CITIZENSHIP, AND SEXUALITY
IN A GILDED AGE CITY

SHARON E. WOOD

THE UNIVERSITY OF NORTH CAROLINA PRESS
Chapel Hill and London

© 2005 The University of North Carolina Press
All rights reserved

Designed by Lou Robinson
Set in Bembo by Keystone Typesetting, Inc.
Manufactured in the United States of America

The paper in this book meets the guidelines for permanence and durability of the Committee on Production Guidelines for Book Longevity of the Council on Library Resources.

Library of Congress Cataloging-in-Publication Data
Wood, Sharon E.
  The freedom of the streets : work, citizenship, and sexuality in a gilded age city / Sharon E. Wood.
    p. cm. — (Gender and American culture)
  Includes bibliographical references and index.
ISBN 0-8078-2939-0 (cloth: alk. paper)
ISBN 0-8078-5601-0 (pbk.: alk. paper)
  1. Women—Iowa—Davenport—Social conditions—19th century. 2. Women—Employment—Iowa—Davenport—History—19th century. 3. Prostitution—Iowa—Davenport—History—19th century. 4. Sex role—Iowa—Davenport—History—19th century. I. Title. II. Gender & American culture.
HQ1439.D8W66 2005
305.42'09777'6909034—dc22
2004019083

Frontispiece: "On the way to the park for bird-watching, Davenport, Iowa" (State Historical Society of Iowa–Iowa City).

cloth 09 08 07 06 05 5 4 3 2 1
paper 09 08 07 06 05 5 4 3 2 1

THIS BOOK WAS DIGITALLY PRINTED

*For my father,
Lee Wood,
and in memory of my mother,
Roberta Forest Wood,
1927–1996*

CONTENTS

	Acknowledgments	xi
	Introduction: The Belva Lockwood Club	1
1	Women in the City: Law, Reputation, and Geography	14
2	Women's Citizenship and the Problem of Employment	30
3	A Place in the City: The Working Woman's Lend a Hand Club	48
4	Lives without Choices: Prostitution as Employment	79
5	The Police Matron Campaign and the Reform of Urban Environments	102
6	Sporting Men and Little Girls	132
7	Making the City Safe for White Men: Regulated Prostitution	158
8	Protecting Men by Reforming Girls: Good Shepherd Homes	186
9	Women, Men, and the Businesses of Bucktown	213
	Conclusion: The Popular Young Lady in Business Life	245
	Notes	259
	Bibliography	285
	Index	305

ILLUSTRATIONS & MAPS

Illustrations

Ted Neuhaus costumed for Belva Lockwood Club parade, c. 1888	2
Rock Island and Davenport, c. 1872	11
Second Street east of Brady, c. 1888	25
Residents and staff of the Clarissa Cook Home, c. 1900	50
Lettie Meacham, c. 1880	55
Dr. Jennie McCowen, c. 1895	58
Brady Street looking north, c. 1882	63
Lend a Hand club membership card	69
Perry Street, looking north, c. 1888	103
Police chief Frank Kessler, c. 1900	115
Bird's-eye view of Davenport, 1888	117
The *Verne Swain*	141
Perry street, looking south, c. 1884	142
Mayor Henry Vollmer, c. 1900	165
Police matron Sarah Hill, c. 1900	167
Prostitute's health certificate	169
Good Shepherd Convent, Omaha, c. 1920	205
W. W. Hovey's saloon business card	220
The Beauchaine residence on Brady Street	224
Second Street, looking east from Harrison Street, c. 1902	230
Second Street, looking west from Brady Street, c. 1907	230
Advertisement for Brick Munro's Pavilion	233

Maps

1. Homes and workplaces of Lend a Hand members, 1888–89	82
2. Brothels and assignation houses, 1888–89	83
3. Brothels, 1895	216

ACKNOWLEDGMENTS

WRITING A BOOK IS A SUBTLE PLEASURE, but writing acknowledgments is a joy. Looking back on all the people who have contributed to this book's completion leaves me heartened and humbled. So many friends, colleagues, and perfect strangers have given of their time and wisdom that I fervently hope the final product lives up to their expectations. It is an honor to acknowledge them here.

My first thanks go to Linda Kerber, who effortlessly made the transition from dissertation director to friend. Her faith in me and in this project have meant more than she suspects. She has read and commented on many drafts, and her advice on the practice of history has always been welcome and wise. I truly cannot count the number of times she and Dick Kerber have opened their home to me, and their kindness and hospitality have made visits to Iowa like visits home.

Lauren Rabinovitz and Shel Stromquist were also part of this project from the beginning. Shel was the first one to teach me about the possibilities of social history, and Lauren has always challenged me to think more clearly about gender and more theoretically about leisure. She has also reminded me that leisure should not be limited to the realm of theory, a lesson graciously reviewed whenever she and Greg Easley welcomed me as their guest during my research trips through Iowa.

Indeed, I have relied on the hospitality of many friends while researching this book. Florence Babb, Sandy and Don Heistad, Mac Marshall and Margery Wolf, Margaret Richardson, Andrew Sandoval-Strausz, and my sister, Sheila Wood, and her husband, Eric Seaberg, have all been generous and thoughtful hosts.

In spite of that long list of hosts, much of the research for this book was, by necessity, long distance. Telephone and e-mail put me in touch with librarians, clerks, and volunteers at historical societies, courthouses, and public libraries all over the country as I tracked down clues and followed a few red herrings. Although I cannot name them all, I honor them all.

The efforts of the special collections staff at the Davenport Public Library made this book possible. Amy Groskopf, Mary Ann Moore, Sarah Wesson, Karen O'Connor, and Mary Herr have been patient, thorough, and enthusiastic in answering my endless queries. They became so familiar with this project that they starting sending me newspaper clippings and court documents they discovered on their own, and many of these items made their way into the book.

At the State Historical Society in Iowa City, Linda Brown-Link in the library, Mary Bennett in manuscripts, and Marv Bergman and Ginalie Swaim of the publications division have been equally treasured as friends and advisers to this project. Richard, Lord Acton, with whom I often shared a table at the historical society, offered welcome advice, inspiration, and insight into the Forty-eighters.

In Davenport—or, rather, the Quad Cities—Bill Roba shared his knowledge of local history, Lisa Mohr gave me a memorable tour, and the owners of the extremely rare *Hell at Midnight in Davenport* (who prefer not to be named) kindly permitted me to examine their copy.

Phyllis Field and Stacy Cordery both took time to look at local history sources and answer questions from a historian they had never met. Leslie Schwalm and Dan Goldstein generously shared their research, and Alison Kibler spent an entire day helping me photocopy hundreds of pages of crumbling police dockets. At the Provincial Archives of the Sisters of the Good Shepherd in St. Paul, Minnesota, Sister Thomas Nestor willingly scouted the archives for records she was not entirely sure existed. She remains memorable as the only archivist who ever brought me ice cream while I worked.

As the project entered the writing stage, I learned much from the thoughtful responses of colleagues in the Nineteenth-Century Group at the University of Nebraska, Lincoln (especially Emily Greenwald and Tim Mahoney), the Social History Workshop at the University of Chicago, and the Urban History Seminar at the Chicago Historical Society. A timely and welcome fellowship at the Charles Warren Center at Harvard gave me access to several wonderful libraries, time to write, and a group of terrific and helpful colleagues, including Laurel Ulrich, Claudia Goldin, John Bezis-Selfa, Leon Fink, Sue Levine, and Karen Sawislak.

Fellowships from the University Committee for Research at the University of Nebraska at Omaha and the Charles and Mary Caldwell Martin Fund for History helped with travel to archives. I also thank my colleagues in the history department at UNO—especially Bill Pratt, Jerry Simmons, Tom Buchanan, Harl Dalstrom, and Mike Tate—for their interest and support. At the University of Chicago, Claudia Schmidt assisted with German translations, and Michael Creswell checked my French, as did Bruce Garver at UNO.

A number of people read and commented on all or part of the manuscript, including Tom Buchanan, Cathleen Cahill, Ken Cmiel, Barbara Hanrahan, Ann Keating, Sue Levine, Andrew Sandoval-Strausz, and Allen Steinberg. Their comments have rescued me from more than one mire of error and awkwardness, but I am certain I have still strayed from time to time. The fault is mine, not theirs. I am especially grateful to the readers for the University of North Carolina Press—Sally Deutsch, Patricia Cline Cohen, and Ruth Alexander—whose thoughtful and chal-

Acknowledgments

lenging reports prodded me to rethink and reorganize parts of this book. My editors, Kate Torrey and Ron Maner, have been patient, thoughtful, and very wise. I thank them.

Terri Snyder and Kathy Jellison have long been the best of friends and colleagues, equally ready to commiserate or to celebrate. Their work is my inspiration, their friendship my comfort.

Sheila Wood and Carol Wood Brooks embody the best meanings of "sisterhood," and my Great-Aunt Frances Forest Frymoyer always let me know how delighted she was that I shared her interest in old books, remnant prairies, and the history of ordinary people. Her death in 2003, at the age of ninety-eight, opened a rift with my own past that will never be mended.

No one has given more to this project than John Hankey. Since coming into my life, he has proposed romantic getaways to the Davenport Public Library, side trips to Havana (Illinois) and Lebanon (Ohio), and even pitched in at the microfilm reader when time got short. He trolled eBay for illustrations and searched antiquarian bookstores for rare and unexpected sources. He also shared his sharp editorial eye and his encyclopedic knowledge of American history. This book, and my life, are immeasurably richer because of him.

Finally, I thank my parents. My mother, Roberta Forest Wood, grew up in another Mississippi River city (Clinton—or more properly—Lyons, Iowa), and from her I first understood how complicated and fascinating these places could be. She started me on the way to this book by teaching me to read, to argue, and to see the history embedded in objects and landscapes. She read an early draft eagerly, but she did not live to see it finished. When my father, Lee Wood, remarried, he made his new wife, Terri Franklin, read my dissertation. I knew then how much he loved me and how much she loved him. They should have waited for the book.

The Freedom of the Streets

INTRODUCTION:
THE BELVA LOCKWOOD CLUB

IN THE LATE FALL OF 1888, just a few days before Election Day, thirty men dressed in gowns and bonnets paraded by torchlight through the streets of Davenport, Iowa. Led by a regimental band and a Civil War veteran, the parade burlesqued the presidential campaign of Washington, D.C., attorney and suffragist Belva Lockwood. A youthful attorney, William Chamberlin, played the part of Lockwood, riding in a carriage behind the marchers with library janitor Jacob Busey, who also wore women's clothes. Shortly after eight in the evening, along streets thronged with a few thousand cheering onlookers, the marchers paraded down Brady Street in the heart of the business district. Then, turning west, they wound their way through the prosperous and respectable part of downtown, finally circling back to end at Brady and Fourth. Under a large transparency reading "Protection-Belva," the glee club sang, "We Will Vote for Belva." Then Busey rose from his seat, "smoothed down the wrinkles in his mother hubbard gown," and introduced Lockwood to the waiting crowd. Chamberlin, warming to his part, proclaimed the downfall of the old political parties and urged women to claim the ballot. I propose, she concluded, "to win this campaign or 'bust.' "[1]

Introduction

Ted Neuhaus, a hardware wholesaler, models the dress he wore in the Belva Lockwood parade, c. 1888. (From W. L. Purcell, *Them Was the Good Old Days in Davenport, Scott County, Iowa*, 1922.)

On one level, this was straightforward parody, with cross-dressing men lampooning Lockwood, who ran for president in 1884 and 1888 as the candidate of the Equal Rights Party. But the symbols deployed and the political context made for complicated satire, especially in Davenport, where the city was four years into a policy of civil disobedience on a grand scale. The saloons that lined the streets of downtown, providing lunch, leisure, and sociability for men, were all illegal. In 1884, the Iowa legislature prohibited the manufacture or sale of all alcoholic beverages, including wine and beer. That same year, Davenport elected its first German American mayor. Democrat Ernst Claussen declared that an elected official might have a duty to enforce the law, but "it isn't his duty to make himself a smelling committee." The *Davenport Democrat* lent its voice to open defiance, pronouncing Prohibition a failure and urging the city to collect license fees from the 130 saloons still operating. Over the next few years, the city did just that. By the early 1890s, the number of saloons had grown to more than 200, and Mayor Claussen had been reelected to a total of seven terms. Davenport's refusal to enforce the Prohibition law was no secret. In 1887, Prohibition governor William Larrabee directed Iowa's ninety-nine counties to report the number of illegal saloons operating in each. Scott County was one of three to thumb their noses at the governor, declaring they simply did not know. Given that Davenport was issuing licenses to illegal saloons, that answer was less than credible.[2]

To members of Davenport's German community, resistance to Iowa's Prohibition law recalled the Forty-eighters' struggle for a united Germany, universal male suffrage, and freedom of speech. Years later, historian and editor August Richter reported that Germans jokingly called their Prohibition-insurgent home on the Mississippi "die Frei Staat Scott," deliberately echoing the rallying cry for "die Frei Staat Schleswig-Holstein." The link was more than just rhetorical: Mayor Ernst Claussen was the son of Hans Reimer Claussen, a leader in Schleswig-Holstein's campaign for independence from Denmark and later a member of the Frankfurt Parliament that drew up a constitution for a united Germany. In old age, the elder Claussen regained his reputation as a freedom fighter when he discovered the legal "technicality" that led the Iowa Supreme Court to overturn an 1882 Prohibition amendment to Iowa's constitution.[3]

By 1888, Davenport citizens who opposed Prohibition must have felt besieged but defiant. Pressure on the governor and legislature in Des Moines to enforce the state law against Davenport's saloons came from both within Iowa and around the nation. In the election-year politics of 1888, women played vital public roles. J. Ellen Foster, an attorney from Clinton, had been a key Republican strategist in the successful 1882 campaign to put Prohibition in Iowa's constitution—the same provision H. R. Claussen persuaded the court to overturn. In 1888 Foster was president of the National Women's Republican Association and helped draft the temperance plank of the GOP platform. Women were even more prominent in the Prohibition and Home Protection Party, which took its name in part from the motto of the Woman's Christian Temperance Union (WCTU). Women served on the party's national committee, and some years as many as 30 percent of convention delegates were women. Nationally, Lockwood's 1888 campaign received far less attention than her first run in 1884, but Iowans had a particular reason for focusing on Lockwood in 1888: the Equal Rights Party convention that nominated her took place in Des Moines in May of that year. By focusing their satire on the one woman who dared to run for president, these Davenport men expressed their anger at all women who threatened their refuge in the city center by working publicly on behalf of Prohibition.[4]

Though no newspaper reported it as such, the Lockwood parade was probably the project of Davenport's Democrats. Not only was William Chamberlin the son of a Democratic officeholder, but the Democrats were the only party in 1888 ready to skewer the slogan "Protection." The Republicans—the party behind Iowa's Prohibition law—made "protection" for American industry a major campaign issue by backing a high tariff. The Prohibition and Home Protection Party incorporated the word into its name. And while the real Belva Lockwood backed a modest tariff, her association with the temperance and woman suffrage movements meant that opponents were unlikely to bother with fine distinctions about her political platform. The word "protection" carried more than one meaning in 1888, but each valence linked it to temperance and woman suffrage.[5]

For women in the WCTU, "home protection" had justified their increasingly successful forays into American public life as they championed not just Prohibition but police matrons, censorship of theatricals, and a dozen other reforms. But what women considered "protection," some men saw as assaults on their prerogatives and pleasures. Drinking and the rituals of sociability that accompanied it were not the only pastimes threatened by "protection." Just two years earlier, the Iowa assembly, responding to lobbying by the WCTU and others, rewrote Iowa's rape law as part of an effort to curtail the entry of young girls into prostitution. The legislature raised from ten to thirteen the age at which a girl's consent to sexual intercourse shielded a man from prosecution for rape. Commonly called the "age of consent," advocates liked to call it the "age of protection." But opponents argued that raising the age of consent would render a man "liable to imprisonment for life for yielding to the solicitation of a prostitute," since prostitutes were often very young. What protected girls endangered men and threatened a well-established form of male leisure.[6]

In the Belva Lockwood Club parade, humor veiled hostility. Cross-dressing can sometimes be a strategy for celebrating androgyny, but in the nineteenth century it more often emphasized the physical appearance of sexual difference. Men who looked ridiculous in women's clothing proved the absurdity of stepping out of place, of becoming men-women—precisely the charge leveled at women who left their "sphere" to enter politics and public life. Satirists delighted in cartoons of cigar-puffing women in trousers, and an 1891 episode in Moline, just across the Mississippi River in Illinois, made a similar point about local women's politics. There, when the local WCTU protested a traveling burlesque show, they were themselves burlesqued. "When the curtain went up a number of sylphs in pink tights were revealed," reported the *Davenport Democrat*. "Then came two less shapely forms introduced as the WCTU ladies who signed the petition to ... have the show suppressed. The names were given." Their "exceedingly scrawny figures" belonged to two men in dresses, and the audience roared with delight at their revenge.[7]

But the Belva Lockwood parody in Davenport went even further. Both Busey and Chamberlin wore not merely women's garments but the Mother Hubbard, a loose gown of gathered fabric falling from a round yoke, worn without a corset. Originally a dressing gown intended for home wear, by the 1880s the Mother Hubbard had become the costume of prostitutes. In some cities, any woman appearing on the street in a Mother Hubbard was subject to arrest. By impersonating Lockwood in prostitute's clothing, Chamberlin and his companions associated women's activism not only with gender transgression but with sexual promiscuity. The women who sought to protect girls from prostitution became the equivalent of prostitutes.[8]

If the gender symbolism of the parade was elaborate, the racial dimension was enigmatic. Jake Busey, the library janitor who rode alongside Chamberlin, was a former slave from Kentucky, popular with men's organizations in Davenport as a singer and entertainer. He was also a graduate of Davenport's high school who had spent time in the late 1870s in Tennessee and Kentucky teaching in black schools. Parade organizers may have intended his presence to boost the carnival element of the parade, signifying the disruption of race hierarchies in the same way that cross-dressing disrupted gender hierarchies. On the other hand, they may have had a more specific reference in mind. Belva Lockwood's vice presidential candidate was Alfred Love, a white man, but Lockwood was not the first woman to run for president. Sixteen years earlier, Victoria Woodhull had declared her candidacy, choosing as her running mate a dismayed Frederick Douglass. Busey's presence might have been meant to evoke that campaign and with it Woodhull's scandalous reputation. Like the Mother Hubbard gown, a reference to Woodhull associated Lockwood and other political women with sexual license. But if Busey stood for Douglass, his feminine apparel added a perplexing layer of meaning. His skirts may simply have suggested that a man who supported woman's rights—as Douglass certainly had—emasculated himself or may have reflected the organizers' sense of appropriate race and gender symbolism: a dignified black man in coat and trousers seated next to a white man in a frilly gown and bonnet confused the message. Or perhaps Busey simply thought that dressing up looked like good fun and did not want to be left out. As the *Tribune* reported under the headline, "Belva's Bustle," the whole club cross-dressed.[9]

Victoria Woodhull claimed Douglass as her running mate in 1876 because suffragists of the 1860s and 1870s linked black suffrage and woman suffrage as kindred calls for justice and because Douglass had long been a supporter of woman's rights. But by 1888, some would have seen Busey's presence as a symbol of the danger of giving civil rights to African Americans. In a world turned upside down by women who challenged the saloon and demanded the vote, white men would lose their dominance and "amalgamation" would become the order of the day. In the South, the crisis in white manhood lead to lynchings, terrorism, and the constitutional disfranchisement of the black population. In Davenport, with its tiny black population and its defiance of the state Prohibition law, Jake Busey stood for the unholy alliance of African American voters and Prohibitionists within the Republican Party.[10]

According to the *Democrat-Gazette*, the Belva Lockwood parade attracted the largest audience of any parade during the fall campaign season. The *Tribune* estimated the crowd at eight thousand, noting that "large delegations came from across the river." Humor and novelty no doubt were strong draws, but the parade may also have expressed the sentiments of many Davenport men. In 1888, women were taking increasingly prominent roles in politics and public life, threatening the comfortable order that protected men's pleasures. If the parade's symbolism was in any way ambiguous, newspaper coverage of municipal politics in Kansas that year made the point more than clear. In Kansas, readers could discover, granting women municipal suffrage had led to the closing of billiard halls, the removal of spittoons from city council chambers, the end of sales of hard cider, and the imposition of strict morals. The town of Oskaloosa, Kansas, took on "a henpecked air and the male citizens have an appearance of weakness." The real Belva Lockwood posed no threat to Davenport's men, but William Chamberlin in a Mother Hubbard embodied their anxiety: that as local women demanded a greater role in the public life of the city, they would jeopardize not just men's pleasures but the sense of manliness men derived from the rituals of masculine leisure.[11]

The men who marched out on that chilly October night never doubted for a moment their right to turn the streets into a site of political expression. After all, political parades had a long and honored history in the United States, and most white men in the 1880s took for granted their right as citizens to move freely along the streets of any city. Yet when the parade turned west instead of east from Brady Street, the marchers acknowledged that all streets were not hospitable to all citizens. East of Brady Street, Davenport tolerated brothels. Many men in the crowd would have felt uneasy bringing their wives and children into the district known as Bucktown to watch a parade, and many women would have been uncomfortable as well. So even as they burlesqued women in politics by dressing in the garb of prostitutes, the men of the Belva Lockwood Club literally turned their backs on the real prostitutes who worked in Davenport. The parade route acknowledged the city's gendered geography: respectable women to the west, prostitutes to the east. Men, of course, chose their own paths.[12]

Gendered geography was by no means unique to Davenport. It had been characteristic of American cities for nearly half a century. By the 1870s and 1880s, however, middle-class women began to demand the same freedom of the streets that men took for granted. Defying the expectation that they would confine themselves to the parks, galleries, and public spaces set apart for them, women moved visibly into established professions such as medicine and law and created new professions such as nursing and social work. Clerking in stores and office work became increasingly feminized as well, and more and more middle-class women and girls began working and living downtown along the streets where prostitutes plied their trade. These middle-class workers discovered what poor and working-class women had known all along: when women intruded into streets considered men's territory, they compromised their safety and respectability. The loitering man from the middle class was a flaneur, taking pleasure from his power to observe the city and discover its secrets, but the loitering woman was merely a streetwalker, the object of men's aggression or police restraint.[13]

For both men and women, respectability was a kind of capital: the greater the investment, the richer the social and employment opportunities. But a woman's reputation was more fragile than a man's, its loss more devastating. Nineteenth-century Americans revealed their view of the matter in the language they employed: a "ruined" man was a bankrupt who might recover and resume his place in society, but a "ruined" woman had no recourse but the brothel. Reputation was something no woman risked lightly.

At the same time, women's employment was beginning to take on a political significance. In the 1850s and 1860s, as the United States became increasingly industrialized, men who saw their future as wage earners, not masters, began to articulate a claim to political rights based on their identity as workers. By the Civil War era, women were beginning to adopt the same position and the question of women's paid employment became a full-fledged social problem. Caroline H. Dall, in her 1860 work, *"Woman's Right to Labor"; or, Low Wages and Hard Work*, declared "that a want of respect for labor, and a want of respect for woman, lies at the bottom of all our difficulties." Beginning with Virginia Penny's *The Employments of Women* in 1863, dozens of books sought to identify the fields of employment respectable women might enter and to weigh the advantages and drawbacks of those fields. The Association for the Advancement of Women, organized in 1873, made the defense of women's paid employment a central concern. In 1873 as well, Louisa May Alcott made her own contribution with a novel, *Work*, whose structure mirrored nonfiction guidebooks such as Penny's. In chapters including "Servant," "Actress," and "Seamstress," the protagonist seeks work to support herself. In the end, she is drawn to meetings where working women discuss their problems and resolves to dedicate herself to this "new emancipation."[14]

Like many who advocated greater employment opportunities for women, Alcott believed that paid employment was key to ending women's social and political dependence. Calling it the "new emancipation," she invoked not just the liberation of slaves but also the assumption of civil responsibilities. An "emancipated" minor, after all, is one to whom the courts have granted the rights of adulthood: to make contracts, to bring suits at law, to own property. (These were also the rights that women lost at marriage and that the movement for married women's property laws sought to restore.) Like a child entering adulthood, a woman earning an income earned a degree of civil autonomy. As Alice Kessler-Harris has observed, the political implications of this autonomy electrified some Americans, while others found it "abhorrent."[15]

Alcott also explicitly linked her vision to Republican free-labor discourse. In *Work*, an escaped slave teaches the white protagonist that no work is degrading if the worker is paid. But in giving free labor a gendered significance, Alcott introduced an element that was not part of the free-labor vocabulary. In the closing scene of the book, when women workers invoke cross-class, interracial solidarity by clasping hands across a table, the former slave is joined by a "fallen woman" who has reclaimed her respectability through honest work. By introducing the shadow of sexual danger into a narrative about redemption through labor, Alcott suggests a flaw in the free-labor vision: one kind of paid employment is inherently degrading. As a new generation of women workers took to the streets, they shared those streets with prostitutes, and prostitution became the demon haunting the political promise of women's employment in Gilded Age America.

Those who endorsed paid employment for women and those who believed women should confine their labors to the domestic sphere sealed their arguments by appealing to the same fear: paid employment put women in danger of becoming prostitutes. For the former, the danger lay in the unjustly low wages women earned; for the latter, the danger lay in the perils of the heartless world beyond the shelter of home and hearth. In the 1880s, these fears began to coalesce into an old image with a new gender: the white slave. As David Roediger has argued, labor activists in the 1840s and 1850s commonly used the expression "white slavery" to characterize conditions of work that deprived white men of the independence and dignity of citizens. At the same time, the term naturalized the dependence and debasement of black slaves. In the antebellum era, "white slavery" might also describe women, even prostitutes, but only to the extent that they resembled degraded white male workers. As late as the 1880s, a white slave could still be a man or a respectable working woman; by 1910, however, when Congress passed the White Slave Traffic Act, a white slave could only be a girl or woman held as a prostitute.[16]

The American "white slave" of the late nineteenth century had a complicated genealogy. She was born not only of discourses of exploited white labor but also of the abolitionist strategy that emphasized the sexual exploitation of black women slaves. She had an international pedigree as well: in Orientalist art that dwelled on the luminous white skin of the Circassian in a Turkish harem, in missionary press reports of the sexual exploitation of "heathen" women in seraglios, and in stories of organized trade in women by Chinese brokers or by Russian Jews. But the American "white slave" was not Chinese, black, Jewish, or "heathen." She was "white" and therefore potentially a mother of the middle class. When she emerged in the 1880s, she posed a cultural counterpoint to the promise of free labor for women. If access to employment heralded social independence for the middle-class women who adopted the free-labor ideal, the "white slave" warned of the sexual danger lurking outside the protection of home and family. No competent, self-owning woman citizen, the white slave was instead naive, a prisoner, and in need of protection. For her, the streets were sites not of freedom but subjugation.[17]

This book examines how women who embraced the free-labor promise took up the tools of public and political life to assert the respectability of paid employment and to confront the demon of prostitution. It also examines how the policies these women championed were transformed in the hands of men who held very different views of male sexuality and political necessity—and far greater power. In the last decades of the nineteenth century, the law of prostitution was primarily a matter of local and state jurisdiction, and cities enforced policies regarding prostitution at the level of individual streets and neighborhoods. While the issues—including tolerated prostitution, women's access to paid employment, and reform of urban environments—were debated at national and even international levels, the problems and the politics were local.

To see how working women encountered urban life and sought to shape public policy, I took my questions to the streets of one particular Gilded Age city: Davenport, Iowa. In the period 1875–1910, Davenport was not Everytown, but it was far more typical of urban America than emerging giants such as New York or Chicago. In 1880, more Americans lived in urban places of twelve thousand to seventy-five thousand than in cities with populations of half a million or more. A regional entrepôt at the intersection of Mississippi River traffic and major railroad networks, Davenport's population grew from about twenty thousand and about forty thousand in this period. It was just one of more than 150 midsized cities scattered across the United States, providing markets, services, employment, entertainment, and an impression of city life for their rural hinterlands.[18]

Nearly every study of urban women in the nineteenth century has focused on one or another of America's largest cities, but most Americans experienced urban life in smaller places. Where cities are concerned, size really does matter. A city of thirty thousand is not a village where everyone knows everyone's business, but it is a place where most people share the same geography. Davenport had one high school, two railroad passenger depots, and one bridge across the river to Illinois. In contrast, Polish immigrant Hilda Polacheck, who arrived in Chicago in the 1890s, recalled living eight years on South Halsted Street before she finally saw Chicago's defining feature, Lake Michigan. It is impossible to imagine a girl like Polacheck living eight years in Davenport without a glimpse of the Mississippi.[19]

Introduction

This book has a second goal as well: to open up an examination of the leisure culture of youth in the nineteenth century. For two decades, Kathy Peiss's *Cheap Amusements* has been the touchstone for historians writing about the 1870s and 1880s, even though that work examines early-twentieth-century New York City. It is a tribute to Peiss's vivid writing and compelling argument that *Cheap Amusements* has been read back onto earlier decades it never claimed to explore. Youth culture is part of the fabric of urban life in Davenport, and some conclusions in this book raise new questions about young women's lives in the city.[20]

As an urban place, Davenport shared much with other cities in the Midwest. Traveling the Mississippi in 1882, Mark Twain recorded a "glimpse of Davenport, which is another beautiful city, crowning a hill." The phrase, he wrote, "applies to all these towns; for they are all comely, all well-built, clean, orderly, pleasant to the eye, and cheering to the spirit; and they are all situated on hills." Twain's party did not stop at Davenport. If his steamboat had drawn up to the landing, he might have seen something different.[21]

Davenport in 1880 was a city of twenty-two thousand, spread along the north bank of the Mississippi River and rising up the gentle bluffs admired by Twain. More than twelve miles of horse-drawn street railways linked its outer reaches to the city center, but Davenport remained in many ways a walking city. Distinct neighborhoods pressed close together, and the distance between affluence and poverty, between respectability and disorder, might be no more than a city block. The verandas of the wealthy who built their homes on the heights commanded spectacular views of the river; of Davenport's sister cities in Illinois; of Arsenal Island, whose green parks and munitions factories stretched to the east; and of the shacks of the poor, clustered in the flood-prone low areas of the city and along the slough, where pork packers' offal and waste from the vinegar works mingled to produce a particularly memorable effluvium.[22]

From the earliest days of European American settlement, Davenport played a central role in the development of the Upper Mississippi Valley. Located just below the Upper Rapids, Davenport was ideally situated to become a regional entrepôt. Steamboats from St. Louis and other southern ports unloaded cargo there rather than navigate the rapids in the low-water season. Arsenal Island ensured the site's selection for the first bridge across the Mississippi, linking rail lines east and west in 1856. The bridge made the Tri Cities region a national crossroads of trade where river and railroad intersected. In 1869, completion of the Union Pacific railroad linking California with Omaha secured Davenport's status by placing the city along the line of the first transcontinental railroad.[23]

From the tops of the bluffs, residents in the 1880s could trace the winding tracks of the Chicago, Milwaukee, & St. Paul railroad and the Chicago, Rock Island, & Pacific. To the south, the Rock Island & Peoria and Chicago, Burlington, & Quincy snaked along the river in Illinois. Long before the 1880s, Moline was famous as the

Introduction

Rock Island and Davenport, c. 1872. (From *Picturesque America; or, The Land We Live In,* 1872.)

site of the extensive John Deere Plow Works, whose buildings stretched along the river, each roof topped by a gilt-antlered stag. Other heavy manufacturing took advantage of the waterpower provided by a dam at the eastern end of the Illinois channel. Over the next decades, the Illinois cities expanded their manufacturing capacity, drawing immigrants from all over Europe.

Across the river, Davenport followed a somewhat different pattern of development. It was dominated by just two groups: old-stock white Americans and Germans, whose settlement there dated from the 1850s and the arrival of refugees from Schleswig-Holstein. Beginning as a mercantile center that supplied goods to the West and provided a market for the products of its agricultural hinterlands, Davenport developed a manufacturing base as well by the 1880s. Most industrial workers found employment in lumber milling and the production of sash windows, doors, and blinds. Others worked in flour milling, agricultural implement production, meatpacking, and the manufacture of work clothes for the men who labored in all those industries. During the Civil War, Davenport's railroad shops expanded dramatically, and the city became more completely integrated into the nation's sprawling railroad network. Two decades later, the city remained an important division point on the Rock Island line, providing employment for hundreds of skilled and unskilled workers. But Davenport was also the shopping and entertainment center for the trans-Mississippi region. In 1880, Davenport boasted an opera house seating two thousand, a German theater seating eight hundred, four public halls for lectures and concerts seating a total of thirty-four hundred, and several beer and concert gardens with room for perhaps two thousand. By contrast, Rock Island had an opera house seating a thousand, three small meeting halls, and no concert gardens. That same year, Davenport's directory counted fifty-one law offices, ten dressmaking establishments, twenty-two tailors, thirteen milliners, six newspapers (two German), three breweries, eighteen boarding houses, twenty-one restaurants, twenty-nine hotels, twenty-six billiard parlors, and 180 saloons.[24]

As a major crossroads of river and railroad, Davenport had a transient population and an urban feel characteristic of much larger cities. Soldiers stationed at Arsenal Island, rivermen and railroad workers, tramps following farm work, and lumbermen working the great timber rafts that supplied the riverside mills all passed through the city. The river itself carried a truly floating population: shanty boat dwellers who tied up to willow islands for a few days or a few months, fishing and working as casual laborers. (Or as city folk suspected, casual thieves.) Even some businesses took to the river, like J. P. Doremus's flatboat photographic studio.[25]

The Gilded Age city was a magnet for another kind of migrant as well. In the last third of the nineteenth century, increasing numbers of women left small towns and rural areas, swelling the population of the cities. Davenport was no exception to this pattern. In 1880, there were 945 men for every 1,000 women, reversing the overall state ratio of 916 women for every 1,000 men. Women sought work in department stores, hotels, dining rooms, or in the various light industries located in Davenport, primarily men's clothing and cigar making. Women later found work in various kinds of food processing, in woolen mills, and by the turn of the century as button makers who turned muddy mollusks into pearl buttons for the shirtwaists of clerical workers and saleswomen. Many more women took jobs as domestic servants. In the language of the census bureau, migrant women who lived outside of families were "adrift," reflecting the fear that without the anchor of a patriarchal household, women would be swept along by the eddies and currents of the city. Davenport's newspapers stood ready to report on the fate of rudderless women, noting those who came for abortions, to leave unwanted infants at "baby farms" (private homes where indifferent care often led to early death), or to work in the brothels.[26]

German immigration brought a distinct culture to Davenport, including an interest in socialism and various kinds of radical thought, strong opposition to woman suffrage, a wealth of musical organizations, and beer. The size and political strength of Davenport's German population meant that whatever Prohibition laws the state of Iowa passed were sure to be ignored in Davenport. Beer was too central to German culture. On a typical Sunday afternoon in the summer of 1880, more than fifteen hundred people visited Davenport's two largest beer gardens, Washington Gardens and P. N. Jacobs's Summer Garden. Scores of others dallied at smaller resorts scattered about the city. The Turnverein and the German theater served beer, and Germans owned and patronized many of the 180 saloons. Where liquor was concerned, Davenport was an open town, a situation that made it a regional center for entertainment. But not every establishment was as respectable as Turner Hall.[27]

In the 1870s, Davenport's largest and most notorious brothels lay on the northern edge of town, clustered around the fairgrounds (and convenient to the northern terminus of the street railway). By the early 1880s, prostitution had begun to move south into the downtown commercial district, with some brothels fronting as cigar stores and others as saloons. This, then, was the city where the Belva Lockwood club paraded: "clean, orderly, pleasant to the eye"—but only if, like Mark Twain, one stayed on a boat in midriver.[28]

For the historian, a smaller city is a more intimate canvas, opening up possibilities for research that would be impractical in a great city. Like the lives they document, the records used in this study are ordinary. Court and police dockets, newspaper reports and tax lists, census schedules and city directories—this paper reckoning of a city's life could be found anywhere. Its power lies in the possibility that the detail can be concentrated on a single canvas. The woman who signs a petition in Brooklyn or the girl arrested on a street corner in Chicago surfaces briefly in the historical record, a name on paper. In all but the rarest cases, she disappears again into the throng of ordinary people, lost to the historian who may wonder about her home, her life, her future.

The primary research method used in this book was inspired by Suzanne Lebsock's pathbreaking book, *The Free Women of Petersburg*, and can easily be summarized: choose a place small enough to see whole, and read everything. In Davenport, the historian can trace an individual through a variety of records and over the course of years, even decades. Fragments come together into lives, and occasionally one of the poor, the illiterate, or the children steps out of the crowd to become the center of her own story. The issues animating women's politics and men's protests in Davenport permeated American culture because they shaped ordinary lives. By opening these lives to view, the small city, the intimate canvas, becomes a window on an unseen world. "God is in the detail," wrote Carlo Ginzburg.[29] Great questions can be asked in small places.

1

WOMEN IN THE CITY
Law, Reputation, and Geography

Lust is a better paymaster than the mill-owner or the tailor.
—Caroline H. Dall, *Woman's Right to Labor* (1860)

IT WAS JUST PAST 11:30 P.M. ON A SULTRY JULY EVENING IN 1880 when four police officers arrived at a dark, quiet house facing an alley on the outskirts of Davenport, just north of the fairgrounds. Three officers took up positions around the house, watching the roof and second-story windows; the fourth, carrying an arrest warrant, rang the front bell. A gracious Belle Walker answered the door, offering the policeman a "luxurious seat" in the parlor. She called to the officers posted outside, urging them to come in. Puzzled, they entered; the visit was not going as expected. Searching through the house, they found no occupants besides Mrs. Walker and a cook in the kitchen. "Where are the girls?" they finally asked. "O, my daughters are all out enjoying the cool air riding," replied Walker, perfectly cool herself. The policemen, thwarted in their efforts to catch a house of ill-fame in full swing, arrested Walker, giving her notice to appear in court the following morning. Her attorney appeared for her and posted a six hundred dollar bond, and Walker remained free.[1]

The report of the foiled raid on Walker's place appeared on the front page of the *Davenport Democrat* just one column distant from the paragraph noting Dr. Jennie McCowen's arrival that day to open a medical practice in Davenport. At first glance, these two women could not have been more different from each other: McCowen was a respected professional woman, well educated and articulate, soon to be a leading citizen of the community. Walker was the proprietor of a bordello. Setting these two women alongside each other, as the newspaper did that steamy July day, calls attention not only to their differences but also to the way gender shaped the possibilities each found in her life. Both Walker and McCowen were in their mid-thirties in 1880. Both women had traveled far from the scenes of childhood and family as they sought ways to earn a living. Neither was married. Despite the honorific "Mrs.," Walker, whose real name was Rachel Armstrong, was not married to her partner, Charles Walker. Armstrong and McCowen, each in her own way, had rejected the expected pattern of a woman's life, a pattern that led from girlhood to marriage to motherhood, a pattern strongly associated in the dominant culture with pastoral retirement to the domestic sphere. As different as their lives were, both Armstrong and McCowen had chosen a course likely to place their names where most women's names rarely appeared: on the front page of the newspaper. Far from retired, both were ambitious, and both were successful. Rachel Armstrong was a businesswoman, a property owner, and a taxpayer; McCowen would become all three as well.[2]

In the judgment of most middle-class Americans, Rachel Armstrong ought to have been an outcast, shunned by her family, miserable, and alone. Or, conjuring another stock figure from the catalog of imagined prostitution, she might have been a monster—"diabolical," one newspaper writer called her. Yet when Armstrong died in 1883, her funeral revealed a woman very different from those caricatures. Indeed, a reporter attending the service seemed fascinated by the way it violated his expectations. Armstrong's brother came for the funeral—a brother Armstrong had tenderly nursed through the months of his recent illness. "Most of the women of her class in the city" also came, and far from being blasphemous harridans, they knew the hymns and sang them with "readiness and harmony," suggesting, perhaps, a history of churchgoing. In "the strange company about that grave," the reporter observed genuine grief. Few women in Davenport would have wanted to trade their lives for Armstrong's (though assuredly, some would have done so gladly), yet in her life, Armstrong had friends, family, and financial comfort. Her money protected her from the sordid business of police-court appearances, and it gave her the stability to form a longtime partnership with Charles Walker. She acknowledged his importance in her life by making him the sole heir to her real and personal property—worth forty thousand dollars, by one probably exaggerated estimate—and the executor of her will.[3]

When Rachel Armstrong and her mourners failed to conform to expectations, they blurred the line that was supposed to separate "virtuous" women from the "fallen." Most nineteenth-century writers who dealt with prostitution in America insisted that the line was unambiguous: loss of sexual purity irrevocably transformed a woman. "Good women," explained philosopher Ellen Mitchell, "feel that between them and their erring sisters is a great gulf fixed." Good men shared the same view. After John Warren, a veteran New York City detective, helped a distraught father trace his missing daughter to a brothel, the man refused to rescue her. "It wouldn't be my Annie, you know, she's gone," he mourned. "I shall never see *her* again." Kate Bushnell of the Woman's Christian Temperance Union was more sympathetic to such women but voiced a similar certainty. The "fallen woman," she wrote, "is an exposed criminal; she cannot keep her crime hid as man can. It tells too painfully on her health; it lies too weightily on her conscience; or the offspring of lust enters the world through her bedchamber. So that in some way or other, either by haggard look or confession or enforced motherhood, the lightening-shaft of God's seeming-judgment descends, and she becomes a castaway." Once a girl or woman was "ruined," the transformation showed in her face and demeanor, and she became an outcast—or so most writers insisted.[4]

Yet the certainty of middle-class writers seems an almost calculated defense against the ambiguity of the streets. In life, what separated "pure" women from the "fallen" was less a bright line than a broad penumbra. Where writers asserted manifest difference, civil authorities found the need to impose distinctions. Prostitution districts were among the first forms of zoning devised by cities in the nineteenth century. Yet the spaces set apart for "fallen" women were rarely empty of others. Brothels had neighbors, and on the sidewalks prostitutes strolled alongside other women. This mingling bred confusion and anxiety, as urban dwellers fretted about how to distinguish among strangers: which women were prostitutes, and which their respectable neighbors? In Davenport, one newspaper expressed the fear quite candidly: when prostitutes mixed with other women, any man might be "dupe[d] . . . into marrying a disguised trull for a virginal bride."[5]

The spatial confusion had its parallel in uncertain social boundaries, as self-supporting women found themselves immersed in a debate over wage earning, prostitution, and respectability. When a woman earned an income of her own, she placed herself—at least symbolically—outside the reciprocal obligations of marriage. In the middle-class model of companionate marriage, a wife owed sexual love and domestic labor to her husband, who provided economic support in return. But the self-supporting woman could resist this bargain, sundering the terms of the exchange. Having no need of a breadwinner, she no longer owed her sexuality to one man alone. Indeed, having defied the feminine modesty that ought to make her timid in the masculine business world, a wage-earning woman might be expected to reveal other kinds of boldness, even sexual assertiveness. Seen through this lens of gender ideology, a woman who moved into the realm of paid employment implicitly compromised her sexual reputation.

Those who argued for expanded economic opportunities for women were uncomfortably aware of this problem. A writer in the popular educational journal *Chautauquan* hesitated to recommend well-paid craft work to women in need of income because its practitioners were "not always moral, and the association is thus dangerous." Characteristically, Ednah Dow Cheney of the Association for the Advancement of Women acknowledged the same problem but took the opposite stance, urging "every woman, rich or poor, to do something for pay, to show that it is not disgraceful." Others, including politicians debating the tariff, associated women's paid employment with prostitution by tracing the inevitable line from low wages to the bordello. John McEnnis of the Knights of Labor alleged that among St. Louis knitting girls, "prostitution was one of the conditions of getting and keeping work, and that many girls could not make enough money to buy bread and fuel without resorting to the streets." As the keeper of one brothel reportedly explained, "What's the use, as long as men pay reluctantly the smallest wages for the longest day's hard labor, and pay the highest demanded price, in these houses, they will be continued." A writer in the suffrage paper *The Revolution*, addressing American women, expressed the problem in the bleakest terms: "Few professions are open to you; and in most of these, social degradation attends your entrance.... To her, therefore, who must earn her own bread, and whose affections do not prompt her to married life, there are but these alternatives—Scanty Earnings, Unloving Wedlock, Death, or Nameless Shame." When the distance from paid employment to the brothel seemed so short, the taint of sexual impropriety could stigmatize the most ordinary employments for women. A "boarding house for ladies" was code for a bordello, the proprietor tagged as a brothel keeper. "Cigar store keeper" became a euphemism for prostitute in some locales, while "shirtmaker" or "sewing girl" were used in others. Even a milliner—that most characteristic of women's trades—could face claims that she kept "a cozy room in the rear, and an inviting lounge" for male callers. Working for pay left a woman's respectability open to question.[6]

When Jennie McCowen arrived in Davenport to open her practice, she came with an introduction to the community from Abbie Cleaves, the physician McCowen replaced. Though a stranger to Davenport, McCowen's respectability was unquestioned. Women without her resources—her education, skill, savings account, manner, and reputation—faced greater obstacles making a place for themselves in the city. "Making a place," physical as well as social, was key to a woman's success in establishing her reputation in a new city, but this was far from simple. Without a written "character" to introduce her or a local reputation for probity, a woman could find herself caught in a double bind: barred from respectable work or lodgings, she might be forced to seek both in places less reputable. Ironically, the legal construction of prostitution in the late nineteenth century focused not on specific actions but on reputation and physical location. In a culture that allowed women few choices about where to work and how to live, a woman on the margins of respectability often found herself deprived of one more choice: whether to accept the identity of "prostitute."

The 1880 raid on Rachel Armstrong's place was the second that week, part of Davenport authorities' new determination to suppress several brothels that had flourished for years just north of the city limits. Two days earlier, a visit to Claude Merrill's resort in the same neighborhood had been more exciting but hardly more successful. Of eighteen people in the house, police captured only Merrill and two women who worked for her. The others, men and women, fled through windows and into the cornfields nearby. One young man "made a flying dash through a second story window, taking sash, glass, and all, landed on a shed roof, from which he got to the ground, and thence into a cabbage patch, where he and some others did serious damage with their wanderings in search of a lone lane to town."[7]

Set down amid cabbage patches and cornfields, these brothels lay near the northern terminus of the Brady Street car line, making them easy for patrons to reach. Nearby was the fairgrounds racetrack, a hub of Davenport's male sporting culture. In the early 1870s, there were few neighbors to trouble, and authorities permitted the brothels to operate relatively undisturbed. But the same car line that made the brothels accessible also drew new residential building. Developers platted a subdivision in the area north of the fairgrounds in the 1870s, and as more respectable neighbors moved in, they pressured authorities to move brothels out. The raid on Walker's place (called "the Farm") was prompted by a complaint from an actual farmer, while the arrests at Merrill's followed a protest from another neighbor about "carriages driving to and from at all hours of the day and night—in full view of all the children and women in the homes in the vicinity." This citizen expected city authorities to redefine the space of his neighborhood, making it a respectable place for wives and children at home by removing the women of doubtful character. On another occasion, one of Merrill's neighbors, a broom maker named George Wilkinson, reported that "at times there is a good deal of noise in and around this house & it had become a nuisance in the neighborhood."[8]

While noise, traffic, and the mixing of "bad" women among "good" wives seemed to be the primary complaints against the brothels around the fairgrounds, neighbors grew to fear violence as well. The Black Hills, a resort on Dubuque Road just north of the streetcar depot, was a particular focus of anxiety. Consisting of two frame buildings, a saloon and a dwelling house, the Black Hills in 1877 was kept by a couple named Heinrichs. He ran the saloon, while she had charge of the house. That April, two young coal miners, Richard Thomas and Ambrose Bone, stopped by one afternoon to drink at the saloon, but it was closed because of Mr. Heinrichs's illness. Mrs. Heinrichs offered to serve them beer in the house. While they were there, Bone argued with a young woman resident, Minnie Brennicke, and as he was leaving, he turned and shot her through the head. Police arrested Thomas almost immediately, but Bone escaped. After more than a week's manhunt up and down the Mississippi Valley, Bone turned himself in to the Davenport police.[9]

This story might be just one more in a series of grim episodes involving prostitutes, drunken young men, and pistols, except for what the newspaper reports suggest about Brennicke. The reports never wavered in their conviction that Minnie Brennicke was a prostitute—"One of the Unfortunate Inmates," a headline called her. Thomas, in fact, testified that the argument between Brennicke and Bone began after they had gone upstairs together, with Bone complaining as he returned to the parlor that "you are a great girl to use a fellow in that way." Mrs. Heinrichs, on the other hand, testified that the men "were indulging in smutty talk" and that when Brennicke protested that "this is no place for any such talk as that," Bone was so provoked he shot her.[10]

At first glance, this seems more than peculiar. What place could be more appropriate for "smutty talk" than a bordello? But the testimony of others acquainted with Minnie Brennicke suggests that while she may have drifted into prostitution, she had hardly chosen it. She seemed instead to be resisting the identity even as she was residing in a brothel. According to one witness, when Thomas and Bone made "overtures" to Brennicke using "obscene language," she "resented" it, especially "when they called her an improper character." In fact, on the day she was shot, Minnie Brennicke had been living at the Black Hills only six days. In the weeks before, she had boarded at several respectable places in Moline. One of her Moline acquaintances identified Brennicke as a "hairdresser by trade." Hairdressing was certainly a trade that might have brought Brennicke into contact with prostitutes, especially if she were desperate for money. But this friend insisted he had seen "nothing immoral in her conduct." The portrait of Brennicke that emerged from the stories told after her death is of a young woman struggling to make a living in a world of few choices. Born Minnie Wilson in Michigan, the twenty-four-year-old Brennicke was the daughter of an English father and a German mother. Like thousands of young women in the 1870s, she and a sister had migrated to Chicago, probably seeking work after their parents died. In Chicago, both sisters married, but Minnie's husband abandoned her. With a small daughter to support, Minnie returned to Michigan to place the girl with people she knew, then traveled again in search of work. Her search brought her to Moline, then to the Black Hills. Six days later she was dead.

Was Minnie Brennicke a prostitute? Thomas, Bone, and the newspapers all seemed to think so. So did the men taking testimony at the coroner's inquest. They carefully inquired about a third woman present in the house, Jennie Creckbaum, who had worked in the kitchen at the Black Hills for two or three months and who had fled, terrified, after the shooting. Mrs. Heinrichs testified that she paid Creckbaum $1.50 a week and charged her nothing for board and that Creckbaum's room was downstairs while Brennicke's was upstairs. The investigators apparently intended these questions to establish that Creckbaum was simply a servant, not a prostitute. No one asked whether Mrs. Heinrichs paid Brennicke a wage; her status was never in question. At the same time, Mrs. Heinrichs disagreed with Richard Thomas about whether Minnie Brennicke had gone upstairs with Ambrose Bone, and she insisted that she had seen "no money except that paid for beer." This may have been simply Mrs. Heinrichs's attempt to avoid admitting that she kept a brothel, but in the end, the evidence was ambiguous: Minnie Brennicke clearly died with the reputation of a prostitute, a reputation that stemmed primarily from being in a place identified with prostitution. Yet she resented being called one and objected to "smutty talk." And her friend saw "nothing immoral in her conduct." Even Bone's alleged complaint—"you are a great girl to use a fellow in that way"—suggests that Bone had not got what he expected out of a trip upstairs. All of this evidence sifts from testimony given in a case where Brennicke's status as a prostitute was irrelevant: only Mrs. Heinrichs had an interest in shaping her testimony on that point. To the newspapers and the men who visited the Black Hills, Brennicke appeared to have crossed that bright line separating prostitutes from other women, but she seems to have resisted this step, clinging to the privileges of respectability. Her reluctance to adopt the role of "fallen woman" so provoked Ambrose Bone that he killed her.

This evidence of how Minnie Brennicke responded to being labeled a prostitute—of her subjective experience—is certainly more suggestive than conclusive. Still, it is rare for a historian to find any such evidence at all. Most women and girls who worked the streets and brothels left no record of themselves. In Brennicke's case, her violent death alone led authorities to interview and record the impressions of those who knew her. Yet these glimpses of Brennicke—her reluctance to be called a prostitute, her objections to impolite speech—become even more significant in the context of nineteenth-century law. In the courtroom, appearance and reputation were more important than actions in determining who was a prostitute.

Under the law, no single action redefined a woman into a prostitute. Definitions that might seem commonsense to later generations—for example, the "practice of engaging in sex acts for hire"—did not apply in the late nineteenth century. Courts agreed that taking money for sex was not an essential element of being a prostitute. "Her avocation may be known from the manner in which she plies it, and *not from pecuniary charges* and compensation gained in any other manner," averred S. M. Weaver, writing for the Iowa Supreme Court. Nor was sex itself an essential element of being a prostitute: courts did not require evidence of acts of sexual intercourse to establish that a woman was a prostitute. "It is certainly true, we think, a woman may be a prostitute and carry on the business of such if she so holds herself out to the world," explained another Iowa Supreme Court justice in 1881. Submitting "her person to illicit sexual intercourse with various persons" was not the essence of the law.[11]

A woman's "manner" and how she "held herself out to the world" were central to the nineteenth-century understanding of "prostitute." It was an identity far more than an action, a reputation more than a vocation. Indeed, "reputation" was a keyword in this matrix of meaning. "House of ill-fame" was the most common term used in statutes referring to brothels. Public impression—"fame"—was so central to the definition that an Iowa statute specifically authorized courts to accept evidence of the "general reputation" of a house in trials for "keeping a house of ill-fame." Such evidence was not *necessary* for a conviction if the prosecution could establish that people "resorted" to the place "for purpose of prostitution or lewdness" but could be *sufficient* when the prosecution had "shown that lewd women made [the house] a place of resort, and that men of licentious repute visited the house." In other words, the presence of individuals with the reputation of prostitutes and sporting men was conclusive evidence that the place itself was a house of ill-fame.[12]

Turning from state law to local ordinances reveals how completely nineteenth-century definitions of prostitution were bound up in appearances, reputation, and hearsay. Under state law, the presence of "lewd women" and "men of licentious repute" automatically made a place a "house of ill-fame." City ordinances sought to draw a bright line around prostitutes: "every person found in any house of ill-fame" was guilty of being "an inmate" of the house, and their presence was deemed "prima facie evidence that they were there for the purpose of prostitution." In other words, the presence of those reputed to be lewd made any place a house of ill-fame, and any woman in the house was therefore a prostitute. Minnie Brennicke may have resented being called an "improper character," but as long as the Black Hills was by reputation a brothel, Minnie Brennicke was by law a prostitute. That identity set the value of her life. In spite of eyewitnesses to the crime, Ambrose Bone suffered little for his act of murder. Within three years he was living in his mother's house in Jackson County, Illinois, working on the railroad.[13]

As residential building increased in the neighborhood north of the fairgrounds, the large brothels became increasingly vulnerable to prosecution. In 1879, the Black Hills was under new management, and Millie Dillon's efforts to keep a tight rein on activities so infuriated Davenport's young sporting men that they repeatedly attacked the house, assaulting the inmates and shooting Dillon. These episodes led the police to close the Black Hills that July, and over the next year or two, several other brothels shut down as well. Given the role of reputation and hearsay in proving cases against them, these large brothels with their carriage traffic and noise were sitting ducks. As the women abandoned these brothels, another presumption of bawdy-house law guided their choices as they set up business elsewhere. Judges had long adhered to an interpretation of the law that held that a woman alone could not be the keeper of a house of ill-fame. As a North Carolina justice expressed it in a case often cited, "the residence of an unchaste woman—a single prostitute—does not become a bawdy house, because she may habitually admit one or many men to an illicit cohabitation with her. The common law did not undertake the correction of morals in such cases, but left the parties to spiritual supervision and penances." Women seem to have known this. A Davenport saloonkeeper testified of a neighboring woman arrested for keeping a house of ill-fame, "At least two or three times she kept a girl for a few days, but she told me that she did not dare to keep one long. As she could not be disturbed if she was alone." A woman alone—and the men who visited her—might be prosecuted for "lewdness," but even then the law insisted that their conduct had to be notorious and public: "secret or private lewdness" was not subject to prosecution.[14]

By the early 1880s, many of the women who had worked in large brothels dispersed into one-woman enterprises, often fronting as downtown cigar stores. Claude Merrill, for example, set up shop at 106 East Fifth Street. Millie Dillon, who operated the Black Hills at the time it closed, ran a cigar store at 204 East Second Street. These women joined perhaps dozens of others "in several localities on nearly every business street in the city." Setting up shop required buying a five-dollar annual license; stocking a display case with cigars, candy, and fruit; and waiting for the all-male clientele typical of a cigar store. The proprietor "leads a quiet life, and being wary and sharp, an appearance of wrong-doing is rarely observed about the premises," explained one newspaper reporter. Police and neighbors suspected most cigar stores run by women of being fronts for prostitution, though one newspaper, after reporting arrests at "a cigar stand kept by ladies," made the point of asserting, "By the way, there are several cigar stores in this city, kept by *ladies*." Those women attempting to earn an honest living selling cigars must have found their situation increasingly difficult as the business became identified with prostitution. The phenomenon became so prevalent that in 1884 the Iowa legislature passed a statute specifically aimed at cigar stores, along with boardinghouses and hotels—two other businesses that, when run by women, were often alleged to be fronts for prostitution. The law distinguished cigar stores from the category "house of ill-fame" (thus eliminating the legal requirement that there be more than one woman on the premises) and made "evidence of the general reputation" of a cigar store admissible in court—the same standard that already applied to conventional brothels.[15]

The emphasis on reputation in the case of brothels and cigar stores and on notoriety in lewdness prosecutions reveals the extent to which these laws were concerned more with establishing social boundaries than with punishing specific acts. "Vagrancy," another charge commonly laid to prostitutes, shared a similar emphasis. Vagrancy was an ancient offense, part of the panoply of common law carried into the American system from its British roots. Vagrancy comprised streetwalking as well as begging, but authorities required no exchange of money, no direct solicitation, to establish the breach. It was instead a status offense, and police had extensive discretion to decide who was a vagrant. Appearance, location, and conduct in public were the markers by which authorities judged women's status. Police rarely explained how they made their decisions, but judges revealed their own criteria in cases where a woman's unchaste character was in dispute. Just as a woman could be a prostitute without having sexual intercourse, a woman could be unchaste without "actual commission of the unchaste act," as Justice William G. Woodward of the Iowa Supreme Court delicately expressed it. "Obscenity of language, indecency of conduct, and undue familiarity with men . . . serve to indicate the true character," he explained. Police magistrate Samuel Finger of Davenport made judgments by the same method. When Cora Battisfore appeared in his court accused of vagrancy, she "pretended to be very innocent." But Finger had seen her a few days earlier, riding the streetcar, and had "sized her up for just the kind of a creature she was charged with being." Battisfore was not arrested for anything she had done on the streetcar that day, but Finger knew how a "decent woman" comported herself in public: Battisfore got thirty days. Under vagrancy law, a woman who was flirtatious or boisterous on the streets, who dressed flashily, or who lingered around places considered inappropriate for "decent" women risked being judged a prostitute.[16]

As prostitutes sought smaller, more discreet locations for their business, the visible center of prostitution moved south, from the outskirts of town into Davenport's commercial district. Prostitution was by no means new to downtown. Saloons on Front Street along the Mississippi River and on the blocks near the railway passenger depots had long attracted prostitutes serving travelers, soldiers, and local men. But the early 1880s brought an increase in both concentration and visibility. Between 1881 and 1883, court records and newspapers reported specific addresses of thirteen brothels, cigar stores, and other sites of prostitution. Of these, nine were in the downtown commercial district, primarily along Front Street facing the river and in a cluster near the intersection of Brady Street—the commercial spine of downtown—and the Fifth Street tracks. By the end of the decade, the shift was nearly complete. Of nineteen sites of prostitution reported between 1887 and 1889, eighteen were downtown—nearly all of them in the blocks just east of Brady Street, along Front Street, or along the north side of the Fifth Street tracks. These downtown sites were small compared with the large brothels that flourished north of town in the 1870s and were dispersed through streets devoted to a variety of activities.

Just how much variety lined these streets becomes clear by matching up the 1885 Iowa manuscript census with an 1886 Sanborn fire insurance map and an 1885 city directory. Together, these documents create a composite snapshot of the urban neighborhood, making it possible to see downtown prostitution as part of a complex urban milieu. The heaviest concentration of brothels lay within a triangle bounded by Front Street along the river to the south, Brady Street to the west, and the Chicago, Rock Island, & Pacific (CRI&P) embankment starting at the foot of Government Bridge and angling northwest toward Fifth Street. Focusing tightly on these few blocks reveals much about the kinds of homes and businesses that lined the streets where prostitutes plied their trade and about the role of the neighborhood in the larger community.[17]

Like most central urban neighborhoods in the 1880s, this was a mixed-use district where dwelling places, factories, and shops crowded close together. Near Brady Street, buildings were three or four stories, with upper floors occupied by residences, public halls, or workshops, while the street level housed retail stores. East of Perry Street, building density dropped off rapidly, and houses built for a single family (but often occupied by several) mingled among small factories and other businesses. Davenport's major passenger depot, the CRI&P, lay within this neighborhood, and along the streets nearby clustered about a third of the city's hotels. Three-quarters of the city's livery stables operated in this neighborhood, as did about a fourth of the saloons. The Burtis Opera House, which offered concerts and theatrical performances by touring companies, stood next to the depot on Perry Street. Around the corner was a roller rink where young people skated to the music of a German band.[18]

Further tightening the focus illustrates how these elements shared the space. A shopper strolling down two blocks of East Second Street would pass a good sample of the neighborhood's features. Walking east from Brady Street on the north side of East Second, the shopper might linger over the window displays of a dry goods store and a clothing shop. Above her, the staccato rhythm of typing practice floats down from the windows of the Iowa Commercial College on the second and third floors, where dozens of young women and men study shorthand, typing, bookkeeping, and business methods. As she passes on, the aromas of tannin, leather, and oil drift from the harness shop next door, followed by the beer-and-cigar scent of a saloon, then the steamy fragrance of a bakery blended with the tang of coal smoke. The shopper might next pause at another clothing store with offices upstairs. The rest of the north side of the block was taken up by sheds, probably part of a carpentry shop on the alley. At the corner, she eyes the muck of Perry Street before venturing a step, and as she waits for her chance to cross, she keeps her distance from the entrance to a corner saloon. Along the south side a similar miscellany stretched from west to east, including two saloons, wholesalers and retailers, workshops, an upstairs meeting hall, and, on the corner, Nicholas Kuhnen's factory, with nearly two hundred women molding cheap cigars in the dank, reeking workrooms.

Safely across Perry Street, the shopper might find the next block of her walk less appealing. She must skirt two more saloons, two cigar stores, and a barbershop—businesses that respectable women know to avoid—before reaching the inviting

Second Street East of Brady, c. 1888. In this block, signs for "cream," "teas," and "clothiers" drew women shoppers, but in the next block, several businesses were fronts for prostitution. (Courtesy of the Richardson-Sloane Special Collections Center, Davenport Public Library.)

outdoor tables and shady arbors of Fred Wulf's summer garden down on the corner. Wulf's place, the third saloon on the block, caters to both men and women, and if the shopper is German, she might even stop for a cool glass of wine. On the alley behind the summer garden was the glass hothouse of a florist. Along the south side, the Reimers and Fernald candy factory (another employer of young women) anchored one corner and a small confectioner's shop the other. In between are workshops, a vacant lot, and a ramshackle dwelling. Walking just two blocks of East Second Street takes the shopper past homes, factories, retail and wholesale stores, a school, and seven saloons.

Woven among these businesses were the residences of twenty households, comprising sixty-seven adults and twenty-six children. A closer look at those households begins to reveal something else about this neighborhood: women headed seven. Of the businesses in these two blocks, women operated five: the bakery, the confectionery, the florist, and the two cigar stores. These two blocks represent another characteristic of the neighborhood where prostitution had clustered: a disproportionate number of homes and businesses headed by women. In all of the neighborhood, more than one in five households were headed by women, and nearly half of all Davenport businesses run by women lay along these few streets. Most of these were small, low-profit operations like toy stores, fancy-goods stores, and fruit and candy stores. Davenport's large department stores, by contrast, all lay west of Brady Street.[19]

The presence of so many woman-run businesses and woman-headed households probably reflects lower rents. As a living environment, this neighborhood was not likely to draw residents who could afford to live elsewhere. The CRI&P yard—with its noisy, round-the-clock traffic—lay just east of the tracks. A coal-gas plant spewing noxious fumes loomed nearby. With three-fourths of the city's livery stables in the neighborhood, residents endured more than their share of dung heaps and horseflies. Some of the more affluent neighbors had already moved away. The old Episcopal Church building stood just outside the district at the corner of Fifth and Rock Island, vacant and for sale in 1886. Other residents found their options limited by low income and racism. Davenport's African American population was tiny in 1885 (about 244), but half of them lived along these few streets. So did the city's seven Chinese residents. And while women outnumbered men in Davenport as a whole by a slight margin, this neighborhood had only about eighty-seven women for every hundred men, reflecting the concentration of hotels and boardinghouses. This was a neighborhood of single men and single mothers, and some of the poorest women in Davenport dwelled along these streets. When the Ladies Christian Association published the names and addresses of destitute women seeking work as seamstresses or laundresses, all of them lived in this neighborhood.[20]

Scattered among these businesses and households were a handful that shaded into what Davenport newspapers liked to call the "demi-monde." Among the seven woman-headed households the imagined shopper passed on Second Street, three were headed by women with a history of arrests for prostitution. Of the five businesses owned by women, two were cigar stores that fronted for brothels. Yet just 10 of the neighborhood's 292 households were clearly associated with prostitution. (However, those 10 represent almost 16 percent of the woman-headed households.) This was not a vice district in the common sense, where brothels formed the most prominent kind of business. Instead, it was a neighborhood where prostitutes plied their trade alongside other struggling women and where legitimate businesses rubbed shoulders with illicit ones.

This tincture of disreputability gave a cast to the whole neighborhood. Respectable women sometimes found their homes invaded. Jane Krebs, who lived near the corner of Front Street and Iowa Street, once awoke to discover men in her house at 2 A.M. They expected to find prostitutes, but instead they found an angry Krebs. "I drove the men—there were two of them—downstairs with a club," she testified. Others found their reputations sullied in print. When police found an eleven-year-old runaway from Clinton in Lizzie Hampton's home near Second and Iowa Streets, the *Times* reported that the girl had been enticed by a "procuress" to enter a house of ill-fame. Hampton's father, who lived with her, went in person to the *Times* office to protest the accusation. "She is washing, ironing and sewing for a living and helping to support her old father and mother," he insisted. Even the skating rink saw its respectability tarnished. A police patrolman called it "worse than all the houses of ill-fame in the city." In the beginning, he reported, "many of the most respectable people, young and middle-aged went. But it grew from good to bad and bad to worse, until it became a free-for-all place." Saloons too suffered from the taint of the neighborhood. In a city where beer stood for German cultural identity and personal liberty, newspaper editorials frequently scoffed at those who called the saloon "a public nuisance and a pest." No, one writer insisted, the saloon is "the resort, almost exclusively of reputable and respected citizens, who enter therein to indulge in a quiet chat with a friend even more than to sip a glass of beer." But even this sympathetic writer made an exception for the saloons on Front Street, calling them "veritable dens."[21]

On the streets, the lack of clear boundaries separating the vice district from legitimate businesses sometimes made for unexpected encounters. When one husband announced to his wife that he would be in town on business that evening, she took advantage of the free time to go shopping. Downtown, she spotted her husband near Fourth and Brady flirting with two young women who were "not such as she cared to have him associate with." She caught up with the trio, "pounded" the two women, then grabbed a whip from a nearby buggy and thrashed her husband. Another wife used not a whip but a rock to attack her husband when she unexpectedly spotted him on Second Street "with one of the most degraded creatures of the town." On another occasion, a young woman chanced to meet her fiancé "in company with a woman whose companionship on the streets he would have avoided in the day time." After protesting his behavior, she left, then returned with a revolver, firing several shots at him. When another man intervened to take the revolver from her, she ran toward the river and was narrowly averted from suicide. A similar encounter ended more tragically, with the shamed woman returning home to end her life with a dose of morphine.[22]

Most such encounters must have gone unrecorded. Like Minnie Brennicke's life, these were preserved for the historian only because they ended in violence. Yet just as scores of other, unnamed women worked in Davenport's brothels, scores of other, unrecorded encounters between prostitutes and respectable women took place. In 1889 (the first year for which police records exist), twenty-nine different women were arrested for keeping houses of ill-fame and twenty-nine more for working as prostitutes. Most of these arrests took place downtown, along streets lined with legitimate businesses, homes, and schools. The line distinguishing respectable women from prostitutes was not drawn through city streets, nor was it regulated by the clock. The hours between 7 A.M. and 10 P.M., when respectable women were most likely to be out on the streets, were also the most likely hours for prostitution arrests. More than twice as many such arrests in 1889 took place during those hours as in the remainder of the day. Arrests in the afternoon—between 3 P.M. and 7 P.M.—were especially common. This concentration of arrests may reflect the desire of police to protect respectable people from encounters with prostitutes; nevertheless, it documents the presence of women deemed prostitutes on the street. The geography of prostitution in the 1880s made it nearly inevitable that men seeking prostitutes and prostitutes seeking men would share the streets with women on their way home from cutting caramels at the candy factory, hurrying to shorthand class at the commercial college, or off to an evening club meeting.[23]

The pattern of Davenport's urban development encouraged the movement of the most visible prostitution from large, isolated brothels on the outskirts of town into small establishments like cigar stores in the heart of the city. As sites of prostitution became especially concentrated along the same few streets where most woman-run businesses lay and in the same neighborhood where many woman-headed households clustered, those women identified as prostitutes shared their neighborhood streets every day with women who claimed sexual respectability.

This shift in the geography of vice in Davenport echoed changes taking place in cities all over the United States. As the country's urban landscapes changed in the early phases of industrialization, first separating "home" from "work," members of the middle class increasingly associated respectability with wives and daughters who remained at home. In the antebellum period, those on the streets were primarily poor and working-class women, including African Americans, whose claims to sexual respectability were rarely honored by elite and middle-class men. Women who ventured unescorted into public space risked being interpreted as prostitutes, since their location, far more than their appearance, was coded. Yet by the 1880s, the growth of corporate America and its new methods of business management created an insatiable need for office workers, altering the geography of gender once again. Middle-class women were invited back into urban space, but their presence unsettled the spatial codes of the antebellum years. No longer were the only women on the streets those whose class had long rendered them vulnerable to sexual exploitation. A new generation of women office workers and professionals increasingly shared the streets with their poor and working-class sisters.

At the same time, analyses of the "problem" of women's paid employment emphasized the links between work for pay and prostitution. Whether their earnings were great or small, critics claimed, employed women placed themselves at risk of prostitution. Self-supporting women breached the reciprocal obligations of marriage, implicitly freeing them from sexual fidelity to a husband. Poorly paid women could be tempted by the high wages of a brothel. As working women of different classes stood at the precipice, middle-class writers remained insistent that prostitutes were a class apart, recognizably different from women who remained sexually "pure," whatever their social class. Yet the systems of law that defined prostitutes made the difference anything but clear. Prostitution remained enmeshed in questions of association, reputation, and hearsay. A woman whose public demeanor appeared coarse or boisterous, who was found in a place associated with prostitution or in the company of women reputed to be prostitutes, was herself subject to arrest and conviction as a prostitute. Whether she had ever participated in sexual acts—much less whether she had accepted money for them—was, in law, irrelevant. Taken together, these elements—a geography of vice that mingled prostitutes among respectable working women, a cultural debate that saw all employed women as potential prostitutes, and a legal system that gave reputation a greater weight than action—created an urban environment fraught with difficulties for the women who entered the paid workforce. Some sought to confront the problem by reshaping the debates about women's work. Some sought to reshape the city itself. Dr. Jennie McCowen would try both.

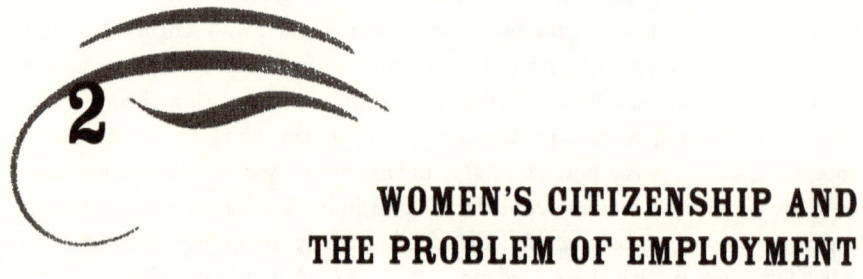

WOMEN'S CITIZENSHIP AND THE PROBLEM OF EMPLOYMENT

Yet, rich as the prizes may be that the world shall gain by the labor of women, the greatest gain will be in the development and improvement of women themselves. For the same causes that have confined women to monotonous toil in a narrow sphere . . . have . . . left injurious effects upon the mind and character of women themselves.
—Laura M. Clay, Association for the Advancement of Women Congress, 1882

AMID THE HORROR AND HARDSHIPS OF THE CIVIL WAR, a onetime schoolteacher named Virginia Penny worried about the women left behind. "At no time in our country's history have so many women been thrown upon their own exertions," she explained. "A million of men are on the battle field, and thousands of women, formerly dependent on them, have lost or may soon lose their only support." For them, Penny published *The Employments of Women: A Cyclopedia of Woman's Work*, detailing more than five hundred occupations open to women and evaluating each for healthfulness, pay, and training required. The crisis of war opened the way for Penny to champion women who "seek new channels of labor," but the need she identified was hardly limited to wartime. Hers was among the first of dozens of books with titles such as *How to Make Money although a Woman* and *Thrown on Her Own Resources; or, What Girls Can Do* published in the last third of the nineteenth century. Most of these books addressed a middle-class audience of girls and women who knew from experience that a changing economy left little room for widows and maiden aunts at home. In a culture devoted to companionate marriage, "spinster" had become a pejorative, but the word still carried the echo of a lost status. A century earlier, when the household had been a center of economic production, an unmarried woman was not a burden but an extra set of hands to spin—or to weed, milk, tend fires, pluck feathers, gather kindling, in short, to do all the woman's work that was "never done." But by the Civil War era, at least in cities, the displacement of household production by a cash economy meant that a husbandless woman without a job was an expense, not an asset. Louisa May Alcott (herself a husbandless woman with many jobs) offered these women a heroine in the character of Christie Devon, who proclaimed "a new Declaration of Independence. . . . I'm going to take care of myself, and not be a burden any longer."[1]

Twenty years after Virginia Penny's book was published, and ten years after Alcott's appeared, the issue had lost none of its urgency. A young woman writing to the *Davenport Gazette* in 1883 begged for "some general system by which girls can be aided to become more able to earn their own living. All girls cannot be teachers no more than all boys can be journalists." But the tone of her letter marked a change. Penny had worried that war would deprive women of the support owed them by husbands, fathers, or sons. This young woman in Davenport saw wage earning as a means to avoid subordination to a husband. She openly scorned marriage: "If I am not going to be an equal partner I would prefer to keep out." Like Alcott's heroine, the writer associated wage earning with the characteristics of a virtuous citizen: "Why should not girls be permitted to be pecuniarily independent and self-reliant?" The trouble she—and all women—faced was that few occupations open to women paid enough to make the worker "pecuniarily independent."[2]

Each in her own way, Penny, Alcott, and the anonymous young Davenport woman sought to shape debate over an issue that emerged as a full-fledged social problem in the 1870s, employment for women. Like most social problems, this one operated on more than one level. For millions of women, the quandary was simple economics: how to pay for food, shelter, and clothing for themselves and their dependents. For millions more, both men and women, the issue was cultural: what did it mean for families, for society, and for women themselves if they left the domestic sphere, competed with men for jobs and pay, and endured the poverty that seemed to haunt so many women workers? As the preceding chapter suggests, a great many people feared that paid employment placed women on the path to becoming prostitutes. Yet by the 1870s, a growing number of women proposed that access to paid employment brought women a step closer to full citizenship. Louisa May Alcott called it the "new emancipation."[3]

WOMEN'S WAGES AND UNION WAGES

As a social problem, women's employment coincided with the struggles over the "labor question" that dominated politics in the late nineteenth century, yet the most popular answers to the labor question only rarely dealt with women's employment. Even within the Knights of Labor, which was on record as favoring equal pay and the organization of women, individual members tended to embrace the idea that in the cooperative commonwealth, women would stay at home. This view shaped the Knights' willingness to admit homemakers to membership, acknowledging that most women's productive labor took place in the domestic sphere. For trade unions, the defining struggle of the era was over the control and conditions of labor in the industrial workplace, a focus that almost inevitably pushed the problems of working women to the periphery. In the 1880s, nearly 55 percent of women wage earners were domestic servants, and a large proportion of the balance worked in the needle trades, often as pieceworkers in their own homes. Isolation from fellow workers characterized wage-earning women's circumstances to an extent male workers more rarely experienced. Even where women worked in industrial settings, the gendered construction of their presence made them outsiders. Only two trade unions permitted women to join (the typographers and the cigar makers), and both did so reluctantly. Union men preferred to argue that the success of unions would give men wages adequate to keep wives and daughters at home and out of competition with men.[4]

Local events in Davenport—especially a pair of strikes by cigar makers in the mid-1880s—may have reinforced the impression that labor unions could offer little of value to working women. Cigar making was a growth industry in Davenport. In 1880, fifteen different shops employed an average total of 102 workers, producing almost $185,000 worth of goods. A decade later, twenty-nine shops employed 273 pieceworkers and another 59 operatives to produce nearly $500,000 worth of goods. Most of these shops were small operations, often with only 1 or 2 workers producing cigars at home. But Nicholas Kuhnen's factory was one of the largest in the West, employing nearly 300 pieceworkers in 1882. In December 1881, cigar makers in Davenport requested a charter from the Cigarmakers' International Union, organizing as Local 172. By September 1882, the union had only about 73 members, none of them apparently women, although women were employed in large numbers at Kuhnen's factory. In October, however, organizing began in earnest, especially among the women. Of the 20 new members who joined that month, about a dozen were women. The following month brought in 31 new members, about half of them women. Two months' organizing brought a 70 percent increase in membership, and about 22 percent of Local 172's members were women.[5]

In November, in the midst of this burst of organizing, Nicholas Kuhnen cut women's piecework rates by 25 percent. Kuhnen claimed that the cut brought his rates into line with those paid by cigar factories in New York City, an argument contested by the Davenport cigar makers, who published their own version of New York City piece rates. The timing of the cut was certainly suspicious, coming just after the union made significant progress in organizing Kuhnen's shop. On 14 November 1882, in response to the rate cut, 90 workers, mostly women, struck Kuhnen's shop. The following day, they were joined by 130 more. Otto Albrecht's small shop, with just a dozen employees, responded to an identical rate cut by joining the strike, which now had the International Union's approval. By December, Kuhnen had raised the stakes, installing equipment to mechanize cigar making and hiring substitute workers—Germans and Bohemians brought in from Wisconsin and unskilled women to work the new machines. "Many of these never saw a leaf of tobacco until within a week," reported one rather dazzled newspaperman, "yet they are expert cigar-makers."[6]

The strike dragged on through the winter and into March before collapsing. In the end, Kuhnen not only kept his piece rate low but accomplished his production goals with a smaller, nonunion workforce. Joining the union had not benefited women cigar makers—indeed, it may have been what brought Kuhnen's wrath down on the workers. The union, in turn, levied fines of fifteen dollars—equivalent to more than three weeks' wages to many of the pieceworkers—on about half the women who had been recruited into the union, presumably for "ratting"—the cigar makers' term for scabbing.[7]

Anyone following the story in Davenport's newspapers would likely have been left wondering what unions had to offer women. It would have been easy to take a skeptical view: rather than leaving well enough alone, the cigar makers' union had persuaded women to turn against their employer, perhaps led to their pay being cut, then fined them when they called the strike a failure and returned to work. Three years later, when a reinvigorated union again began organizing, Kuhnen cannily played the gender card against it. He banned union membership among his employees, then defended himself by claiming that the union wanted to bar women from cigar making. "Those loud-mouthed leaders of the cigar-makers' unions," he charged, "never seem to have observed that one of the most prominent social questions of the day is to open the door to the members of the female sex for better and more remunerative occupations than they have heretofore been allowed to participate in." (Virginia Penny and her cohort were not lost on him.) Kuhnen might know how to talk the talk, replied the union, but he did not walk the walk: Kuhnen paid women piecework rates only 40 to 50 percent of what union members earned in other factories. "Now, you great champion of Woman's Rights, show your magnanimous generosity, by giving those poor, overworked women what justly belongs to them," replied the union's committee. In a letter to the *Democrat* signed by "The Girls in Kuhnen's Employ" (and claiming to have been written without Kuhnen's knowledge), the women cigar makers appeared to insert themselves into the debate on Kuhnen's side. "We claim that we are not overworked and our wages are equal to those paid to women any place," they wrote. These women saw the union's "equal pay for equal work" not as a promise but as a threat. Their wages were "women's" wages, set by custom and reflecting the presumption argued by economist John Stuart Mill: that women need earn no more than "the pittance absolutely required for the sustenance of one human being." The cigar makers understood that if they demanded wages equal to men's, their jobs would go to men. All in all, for the women cigar makers in Davenport, the union's bargain seemed a devil's bargain. Still, they revealed the social consequences of "women's" wages in their plea to keep their jobs: "there is many a poor family in Davenport who depend entirely on this shop for support." Women could support their families on Kuhnen's wages, but their families would be poor as a result.[8]

MOTHERING THE WORKING GIRL

The seemingly inevitable link between women's wages and poverty only reinforced fears that employment for women concealed a moral danger. One response to the social problem of women's employment emerged from the matrix of benevolent organizations—mostly Protestant—that drew together middle-class and elite women in the years just before and after the Civil War. Assuming a moral authority based in gender, members of these groups proposed that, as women, they could offer guidance and protection to their vulnerable sisters. Most of these efforts fell into the category historians have characterized as "class-bridging organizations." They embodied a genuine interest in improving the lot of the workers who made up the preponderance of members yet remained under the control of the founders and reflected their values. Those seeking to help women workers shared common beliefs: that woman's sphere was the home and that work for pay debased a woman and endangered her morals.[9]

Young Women's Christian Associations (YWCAs), which emerged independently in several cities in the 1860s and 1870s and came together in a national organization by 1873, understood their clients as "young women"—or, more often, girls—and fell easily into the language of motherhood. Worrying about newcomers to the city, an 1881 report cast them as lost children: "The poor things wander from place to place, not knowing where to go or what to do." The YWCA's commitment to the domestic ideal found expression in the organization's programs. Believing women who worked for a living to be "unfortunate," the association's solution was to "provide the influence and protection of a Christian home" for "poor, lonely, and isolated" working women. In keeping with these goals, urban YWCAs emphasized Bible classes, employment bureaus, and residences for working girls. YWCAs generally limited participation to those who could provide letters of church membership in one of the evangelical Protestant denominations. Catholics, Jews, Universalists, and those with no church affiliation were either excluded or limited to "associate memberships," with no role in governance. In YWCA homes, watchful matrons supervised residents' morals, enforcing strict rules and encouraging residents to spend their evenings in the safety of the home rather than venturing out to sample the dance halls, theaters, and other amusements that might endanger their souls. Some YWCAs sponsored classes in gymnastics or dressmaking, but equally typical was a housekeeping course designed to teach girls to be "serviceable at home." So immersed in the ideal of domesticity were most YWCA sponsors that they deemed learning to set a table or make a bed key to the development of girls' characters.[10]

The working girls' clubs organized in New York City by heiress Grace Dodge rejected the evangelical Christianity of the YWCA in favor of an open door for Catholics, Jews, and nonevangelicals, but the clubs still embraced the belief that daily toil made girls "as dull as the materials with which they labor" and destroyed their self-respect. Like the YWCA, working girls' club sponsors assumed that domesticity was the ideal toward which members should aspire. Indeed, Dodge began by meeting with silk weavers to instruct them in housekeeping. The club that grew out of this initial contact sought to uplift workers by providing "plenty to interest mind and heart," meeting for discussion and self-improvement, much like the middle-class women in literary societies who were their contemporaries.[11]

The first sponsors of working girls' clubs in New York City in the 1880s were, like Dodge, socially elite young women, often young marrieds not much older than their "girls," who "repeatedly exhorted club members to reach for higher standards of refinement, purity, and domesticity." Clubs turned their energy to developing working-class adolescents into "wives, mothers and homemakers," offering classes in inexpensive cookery, mending and sewing, household management, and manners. The morals of working girls were a particular worry for Dodge, who in her writings and "practical talks" warned against "the sacrifice of purity of thought." Dodge admonished her charges, "until you are married you must not behave as if you were." As the movement grew in size and spread to other cities, the clubs began to expand their programs. They offered classes in typing, bookkeeping, millinery, dressmaking, and even typesetting and glasswork. Employment bureaus helped members find better jobs. Still, for many members, the chief benefit of the club continued to be the opportunity it offered for respectable sociability, and some members clearly valued the guidance in matters of dress and deportment offered by elite sponsors.[12]

Both the YWCA and Grace Dodge's working girls' clubs saw their clients not as self-supporting women but as girls—girls for whom employment was a temporary status, girls who would soon leave the factory or office to enter their true calling as wives and mothers. Indeed, most working girls would do just that. But this was not the only view of working women adopted by class-bridging organizations. The Boston Women's Educational and Industrial Union (WEIU), founded in 1877 by a group including prominent professional women, sought to aid "*all classes* of women," not just those who worked for a living. Its expansive social vision led it to experiment with an impressive array of social programs. It opened lunchrooms for women, an employment bureau, evening classes, and club rooms where members could meet in the city center. Its program of social investigation led to services for children, including school lunches and milk distribution. Yet as Sarah Deutsch has argued, what began with an emphasis on the cross-class unity of women gradually shifted as the elite women who led the WEIU sought allies and collaborators among politically powerful men. Indeed, their interest in shaping public policy led them to seek—and find—real political power. Similarly, the young Florence Kelley helped a group of teachers found the New Century Working Women's Guild in 1882. Renting a mansion in downtown Philadelphia, the guild offered day and evening classes, a reading room, and social activities.[13]

THE ASSOCIATION FOR THE ADVANCEMENT OF WOMEN

"Among the various problems that wait for solution at the hands of women in the present age, that of her self-support presses foremost," declared the Reverend Augusta Cooper Bristol in an address to the Association for the Advancement of Women (AAW) in 1885. That October, two hundred delegates, including a group from Davenport, gathered in Des Moines for the AAW's first meeting west of the Mississippi. Bristol's was not the only speech at the congress to raise the issue of women's work. More than half the presentations dwelled on some facet of the problem. But as woman after woman rose to address the assembly, listeners would have drawn a very different conclusion about the problem of women's employment than that offered by the organizers of the working girls' clubs or the YWCA. Where those women praised the home as woman's province and saw paid work as inferior, perhaps even dangerous, the women of the AAW embraced paid employment as a source of personal and social virtue. Their analysis evoked antebellum Republican free-labor discourse but took a radical turn by applying the promise of independence to women.[14]

In the decades before the Civil War, those who came together to form the Republican Party articulated a set of beliefs about work and social order that were encapsulated in the expression "free labor." When northerners spoke of free labor, they meant it in contrast to the slave labor of the South, but the difference was complex. "Labor" they used in an expansive sense, encompassing small businessmen and farmers as well as wage-earning mechanics and menials. Free labor was labor with the opportunity for social mobility, labor that had economic choices and could perhaps work its way out of the wage-earning class and into an "independence."[15]

The desire for social mobility, to lift oneself out of the wage-earning class, had a political dimension as well. In contrast to black slaves, whose enforced dependency was both economic and political, free white men expected to participate in the civic life of the American republic. Economic self-sufficiency—or at least the promise of sufficiency—enabled a man to enter the public sphere on terms of equality. Antebellum Republicans resisted the idea that industrialization might bring with it a hardening of the difference between worker and owner, between wage earner and petty capitalist. The creation of classes struck them as inconsistent with self-government: "wage slavery" deprived men of the dignity of citizenship, placing them on a level with chattel slaves. To be dependent on another for a livelihood was to be beholden: it was "antithetical to citizenship."[16]

While antebellum Republicans may have wanted to believe, with economist Henry C. Carey, that "the interests labor and capital" were "in perfect harmony with each other" and that free labor would keep social classes fluid, the transformation of American industry that was becoming evident by the 1850s made it increasingly hard to argue that any man could, through hard work and frugal ways—or pluck and luck—turn himself from wage earner into capitalist. The emergence of a permanent wage-earning class threatened the ideal of an independent citizenry that underlay workingmen's claims to a political voice. How could a class of wage earners claim the independence necessary to republican citizenship? As Nancy Fraser, Linda Gordon, and Alice Kessler-Harris have all suggested, one strategy lay in the reconfiguration of "dependence" and "independence" around gender.[17]

No longer able to claim independence as self-employed producers wielding craft knowledge and the tools of their trades, wage-earning men gradually embraced a consumer's model for defining independence: the "family wage," meaning a wage sufficient to support a wife and children who were not employed. Men became "independent" by virtue of having others dependent on them. This was why union men preferred to imagine their wives and daughters at home, not in the workplace or the union hall. This new model of independence also fit increasing numbers of middle-class men—managers, salesmen, and engineers—who worked in the expanding corporate economy as well as their working-class counterparts. Whereas in the preindustrial household, the labor of subordinates was valued as economically necessary to the household, in this new industrial-age model, women's dependence defined men's independence, and women's household labor was redefined into leisure, a process Jeanne Boydston has called "the pastoralization of housework."[18]

The figure of the housewife, Fraser and Gordon have noted, "melded woman's traditional sociolegal and political dependency"—coverture—"with her more recent economic dependency in the industrial order." But "dependency" had changed its meaning with industrialization. The new language of dependency now placed wives in a category also occupied by two excoriated "others": "paupers," who were presumed corrupted by their dependence on charity, and "slaves" or their colonial counterparts, "natives," who were considered uncivilized, childlike, and in need of the guidance of a "superior race." The language of "separate spheres"—always flexible, always handy—emerged to mask the implied derogation. Woman, though dependent, was not inferior, went the logic. She was outside, perhaps *above*, the brutal world of men and commerce. This was the position adopted by the organizers of the YWCA and the working girls' clubs. "Protected" from labor by the men who supported them, these women embraced their outsider status as ground for moral authority. Even as wage-earning men claimed the independence required for republican citizenship by virtue of supporting dependents, dependent wives and daughters mediated their citizenship through familial obligations, espousing causes that could be construed as "maternal."[19]

Not everyone joined the rush for the pedestal. Reaching back to the antebellum rhetoric of free labor, the women of the AAW embraced the promise of independence and social mobility, even as they named and scorned the new meanings attached to dependency. For many of these women, "free labor" was their native tongue, the political discourse of their coming-of-age. Longtime member Laura Clay was the daughter of Cassius Marcellus Clay, an antislavery Kentucky Whig who helped form the Republican Party. Laura Clay's father was absent during much of her childhood, but her mother, Mary Ann Warfield Clay, shared her husband's politics, defying local elites to supply the U.S. Army during the Civil War. When the Clays divorced in 1878, Laura and her sisters received an object lesson in the dangers of dependence. After years of laboring without her husband to build up the farm and free it from debt, Mary Ann Clay was forced to give up even her dower right to the property. Ada Sweet, another woman who used the AAW as a forum to defend women's employment, was the daughter of a Republican state senator in Wisconsin who received a commission as an army major when the Civil War began. Her appointment as a federal pension agent after the war came as a political favor from President Ulysses Grant. And Dr. Jennie McCowen of Davenport, who spoke on "Women Physicians in Hospitals for the Insane," lost her only brother in the war and maintained her link to the politics of the 1860s through her longtime membership in the Women's Relief Corps of the Grand Army of the Republic.[20]

These women understood the conflation of economic and political independence, and they claimed the right to labor for pay as a step toward securing the rights of citizenship. Their position was well within the mainstream of the woman's rights movement, echoing the resolution offered by Lucretia Mott at the Seneca Falls convention of 1848: "*Resolved*, that the speedy success of our cause depends upon . . . securing to woman an equal participation with men in the various trades, professions, and commerce." Like the young woman in Davenport who sought employment but scorned marriage, they emphasized pay as the key to women's autonomy and challenged the political premise of the "family wage." AAW speakers were not terribly concerned about whether a woman's income came from wages, self-employment, or the investment of capital. Where for a man, wages might imply dependence on a master, for a woman, wages meant freedom not to be dependent on a husband. At a level both personal and political, women's wages threatened men's new understanding of "independence."[21]

THE POLITICAL MEANING OF WOMEN'S EMPLOYMENT

To their audience in Des Moines and to a wider audience that read the published proceedings, AAW speakers explained that the problem of woman's self-support was both structural and moral. To achieve economic independence, women needed access to jobs with sufficient pay. This meant challenging the gendered division of labor and developing strategies to improve women's wages. To achieve political independence, all women needed to embrace the obligation of self-support, thus freeing women from stigmatization as a dependent class. This meant defying the social condemnation that followed women in the workforce.

The women of the AAW sought first to claim women's labor as a positive social good. Alida Avery proclaimed work as "joy." To physician Julia Homes Smith, "work mean[t] self-respect." Not only did women who did not work lose those satisfactions, but their dependency endangered democracy, even civilization itself. In her speech, Sweet outlined the argument of social theorist Herbert Spencer: "It is not until an individual or community begin to recognize . . . the blessedness and happiness of work and cease to regard it as a curse and something to be shunned, that any great advance in civilization can be claimed." But Sweet gave Spencer's argument a gendered spin the eminent philosopher would not have recognized. As long as women expected to be supported as dependents, she proposed, their idleness would hamper the ascendancy of American civilization. "Contempt of manual labor, want of sympathy with those who are engaged in it, social caste, vanity of riches, worship of rank, these are commonly met with in some countries, in men and women," wrote Sweet, "but in our country, women are the only ones, with a few insignificant exceptions, that cultivate and stimulate these relics of the ages of ignorance and barbarism." Avery, in turn, clarified the way that dependency placed women in the same class as paupers. Drawing on scientific analyses of the urban underclass that were shaping the charity organization movement, Avery shrewdly compared "girl-life in the U.S.A." with the upbringing of "pauper children." Just as almsgiving taught the poor that they need not work, gender conventions taught American girls a similar lesson of idleness rewarded. Girls grow up "in a moral atmosphere well-calculated to make them, throughout their lives, burdens upon the people," wrote Avery. "Their characters are warped, their self-reliance is utterly destroyed, and the foundations of useless and miserable lives are laid"—all because girls were "not taught to work." Housework, insisted Avery, did not count. Necessary though it might be, the "endless routine" of household labor cannot produce "the inspiration that comes from the sense of growing power, of increasing skill." Girls' education in dependency even thwarted the development of society. "We shall not find the true worth of woman in the work of the world until the girl breathes freedom in the cradle; until she learns to listen for her call; until she realizes that there is for her a vocation, and that she fails both in duty and in privilege if she does not discipline her powers to its faithful following."[22]

Other speakers were explicit in declaring nonemployed women a threat to democratic government. The "limited experience and narrow life of the mass of women" who do not work, argued Sweet, made women "the last to throw off prejudice or superstition, and walk by the light of reason." At the 1882 AAW congress, Laura Clay made the point with even greater force: "Lack of independence is also shown by the blind adherence to leaders which politicians and historians have noted," she warned. "It has also caused [women] too often to be found among the supporters of tottering tyrannies." Dependency made women the dupes of demagogues. Work, in turn, was not merely the basis of economic independence. "The richest woman must become a worker in one field or another," argued Antoinette Brown Blackwell in 1886, "or else she will assuredly lose half the value of an earnest life." Work brought strength of character, breadth of experience, and self-reliance—the keys to virtuous citizenship.[23]

In celebrating employment as a source of social virtue and the key to the rights of citizenship, the AAW chose a different political path from the one historians have associated with the suffrage movement of the 1870s and 1880s. Antebellum suffragists had argued that women possessed the same natural rights as men and therefore should have the same political rights. In the decades after the Civil War, supporters of woman suffrage were more likely to argue that women deserved the right to vote because of their special moral authority, an authority grounded in their role as mothers. Susan B. Anthony and Elizabeth Cady Stanton briefly tried to build a suffrage movement around wage-earning women, but as Ellen DuBois has argued, their vision of "independence and equality with men" had little meaning for most wage earners, whose pay was below subsistence levels. Anthony and Stanton found a more receptive audience among middle-class women who saw politics in terms of "Home Protection." In the AAW, the ideal of a movement for women's equality based on economic independence lived on.[24]

While proposing that women's failure to work for pay posed a serious social problem, AAW speakers were well aware of the difficulties faced by women who did enter the workforce: narrow opportunities, low pay, and social isolation, at least for those who aspired to middle-class respectability. For AAW members more than for those who assumed that all working women would be working class, these three problems were inextricably linked. The crowding of many women into few occupations depressed pay for everyone, yet women channeled themselves into a narrow range of occupations in part because those few occupations were the only ones considered socially acceptable. Teaching was "possibly proper" and "not to be despised"—though there was the danger that if a woman taught for too long, she would get "those stiff, precise, schoolma'am ways that men so hate." But when so many women entered teaching, the market became glutted and "salaries [were] cut to starvation rates." On the other hand, "The day the girl begins to sew, to wait in a shop, to practice telegraphy, or use the typewriter or short-hand, that day she is socially ostracized." In contrast, "Idleness is respectable. A song, a smile, a grace are worth more than a hard day's work" in the currency of the parlor.[25]

The AAW offered two solutions to the problem of social ostracism. The first was for elite women to join their sisters in making employment honorable by power of example. Some, like Ella Lapham and Ednah Dow Cheney, proposed that this could be accomplished by all women entering the workforce. As Cheney argued in 1887, "The fallacy that it is an ungraceful thing for women to work for money has lessened the respect of the public toward women workers. It is the duty of every woman, rich or poor, to do something for pay, to show that it is not disgraceful." Julia Holmes Smith proposed a more modest effort based in rituals of sociability. She urged taking a lesson from "business men, who habitually invite to their houses the young men in their employ who . . . manifest right dispositions and good abilities. No questions are asked concerning genealogy, or family connections." By inviting working women into their homes, elite women could counteract the "feeling of caste" that separated women from each other and made idleness respectable and self-support unseemly. Augusta Bristol agreed, calling it women's duty to make business opportunities "attractive by all the social prestige we can throw about them."[26]

The second strategy circled back to the linked problem of narrow opportunities. The AAW sought to identify all the employments they could possibly claim as respectable for women, focusing especially on fields not yet segregated by gender. As Imogene Fales explained, "woman should enter fields of employment where labor is not yet a drug on the market." Over the decades of its existence, AAW members heard papers on "Women in Journalism," "Women in Dentistry," "Women as Architects," "The Necessity of Woman Professorships in Mixed Colleges," "Opportunities for Women's Work in the Southern States," and "Bee Culture" as well as dozens of other possibilities. Such papers followed in the footsteps of Virginia Penny's *Cyclopedia of Woman's Work*.[27]

While some AAW members urged "Women's Need of Business Education" and looked for "Better Business Opportunities for Women," others went a step further, urging that businesses owned by women offered an especially promising field for advancement. "Pecuniary success," argued Ella Lapham, was more likely to come to the woman who worked as an "independent producer" because she could avoid discriminatory wages. "Her handiwork she can sell upon its own merits," explained Lapham, "her labor she is too often forced to sell as a woman's." Antoinette Brown Blackwell, observing that "man's industrial work is almost wholly the product of associated effort in some form," encouraged women to think big: "What women especially need is more co-operation among themselves; more large enterprises which are either wholly or in part under their own management and patronage."[28]

The desire to claim new fields of labor for women led the AAW to take a particular interest in documenting the precise boundaries of women's advancement into new occupations. For example, in 1878 the AAW sent a petition to the U.S. Senate urging that women be employed as census enumerators in equal numbers with men and that effort be made to count all women workers. Indeed, the need to count, to establish just what fields of labor were open to women, became a theme of AAW activities in the 1880s. Increasing numbers of papers on women and work appeared on the annual program, culminating in an 1886 "labor symposium."[29]

As they identified employments for women, AAW members also asserted that altering the gendered divisions of labor would not jeopardize "natural" gender differences. After all, argued Augusta Bristol, man had entered virtually every kind of work, and no one worried that this endangered his manhood. It surely followed that sauce for the gander was sauce for the goose: "Why will not woman, with every avenue of business activity open to her, retain her womanliness as naturally and surely as man has retained his manliness?" If there were occupations for which women were naturally unsuited, they would soon discover this and abandon those fields. "Remove the artificial barriers which hinder women's power of self-support, and she will find her natural limitations," urged Bristol. Admitting that women who are the first to enter a new field "do often exhibit a forcefulness and antagonism of character which is not in harmony with the popular idea of womanhood," Bristol insisted this was the effect not of work itself but of "the obstacles [women] are obliged to overcome in order to reach and hold the position." As pioneers, these women had to build their own highway. "Honor and gratefulness be to them; for along this now rugged road our daughters' daughters shall walk a path made smooth and easy, and with that dignity and grace which accompanies attractive womanhood," she promised.[30]

Honor and gratefulness be to *us*, she might have said, for the AAW's membership roster was dense with the names of pioneering professional women. Bristol was an ordained minister. Astronomer Maria Mitchell, poet and race woman Frances E. W. Harper, physicians Marie Zakrzewska and Eliza Mosher, attorneys J. Ellen Foster and Belva Lockwood, activist Frances Willard and social theorist the Reverend Antoinette Brown Blackwell all took out memberships. Created in 1873 to promote "practical methods for securing to women higher intellectual, moral, and physical conditions," the AAW was self-consciously an elite organization, though its elitism was based in achievement rather than mere social caste. Unlike the Woman's Christian Temperance Union or the YWCA, with members numbering in the thousands or tens of thousands, the AAW never counted more than about five hundred members.[31]

THE PROBLEM OF WOMEN'S EMPLOYMENT IN IOWA

The Des Moines meeting of the AAW proved to be one of several episodes that converged to inspire women in Davenport, led by physician Jennie McCowen, to organize on behalf of working women in the city. McCowen joined the AAW in 1881 and became its vice president for Iowa in 1884. As a woman who had become self-supporting at sixteen, earned a medical degree at thirty, and had come to Davenport to open a medical practice in 1880, Dr. McCowen was already personally interested in the problem of women's employment. In the AAW, she found a forum in which women like her were attempting not only to solve the problems of self-supporting women but to recast women's employment from a social danger to a social strength.

Much of the organization's work took place through its Committee on Reforms and Statistics (CRS), headed by Antoinette Brown Blackwell. Each year, the CRS drew up a plan for research on economic and legal issues relating to women, including a set of questions for the state vice presidents. The primary duty of their office was to prepare annual reports responding to these questions. In 1883, the CRS queried vice presidents about the numbers of men and women employed in "prominent industries," about their relative wages, about growth fields for women, and about women in "fields of labor unusual to their sex." A typical response filled one page of the AAW *Annual Report*, and the report submitted by Iowa's vice president that year was no different, asserting, "In Iowa women are taking advanced positions in every direction," and offering a handful of examples. That answer apparently did not satisfy Dr. McCowen. When she succeeded to the vice presidency in 1884, she chose to research not only the newly assigned questions on the relationship of women to taxes and property ownership in the state but those from the previous year as well. Drawing on the 1880 census and on her own surveys of women's condition, McCowen delivered a ten-page report on the status of women in Iowa, cataloging the diversity of occupations held by women, their property and inheritance rights under Iowa law, and nearly every other benchmark she could imagine, from the comparative number of male and female prisoners to the number of oratorical prizes taken by college women to the progress on a suffrage amendment in the Iowa General Assembly.[32]

McCowen's thoroughness was dazzling. She uncovered two women bank presidents and three women stockbrokers. She found that more than half of Iowa's twenty-three colleges and universities had one or more women on the faculty, "with the title professor and the corresponding salary," and that fully half the "tutors and instructors" in those institutions were women. Her catalog included the unexpected (women boilermakers, blacksmiths, barbers, and detectives) and documented the better known (the feminization of clerical work and teaching). By 1884, one in eleven Iowa school superintendents was a woman, including the young woman then known as Carrie Lane but later remembered as Carrie Chapman Catt. In recognition, perhaps, of this tour de force, McCowen found a place on the reforms committee and on the AAW program. Indeed, her impressive report likely played a role in persuading the AAW leadership to bring the congress to Des Moines the following year.[33]

Jennie McCowen's interest in changing the debate on women's employment led her to seek out a wider audience than the AAW for her research. That same year, 1884, she submitted a slightly different version of the report to the Iowa Commission for the World's Industrial and Cotton Exposition in New Orleans. The essay, which was also published in the State Historical Society's journal, *Annals of Iowa*, shifted some of the emphases of the AAW report and opened with the heartfelt gratitude of an adopted daughter: "No description of Iowa can be complete without some mention of the progressive and liberal attitude of the State toward women. In no state has it been more freely conceded that human interests are not one but many, and that the work of the world, broad and varied, must fall not upon one sex, nor upon one class, but that each individual, in return for benefit received, is in honor bound to bear his or her share of the burden." From there, McCowen moved on to justify women's departure from the "domestic circle" with a nod to the inexorable progress of Yankee ingenuity. Man has "invaded" woman's sphere, taking over her former tasks with "the invention of machinery." McCowen's argument echoed one offered by Susan B. Anthony and other nineteenth-century advocates of expanded employment for women. It is clear as well that McCowen had read and pondered the words of fellow AAW members on the topic. When she wrote, "It was inevitable that women would adapt themselves to the changed circumstances, . . . with too much self-respect to be a useless weight upon the industries of others," it is hard not to assume that she had been perusing Laura Clay's paper from the 1882 congress. "Impress [girls] with the noble desire for self-maintenance," urged Clay, "make them ashamed of hanging as useless weights on the industry of others."[34]

McCowen's essay operated on the loyalty of Iowans by making advanced women a point of pride. She had already experienced the power of Iowa boomers' desire to show up the conservative East. A year earlier, her colleagues in the Scott County Medical Society had elected her president, a position to which they would soon unanimously reelect her. The men of the medical society were well aware that they were making history, and newspaper reports suggest they expressed some glee at the fact. By contrast, women in Massachusetts were engaged in an ongoing struggle merely to win admission to medical societies—they hardly dreamed of winning the presidencies. In her column for Clara Bewick Colby's suffrage paper, the *Woman's Tribune*, McCowen regularly noted women's advances in the medical professions, soliciting contributions from readers by noting, "Iowa is a glorious state to live in and to work in, but I have no desire unduly to exalt it."[35]

When the CRS first queried the vice presidents on the employments of men and women, the committee offered the helpful suggestion that "the annual State Report on Labor and Industries will readily supply, to most of these queries, the answers." But in 1883, Iowa was still a year away from establishing a bureau of labor. Jennie McCowen had to assemble her data on her own. When the legislature set up the bureau, McCowen, in her capacity as vice president of the AAW for Iowa, wrote urging the new bureau to remember the women and to include on its questionnaires "such queries as would show adequately the relations of women to labor." When the first biennial report for 1884–85 came out, labor commissioner E. R. Hutchins openly admitted that he had failed on this account. Defending himself, he blamed the absence of data on the lack of interest from working women and from prominent women of the state. The implication was that women's labor was part of woman's sphere, and Hutchins apparently accepted the growing belief that public policy for women was the special province of women.[36]

Hutchins's implied challenge helped spark the third episode that inspired Davenport's women to organize. In the winter of 1886, Dr. McCowen called on two friends who were also self-supporting women, Lettie Meacham and Lile Bickford. The three constituted themselves a committee and assumed the task of collecting statistics on women's labor for the next reporting period. Their action was typical of the liminal position women occupied in relation to public policy in this era: they were self-designated, yet acknowledged—even valued—by officials; and they were outside the governmental structures that provided funding, continuity, and real authority. The women's committee examined the questionnaire Hutchins had used and recommended "improvements," which he adopted. When the new report appeared, with charts and tables on women, Hutchins could hardly contain his gratitude: "Had it not been for this one person in the State, whose zeal in this excellent cause has never flagged—whose active life in the interests of womanhood has already been felt far outside the limits of her own State—had it not been for this person, the prominent absence of data upon this subject would have again shown itself in this report. This person interested herself in the personal distribution of blanks, and had her time been less occupied, the results would have been much larger." That "one person," of course, was McCowen. Even with her efforts, only 155 women (out of some 80,000 employed women in the state) responded, and it is difficult not to suspect they all lived in Davenport.[37]

The questionnaires provided direct evidence of the difficulties faced by Iowa's working women. A nurse with an "intemperate husband" explained that she had begun work when her firstborn was six weeks old and continued through the births of eight more children. "They are all a blessing, and while I have to be away from them so much, it is not a hard task to work for them." A clerk in a shoe store assured McCowen and her associates, "I am much interested your work; am much in favor of the advancement of my own sex; for my part will do all I can." Continuing, she bemoaned the discrepancy in pay between herself and the men she worked with, "although this day I am six hundred sales ahead! Call this justice? But I have to grin and bear it, because I am so unfortunate as to be a woman." A stenographer wrote, "I am happily situated, but my heart goes out to the number of poor, hard-working, [h]alf-paid, half-starved female wage-workers, and would do a great deal to raise their wages—and in that way their spirits."[38]

The 155 women who responded to a decidedly unscientific survey can hardly be taken as representative wage earners. But knowing how the survey was administered makes their answers significant in a different way. Because Bickford, Meacham, and McCowen were personally responsible for distributing and collecting a majority of the questionnaires, the answers reveal the way these women in particular encountered wage-earning women. As a group, the women surveyed were much older than the teenage working girl who was the typical female wage earner of the period and the focus of YWCAs and working girls' clubs. The thirty-one dressmakers averaged twenty-eight years old; the nineteen house servants thirty-three years old; and the thirteen printers thirty-four years old. Only store clerks, bookkeepers, and telegraph operators (of whom there were forty-six altogether) averaged between eighteen and twenty-two years old. Most of the 155 women earned less than three hundred dollars a year, and most supported two or three people in addition to themselves. Significantly, none of the women surveyed were factory workers. There were no cigar makers, no candy factory or woolen mill operatives, no girls from the Amazon Pickle Works. Factory jobs were the ones most likely to be held by unskilled teenagers working only until marriage. The women surveyed were attached to the labor force; they were predominantly skilled or semiskilled workers; they were supporting themselves and dependents; and they were in it for the long haul. They were the women for whom the "problem" of women's employment had immediate and enduring significance.[39]

By the winter of 1886, this confluence of episodes—the 1885 AAW Congress in Des Moines with its emphasis on women's labor, McCowen's research for her report and essay, and the investigations begun by the women's committee for the Iowa Bureau of Labor—contributed to the perception shared by McCowen and her colleagues that something ought to be done to assist working women. A year earlier in Des Moines, Julia Ward Howe had praised the "possibilities of co-operation" to "promote the industrial interests of women," anticipating the creation of a "great industrial association." To ears familiar with the language of labor organizations in the late nineteenth century, Howe's choice of words might seem to imply a kind of labor union, one organized along the lines of the Knights of Labor or perhaps anticipating the industrial organization of the American Railway Union. But when Bickford, McCowen, and their circle decided to seek strength in the "co-operation of others," the model they chose was not a labor union but a club.[40]

The club—especially the woman's club—might not seem an ideal form in which to organize working women. Woman's clubs evoke a set of images more easily associated with middle-class women of leisure than with self-supporting workers: afternoon teas and earnest papers on Shakespeare and Milton. But the woman's club of the 1880s carried another set of associations as well. Women's organizations frequently proposed themselves as the feminine counterpart to the masculine public sphere. Largely excluded from elective office and marginalized within political parties, women found in their organizations a means to claim authority and bring their concerns to bear on public policy. Indeed, the annual Woman's Congress of the AAW began from just such roots. *New York World* columnist Jane Croly called for a meeting as a way to bypass the suffrage issue. "There is no need of waiting till men give us a vote," she insisted, "we take it without asking, and we apply ourselves at once to an examination of the causes of the evil we deplore and of the remedy to be applied." In Croly's vision, women's organizations could constitute an entire shadow government. "There is no reason why women should not elect their president and the entire corps if they choose of representatives," she declared. "They should keep a cabinet or standing executive committee, always in session. They would soon have official organs, and might erect a Capitol of their own in New York City." While this original plan might seem, as Julia Ward Howe thought, "vast and vague," its echo can be heard in the decision to call the AAW annual meeting the "Woman's Congress." Exclusion from the male public sphere enforced separate organization, but separatism became, as Estelle Freedman has argued, a strategy: women increasingly relied on presumed gender difference to claim expertise on public policy relating to women and girls. In Davenport, Dr. Jennie McCowen became the center of a circle of women who sought to use a club to advance the interests of working women. In so doing, McCowen and those who worked with her negotiated a delicate balance, seeking to claim employment as the basis for women's political equality while exploiting the growing belief that gender difference gave women special authority on policies relating to women.[41]

A PLACE IN THE CITY
The Working Woman's Lend a Hand Club

> That No Woman's Land, which occupied a forbidden tract between domestic duty and business bread-winning, which a few years ago no girl or woman could enter without being regarded by her own sex as unsexed, and by men as intruding upon their special prerogatives and preserves, is now swarming with female "boomers." They have camped there and have gone to stay.
> —*Davenport Times*, 30 January 1889

CHRISTMAS DAY 1886 DAWNED COLD AND CRISP in Davenport. The weather had been mild, but earlier that week, a cold snap put a hard surface on the muddy streets and turned the Mississippi River into an ice bridge over which folks safely walked to reach the cities to the south, Rock Island and Moline, Illinois. A light snow fell in the afternoon, veiling the layers of coal smoke and grime in two inches of glittering white. For those who strolled out to make Christmas calls, the city must have presented a picturesque sight: street upon street of houses climbing up the gentle bluffs, the warm glow of their windows reflecting on the snow in the early twilight. Along the riverfront, the lumber mills and factories lay quiet, their smokestacks as cool as the church steeples. Across the river, other houses climbed other bluffs, rising above other mills and factories, a mirror image across the mile-wide plain of ice.[1]

Two women who ventured out that day, Dr. Jennie McCowen and Anna J. S. McCrum, made their way across town to one especially handsome home on the city's west side. Set back on a broad lawn, with verandas framing the tall parlor windows, it was the picture-perfect setting for a traditional Christmas celebration, an image straight out of a holiday lithograph. No matter that the "traditional" Christmas of 1886 was just over a half century old. Neither McCowen, age forty-one, nor McCrum, thirty-seven, was old enough to remember the raucous working-class street carnival that had preceded the child-centered festival of domesticity. Indeed, their city had no Christmas traditions older than the ones now celebrated, having been platted on the site of a Mesquakie village barely fifty years earlier. So as they stepped into the high-ceilinged hall, with its elegant staircase and dark polished woodwork, either woman might have paused to reflect with irony or wistfulness: on the holiday dedicated to home and family, McCrum and McCowen joined a gathering at the Clarissa Cook Home for the Friendless, celebrating that year, as every year, without family.[2]

Sixteen elderly women lived at the Cook Home that winter. As they gathered in the dining room and saw the feast and small gifts laid out for them, one exclaimed, "This does not look as though we are friendless." And truly, the Cook Home was not built for women without friends. Opened in 1882, it had been endowed by the wealthy widow of Ebenezer Cook, an officer of the Chicago, Rock Island, & Pacific Railroad. Clarissa Cook's will provided a retirement home for women over sixty, "without distinction as to nationality or color." It was a haven for women who may well have had friends but who lacked family to care for them in old age. This was a condition common enough anywhere in the United States, but it was especially true in places like Davenport, where every woman over sixty had come from somewhere else, often leaving family behind and often sending children on to yet other places. The same railroad that generated the endowment for the home also created its clientele.[3]

The Cook Home represented what Americans in the 1880s liked to call "woman's work for woman": philanthropy initiated by women on behalf of the less fortunate of their sex. As charity, it came with a paradox. While appearing to uphold the nineteenth-century gender ideal that confined women to a separate sphere of private, nurturing duties, "woman's work for woman" often subverted that ideal by inventing professional employment opportunities for women. Clarissa Cook's will established not just a home for elderly women, it created an enduring institution staffed and managed by women who became self-supporting as a result. The Cook Home also recognized another change that followed the network of railroads overspreading the country: the home offered temporary shelter to transient women of "good character"—those who came with an introduction. Easy mobility meant not only that aged women might be left without families but also that younger women might travel far from home and family in search of employment. The Cook Home offered assistance to these women as well, acknowledging that, from choice or chance, not every woman remained within the domestic circle.

After the Christmas feast and entertainments had ended, five women lingered on in the dining room. These were not the elderly clients of the home but the working women who staffed it. Dr. Jennie McCowen was the home's physician on call. Miss

The Lend a Hand Club

Residents and staff in front of the Clarissa Cook Home for Friendless Women, c. 1900. Lettie Meacham is standing in the light-colored dress at the far right. (Clarissa C. Cook Home, Davenport, Iowa.)

Lile Bickford, thirty-one, was the home's matron; Miss Lettie Meacham, thirty-four, served as assistant matron. May Santry, twenty, was a seamstress employed by the home. Anna McCrum joined them as "a mutual friend of all." That afternoon, marking the holiday in the intimate circle of friendship, they determined to create from those friendships an organization. "Hoping to widen their opportunities as well as to be strengthened by the sympathy and co-operation of others," the five women resolved to draw others into their circle, creating the Working Woman's Lend a Hand club. While the name echoed Grace Dodge's working girls' clubs, the Davenport women rejected Dodge's insistence that her clubs showed "the true advancement of women—not desirous for men's work or place, but remaining where circumstances have placed them." Instead, the Lend a Hand organizers lifted their statement of purpose exactly from the Association for the Advancement of Women: "to promote the best practical methods of securing higher intellectual[,] moral[,] and physical conditions" for women. For those women whose lives led them out of the domestic circle and into the realm of paid employment, the Working Woman's Lend a Hand club provided a network of support, both practical and visionary. During its first decade, the Lend a Hand proclaimed the social virtue of women's employment, urged the entry of women into new fields of labor, and developed a range of programs to aid women workers and promote women's ownership of businesses. It created a network of support for newcomers to the city and embraced an ethos of mutuality, seeking social transformation by assisting individual women toward upward mobility. And it became a significant factor in reshaping the gendered geography and politics of Davenport.[4]

MEETING THE NEEDS OF WORKING WOMEN

Barely a year after that first meeting of five women in the dining room of the Cook Home, the Lend a Hand counted more than eighty members, all "women . . . dependent upon the work of their own hands for support." Growth did not come gradually. Seven months after its creation, the Lend a Hand had attracted only eight new members. That small group, however, already recognized what working women needed most. The members plunged enthusiastically into raising money for club rooms, and in September 1887, the Lend a Hand opened the doors to two "large and sunny rooms" on the third floor of the Ryan Block, at the corner of Brady and Second Street. The club rooms were a magnet, and scores of working women joined up.[5]

The club's location placed the Lend a Hand rooms in the heart of downtown Davenport, close to businesses where members might work. The buildings on the adjacent blocks were primarily three and four stories tall, with retail businesses on the first floor and residences, meeting halls, factories, and other establishments on the upper floors. Directly across Second Street were the classrooms of one of Davenport's business colleges, while another business college occupied the upper floors diagonally across Brady Street. Just down the block to the west was the Newcome House, one of Davenport's more impressive hotels, where black men waited tables in the dining room and white women cleaned the rooms. To the west as well stood Davenport's three largest department stores, where dozens of women worked and hundreds shopped. A block to the east of the Lend a Hand rooms stood Nicholas Kuhnen's cigar factory, the single-largest employer of women in the city. Dr. Jennie McCowen's office and rooms were just two blocks north of the Lend a Hand on Brady Street.

Open from nine in the morning until nine at night, the club rooms held a cabinet organ, a desk "supplied with stationery neatly stamped with the monogram of the club, for the use of the members," and a library with so many books and periodicals that they overflowed the bookcase and lined the deep windowsills. Plants, pictures, carpeting, comfortable chairs, and sofas made the space inviting, and when the folding doors were opened for evening lectures or concerts, the rooms could seat 125. For downtown workers who carried a lunch, tables provided a clean, sociable place to eat, and a "neat dressing room" enabled them to tidy up afterward or change their attire at the end of the day. Both club members and nonmembers found the rooms congenial. Club members used the rooms free of charge, while a seventy-five-cent ticket gave any woman three months' access. The rooms soon became a popular resting place for rural and small-town residents who came to Davenport for a day's shopping. The Lend a Hand rooms proved "a pleasant place to wait for the street car, or to meet a friend."[6]

As reported in the papers, the Lend a Hand rooms took on a distinctly feminine cast, like outposts of domestic space, but to view them as extensions of the home is to isolate them from their urban context. The Lend a Hand's rooms met the practical needs of women workers in a downtown filled with institutions catering to the needs of men. Labor unions, fraternal associations, and other men's organizations all had meeting and social rooms in downtown Davenport. But the most important institution for downtown workingmen was the saloon. Eighty-eight saloons clustered along Davenport's downtown streets; twenty-four lay within a two-block walk of the Lend a Hand rooms.[7]

Young workingmen typically built their social lives around saloons. Much more than places to drink, saloons provided their patrons with a range of services, some especially valuable to young men of modest means. Saloons played the part of banks, cashing paychecks and holding savings on account. They served as clearinghouses for employers and men seeking work and offered meeting spaces for all kinds of men's groups, including ethnic, fraternal, and labor organizations. Saloons also provided for the most basic needs of workingmen: toilets (often the only public ones around) and most famously, the free lunch. Saloons served up pounds of meat, bushels of potatoes, and dozens of eggs as well as bread, oysters, pickles, smoked fish, even vegetables. For the price of a nickel beer—and not even that if he was clever enough to avoid detection—even the poorest workingman was guaranteed a full stomach once a day.[8]

The saloon was also a retreat for men, the anchor of a social network that drew middle-class and working-class men together in a shared culture of masculinity. Few women crossed the threshold, and those few were likely to be prostitutes who served men's recreational and entertainment needs. For other working women, there was no parallel to the saloon, no institution that provided sociability and served their basic needs in the city center. The commercial downtown had evolved in the mid–nineteenth century as gendered, masculine space. When the workforce changed in the last decades of the century, the gender of downtown space rapidly became outdated.[9]

The gendered social geography of urban space first emerged from concerns raised by the rapid urbanization of the United States. In 1800, census takers counted only thirty-three towns with a population above 2,500 in the United States, and all of these lay along the eastern or southern seaboard. By 1880, more than nine hundred towns exceeded 2,500, and thirty-five cities had populations over 50,000. Urban places were no longer clustered in the East but were scattered broadly across the country. In 1880, twenty-two of the thirty-eight states (plus the District of Columbia) could claim at least one city with a population over 20,000, and these cities were home to nearly 14 percent of the population. Increasingly over the course of the century, Americans lived in urban places where they could not expect to know fellow citizens by name or face. The extraordinary territorial expansion of this period, coupled with Americans' mobility, also meant that families rarely had deep histories in the cities where they lived. The nineteenth-century city truly was, in Lyn Lofland's evocative phrase, "a world of strangers."[10]

To impose order on the confusion and variety of the city, urban dwellers developed elaborate codes of behavior and what Mary Ryan has called "cartographies of gender." First elaborated by journalists exploring New York City, the iconic metropolis of the 1830s, these cartographies of gender imposed social order by distinguishing between respectable and disreputable women. To a great extent, this difference lay in class. Elite and middle-class ladies confined themselves to respectable spaces, encountering other districts only under the protection of a male escort if at all. They did not attend theaters, where prostitutes solicited in the "guilty third tier." Ladies did not acknowledge or make acquaintance with the strangers who surrounded them. Poor and working-class women, for whom the streets were places of work and sociability, mixed more freely in the crowd and found themselves labeled disreputable, even sexually available, by more elite observers.[11]

To reinforce this distinction, many kinds of urban places, both public and commercial, formally segregated women, creating the respectable spaces to which ladies confined themselves. Hotels offered "ladies' parlors," and even post offices provided separate windows for women so they would not have to wait in a queue with men. The midcentury movement to establish urban parks quite explicitly addressed fears of gender disorder, envisioning parks as places where ladies with children could "enjoy themselves in a home-like manner." But by the 1870s and 1880s, the presumption that respectable women would limit their movements had become a point of increasing social tension. Downtown businesses began attracting two new groups of women to the city center: shoppers and middle-class workers. Managers of downtown department stores continued the pattern of segregation by turning their stores into self-contained islands of women's territory—"Adamless Edens," in the words of store owner Edward Filene. By the 1890s, shoppers could find child care, restaurants, lounges with desks and stationery, and a multitude of other amenities, all enclosed in spaces designed to evoke opulence and encourage consumption.[12]

Working women did not have the luxury of confining themselves to these islands of respectable space. As waves of middle-class women entered occupations once pursued only by men—occupations such as medicine, journalism, bookkeeping, clerical work, law, and sales—their presence downtown upset the codes of conduct established decades earlier. When they mixed with the world of strangers, both middle-class and working-class women risked their reputations. The requirements of employment turned conventional decorum topsy-turvy. An etiquette book published in

Des Moines in 1890 urged "great prudence and caution" in choosing to introduce two ladies to each other, or a gentleman to a lady, "as a lady cannot shake off an improper acquaintance with the same facility as a gentleman can do, and her character is much easier affected by *apparent* contact with the worthless and the dissipated." But the woman whose work involved any degree of contact with the public did not have the luxury of declining an unseemly acquaintance. The same writer offered tips for "business woman's dress" but seemed unable to imagine how other aspects of a working woman's day—including her hours of employment—might confound his rules. "After twilight," he asserted, "a young lady would not be conducting herself in a proper manner, by walking alone," but most women's workdays ended after twilight, especially in the winter months. Obtaining an escort home was hardly practical for many of these women, especially those who had left fathers and brothers behind when they came to the city for work. Some etiquette writers attempted to acknowledge the new order by proclaiming that working women could protect their reputations by adopting a suitable reserve in dress and deportment. "The woman or girl who is plainly absorbed in some earnest and dignified work is shielded from misinterpretation or impertinent intrusion while engaged in that work," insisted one writer in 1899. "She may go unattended to and from her place of business, for her destination is understood, and her purpose legitimate." The implication, of course, is that any woman who attracted "impertinent intrusion" must be to blame, since she failed to radiate the dignity and legitimacy that would distinguish her from a prostitute.[13]

The Lend a Hand rooms challenged this restrictive gendering of city streets by creating a new kind of space in the heart of the city. Where young men turned to the saloon for sociability and services, the women of the Lend a Hand created an alternative that did not jeopardize their respectability. No longer restricted to the narrow path from home to work—or to the role of bourgeois consumers—Lend a Hand members could choose to linger in their congenial downtown rooms just as men did, pursuing leisure activities outside the purview of home and family. Further, by making their rooms available to rural homemakers and other women who did not work for wages, Lend a Hand members inverted the common assumption that wage-earning women were vulnerable and in need of assistance. By opening their rooms to other women, they became the ones providing assistance; *they* became the patrons of others.

MIGRATIONS, SISTERS, AND THE JOURNEY OF LETTIE MEACHAM

The emphasis on claiming a space in the city and insisting on the respectability of working women reflects the experiences of the five women who organized the Lend

Lettie Meacham, c. 1880. (Putnam Museum of History and Natural Science, Davenport, Iowa.)

a Hand club that Christmas Day in 1886. Jennie McCowen, Lile Bickford, Lettie Meacham, Anna McCrum, and May Santry knew well the difficulties working women faced because these women were unmarried and self-supporting, and all had migrated to Davenport as adults, independent of a domestic, parental household. Only the youngest, May Santry, ever had kin in Davenport, and only she ever married. The others lived out their lives embedded in geographically expansive networks of sisters and friends. At a time when middle-class women's respectability was tightly bound to an ideal of domesticity, these women sought lives of movement, change, and independence, embracing an ideal of self-support and productive labor. Though their family origins ranged from comfortably middle class to tenuously working class, in Davenport these women claimed an identity based in their own achievements. The club they created drew on their experiences, seeking to translate the informal networks of support on which they had relied into an institution of "sympathy and cooperation" for other women like themselves.[14]

Meacham, assistant matron of the Cook Home, began life as a New England farm girl. Born Electa Meacham about 1848, she was the youngest of eight children, six of them daughters. Her father, Calvin Meacham, was a tenant farmer in the rocky, rugged hills of Berkshire County, Massachusetts. Tilling that stingy soil did not bring prosperity to match the growing size of his household. By 1860, Calvin Meacham claimed a personal of estate of just $492, no real estate, and a household of a dozen people, including his wife, Elvira; several grown children; two young children; and four grandchildren. The family had relocated from rural Savoy closer to Adams, a textile mill town of about four thousand where the Meacham daughters found work. Lettie's sister, Abbie, worked in a cotton mill, while other sisters, Emily and Laura, were domestic servants. Their wages no doubt helped eke out the living procured by a marginal farmer and his wife's home production. Life in Adams also gave Meacham a memory she would hold very dear: it was the birthplace of Susan B. Anthony, and Meacham recalled with pride seeing and meeting Anthony on her visits to the town.[15]

Four of the Meacham daughters married into local farming families, but Abbie, the mill girl, broke that pattern. In November 1865, she married Illinois-born William Craton and moved with him to a farm not far from his mother's residence in Fulton, Illinois. They were not destined to grow old together. Ill and broken after six months in a Confederate prison, Craton succumbed to chronic diarrhea and lung disease less than a decade after his wedding.[16]

Lettie Meacham was just seventeen when Abbie and William wed, and their journey west may have offered an irresistible opportunity for an adventuresome girl. Berkshire County, like other parts of New England, was experiencing a significant outmigration of young men of marriageable age. In 1860, the white population between the ages of fifteen and twenty-nine was just over fifteen thousand, but in that group women outnumbered men by more than a thousand. The loss of young men during the Civil War only increased the perception that some women would remain outside the sacred circle of domesticity so praised in nineteenth-century rhetoric. These were the women Virginia Penny sought to aid with her *Cyclopedia of Women's Work*. Essayist Mary Livermore called them "Superfluous Women" and offered advice on how to make their lives useful. Livermore found it outlandish to imagine that New England women might migrate themselves ("Heaven only knows where," she wondered), but for Lettie Meacham, migration brought opportunity and purpose.[17]

Meacham may have accompanied the newlyweds to Illinois, or she may have followed a bit later—to assist during Abbie's pregnancy or to help out as William's bouts of illness became increasingly severe. Lettie was at Abbie's side when Abbie gave birth to Lenial Craton in September 1867, and the 1870 census shows her living with William and Abbie in the river-port village of Albany, Illinois, where William worked in a warehouse and Lettie found employment as a domestic. In 1874, Lettie nursed William during his final illness. With his death, Lettie apparently assumed responsibility for supporting her sister and her infant nephew, a decision that led her to travel again, this time in search of employment.[18]

Like many women with experience caring for family members, Lettie Meacham adopted nursing as a vocation, and her search led her 140 miles away, to the Iowa State Hospital for the Insane in Mount Pleasant. Meacham first worked there as a ward attendant, a job that could be physically demanding, even dangerous. By 1877, she had risen to the responsible position of "assistant supervisor" of female employees, earning a salary of seventeen dollars a month plus board. At the hospital, Lettie Meacham found a friend who helped shape the course of her life. Among the staff physicians in 1877 was Dr. Jennie McCowen. McCowen left the hospital in 1878. Around the same time, Meacham returned to her sister's home in Illinois. Still needing to earn a living, twenty-eight-year-old Lettie found work in a paper mill on the banks of the Rock River. Four years later, when the Cook Home in Davenport needed a nurse, McCowen drew Meacham to Davenport.[19]

GILDED AGE INSTITUTIONS AND THE MAKING OF A PROFESSIONAL: DR. JENNIE MCCOWEN

Lettie Meacham, domestic servant and mill hand, was hardly the middle-class matron usually associated with club work in the Gilded Age, and in many ways her life differed markedly from that of the woman who befriended her in Mount Pleasant. Yet the two also shared much. Both had worked since their teens, both had migrated far from their childhood homes, and both linked their migrations not to a paternal household but to a network of sisters and friends. Jennie McCowen was born in Warren County, Ohio, some thirty miles northeast of Cincinnati, in 1845. Years later, as a professional woman living in Iowa, she gave out the story of her childhood in a way that emphasized both its respectability and its romance. Her father, most biographical sketches reported, was a "well-known physician in southern Ohio," and her mother was a Quaker. In spite of these comfortable origins, McCowen chose to portray herself as a self-made woman. She was, most sources reported, "thrown upon her own resources" at the age of sixteen, compelled to earn a living as a schoolteacher. The phrase suggests she was orphaned, and more than one article reported that her father's death propelled her into the workforce. The truth was more complicated, involving a troubled family divided by politics.[20]

Dr. Jennie McCowen, c. 1895. The pin on her collar is the emblem of the King's Daughters. (From Irving A. Watson, *Physicians and Surgeons of America*, 1896.)

Maria Taylor, Jennie's mother, was indeed a Quaker, and she and her three sisters all affiliated with an abolitionist sect of Friends in the early 1840s. In 1839, Ohio-born Maria Taylor married John McCowen, a Presbyterian widower from Maryland. They spent the early years of their marriage in Warren County, where Maria gave birth to three children: Israel, named for Maria's father; Jennie, then called Jane; and Mary. Even before their marriage, John McCowen was an ambitious man, eager to take advantage of economic opportunities in the expanding Midwest. By 1846, McCowen had decided to move his family to Mason County, Illinois. He purchased several parcels of land, probably as a speculator. John McCowen was no prairie farmer—and he was apparently no physician, either. The 1850 census shows the family living in the village of Havana, where John McCowen operated a store. In

Illinois, Maria gave birth to two more daughters. Then, sometime between 1855 and 1859, Maria apparently died. John moved his family back to Ohio, where in 1859 he married Elizabeth Stokes, the sister of a prominent banker in Lebanon. Jennie was then fourteen years old.[21]

Although Jennie repeatedly implied that she had been orphaned at sixteen, her father did not die that year. Indeed, John McCowen lived on until 1878, when Jennie was thirty-three. What did happen when she was sixteen, and what may have provoked a split in the family that left her feeling a spiritual orphan, was the outbreak of the Civil War. Jennie was fifteen when the war began in April, but for her the significant moment probably came in June. A few days after her sixteenth birthday, Jennie's only brother, Israel, enlisted in the U.S. Army. That Jennie's mother belonged to an abolitionist sect of Quakers, that her brother was an early volunteer in the war, and that she became a longtime active member of the Women's Relief Corps of the Grand Army of the Republic suggest a mother and children strongly committed to the Union cause, perhaps even to antislavery politics. Jennie's father, however, was a Marylander and a Democrat, and his new wife's family were leaders in the local Democratic Party. If Jennie felt "thrown upon her own resources" in 1861, it may have been because she and her father disagreed about the war. She and Israel were not the only ones to break with their father. Maria Taylor McCowen's children all left their father's household at relatively young ages and made their lives far from southern Ohio.[22]

Jennie McCowen later reported that she turned to schoolteaching to earn a living, attending the local normal college, which awarded her a teaching diploma in 1865. If Jennie did indeed become self-supporting in 1861, the rift with her father must have been significant. John McCowen was by then a substantial merchant in Lebanon, owning and operating a drugstore on the main street, Broadway. Jennie always identified her father as a physician, and indeed, John McCowen occasionally used the title "Dr." But John McCowen did not practice medicine as his usual occupation, nor was he trained in regular medicine. Judging from an 1838 letter from James Boggs (probably John McCowen's half-brother) both McCowen and Boggs embraced the Thompsonian system of botanical medicine, placing them at odds with the emerging hegemony of allopathic physicians. With some sarcasm, Boggs wrote that he and the physicians of his town got on "very well. They go civily by & I let them." After the 1830s, John McCowen's primary connection with medicine seems to have been through the sale of pharmaceuticals and a variety of patent medicines. At his death in 1878, his books were valued at less than fifty dollars, hardly suggesting an extensive medical library. But in the 1860s, the *Lebanon Western Star* carried advertisements for "Ayer's Sarsaparilla and Ague Cure," "Dr. Roback's Blood Purifier," "Duponco's Golden Periodical Pills," and "Cheeseman's Female Pills"—all available from "John McCowen, Druggist and Apothecary!"[23]

By the summer of 1864, Jennie McCowen was apparently ready to put even more distance between herself and her father. Israel died in battle at Lynchburg, Virginia, on 17 June 1864, two days after Jennie's nineteenth birthday and two days before the close of his three-year enlistment. A few weeks later, Jennie McCowen journeyed to a sparsely settled county in western Iowa where her mother's sister, Hannah Taylor Ballard, farmed with her husband, William, and their five daughters. There, Jennie found work as a schoolteacher.[24]

If Jennie McCowen kept a diary on that trip west or wrote letters to her sisters, those documents have long since vanished. But it is easy to imagine some of the things she might have written. The nation was at war, and the railroads, still fairly primitive, were not run for the convenience of lady passengers. Smoke, cinders, and dust flew in open windows, and the floors of passenger cars were filthy with tobacco spit. Even stopping at a hotel could be uncomfortable for a woman traveling alone. "Ladies without escort should not stop over-night before reaching their destination—remember this," warned an 1861 travel guide. Despite these drawbacks, train travel was so much easier than the alternative that women were increasingly likely to undertake long journeys alone. Still, McCowen could not travel the entire distance to her posting by train. A railroad serving Audubon County had yet to be built. The last fifty miles would have been by coach or wagon, in the sweltering heat, humidity, and dust—or the thundering torrents of rain—of a prairie summer. If it was a physically grueling trip, it must also have been emotionally draining. In less than a decade, Jennie McCowen had lost her mother and brother and become alienated from her father. Now she was moving far from her sisters and the familiar scenes of her childhood to earn her living in a country school.[25]

For the next few years, Jennie McCowen lived the life of a typical schoolmistress in a rural county of straggling settlements. Like any teacher, she boarded around with farm families and attended the local county teachers' institutes in August. But in 1871, at the age of twenty-six, she did something far from typical. She became a candidate for elective office, losing the race for Audubon County superintendent of schools by just fifteen votes (out of about three hundred eligible voters). The spectacle of a woman running for office was so novel that just two years earlier, when Julia Addington was elected superintendent of schools in Mitchell County, Iowa, cautious officials consulted the state attorney general to determine whether Addington could legally serve. She could.[26]

Over the course of the 1870s, women as elected county superintendents became increasingly common in the Midwest, but in 1871 choosing to run for office took more than a little audacity. In Wyoming and Utah Territories, women could vote, but everywhere else in the United States, woman suffrage was at best a matter of controversy. Even leaders of the national suffrage movement were bitterly divided over the Fifteenth Amendment, which gave the vote to black men but left white and black women disenfranchised.

Audubon County in 1870 had one of the state's smallest school systems: just ten ungraded schools, 317 students, and seventeen teachers. No newspaper reports of McCowen's candidacy remain, so the issues that led her to take such a step are left to speculation, but one of her concerns may have been pay. The average salary of Audubon County's seven male teachers was 37 percent higher than that paid their female counterparts. Fifteen years later, McCowen noted that women earned 20 percent less than men as schoolteachers, but she observed that this was "not so great a disparity as formerly." Whatever the particular issues drawing McCowen into the race, what seems certain is that as a public employee, McCowen saw clearly that the actions of the state affected her directly. Public policy determined how well women could support themselves and their dependents, so public office could not be solely the concern of men.[27]

Jennie McCowen never repeated her run for office, perhaps because the possibility of another future suddenly opened out before her: the state university in Iowa City announced a new medical department. Since its opening in 1855, Iowa's university had admitted men and women to its degree programs on an equal basis. The new medical department continued this tradition, and among the thirty-seven medical students who matriculated in the fall of 1870, eight were women. As she would later tell the story, McCowen had dreamed since girlhood of becoming a physician. She claimed to have read medicine in her father's library, deterred neither by "much opposition" nor, apparently, by a paucity of books. Two years after the medical school opened, Jennie McCowen left teaching, took her savings, and began the studies that had once seemed beyond her reach. She would not be alone in Iowa City. Jennie joined her younger sister, Mary, who was studying pedagogy at the university.[28]

Entering medical school in the fall of 1872, the twenty-seven-year-old McCowen found a colleague—another single woman—who opened paths for her, just as she opened paths for her sisters and friends. Margaret Abigail Cleaves was among the eight women in Iowa's initial medical school class, and she graduated at the end of McCowen's first year. Abbie Cleaves and Jennie McCowen were close in age and parallel in experience. Born in eastern Iowa in 1848, Cleaves was the third of seven children, all girls except one brother who died of pneumonia at seven months. "From that time on," she recalled, "I was my father's 'boy' and we were close companions and comrades." Cleaves's father, a physician, died when she was about fifteen, and she turned to teaching when her family disapproved of a medical career. Like McCowen, when the state university opened its medical department, Cleaves left the schoolroom for the medical education she had long desired. When she graduated in March 1873 at the top of her class, Abbie Cleaves immediately joined the staff of Iowa's state hospital for the insane. The use of women as staff physicians was a controversial innovation, and Dr. Cleaves was only the second woman in the United States to hold such an appointment. Mark Ranney, the superintendent of the asylum, was also a professor in the medical school, and he may have eagerly recruited a promising young physician for his staff. When Dr. McCowen graduated, taking the thesis prize in her class, Ranney recruited her as well, and she filled the vacancy created when Dr. Cleaves resigned in 1875 to enter private practice in Davenport.[29]

It has become almost a convention in the history of women's education to suggest that the women's colleges that sprang up in the East between 1865 and 1890 provided a superior environment for nurturing activist women. But some scholars have recently challenged this interpretation. Glenda Gilmore has argued that African American women in the South, for whom single-sex education was rarely an option, gained specific benefits from coeducation. Shared classrooms gave women the self-confidence to compete with men and the ease to work with them as colleagues. When relations were less than collegial, women in coeducational institutions learned to cope, a skill that served them well in later years as they sought to take part in a public sphere that was definitely not single sex. Kathryn Kish Sklar has made similar observations about the experience of Florence Kelley, who attended coeducational Cornell University in the late 1870s.[30]

In the Midwest, coeducation was the rule, and it may have had as much impact on men as on women. Jennie McCowen and Abbie Cleaves experienced their share of harassment in medical school, where the subject matter, with its emphasis on bodies and functions, continually called attention to the sexualized status of women students. Neither McCowen nor Cleaves appears ever to have alluded to this trouble, but decades later, a male classmate remembered the hazing they had endured. "I recall with shame the treatment we hoodlums accorded those pioneer women in the medical school.... In discussion, we soon learned [McCowen] could 'floor' us and our note writing gave way to wholesome respect." His memory had probably taken on a rosy tint with age, but the careers pursued by both McCowen and Cleaves suggest that midwestern medical men—many of them products of coeducational schools—may indeed have learned "wholesome respect" for the women who were their classmates and colleagues.[31]

After five years in private practice, Abbie Cleaves left Davenport to take charge of the Female Department of the Pennsylvania State Lunatic Hospital in Harrisburg in 1880. At Cleaves's suggestion, Jennie McCowen moved to Davenport to pursue her career in a city that had already shown itself receptive to women in medicine. When she arrived in Davenport, Jennie McCowen stepped into the spaces—physical, social, and professional—vacated by Cleaves. McCowen moved into rooms directly across the street from the home where Cleaves had lived and where Cleaves's widowed mother and sisters still resided. She took over Cleaves's office in the Forrest Block in downtown Davenport. She was invited to join the Scott County Medical Society, which, unlike its counterparts in eastern cities, had welcomed women as members since 1863. The departure of Abbie Cleaves left open the office of secretary, and members immediately chose Dr. McCowen to fill it, reelecting her in January 1881 and again a year later.[32]

The Lend a Hand Club

Brady Street looking north, c. 1882. The building at the center is the Forrest Block, where first Dr. Abbie Cleaves and then Dr. Jennie McCowen had their offices. (Putnam Museum of History and Natural Science, Davenport, Iowa.)

October 1882 brought the opening of the Cook Home. In December, Jennie McCowen applied for the position of staff physician, securing a "full and hearty endorsement" from the men of the county medical society. The managers granted Dr. McCowen the appointment. Her new affiliation allowed McCowen to rescue Lettie Meacham from her job in the paper mill, and Meacham joined the staff as a nurse. McCowen's association with the Cook Home continued almost forty years, and it became one more in a series of institutions—including the University of Iowa and the Iowa State Hospital for the Insane—that linked her with other women in a network of organization, employment, and friendship.[33]

SEARCHING FOR OPPORTUNITY IN THE CITY

A third founder of the Lend a Hand also came to Davenport to work at the Cook Home. Lile Bickford, employed as the home's matron, was born Eliza Bickford in New Hampshire about 1854, the daughter of a stationary engineer on the Concord & Northern Railroad. She grew up in Concord, with three older sisters and a younger brother. Like Jennie McCowen and Abbie Cleaves, Bickford began teaching school in her mid-teens, and she too used teaching as a springboard to a different career, in this case, institutional administration. When the board of managers of the newly organized Cook Home recruited her, one Davenport newspaper reported that Bickford was already "a lady of considerable experience in similar work." By then Bickford was living in Manchester, New Hampshire, where she may have worked in one of several public or private institutions, including a juvenile reformatory, a home for the aged, or the state hospital for the insane. At twenty-eight, Lile Bickford was apparently ready to take the next step in her career, even if it meant traveling across half a continent to a city where she had neither family nor friends. She did, however, have a sister living in western Iowa. Like the McCowen sisters and Lettie and Abbie Meacham, one sister's journey drew others in the same direction.[34]

Lettie Meacham and Lile Bickford grew up only about 125 miles apart, but each traveled more than a thousand miles to the place where they finally met and lived under the same roof. Each migrated as an adult, leaving her birth family and following a path chosen in part for the employment opportunities it presented. This was a new kind of migration that would have been far less likely before the improvement of railroads annihilated time, distance, and the gendered barriers to travel in the years after the Civil War.[35]

In creating the Lend a Hand, Meacham, Bickford, and McCowen were joined by two other women whose journeys to Davenport followed different patterns. Anna J. Somerville McCrum was born in Kentucky about 1849. Her Irish-born father, William McCrum, a veteran of the War of 1812, moved with his wife and daughter to Lawrence, Kansas, about 1858, probably as part of the migration of antislavery Republicans into the territory. By 1860, however, the family had relocated to Columbus City, Iowa, where eleven-year-old Anna would have been a schoolmate of Abbie Cleaves. William McCrum was a modestly successful merchant; he told the census taker he owned real estate valued at $4,000 and personal property worth $1,000. Anna was the only child in the household. By 1870, William McCrum had retired, and he was apparently spending down his capital. His real estate holdings came to only $1,900 that year, and his personal estate amounted to $1,400. Anna's mother died in 1872, and her father died the following year, when Anna was twenty-four. By 1880, Anna had moved to Davenport. The city directories and censuses are resolutely silent about her occupation. According to tax records, Anna McCrum owned one small piece of property in a residential area east of downtown, assessed at just $485. She did not live there, so she probably relied on it for rental income. Perhaps, through frugal habits and careful investment, she was able to live more than forty years on the nest egg bequeathed by her parents. But one reason for a young, single woman to move to Davenport would have been the employment opportunities afforded in an urban center. Anna McCrum probably worked in the casual market for a woman's labor: sewing, nursing, "help."[36]

May Santry, the fifth organizer of the Lend a Hand, was a generation younger than the other women. Barely out of her teens, she was at a transitional moment in her life, still linked to her family while emerging into the women's community embodied in the Lend a Hand. As if to confirm this intermediate identity, Santry was recorded twice in the 1885 Iowa census: once living among the women of the Cook Home and once as a boarder in the large, working-class household of an Irish blacksmith. Only one other person in Davenport shared her surname, another boarder in the blacksmith's household who was probably May's younger brother. May and William Santry, Wisconsin natives, were both children of Irish immigrants and may have migrated to Davenport together. Eighteen-year-old William Santry was a blacksmith like his landlord and probably worked for him. Like Lettie Meacham, May Santry came from a working-class family, and when she married in the mid-1890s, she confirmed her working-class identity by choosing a blacksmith from Springfield, Illinois, William Sauer.[37]

These career paths and migrations distinguish the Lend a Hand founders from the typical clubwoman of the 1880s as historians have characterized her. These were not middle-class and elite matrons who looked to club activities to enrich their leisure hours. Nor were these women who subscribed to the "true advancement of woman" imagined by Grace Dodge: not one was satisfied to remain where circumstances had placed her. Typically, historians assign women to a social class based on their husbands' or fathers' occupations. But in Davenport, no one knew these women's fathers. McCowen and McCrum, daughters of shopkeepers, certainly came from solidly middle-class families, but Meacham's and Santry's homes were distinctly working class, and McCrum's position in Davenport was at best ambiguous. In Davenport, however, these women were known not by their families but by themselves. In founding the Working Woman's Lend a Hand club, they laid claim to the identity of worker. As migrants to the city, they understood the importance of establishing their respectability in a world of strangers, and the networks of sisters and friends that guided their migrations suggest one of the ways a newcomer to the city obtained an introduction: Abbie Cleaves introduced Jennie McCowen, McCowen introduced Lettie Meacham, and the managers of the Cook Home introduced Lile Bickford. Given their childhood acquaintance, it is possible Abbie Cleaves introduced Anna McCrum as well. Like links in a chain, these networks anchored women to a respectable identity and helped guarantee their welcome. It was no accident that when Jennie McCowen sought a home in Davenport, the rooms she found were directly across the street from Abbie Cleaves's mother.

THE PRACTICAL REFORMATION

Given their personal histories, it is not surprising that the founders of the Lend a Hand embraced an ideal of self-support for women. Yet while they sought independence, they also embraced mutuality. They made their commitment clear in their choice of a name. To Americans who participated in the popular reading culture of the 1870s and 1880s, "Lend a Hand" had a specific reference: it was the fourth of the "Wadsworth Mottoes" popularized by writer and liberal clergyman Edward Everett Hale. By 1886, it was also the title of the journal he edited. Now remembered chiefly as the author of the patriotic short story, "The Man without a Country," Hale in the 1880s was an established member of America's literary elite, prolific and widely read.[38]

In 1870, Hale published a novel, *Ten Times One Is Ten*, in which he offered his vision of "the practical reformation" (as early editions were subtitled). It told the story of "the strangest Club that ever came into being," a circle of ten strangers brought together for the funeral of their mutual friend, Harry Wadsworth. As they wait for a delayed train, the strangers share their stories of the friend they had lost, "the most manly and most womanly fellow" they had ever known, one whose practical kindness and courage had transformed their lives. They resolve to write to the narrator whenever "anything turned up which brought Harry" to mind. The ten strangers carry Wadsworth's spirit with them, and the letters they write gradually tell the story of a spreading movement. More and more people who never knew Wadsworth are inspired by his life and pass their enthusiasm on to others. The movement is embodied in a set of mottoes: "Look up not down, look forward not back, look out not in, lend a hand."[39]

It is a religion of sorts, but a practical, secular one. "The freemasonry of it was that you found everywhere a cheerful outlook, a perfect determination to relieve suffering, and a certainty that it could be relieved," explained one adherent. Another insisted, "Our notion is that man had better not talk much about his religion, certainly had better not think about saving his soul." Instead, the readiness to be of real help to others spread the spirit, and as the letters pour in, the narrator discovers that the number of people in the movement multiplies by a factor of ten every three years ("ten times one is ten"). Twenty-seven years proves enough to reform the world, so that newspapers have no wars or crimes to report and devote themselves instead to publishing fiction. "Pretty country jails," bereft of prisoners, begin taking in summer boarders, and the classified ads fill up with offers of assistance. ("A widow with four children will take into her family a paralyzed woman, or any blind person. Two sons good at lifting invalids.")[40]

As a utopian vision, *Ten Times One Is Ten* had much appeal. Although it explicitly poked fun at sectarian Christianity (the last holdout in the world is a New England divine who worries that "lend a hand" is "a Covenant of Works, and union with the

Devil"), it also echoed the familiar story of the spread of Christianity through the witnessing of the apostles. More important, the story made every individual directly responsible for bringing on "the practical reformation" by living the Wadsworth Mottoes in her own life. Hale's work must have had special appeal for the women who created the Lend a Hand club, for a recurring theme of the book is the mobility of Americans. Not only is the club formed in a train station (in memory of a freight agent), but railroads, boats, and travel generally are the keys to the movement's spread. "Happy country," cries one character, "where no man settles down!"[41]

Long before Hale began publishing the journal *Lend a Hand* to record the progress of the practical reformation, groups were organizing themselves around the promise of the book. The "Look-Up Legion" and sundry "Wadsworth Clubs" and "Ten Times One Clubs" joined other "Lend a Hand" societies around the country, yet among all these, the Davenport entry seems to have been, as Jennie McCowen called it, a "unique infant" indeed: the only Lend a Hand devoted explicitly to the needs of working women. At Hale's death in 1909, Davenport club members remembered him as the "honored father of the Lend-a-Hand."[42]

The ethos of mutuality embodied in the "Ten Times One" ideal led the founders to take steps to protect the egalitarian spirit of the club. Renting club rooms was expensive, especially for a group of working women. As late as 1892, one report estimated that most members earned between $2.50 and $5 a week. From the beginning, the organizers seem to have recognized that to survive, the club would need patrons; however, patronage threatened their ethos of mutuality. To address this, they created a separate organization, the King's Daughters, open to sympathetic but more affluent women—though in fact it too remained predominantly an organization of single, self-supporting women. The Order of the King's Daughters, an ecumenical Protestant group dedicated to "silent service," had been established in New York the previous year, and four of the Lend a Hand founders organized themselves under its auspices. Circle Number One of the King's Daughters, though based in Davenport, reflected the geographic networks created by the migrant women who created it. Members lived not just in Davenport but in nearby Muscatine, in the state capital at Des Moines, and even farther afield, including Meriden, Elwell, and Hull, villages in western Iowa. Two other members lived in Chicago and Lincoln, Nebraska.[43]

Perhaps because the organizers recognized the potential for the more affluent King's Daughters to dominate the Lend a Hand, from the beginning the structure of the working woman's club encouraged the autonomy and independence of the membership. While the whole club met weekly, Lend a Hand members were also organized into smaller groups called "tens" (another echo of Hale's "Ten Times One" prototype), though they often numbered more than ten. These tens elected their own officers, met on their own schedule, and organized projects according to their own interests. Each quarter, the groups reported their activities to the rest of the club. The board of directors of the Lend a Hand consisted of the presidents of these tens plus the Davenport residents who belonged to Circle Number One of the King's Daughters. Effectively, "Davenport residents" meant McCowen, McCrum, Bickford, Meacham, and Miss Martha A. Cooke, a Davenport schoolteacher who later joined the faculty of Monmouth College in Illinois. By the end of the first year, the presidents of the tens easily outnumbered the representatives of the King's Daughters, assuring that control rested more heavily with the membership than the founders.[44]

THE MEMBERS OF THE LEND A HAND

Though no membership lists from the early years of the Lend a Hand remain, newspaper reports reveal the names of fifty-one women who joined during the club's first five years of existence (1887–91). Other sources, especially the 1885 Iowa manuscript census and city directories, fill in details about the membership, including age, occupation, residence, and workplace. While the information is far from complete and is almost certainly richer for the more socially elite members, it does offer a glimpse of the kind of women who joined the Lend a Hand in its first few years.

The Lend a Hand may have drawn a disproportionate number of its members from the clerical and professional occupations. Clerks and teachers made up almost half the membership reported in the papers, outnumbering factory hands, domestic servants, and seamstresses, who counted for about a third.

Initial Occupations of Lend a Hand Members Who Joined 1887–91

Clerks/bookkeepers	12
Teachers	9
Domestic servants	4
Factory hands	4
Seamstresses	4
Institutional administrators	3
Physician	1
Photo retoucher	1
U.S. Revenue stamp deputy	1

Biases inherent in the sources may overstate the proportion of teachers and clerical workers, however. Women in both of these occupations were far more likely to be listed in the city directories than were domestic servants. It seems plausible as well that those with more education felt greater confidence in accepting club offices,

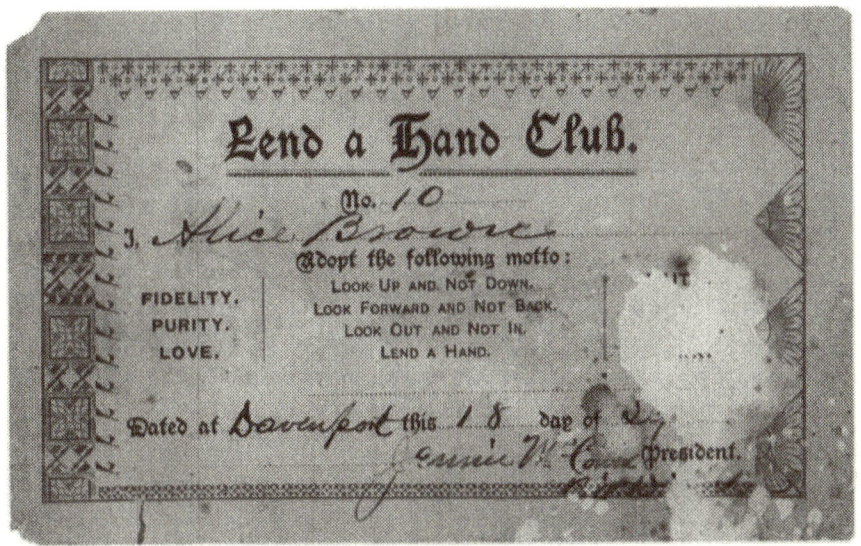

Lend a Hand club membership card. At the time she joined, Alice Brown was assistant matron of the Cook Home. (Putnam Museum of History and Natural Science, Davenport, Iowa.)

and club officers were more likely to be mentioned in the newspapers. Either of these phenomena would tend to overstate the number of clerks and teachers among club members. If the 1892 report that most members earned between $2.50 and $5 a week is accurate, that would suggest a larger number of servants and factory hands, because teachers generally earned around $11 a week and bookkeepers and clerks generally earned between $5 and $6 a week.[45]

One of the more striking characteristics shared by these women is their spatial proximity to the Lend a Hand rooms. Of the forty-seven women whose residences could be determined, thirteen lived within about five blocks of the rooms. Of the twenty-six whose employers are known, twenty worked within the same distance. In one way, this is not surprising: the concentration of commercial activity in the city center meant a concentration of jobs there, too. Yet this concentration also confirms contemporary observers' perception that more and more women were mixing in the streets of the city center. Whether they lived in furnished rooms, boardinghouses, or with their families, the emphasis placed on the club rooms suggests that Lend a Hand members valued the social space and services provided by the club. When a reporter called the rooms "a pleasant place to wait for the street car," he may have been thinking that in winter, men commonly waited in corner saloons, while "ladies are unable to use these advantages for reasons that are too well known to be repeated" and so shivered on windy street corners. The opportunity to carry a lunch to the club rooms seems to have been particularly important. Denied the free lunch their male coworkers could find at saloons, most women earned too little to afford restaurant lunches. At the Lend a Hand rooms, women could eat, rest, and use the toilet and dressing room before returning to work. Before long, the club decided to purchase a range to accommodate light cooking.[46]

Examining the club's membership also reveals a surprising diversity in age, setting the Lend a Hand apart from working girls' clubs. Of the twenty-nine members whose ages could be determined, ten were born before 1860, eleven between 1860 and 1869, and eight in the 1870s. Many Lend a Hand members were considerably older than the typical teenage working girl of the 1880s. The oldest Lend a Hand member, Mrs. M. A. Thompson, was a stamp deputy in the U.S. Internal Revenue Office when she joined in her late forties, around the time of her husband's death. She remained active until her early sixties, when she moved to Iowa City. The youngest member was Emma Wittig, a cigar factory hand who followed her older sisters into the club while she was in her mid-teens. All three of the Wittig sisters were still associated with the Lend a Hand twenty years later. Indeed, memberships lasting more than a decade, though perhaps not the rule, were hardly unusual. The diversity in ages suggests that the ethos that distinguished the Lend a Hand from class-bridging organizations directed at youthful workers was borne out in its day-to-day activities. Focused on women's identity as workers, its appeal did not diminish as members grew older. Instead, it could remain a source of practical support and social pleasure for women of thirty or forty or more. At the same time, this age integration offered a special benefit to younger members: friendships with older, self-supporting colleagues who provided a model of womanhood not tied solely to home and motherhood.

LEND A HAND PROGRAMS

In the early months of its existence, meetings of the Lend a Hand combined formal programs with informal social hours. At an October 1887 meeting, for example, Miss Anna Meckel, a domestic servant and president of Ten Number One, gave a report on that group's activities over the previous quarter. Miss Alice Brown, assistant matron at the Cook Home and a member of Ten Number Three, led the group in singing an original song written for the occasion, playing the organ in accompaniment. And Miss Bauer, a clerk at Peterson's department store and a member of Ten Number Two, recited a poem, "The Emigrants," in German. This was probably Ludwig Schandein's "Die Auswannerer," written between 1848 and 1852, which opened with a lament for those departing for America, "It always causes so much pain / When one must go so far away," and continued by evoking the power of shared language: "As far as you may travel / You shall not lose the language once learned, / The tongue which is so dear to the heart." Like perhaps a third of early Lend a Hand members, Miss Bauer was the daughter of German-born parents. Her bilingual skills were a matter of both cultural pride and economic value. In a city where about one in five residents was born in Germany, a store clerk who could assist customers in both English and German was a valuable employee.[47]

Education was a primary purpose of the Lend a Hand; it was both high school and business college for women who had left school for work in early adolescence. Indeed, it met a need working women in Davenport had articulated even before McCowen and her colleagues organized the club. In October 1886, a group of women petitioned the school board for a night school for women only, but the board rejected the petition because all the signers were over twenty-one—too old to be eligible for publicly funded education. During its first year, the Lend a Hand sponsored classes in skills designed to improve members' employment options (for example, penmanship, arithmetic, and cash accounts) as well as subjects more likely to enhance members' quality of life (vocal music and sewing). (While some women certainly earned a living by sewing, the consistent appeal of sewing classes probably lay in the fact that ill-paid women could stretch a meager clothing budget to greater heights of fashion when they did some of their own sewing.) In a city where the ability to speak German was an asset for employees who dealt with the public, demand for German language classes was especially high, and the club offered two. Classes were taught by Lend a Hand members whenever someone with the requisite skills could be found, but the club also hired outside teachers when appropriate.[48]

In its search for "practical methods" to secure better conditions for working women, the Lend a Hand freely drew from successful programs initiated by Young Women's Christian Associations or working girls' clubs. To promote thrift, the Lend a Hand set up a dime savings agency, enabling workers to begin bank accounts with less than the minimum deposit accepted by a commercial bank (which could be more than a week's wages for many women). Just as with the club rooms and lunch tables, the dime savings program provided a service for working women that young men might get from their saloons. By issuing passbooks and using standard procedures, the Lend a Hand savings bank also helped a working woman feel confident and at ease when the time came to transfer her nest egg to a regular bank. The club promoted intellectual development through the systematic study program of a Chautauqua reading circle and through organized discussions of current events. The women of the Lend a Hand shared with their contemporaries in the Knights of Labor a respect for literacy and its uses. They were fellow participants in a culture Leon Fink has characterized as stressing "the development of individual capacity" while "striving to elevate humanity." By 1889, the Lend a Hand had published a *Protective Circular for Women*, which outlined basic legal principles of importance to workers: it gave advice about initiating a lawsuit against an employer to secure unpaid wages and about what to expect from landlords when renting rooms, and it offered cautions about purchasing on installment or entering into sewing machine contracts that might be unfairly revoked. The club also attempted to keep its members informed of new frauds aimed at working women who were ambitious to find jobs with better pay and more opportunities.[49]

Of all the goals espoused by the Lend a Hand, none was more successful than the effort "to widen our opportunities." On a week-to-week level, this was pursued through classes in marketable skills. "If their services are less valuable by reason of any lack which instruction can supply we stand pledged to help them remedy the defect," declared Dr. McCowen at the club's first annual meeting. For members whose ambitions reached beyond what the club itself could offer, the Lend a Hand established an educational loan fund to enable members to seek further training. At a more visionary level, the Lend a Hand saw itself as providing a kind of public relations for women workers, countering employers' fears that women were by nature flighty and unreliable employees. The day would come, predicted McCowen, when membership would "come to be recognized in the community" as a sign that "no matter what work the [woman] is engaged in, it will be well and carefully done, that she can be trusted with not only the work assigned her, but with the property, the reputation, the honor" of her employer. "Personal character, helpfulness to others, integrity of purpose, fidelity to duty are the foundation stones upon which our edifice is to be reared." In a sense, the Lend a Hand was promising the same kind of quality control trade unions attempted to guarantee.[50]

The success of the Lend a Hand in widening women's opportunities can be documented in the careers of individual members. Fully a quarter of the women who joined during the first five years were upwardly mobile. Some moved within a few years from working-class to middle-class occupations, while others made the transition from worker to proprietor. In a few cases, the role of the Lend a Hand in supporting this transition was quite direct: the club became a seedbed for woman-owned businesses.[51]

The first of these, organized in 1889, was a "first class dressmaking establishment with a full force of experts and the usual complement of apprentices." May Santry, "a Lend-a-Hand girl who is a competent dress maker," operated the establishment, making the transition from Cook Home seamstress to businesswoman. Capital for the enterprise came from the King's Daughters, who intended to underwrite it until it became self-supporting. Dressmaking was a cautious choice for a first business, unlikely to create waves among downtown businessmen. Dressmaking and millinery were the late-nineteenth-century businesses most likely to be run by women. While not directly challenging gender boundaries, this project reflected the Lend a Hand goal of helping working women improve their condition by turning experts into proprietors and training less-skilled workers, through apprenticeships, in a relatively well-paid trade.[52]

While the dressmaking business may have been a judicious choice, it did not necessarily reflect conservatism on the part of the club. Earlier that year, the Lend a Hand became the local agent for Annie Jenness Miller's dress patterns. Jenness Miller, editor of *Dress*, advocated a practical system of dress reform that sought to simplify the process of dressing and undressing and to increase the personal comfort of the wearer. Her garments used no corsets, no bustles, no petticoats, no reed or whalebone stays. She toured the country giving lectures on her system, modeling her gowns and demonstrating the graceful movement they made possible and contrasting it with a comic portrayal of a woman hampered by conventional dress. In May 1889 the Lend a Hand sponsored a lecture in Davenport, where Jenness Miller's "freedom of movement . . . excited the liveliest envy on the part of the audience." For "business women," Jenness Miller proposed a skirt falling "just below the knee," worn with matching gaiters and a suitable jacket and bodice. She preferred the "coat style of waist, which admits of useful pockets." It would be more than thirty years before businesswomen actually shed their corsets and shortened their skirts to the knee, but the enthusiasm with which club members greeted Jenness Miller in Davenport suggests that working women were already discovering the impracticality in the workplace of clothing designed for the respectable matron at home.[53]

A plain sewing and mending bureau established at the same time as the dressmaking business offers further insight into how the Lend a Hand envisioned and pursued its mission. As announced in the newspapers in 1889, the bureau seemed a straightforward proposition: it operated out of the club rooms, providing a clearinghouse for seamstresses seeking household piecework, much as a union hall or saloon might serve as a clearinghouse for workingmen and employers. Through cooperative effort, it hoped to secure steady work for those who relied on less-skilled sewing for their incomes. But a letter written years later revealed another side of the venture. A woman recalled that during a serious illness, club members took care of her and paid her doctor's bills, then strategized to help her get back on her feet. "Finding I had no strength to do an ordinary day's work [as a house servant], and knowing I was alone and must earn my own living, the directors of the club started a 'Mending Bureau' and put me in charge of it; and I didn't know until years after that it was organized for my especial benefit," she recalled.[54]

The mending bureau may have been another example of women's business enterprise, but it was also a gesture of personal charity, the ethos of mutual assistance proclaimed through the name "Lend a Hand." This dual commitment to women's advancement and mutual assistance continued to characterize the club's businesses and projects. The Lend a Hand approach stood in marked contrast to the Woman's Exchange, a popular philanthropy of the 1880s. At its heart, the Woman's Exchange was a consignment shop for women's home production of needlework, cookery, and other goods. On the presumption that working for money humiliated women, organizers went to great lengths to preserve the anonymity—and thus the dignity—of the women whose pies, preserves, embroidery, and children's garments were displayed and sold. Not everyone agreed that exchanges did women a service. Reformer Lucy Salmon protested that keeping consignors anonymous reflected "moral cowardice" by capitulating to backward ideas that women's paid labor was somehow dishonorable. Because the Lend a Hand wholeheartedly embraced the virtue of women's employment, the club welcomed—even sought—publicity for its businesses and successes.[55]

The same year it organized the mending bureau and set May Santry up in the dressmaking business, the Lend a Hand also launched the first professional organization for women in the city, the Davenport Nurses' Association (DNA). The DNA began as an employment bureau. Since most nurses in this period worked in private homes, the association kept a register of nurses, listing their training, experience, and specialty as well as recommendations from physicians. A bulletin board showed which nurses were currently employed and which were available for service. "Instead of hunting from house to house[,] a visit to the club rooms will show at a glance what nurses are at home and open to engagement and what kind of nursing they are willing to do," explained a report. The service was thus a boon to both nurses and the community they served.[56]

At the same time, the association positioned itself on contested terrain. Through most of the century, nursing had been a kind of personal service, a step above the status of house servant but not a profession. The woman who nursed was often a widow whose chief claim to expertise came from having cared for a dying husband. Following the employment of large numbers of women as nurses during the Civil War, a movement emerged to make nursing a true profession for women. Success came slowly. In 1890, only thirty-five training schools for nurses existed in the United States. The DNA, with its central register of trained nurses, sought to claim nursing as a profession with standards and credentials, thus raising its status (and perhaps its pay). To promote professional standards, the association began building a library of books on nursing, organized a lecture series for nurses by the city's physicians, and subscribed to *Trained Nurse*. The King's Daughters donated a subscription to *Health Journal*. Association meetings, the library, and the lecture series were all held at the Lend a Hand rooms, and when Davenport established its first training schools for nurses in the 1890s, members of the Lend a Hand were closely involved. As with other programs and organizations fostered by the Lend a Hand, the DNA sought to support women in their identities as workers, promoting efficiency and professionalism.[57]

A Lend a Hand project that turned members into proprietors yet also embraced the ethos of service was the Home Cooking Company. In the fall of 1893, Mary Colville, a clerk, and Elizabeth Lau, a photo retoucher, resigned their jobs at the Jarvis White Art Company, a photographic studio, and sold their stock in the firm. Colville had worked for the company for eighteen years. In March 1894, the two were among five women filing articles of incorporation for the Home Cooking

Company, with Colville as president, Lau as treasurer, and Lile Bickford as vice president. All five members of the board of directors were Lend a Hand members.[58]

The Home Cooking Company combined a restaurant and bakery with a cooked-food delivery service, providing "all kinds of cookery" to families at home. While restaurants, like dressmaking establishments, were not unusual businesses for women to take up, a cooked-food delivery service was out of the ordinary. Dolores Hayden has documented the creation of such services beginning in the late 1880s as part of a general movement to relieve women of the burden of housekeeping, thus freeing them for more active public lives. Hayden called this movement "material feminism." The Home Cooking Company, however, did not concern itself solely with women trapped at home by housework. Its original plan included a parlor and "toilet rooms for ladies" at its downtown location—an effort, like the Lend a Hand rooms, to provide for women the kinds of conveniences men took for granted. This scheme was thwarted when it became clear that the property did not provide suitable space for such amenities. Disappointment on one front did not, however, discourage the women of the Home Cooking Company from expanding in other directions. In 1895, the company held the first of several professional cooking schools, bringing in caterers and home economists from around the country to instruct students in both nutrition science and cookery. One goal of these classes was to "dignify" cooking, raising it "up from the plane of slavish drudgery." Bickford, who had become an officer in a new national organization, the American Household Economics Association, took a leading role in establishing these schools. The Home Cooking Company operated for about three years under the management of Colville and Lau, employing during that period about five women and two men. When the women sold the business, the new proprietors seem to have continued only the restaurant.[59]

Another venture growing out of the Lend a Hand matrix of service and entrepreneurship was the Hadlai Heights Woman's Hospital. In 1891, Lile Bickford resigned from the Cook Home to take a position as matron of a school for deaf children in Chicago operated by Jennie McCowen's sister, Mary. A year later, Bickford returned to Davenport and joined with Jennie McCowen to purchase eight acres on the western heights of the city for $6,500. The property, which offered a twenty-five-mile view of the Mississippi Valley, included a "spacious, old fashioned house," which the women converted into "a beautiful home for themselves" and a private hospital. Dr. McCowen was chief physician, and Bickford was superintendent.[60]

The Hadlai Heights Woman's Hospital operated until the turn of the century, crowning one of "the two highest hills along the river front." (On the other crest was the residence of the Catholic bishop.) Occupying a site once inhabited by Davenport's founding family, the hospital provided visible evidence of the success of working women. But its service was not only symbolic. During its years of operation, the hospital provided free care to Lend a Hand members and other working women to the value of more than a thousand dollars. In 1900, Lile Bickford moved to Denver, apparently to help care for her aged mother. This, along with competition from St. Luke's Hospital, which had opened in 1895, may have prompted the closing of Hadlai Heights. The property was sold in December 1900.[61]

In addition to these business and organizational ventures, the Lend a Hand also supported women's occupational mobility through its educational loan fund. Published club reports indicate that the fund was regularly used (and regularly repaid), but they do not give information about who borrowed and for what kind of training. Still, it is possible to identify a few likely borrowers. When Meta Wittig first joined the Lend a Hand, she was the teenage daughter of German immigrants, employed to pack cigars in boxes. Over the next decade, she rose to working as a clerk in a dry goods store. Then, in 1901, Meta Wittig moved to Chicago to attend the Armour Institute Kindergarten Training School. A journey to Chicago in 1901 hardly required the same fortitude as McCowen's move to western Iowa in 1864, but Wittig was no doubt happy to draw on the networks created by other Lend a Hand members in the city, just as the earlier generation of migrants had relied on each other. After Armour, Wittig studied with Mary McCowen at the McCowen Oral School for the Deaf. Upon her return, Meta Wittig took charge of deaf education in the Rock Island public schools. The club celebrated her graduation from the Armour Institute with a party in the downtown club rooms, suggesting that Lend a Hand members viewed her success as a shared event. If Wittig financed her education with a Lend a Hand loan, that sense of communal pride must have been even stronger.[62]

Clara Craine was another likely borrower. Craine was in her early twenties when she moved to Davenport and began working as a seamstress. She joined the Lend a Hand about 1891 and soon moved into a new career, beginning formal training in nursing at the new St. Luke's Hospital school in 1895. The educational loan fund existed exactly for cases like hers. For several years, Craine worked as Jennie McCowen's office nurse, taking time out in 1898 to run a wartime Red Cross Hospital in Des Moines. In 1903, when the superintendent of the Davenport Visiting Nurses Association resigned, Craine took over the position, which she held until her retirement in 1935. Clara Craine's new occupation drew her closer to Dr. McCowen, and after Lile Bickford moved to Denver, McCowen and Craine shared a home until McCowen's death in 1924.[63]

These were certainly not the only women who followed significantly upward paths in their careers after joining the Lend a Hand. Meta Wittig's sister, Emilie, left store clerking to study at the School of Civics and Philanthropy of Chicago, worked for the United Charities of Chicago, and then returned to Davenport to become executive secretary of the Lend a Hand in 1909. Mrs. Margaret Thompson had worked alongside her husband at the Internal Revenue Collector's Office in the 1880s. After her husband's death, she opened her own dressmaking establishment in 1896. She advertised Mrs. W. Karr's Hand-Made Corsets ("warranted not to break or burst"). In 1901, Thompson moved to Iowa City to become matron of the university hospital. Emily Haines, a store clerk in 1890, moved into teaching by 1893. And Annie Eldridge, who was a folder at the Egbert, Fidler, Chambers, and Company job printers in 1890 (where her sister, Sadie, was a pager), followed in Jennie McCowen's footsteps and became a physician.[64]

If what the organizers of the Lend a Hand imagined on Christmas Day in 1886 was institutionalizing the networks of support they had improvised for themselves, they seem to have succeeded. The Working Woman's Lend a Hand club took seriously its promise "to promote the best practical methods of securing higher intellectual[,] moral[,] and physical conditions" for women. The downtown rooms provided an environment where working women could eat, rest, and socialize, secure in their welcome and in their respectability. Club social activities promoted a culture of literacy and self-improvement, encouraging members to develop speaking skills and an interest in public affairs. The classes and loan fund gave practical assistance to women who sought occupational mobility. And the businesses and organizations incubated by the Lend a Hand reflected its dual commitment to both mutual service and women's advancement.[65]

At the same time, the Lend a Hand's efforts reveal the limits of self-help organizations among women. While the DNA and the Lend a Hand itself survived and prospered for decades, all the businesses started in the club's early years either folded or were sold. By 1901, the dressmaking establishment, the Home Cooking Company, and the Hadlai Heights Woman's Hospital no longer survived as businesses run by Lend a Hand women. In the case of the hospital and the dressmaking business, the decision to close probably stemmed in part from changes in family obligations on the part of the principals: Lile Bickford assumed the care of her aging mother in Denver, and May Santry married and moved to Springfield, Illinois. Yet in each case, the pool of ambitious, competent, self-supporting women proved too small to furnish a replacement. Or perhaps the profound personalism that underlay these ventures made it difficult for one woman to step into the role originated by another. An 1895 biographical sketch of Jennie McCowen concluded with the information that she had never married but shared "a beautiful home in the suburbs"—Hadlai Heights—with "a life-long friend." The parallel drawn between marriage and the relationship between McCowen and Bickford suggests that Bickford's place in McCowen's life and business could not have been filled easily by someone else.[66]

Small businesses, especially those operated by women, failed at a breathtaking rate at the end of the nineteenth century. Wendy Gamber found that a third of all milliners' and dressmakers' establishments survived less than two years, and 60 percent closed within five years. Women who survived on their own earnings had difficulty generating enough capital to sustain businesses and faced greater difficulty than men obtaining credit. In the nineteenth century, R. G. Dun and Company sent agents to investigate the creditworthiness of large and small businesses across the country. No Dun records for Davenport survive from this period, but a notice appearing in the *Davenport Tribune* exposes the same degree of skepticism that R. G. Dun investigators expressed regarding women's business abilities. Commenting on an 1889 fund-raising effort by the Lend a Hand, the newspaper noted, "Many business men when asked to contribute to the Lend-a-Hand club have refused, saying it was managed by women who knew nothing of business affairs." In response, two "leading financiers" of the city examined the club's financial records and endorsed its practices. If some men were reluctant to donate money to the club because it was run by women, they may have been even less willing to extend credit to businesses managed by these women. Small businesses failed often; when gender compromised access to credit, failure was even more likely. This was precisely the kind of prejudice the Lend a Hand hoped eventually to confound. More than any of these factors, however, the Lend a Hand businesses may have suffered from simple bad timing. The hospital and the Home Cooking Company both opened in 1893, just as the country was sliding into the century's worst depression. Thousands of businesses failed over the next four years, and the Lend a Hand ventures were by no means immune.[67]

The failure of these businesses should not be taken as the failure of the Lend a Hand, however. The club flourished and could point to many women whose individual successes testified to the effectiveness of its programs. The experiments of the 1880s and early 1890s led to some practical conclusions: the club's greatest services lay in providing rest, refuge, and space in the city center; in offering access to education; and in encouraging women's ambitions by giving young women the model of older, successful women in their midst.

The Working Woman's Lend a Hand club began as an unusual entry into the organizational universe of the Gilded Age city. It placed control of the organization in the hands of working women from the start, and unlike its counterparts run by elite and middle-class women of leisure, the Lend a Hand never promoted domesticity or worried that paid employment humiliated women or endangered their morals. Innovating while imitating, the Lend a Hand borrowed freely from the programs of its counterparts, transforming these models with an alternative ethos: the self-confident assertion that employed women were not endangered girls adrift in the city or weak sisters in need of protection but admirable examples of what Jennie McCowen called "the new life animating women everywhere." McCowen and her colleagues understood themselves as a vanguard, challenging common beliefs about the meaning of paid employment in women's lives. But the club's founders quickly discovered as well the limitations of these private efforts to claim a place for women in the city center.[68]

4

LIVES WITHOUT CHOICES
Prostitution as Employment

On either side of us, and across the street, the houses were occupied by prostitutes.... They were boarding houses, dressmaking-shops, hand-laundries, and the homes of working-men whose wives added to the family finances by occasional prostitution.... Their houses were palaces compared with the wretched place that I called home. Needless to say, I had an opportunity, and I heard many suggestions and learned many things that it is not well for a girl to know.
—Anonymous, *Madeleine*, 1919

BY THE 1870S AND 1880S, prostitution had become a fact of everyday life in much of the United States. Folk history has often treated the brothel as exotic, one of the mysteries of the great city, or as a colorful adjunct to mining camps, seaports, or army posts. Academic historians as well have tended to focus on the largest cities, especially New York, or on the mining and lumbering West, where dramatically skewed sex ratios and weak institutions of social control created both demand and opportunity for prostitutes. In truth, however, any market town, county seat, or railroad division point was likely to have a brothel or two—or more. Historians have documented brothels in such places as Grand Island, Nebraska; Sedalia, Missouri; and East Grand Forks, Minnesota. Nor was prostitution generally clandestine, invisible to those who preferred not to know about it. Newspapers described brothel arrests and vagrancy trials in the same columns that reported social events, church services, and the illnesses of neighbors. Middle-class newspaper readers—whether gentlemen checking the markets or ladies perusing charity reports—could easily know the names and neighborhoods of local public women. In cities such as Davenport, knowledge of prostitution could be even more direct. Any visit to the central business district might prove an opportunity for education, welcome or not.[1]

For the working women who joined the Lend a Hand club, education might come on their daily walk to work or as they left the club rooms after an evening meeting. The diffusion of spaces occupied by prostitutes through those occupied by respectable working women becomes clear when the locations of Davenport's brothels in the late 1880s are mapped against the homes and workplaces of members of the Working Woman's Lend a Hand club. Map 1 shows the homes and workplaces of Lend a Hand members in the same period. Map 2 shows the sites of brothels and assignation houses in 1888 and 1889. While three brothels are scattered north of downtown, the rest are located in a concentrated area in the center of the city. One cluster sits on Front Street west of Brady; another lies on Fifth Street east of Brady; and smaller clumps lie on Third Street and Perry Street, with a handful of other locations nearby. While many of the Lend a Hand members lived in the outlying residential areas of Davenport, a distinct concentration lived in the same few blocks where brothels and assignation houses clustered: Brady Street is clearly the spine of this map, with both homes and workplaces along the blocks nearby. To put this spatial relationship in the most personal terms, throughout the 1880s, Dr. Jennie McCowen never lived more than half a block from a brothel. In 1888, any route the Wittig sisters might have walked from their home on East Fourth Street to the Lend a Hand rooms at Second and Brady would probably have taken them past two or three brothels. Lucy Pratt, who taught penmanship at the Lend a Hand, would have faced a similar walk from her home near Fifth and Perry. And Mary Colville, who cofounded the Home Cooking Company, lived directly across the street from a brothel.

Who were the women who worked in these brothels? What distinguished them from their counterparts who joined the Lend a Hand club? Prostitution may have been pervasive, but it was also perplexing. The women who worked as prostitutes violated a fundamental premise of middle-class gender ideology: that women were by nature modest, sexually reticent creatures. Debates over what could cause women to violate their nature filled social and medical journals. Did desperate poverty drive women to prostitution? Did unscrupulous men seduce foolish girls, then abandon them to the brothel? Were prostitutes simply unnatural women who chose their life to satisfy greed, lust, or desire for drink? The best research of the day offered support for all three possibilities. William Sanger and his assistants interviewed two thousand women arrested for prostitution in New York City in the mid-1850s, using a schedule of more than forty questions designed to elicit information about prostitutes' family origins and life histories. Of those interviewed, more than a quarter identified "destitution" as the cause of their entering the life. Nearly as many claimed "inclination," and 181 declared "drink, and the desire to drink." More than 300 said they were either "seduced" or "violated," and another 164 named "ill-treatment by parents, relatives, or husbands" as the cause. Victims outnumbered wantons, but the 513 who claimed to have become prostitutes out of "inclination" shocked even Sanger.[2]

Historians have debated what these brief answers meant—how much they reflected the prejudice of the questioners or the powerlessness of those questioned. A few months before Sanger's *History of Prostitution* was published, fire destroyed the answer sheets that might have linked these responses to the individuals who gave them, ensuring that the women's words would remain forever disembodied fragments. Nevertheless, Sanger's book has remained an important source for historians attempting to understand the origins and motivations of nineteenth-century prostitutes. Most historians addressing the subject have spent at least some time weighing Sanger's fragmentary answers and creating a composite profile of a typical prostitute.[3]

This chapter takes another path into the lives of prostitutes, focusing on six women who worked as streetwalkers, brothel prostitutes, or brothel keepers in Davenport in the 1870s and 1880s. Instead of creating a composite, what follows is a reconstruction of six different lives based on evidence collected from a wide range of historical records. The profiles begin with the women's birth families and continue through about 1893, when Davenport entered a new period of public policy toward prostitution. The effects of that change on these women's lives will be explored in a later chapter. None of these women was a "typical prostitute," but together their lives suggest the experiences that might lead a woman into the commerce of sex.

The evidence that makes it possible to trace these lives is a sign of one difference separating these women from at least some of their contemporaries. Scores of women came and went, working in Davenport's prostitution trade for a few weeks or a few years. These six women, however, stayed near Davenport and Scott County for decades—some for their entire lives. This attachment to place opens their lives to the historian to a degree that is impossible for more transient prostitutes. Yet these women's persistence is not unusual. They are only a handful among more than fifty women whose names recur regularly in the newspapers and police records over these decades. While transience was characteristic of some women's experience in the prostitution trade, persistence was equally characteristic of others. And because these women stayed in the community, they more than their ephemeral counterparts formed the public face of prostitution. They were truly public women, known to the police, to sporting men and others who patronized prostitutes, and to anyone who read the daily newspapers.

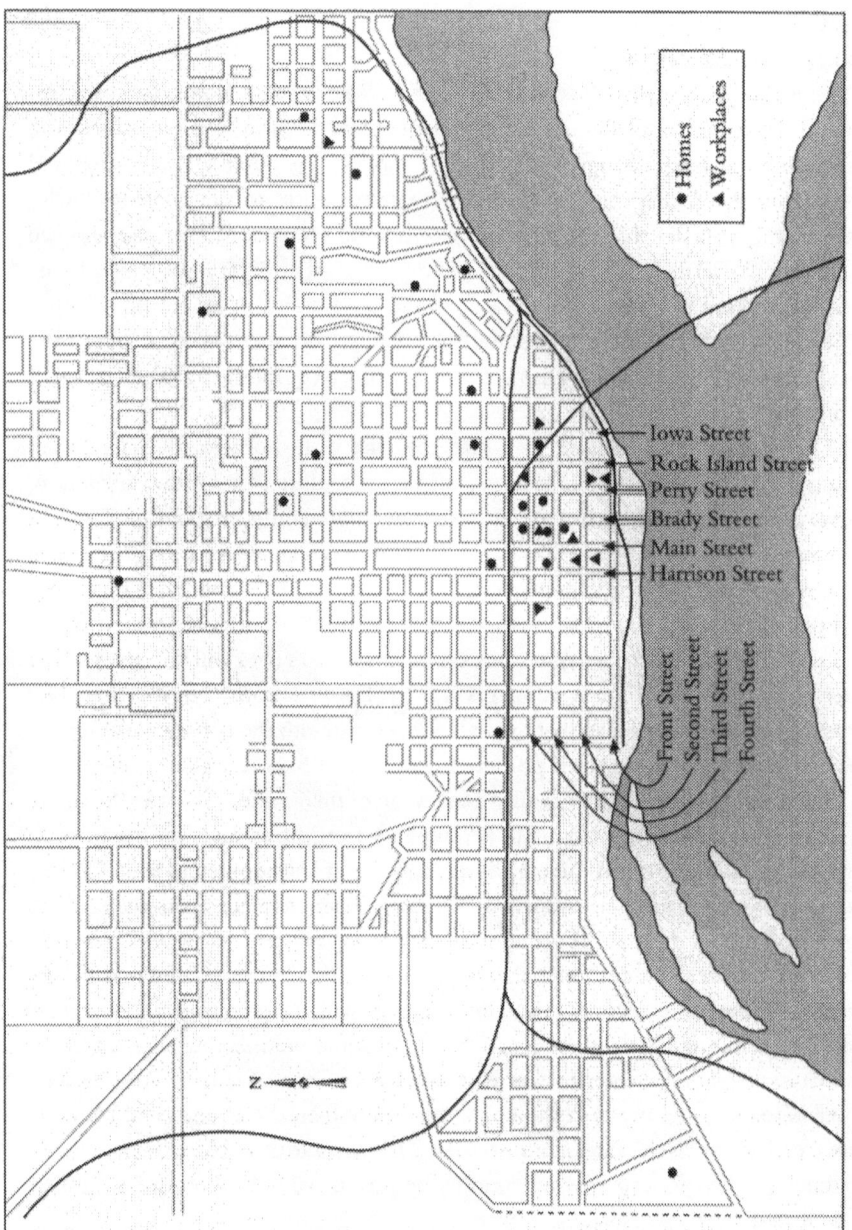

Map 1. Homes and workplaces of Lend a Hand members, 1888–89

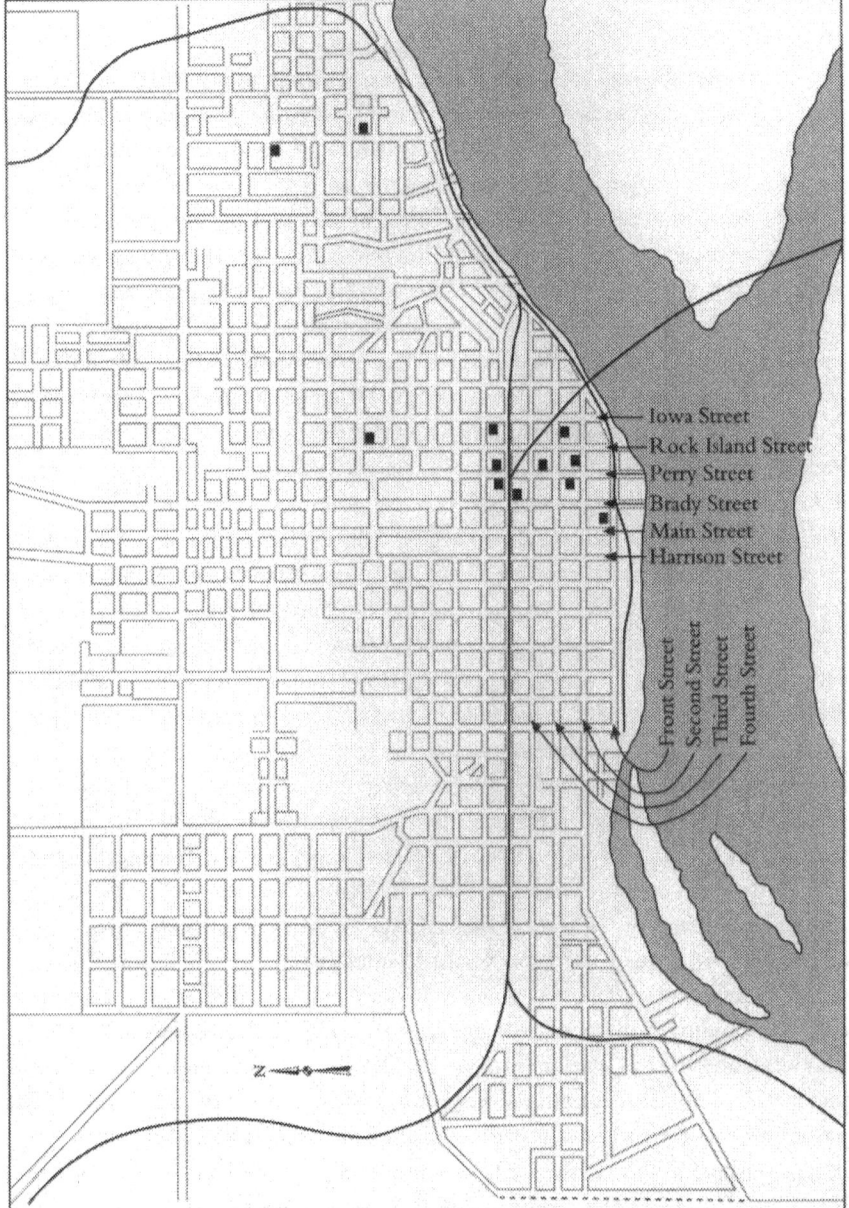

Map 2. Brothels and assignation houses, 1888–89

JOSIE MITCHELL

The woman born Naomi Josephine Fowler went through at least eight surnames and several variations on her given names in her sixty-one years of life, but as a prostitute she was nearly always Josie Mitchell. Her girlhood name, Naomi, was often written Neoma, but she was in no position to correct anyone's spelling in those days. Josie was almost forty years old before she learned to write her own name.[4]

Naomi was born in rural Scott County, Iowa, in January 1851, to Abram Fowler and Margaret Kelso Fowler, natives of Ohio who had been married nearly a year. Abram was a farm laborer, and the couple began their marriage boarding on the farm where they worked. Over the next fourteen years, Margaret bore at least three more children, Sevilla in 1857, Oscar in 1860, and Clementine in 1866. That Naomi did not learn to write reveals something about these early years: such illiteracy was relatively rare in midcentury Iowa. The 1870 census for Scott County recorded only 188 American-born citizens who could not write out of a population of well over 38,000. That Naomi was among these suggests a disrupted childhood in which her parents failed to ensure even minimal school attendance. About 1866, Abram Fowler either died or departed, and Margaret married another farm laborer, John Wiley. She bore him a namesake in 1871. John Wiley, Naomi's stepfather, gave permission for her to marry William Keller in May 1866. Naomi was just fifteen that year, about the same age that Jennie McCowen and Lile Bickford had entered the workforce as schoolteachers. Naomi, by contrast, became the wife of a farm laborer from Maine. Four years later, Naomi and William were living in rural Sheridan Township, just north of Davenport, with their children, two-year-old Lyman and two-month-old Oscar Lafayette, who was named after Naomi's younger brother. Her mother and stepfather lived not far away with their three children.[5]

Naomi spent the first ten years of her marriage pregnant or nursing. Three more children followed Lyman and Lafe: Sevilla Clementine in 1873, William in 1874, and Margaret in 1876—all names chosen to honor family ties. But by 1875, Naomi's family was straining at the seams, her marriage faltering. William suspected Naomi of adultery. Around 1878, the family moved to Davenport, perhaps forced from their home by the economic depression overspreading the country. William found work as a teamster, but it was not a well-paid occupation. The family lived that year in one of the poorest parts of town, the seedy neighborhood along East Front Street where tough saloons clustered and prostitutes strolled. Naomi went to work "to support herself and children," most likely as a laundress. The job was well suited to an illiterate woman with children to care for. In the city, William's suspicions only increased, and in 1880 he moved out, taking "all the personal property and household goods." He sued for divorce, charging Naomi with adultery. Naomi countersued, claiming "inhuman treatment" and asking for thirty dollars in temporary alimony to help meet the expenses of the divorce. Of their five children, she asked custody only of Lyman, her firstborn, who by that time was twelve years old and what contemporaries called "feebleminded." The court sided with William, granting him the divorce and custody of the four younger children. Naomi, as she requested, got Lyman.[6]

At twenty-nine, Naomi Fowler Keller was divorced, illiterate, and had the care of a mentally disabled son. Supporting herself could not have been easy, and she may have turned to her mother for help. By this time, Margaret Wiley was also living on Front Street in Davenport, with her children: Oscar, a teamster; Clementine; and young John Wiley. Within a year of her divorce, Naomi chose the route many women in her position would have taken. In May 1881, she married again, perhaps in love but probably also hoping that her new husband, Frank Mitchell, would be a provider for her and her child. But barely two years later Mitchell was gone for good, and all he provided for Naomi was a new last name.[7]

Naomi, now known more often as Josie or Joe, pursued a variety of employments to support herself and her dependent son. She did washing and took in boarders. She occasionally collected relief from the county. Beginning in September 1883, Josie Mitchell became one of several women sometimes paid by the county to care for the sick poor or to provide lodging for the destitute. It was a kind of public assistance: by paying needy women to care for the poor, the county helped two for the price of one. The cases that came into her home must have hardened her resolve to provide for herself and her children. In December 1883, for example, a woman staying at a downtown hotel—ostensibly awaiting her husband's arrival from distant parts—went into labor. The baby was safely delivered, and when no husband appeared, the overseer of the poor placed the mother and baby with Josie Mitchell. A few days after the birth, he sent the mother out to find employment so she would not remain a county charge. She returned saying she had found laundry work in Rock Island and asked Josie to care for her newborn until she could find a place to have the infant with her. The woman left again for Rock Island and never returned. That same week, Josie was caring for Lizzie Hendricksen, a twenty-year-old woman dying of lung disease. She had become a county charge some weeks earlier when her mother, Kate Huber, refused to take her in. When Hendricksen died at Josie Mitchell's home, the newspapers mourned, "She was absolutely homeless and friendless at the last, though she had a mother living." As Josie Mitchell cared for the county's destitute, her home became a refuge for women and children whose claims on the support of others had been betrayed. Poor though she was, Mitchell attempted to fulfill her own obligations. By 1885, she had her four youngest children with her again, and she had placed Lyman in the state home for the feebleminded at Glenwood. Josie's mother, now widowed and working as a laundress, still lived on Front Street with her fourteen-year-old son.[8]

Josie Mitchell may have tried to fulfill her obligations as a mother, but as she struggled through the 1880s, failure dogged her steps. The court judged Josie an adulteress when it dissolved her marriage to William Keller, but she must have met some minimal standard of respectability from 1883 to 1887 when she boarded county charges. Still, her position was precarious, and she seemed unable—perhaps uninterested—in keeping it. Though in 1883 she drew as much as thirty dollars a month from the county, by 1886 and 1887, her payments dwindled to at most eight dollars a month. She could not hold onto her boardinghouse on the more respectable west side and drifted from street to street in the east side neighborhood now increasingly associated with prostitution. Poverty meant that she could not exercise much selectivity about boarders. She was limited to those who would pay for the crowded, shabby accommodations she could offer—usually tenants rejected by other landladies. Sometimes these were men like Mike Whitty, who boarded with Josie in 1885. Mike, "the irreclaimable do nothing and guzzler," as one paper called him, was one of the notorious Whitty brothers whose crimes figured in Davenport papers for decades. Some of her boarders may have been prostitutes, another group who would pay for accommodations where the landlady looked the other way. By June 1889, the downward spiral of Josie Mitchell's reputation was confirmed by the police department: she was arrested and fined as the keeper of a house of ill-fame.[9]

Whether Josie Mitchell made a conscious choice to take up brothel keeping in the late 1880s or whether doing so was the result of an inexorable drift can probably never be determined. In law, she was a "keeper of a house of ill-fame" if "lewd women made [her house] a place of resort, and . . . men of licentious repute visited." Simply accepting the kinds of boarders who would pay for her rooms put her in jeopardy of the law.[10]

Josie Mitchell's life in that period was one of increasing instability and crisis. Between 1885 and 1892, she married and divorced at least twice and perhaps three times. In April 1888, she wed Charles Robison, a twenty-seven-year-old common laborer. She reported her age to the clerk as twenty-nine, though she was in fact thirty-seven. The clerk also recorded her "color" as "blonde," evoking a blondeness so startling that it displaced the usual entries of "white" or "colored." (Police records usually identified Josie as five-foot-nine and "dark." In the 1880s, "peroxide blonde" was strongly associated with prostitution.) Three years later, in October 1891, Robison fled after being caught in adultery, apparently with his sister-in-law, who decamped with him. In December 1892, after divorcing Robison, Josie married a thirty-year-old drayman named William Hawkins. This time, Josie gave her age as thirty-five; she was forty-one. Four years later, Hawkins charged her with adultery.[11]

In the midst of these marital entanglements, Josie's older daughter was experiencing her own ongoing crises. In August 1885, fifteen-year-old Sevilla married twenty-two-year old laborer Adelbert DeMaranville. How Josie felt about the marriage at the time is impossible to discover. She had married at the same age, and she may have welcomed the possibility that Sevilla would now be supported by someone else. But eight years later, when the couple divorced, Josie expressed her opinion in frank and brutal terms. DeMaranville "is and was a drunkard, a man of ill habits, and wholly immoral," she reported. He forced Sevilla "to have sexual intercourse with men for hire, and took and lived on the proceeds" of his wife's prostitution. According to his mother-in-law, DeMaranville filed for divorce only when Sevilla "refused longer to lead an immoral life for his support."[12]

In addition to prostituting his wife, DeMaranville got involved in a scheme of revenge against a neighborhood saloon keeper's family. DeMaranville; Josie's son, Lafe Keller; and perhaps Josie herself, under coercion, gave false testimony charging the saloon keeper and his wife with keeping a house of ill-fame. This episode will be explored at length in chapter 6, but for now it is enough to say that it clearly added to the strain of Josie Mitchell's already difficult life. In March 1892, in the midst of the campaign of harassment, Josie Mitchell attempted suicide, taking fifteen grains of morphine.[13]

The events surrounding Josie's suicide attempt may have led Sevilla and DeMaranville finally to divorce in the fall of 1893. DeMaranville agreed to leave the couple's three children in Josie's care with the understanding that she would adopt them. Two months later, in December 1893, he changed his mind and went to court to have them removed from their grandmother's house, complaining that Josie was "now a keeper of a house of ill fame" and "addicted to unchaste habits and immoral practices." Josie responded with her blistering charges against DeMaranville and insisted that she and Sevilla "a long time since have been leading chaste and moral lives and are engaged in conducting a boarding house and restaurant and are making an honest and competent living." The court hesitated, apparently suspecting the morals of everyone involved, so Josie and her younger daughter, Maggie, took the children and fled across the river into Illinois, leaving Sevilla in charge of the "boarding house and restaurant."

Josie may have been telling the truth about trying to make an honest living. In the months following June 1891, Josie Mitchell was arrested as a brothel keeper on several occasions, but each time her arrest coincided with events in DeMaranville's campaign of harassment against the saloonkeeper. Their timing suggests that DeMaranville was working with the police to coerce Josie's cooperation. Mitchell did not appear again in the police records until the late fall of 1893, when she was arrested three more times. Those arrests, however, coincide with DeMaranville's divorce action, and the alleged inmates were Mitchell's daughters and daughter-in-law. It would not be the first time an angry husband made charges against his estranged wife's family to bolster his case—charges that seemed plausible because of the histories of the women involved. Josie Mitchell may or may not have been back in the brothel business in the winter of 1893. Significantly, however, she did not appear in court again for almost six months.[14]

As a single mother with no education and few resources, Josie Mitchell worked where she could to support her children, but the neighborhood she could afford and the boarders who would pay left her exposed to accusations of prostitution. Without a reputation to sustain her, she remained vulnerable to arrest, even extortion. Her neighborhood and associations also had consequences for her children, especially Sevilla, who found her own way into prostitution.

KATE HUBER

If Josie Mitchell's slide into prostitution appears linked with her struggle to be a good mother to her five children, Kate Huber's reputation clearly suffered from her public failures as a mother. Huber, whose name was sometimes spelled Uber, was born in Prussia in July 1841, where she was called Catharina. She completed seven years of grammar school, and at the end of the U.S. Civil War, when she was about twenty-two, Catharina emigrated to the United States. She may have gone first to Pennsylvania, where Ernst Huber, the man she married, was born. The couple found their way to Davenport about 1878. There, Ernst Huber pursued his trade, making cigars, and the family lived at first in the German settlement a few blocks west of downtown.[15]

As early as 1881, evidence that this was a troubled family began to emerge. In June of that year, Kate Huber was living in a small shack behind 1022 West Second Street in Davenport. One Monday morning, several neighbors heard a child crying and went to investigate. They saw Kate Huber "whipping" her six-year-old daughter, Lena, with "a stick of firewood as thick as my wrist," according to one woman. Henry Oldendorf, Huber's landlord, "did not think it was any of my business and returned to my work." Doris Schestedt "proposed to go and stop her whipping," but her companion held her back, warning, "she would strike you if you interfered." As the child's cries continued, Oldendorf again considered intervening but did not. Schestedt and her companion "made a noise to attract the attention of Mrs. Huber," but Huber did not stop. Instead, she "seized the child by the arm and drew her into another room," where the neighbors could no longer see what was going on. But, testified Schestedt, they "could hear the blows upon the child and the outcry made by the child from the effect of the blows." Witnesses estimated that the noise lasted between fifteen and thirty minutes.[16]

Although Lena died a few days later, neighbors did not come forward with their stories until after the child was buried. But the whispers about what had happened eventually reached the police, and Lena's body was exhumed and autopsied. Although one of the physicians found that "the head showed effect of a blow from some dull instrument which had affected and injured the brain," they could not conclude with certainty that the beating had caused the child's death. Kate Huber was convicted of simple assault and sentenced to thirty days in jail.[17]

Ernst was never mentioned in the court record, and it is possible that he and Kate had separated by this time. The 1880 census taker had found them living together with their five youngest children in a rear house on West Second Street. Two years later, when Kate turned her desperately ill daughter, Lizzie Hendricksen, away from home, newspapers criticized Kate, reminding readers of Lena's suspicious death, but again never mentioned Ernst. In a move suffused with irony for the historian, the superintendent of the poor placed the dying Lizzie in the care of Josie Mitchell. In 1884, two different city directories placed Ernst and Kate at different addresses, and in 1885, the state census taker found Kate living with three children ages two, seven, and fifteen but no husband at 104 East Front Street. By 1890, Ernst was apparently dead.[18]

Unlike many of the other women who drifted into prostitution in this period, Kate Huber was relatively well educated. But she also had a reputation as a brutish woman who might strike a neighbor and who had probably sent two daughters to their deaths. She was hardly in a position to attract and keep boarders, and she must have struggled to make ends meet. By 1885, she was living in the Front Street neighborhood associated with prostitution. In 1887, she was considered a prostitute herself and was held in contempt even by other women in the trade. That September, Mary Artelle defended herself against accusations that she kept a brothel by arguing that she had simply moved into a house previously occupied by Kate Huber. When neighbors testified that they had seen soldiers from Arsenal Island coming to her house, Artelle insisted, "these people—soldiers etc.—were looking for one Mrs. Huber." Artelle was alleged by neighbors to have proclaimed "that she did not have to sleep with a man for 50¢ the same as Mrs. Huber." To Artelle, Huber was contemptible, a woman who would sell herself for a pittance. Artelle's defense was unsuccessful, and the court sentenced her to three years in the penitentiary. Huber, in turn, did her business quietly, probably by operating alone for several years. With the exception of one arrest—with her eleven-year-old daughter, Clara—in 1892 for disturbing the peace, Huber avoided attention from the police until May 1893.[19]

Huber's 1885 move from the respectable west side to Front Street signaled a change in her status, but it is difficult to discern what was cause and what was effect. If she found in prostitution a reliable income to support her remaining children, a move to Front Street would make it easier to find customers. If she was forced to leave her west side home because her landlord found her an undesirable tenant, Front Street may have been her only alternative and prostitution a ready option.

MINNIE HAGAN

In the spring of 1878, a newspaper in Rock Island reported that an "abandoned creature" had been "making her headquarters in the woods adjacent to the city." She "seems to glory in the life of infamy she is leading" and "keeps in her train a lot of young boys, of from fifteen to twenty years of age." This woodland siren was Minnie Hagan, notorious already at thirteen. When sentenced to thirty days in jail on a charge of vagrancy, "Minnie suggested that it would give her a good rest, and rather seemed to enjoy the prospects of imprisonment." To the newspapers, Minnie Hagan was a hard case, "a very veteran of iniquity," but from another point of view, she was just a homeless girl who lived in the woods and earned money from her only reliable asset. Given her circumstances, a jail sentence might indeed seem a welcome respite.[20]

How Minnie Hagan became a homeless child prostitute is a study in the precarious economic condition of women and girls in last half of the nineteenth century. Minnie Hagan was born Minnie May in about 1865 to Emma Jane May, an illiterate, unmarried, nineteen-year-old Ohio native living in southeast Iowa. In July 1869, Emma May married Andrew Jackson Hagan in Muscatine, Iowa, about thirty miles downriver from Davenport. Jackson, twenty-six, was also a native of Ohio. A year later, when the census taker canvassed rural Seventy-six township in Muscatine County, he found Emma and Jackson boarding on a farm, where Emma worked as a domestic servant and Jackson as a laborer. Minnie was not living with them. Perhaps Jackson did not welcome his wife's daughter, or perhaps their employers were not interested in providing a home for a small child in need of parental care. Emma may have placed Minnie in the care of another family after her marriage; the census taker recorded a five-year-old "Emma Hagan" living with the Lehfler family in Highland Township, Washington County, about thirty miles from where Jackson and Emma resided.[21]

By the spring of 1876, the marriage between Emma and Jackson was over. When Emma filed for divorce three years later, she claimed that Jackson had thrown her out of their house in Moline and refused to support her. Homeless and broke, Emma turned to petty crime. Her daughter was sometimes with her, but just as often, Minnie fended for herself. In late winter, Minnie and Emma were arrested together for stealing watches at a Davenport hotel. The *Davenport Democrat* identified Emma as "Mrs. Maggie Day," perhaps the paper's error for "May" or perhaps her alias. Twelve-year-old Minnie the paper judged to be "about 16," observing that she "seems as hardened in sin as her mother." Two months later, police found Minnie occupying an abandoned house in Davenport. The newspapers were already identifying her as a streetwalker "of low grade," and some women of Davenport took an interest in her case, arranging for her to be released from jail and placed with the Sisters of Mercy. A few days later, Minnie slipped out at five in the morning and fled from Mercy Hospital. She was arrested the following day for vagrancy, but the police-court judge suspended her ten-day sentence on her promise that she would go to live with her stepfather, Jackson Hagan, in Moline. Emma Hagan apparently could not provide a suitable home for her daughter, but no one seems to have considered whether putting the troubled and troublesome Minnie in the home of a stepfather who had already rejected her mother was a good idea. Less than a year later, Minnie was on her own again, living in the woods and making light of a thirty-day jail sentence.[22]

Like Josie Mitchell, Emma May Hagan was illiterate and rejected by her husband, and she could not have had an easy time earning a living for herself and her daughter. Evidence of Emma's activities in this period is sparse: her arrest for stealing watches in Davenport and her unwilling participation in a spectacular horse theft the following August are the only exceptions. She lived for a while on a farm near Andalusia, Illinois, ten miles downriver from Rock Island, where she may have worked again as a servant. If so, her employers might have drawn a line at providing a home for an unruly twelve-year-old as well. Two years later, in December 1879, Emma was living on another farm, this time in Blue Grass, Iowa, just west of Davenport. That winter, she filed for divorce from Jackson, and the following May she became the wife of George Woodruff, a Rock Island laborer.[23]

Unable to make a home with either her mother or stepfather, Minnie followed a path from casual prostitution into brothels, and in October 1882, at seventeen, she married. Her husband was Ezra Murdoch, son of a Davenport shoemaker and himself a hack driver. He was also a sporting man, a habitué of the tough, often violent world of gambling halls and brothels. Either he or a brother was a member of the gang of thugs that repeatedly terrorized the Black Hills resort in 1879, assaulting the women who worked there and shooting the keeper, Millie Dillon. Along with bartending, hack driving was a typical occupation for a sporting man—and for a prostitute's husband. A few weeks after their wedding, Ezra and Minnie were already at odds. She left Davenport, heading west to Council Bluffs, Iowa, then moving across the Missouri River into Omaha. Murdoch followed her, and they patched things up. He then accompanied her north to Sioux City, Iowa, agreeing that she would work in a brothel there for a few months and then rejoin him in Davenport.[24]

In early March 1883, Minnie Hagan Murdoch went to work in Ida Allen's brothel on Second Street in Sioux City. About two weeks later, she moved around the corner to Madame Shaw's Maple Grove, described by one newspaper as the "bon ton house of prostitution in the city." There, Minnie earned a reputation as "a beautiful blonde" and "one of the most attractive ladies" in the house. The men who sought her attention included Joseph Kiter, the twenty-five-year-old son of a Sioux Falls newspaper publisher. Kiter was a sometime bartender and gambler with a history of beating up prostitutes. He was known as a heavy drinker and suspected as an opium smoker. Kiter quickly became enamored of Minnie, who, for her part, responded by encouraging his infatuation and the gifts of money that accompanied it. In early June, a homesick Minnie plotted with Ezra that he would send a telegram warning that her mother was dangerously ill. She used the telegram to persuade Kiter to give her money for the trip home, making a visit to her husband at her lover's expense. According to Ezra, Minnie decided during that visit to move back to Davenport and returned to Sioux City to settle her business. A few days later, she and the other girls from the Maple Grove went shopping together, and while they were out, Kiter ransacked her room, discovering Ezra's letters and Minnie's planned departure.[25]

He returned to the brothel the following afternoon to confront Minnie. They argued, and Kiter pulled out a thirty-two caliber revolver, shooting Minnie in the head. He then fired at his own head and staggered out the back door, down the alley, and across a street. He collapsed in the doorway of a saloon, blood pouring down his face and pooling around him. His wound was quickly discovered to be more spectacular than life threatening, but Minnie Hagan was not so lucky. Two days after the shooting, newspapers back in Davenport reported the "Murder of Minnie Hagan." Kiter's bullet had entered the side of her skull near the temple and exited her forehead. "Brain matter" was "oozing out," and the attending physician "pronounced her chances for recovery poor."[26]

He was wrong. A day later, Minnie Hagan was conscious and asking for her mother. Emma Woodruff, informed that her daughter was not "murdered" after all, set out for Sioux City, arriving three days after the shooting. While Sioux City papers correctly identified Emma Woodruff as Minnie's mother, Davenport papers, either from confusion or discretion, repeatedly referred to "Mrs. Woodruff" as Minnie's aunt even as they quoted from her letter describing Minnie's condition. Ezra Murdoch came as well, and Minnie expressed "delight" at seeing him. The newspapers marveled at her recovery, dwelling at length on her "vitality," "strong . . . organs," and "full lungs." A Minnie Hagan so full of animal vigor became a much less sympathetic character than one languishing on the brink of death. The Sioux City papers began by reporting "universal . . . sympathy" for "the unfortunate young woman, who under more favored auspices possessed the attributes of being an honor and ornament to her sex and society." (Minnie, who asked that newspaper reports be read to her, must have enjoyed that.) But as she recovered, they shifted to sneering that "lots of useless sympathy" had been "wasted" on Minnie, who was simply a "bad, bad woman" who had toyed with Kiter's affections and got what she deserved. The only good prostitute, it seems, was a dead prostitute—or one at death's door.[27]

With or without public sympathy, Minnie Hagan made a complete recovery. She returned to Davenport, though not, apparently, to Ezra Murdoch. However delighted she was to see him in July, their relationship remained volatile. Six weeks after the shooting, Ezra attacked Minnie, striking her violently several times and threatening to kill her. In a matter of days, she had sued for divorce.[28]

Whether Minnie Hagan returned to prostitution after the shooting is not clear. She does not appear in Davenport police reports or court records, but that may simply indicate that she chose to work elsewhere: Council Bluffs or Omaha, Clinton or Muscatine. She appears only once in the Davenport city directory in this period, living on East Third Street (the neighborhood associated with prostitution) in 1888. But absence from the record does not mean departure from the business. Minnie Hagan, after her encounter with Kiter, may simply have learned to be careful and discreet. In October 1893, ten years after the Sioux City episode, Minnie Hagan appeared in police records again, running a brothel with two girls in Davenport.[29]

In contrast to Mitchell and Huber, Minnie Hagan found her way into prostitution not as a mother with children to support but as a homeless child herself. She learned at an early age that men would pay for sex, and her earnings enabled her to survive. But the life she led taught her other lessons as well: survival meant neither comfort nor an escape from violence.

EMMA WEBB WOODWARD

Emma Webb Woodward was a native of Davenport. Born about 1864, she was the fifth of seven children of David and Caroline Auerochs, a carpenter and his wife who settled in Iowa in the early 1850s. David Auerochs had been born in Bavaria; Caroline was from Baden. By 1859, the family had a home on Gaines Street in Davenport, in the heart of a German settlement. In 1870, when Emma was six, David Auerochs told the census taker that he owned personal property valued at just three hundred dollars, not a great deal for a man with two grown sons living at home and contributing to the family income.[30]

By 1880, the Auerochs family was living in a seedy area on East Front Street, suggesting that their economic situation had continued to decline. Among the saloons, cheap hotels, and shabby residences facing the riverfront and train yard was a small broom factory, where a young man named Frank Webb worked along with his younger brother, John. Coming into the neighborhood every day, perhaps lingering on in the evenings after work, nineteen-year-old Frank got to know fifteen-year-old Emma, who had finished eighth grade by then but was not yet regularly employed. Sometime over the next couple of years, the couple courted and married. In 1883 Emma Auerochs Webb gave birth to a son, Edward. The details of their marriage—including the date—are unclear, but there are hints that it got off to a rocky start: in the fall of 1882, Frank faced trial in district court, charged with embezzlement. The episode ended in his acquittal, but facing a trial and engaging a defense attorney must have been a hardship for the young husband. Other troubles are intimated in the record of Edward's birth. According to the register, Edward was Emma's second child, suggesting that an earlier child, perhaps illegitimate, had either died or been given into the care of others. The shadows on their early marriage proved prescient. By 1888, Frank had disappeared from Davenport, and Emma was listed in the city directory on her own. In 1890, the directory identified her as a widow.[31]

Emma's choice of residences in these years reflected her unstable economic situation. In 1888, she lived at the corner of Perry Street and Thirteenth, in a fairly respectable neighborhood. But after Frank disappeared, she moved down to Fifth Street facing the railroad tracks, a block where the saloons and residences frequently appeared in police columns as sites of petty thefts, brawls, and prostitution. By 1892, Emma had moved again, this time back to the Front Street neighborhood where she had grown up. In the 1870s, when Emma was a child, Front Street was already a rough neighborhood catering to river men and railroad workers. By the early 1890s, its reputation as the district of streetwalkers and shabby saloons was secure.[32]

At the same time Emma's fortunes were pulling her back to Front Street, the rest of her family was making the economic climb into better neighborhoods. By 1888, all four of Emma's brothers had found jobs as brakemen with the Chicago, Rock Island, & Pacific Railroad (CRI&P). The two youngest, Louis and David, lived with their mother and younger sister, Kate, in a home on East Tenth Street, while Robert and his wife lived nearby on LePage Street. Only Theo remained in the old neighborhood on Front Street. "Brakeman" was an entry-level position in the railroad running trades, and the Auerochs brothers seemed poised to steer their families toward economic security and the middle class. But it was also an exceedingly dangerous occupation before the late 1890s, when air brakes became common. Brakemen like the Auerochs brothers had to climb atop moving trains and leap from car to car, turning the wheels that set the hand brakes according to signals from the engineer. In the fall of 1893, the worst fears of a brakeman's family came true for the Auerochs, and the family's prospects took a turn for the worse. That October, while Louis was working his usual 6 P.M. to 6 A.M. shift in the switching yard, a collision threw him under the wheels of the car on which he was riding, killing him instantly. A few months later, his widow, Fannie, sued the CRI&P for fifteen thousand dollars, but consistent with liability law of the day, the court ruled that Louis had known the risks and had agreed to them when he took the job. Fannie received no settlement, and not surprisingly, the other three brothers left railroad work. They were probably no longer welcome on the CRI&P, and given the tense relations between railroads and their workers in 1894 (stemming from the Pullman strike and the organizing efforts of the American Railway Union), they may have been blacklisted—formally or informally—by other railroads in the area.[33]

Meanwhile, another Auerochs sibling found himself in court. Theo Auerochs had a long history of drunkenness and violent outbursts, once stabbing the family dog after his wife and children had fled their home in terror. No longer willing to stand his beatings, his wife, Mary, divorced him, gaining custody of their two children, Henry and Nettie, and resuming her maiden name, Cullivan. After the divorce, Theo disappeared from Davenport. Louis Auerochs's and Frank Webb's deaths and Theo Auerochs's disappearance left the Auerochs clan with three single mothers struggling to support children. Fannie Auerochs turned to cigar making. Mary Cullivan took in laundry. Emma Webb followed a different path.[34]

In May 1891, Emma Webb made her first appearance in police records, arrested for keeping a house of ill-fame with one inmate, Bertha Swain. The police record gave her occupation not as prostitute (which would have been usual) but as "housekeeper." This may indicate that, as far as the police were concerned, Emma Webb was not actively pursuing the vice business. Instead, she may have seemed just another woman in poverty who kept boarders with "the character and reputation of prostitutes." By October, however, her new status was confirmed by a second arrest, and in November she was arrested yet again, this time with three young women inmates. Four more arrests followed in 1892: all were for keeping a house of ill-fame, and each involved as many as six inmates. Emma Webb had found a new vocation that would eventually benefit other members of her family.[35]

That Emma Webb would find her way into prostitution seems far from certain, given her beginnings. She had basic education, a family of brothers with good work prospects, and only one child to support. Perhaps the answer lies in the hint of an illegitimate child born before Edward. A respectable woman was supposed to embody sexual reticence, not desire. If Emma Webb's passions led to an early alliance and then to trouble with her husband, they may also have compromised her reputation and her ability to find the work her sisters-in-law pursued. Prostitution may have been her only alternative.

MATTIE BURKE

Mattie Burke was about twenty when she first appeared in Davenport, operating what was sometimes called a saloon, sometimes a restaurant, but most often a "den" on Front Street. She was one of about a half dozen African American women who kept houses of ill-fame in Davenport in the late 1870s, all near Front Street or along the blocks just east of Brady Street downtown. In 1879, the *Democrat* referred to Burke's place as a "resort for colored fo[l]ks," but other reports make it clear that she served whites as well. For example, police raids on Burke and another black woman, Mary Brown, one night in 1880 resulted in the arrests of "five colored and two white girls, and nine young men," and in a deposition filed in 1883, police officer J. H. Howard asserted simply, "Both white and black men go there."[36]

Where Burke lived before coming to Davenport is unclear, though she told the 1885 census taker that she was unmarried and that she had been born in Kentucky in about 1857. If so, she likely spent her childhood as a slave. In 1900, the census taker reported that she could neither read nor write. Through the twenty-some years Burke lived in Davenport, she never married, nor was she part of any clear kin network. Yet her life was intricately entwined with the small African American community. In 1880, Burke employed fourteen-year-old Nannie Phillips, the daughter of longtime residents Mary and Lewis Phillips. Burke often lived next door to another black woman, Sylvia Hutchins, who was close to Burke in age and, like Burke, had been born in Kentucky and was frequently arrested as a prostitute. Their enduring link raises the possibility that the two women might have been cousins or even sisters, though no document identifies them as such.[37]

In 1885, Burke's household included an eleven-year-old girl, Eliza Cleveland, whose family resided across the river in Moline. Her parents, Barney and Jane Cleveland, almost certainly began their lives as slaves. He was born in South Carolina about 1843, she in Mississippi about 1845. Both were illiterate, and Barney worked as a barber. In the thirteen years between 1868 and 1881, Jane Cleveland gave birth to at least ten children; she would bear thirteen in all. The eldest was a boy; the next nine were girls. In this small way, the Cleveland family resembled those into which Jennie McCowen, Abbie Cleaves, Lile Bickford, and Lettie Meacham had been born. In those families, many girls and few boys had been part of the chemistry that produced ambitious women ready to travel far from home in search of opportunities. Poverty and racism, however, would channel the Cleveland daughters in a very different direction. Eliza Cleveland was most likely "placed out" into Burke's household to reduce her family's economic burden; as a single woman running a business, Burke probably appreciated the extra set of hands. At Burke's side, Eliza Cleveland apparently learned Burke's business. By fifteen, she was a known streetwalker, and between 1889 and 1910 she was arrested more than twenty times—mostly for vagrancy, larceny, and public drunkenness. Indeed, of the nine Cleveland daughters whose names are known, seven appeared in the Davenport police records.[38]

Other changes in Burke's life hint at the ways African Americans in Davenport consciously operated as a community. About 1886, after running her business at two or three locations along Front Street for nearly a decade, Mattie Burke moved herself and her "resort" four blocks north to 124 East Fifth Street. Her move coincided with the relocation of another black business owner, Linsey Pitts, a Civil War veteran and former slave from Missouri who arrived in Davenport in the late 1870s. He worked first as a laborer and then as a barber. In 1885, he opened a saloon at 120 East Fifth Street. Both Mattie Burke and Sylvia Hutchins followed him to Fifth Street within a year. Pitts's saloon became the anchor of a cluster of black businesses facing the CRI&P tracks just east of Brady Street. By 1890, four black businesses and households had moved onto the block. A decade later, the concentration had increased to ten. For Pitts, the saloon was also the beginning of a period of investment and property acquisition. In 1889, the only taxes he paid were fifty cents for his dog and a fifty-cent poll tax. Just a year later, he owned the property where his saloon stood, assessed at $340. The following year, his holdings ballooned to an assessed value of $1,740.[39]

The movement of Mattie Burke, Linsey Pitts, and Sylvia Hutchins into three adjacent buildings in 1885–86 appears more than coincidence. They may have seen mutual benefit in creating a small concentration of entertainment businesses open to African Americans, and the location put them just two blocks from the CRI&P passenger depot, with its regular traffic of black dining-car waiters, porters, and of course passengers. In 1888, Burke's business was identified in the city directory as a restaurant, which would have nicely complemented Pitts's saloon. At the same time, she continued to be arrested regularly for operating a house of ill-fame. During the same years when Linsey Pitts parlayed his real estate investments into a comfortable nest egg, Mattie Burke continued to struggle. Because she owned no real estate, the city dunned her only for the fifty-cent dog tax, and she was delinquent in paying even that.[40]

Any woman seeking to earn her living by her own labors faced a daunting struggle, but as an African American, Mattie Burke confronted almost insurmountable obstacles. In the South, domestic service was reserved for African American women, but in the Midwest, employers preferred white farm daughters or immigrants as household help. Stores and factories did not employ black women, and even as laundresses, African Americans competed with white women. Only in providing services to African Americans—meals and lodgings—could black women expect to have the field to themselves, but the black community was too small to sustain such enterprises. Prostitution, which drew both white and black customers, supplemented boardinghouse and restaurant income.

MAMIE MAGEE BEAUCHAINE

Probably the most singularly successful woman in Davenport's prostitution trade was Mamie Magee Beauchaine, an Irish immigrant whose canny investments enabled her to live comfortably well into her eighties and to leave a small fortune when she died in 1949. Born in County Sligo, probably in 1861, Mamie Beauchaine's early history is obscured by her own careful efforts. Her obituary reported what she herself may have asserted: that she had immigrated directly to Davenport with her parents in 1877 when she was ten years old. This is certainly not true, but her real path from western Ireland to the Mississippi Valley is harder to trace.[41]

Mamie Magee probably immigrated around 1880 as a young woman. While she might have come earlier in the company of her parents, they must have chosen to return to Ireland. In the 1901 Irish census, they were recorded living on a farm in

County Sligo with three of her younger siblings. Wherever she grew up, Mamie attended five years of common school, enough to give her basic literacy. Where Mamie lived until 1887 is unknown, but that is almost certainly the year she arrived in Davenport, when she was twenty-six. The first record of her presence is a newspaper note of her arrest in January 1888. From her first appearance in Davenport, Mamie Magee was identified as the keeper of a house of ill-fame, not as a vagrant or an ordinary prostitute. Unlike Josie Mitchell, Emma Webb, and Kate Huber, Magee was not a lone mother with children to support or simply a woman of uncertain principles who kept boarders of unseemly reputation. This suggests that Magee may have come to Davenport with the express purpose of entering the business.[42]

Magee managed her affairs with the acumen of a businesswoman. During 1890 and 1891, her enterprise flourished. She was arrested regularly for keeping a house of ill-fame, always paying the fine, and the number of inmates associated with her increased from one or two to as many as six. Within a year or so of arriving in Davenport, she had purchased her first piece of real estate, a half lot just south of the CRI&P embankment east of downtown. By 1892, she had sold that lot and purchased a nearby property assessed at more than four times the value of her first lot. Magee soon acquired a row of tenements on Rock Island and Front Streets, then the wedge of property at the foot of the Government Bridge that held the landmark Slate House saloon and hotel. In 1893, the assessed value of her properties was almost seven times what it had been in 1890.[43]

At least some people believed Magee achieved her prosperity under the protection of the police department. If true, this would reflect her more systematic approach to the business. As a woman who pursued rather than drifted into vice, Magee would have been in a position to appreciate the return on investment she could achieve through payoffs to the police. But while one newspaper hinted in 1890 that Magee was in cahoots with the night captain, Charles Falkner, a retrospective investigation in 1894 could not prove the allegations. And Magee's apparently cozy relationship with the department did not continue. In 1891, she was prosecuted in district court for keeping a house of ill-fame. Unlike some other women similarly accused, Magee kept her cool throughout the proceedings. Wearing "garb of plain black" for her court appearances, Magee "occasionally wiped[d] her eyes and seem[ed] very humble, and her demeanor show[ed] . . . trustful innocence and sweet simplicity," according to one newspaper report. In spite of "conclusive" evidence against Magee, the jury acquitted her.[44]

By 1892, Magee had withdrawn from the day-to-day business of running a brothel. Instead, she earned substantial income by renting out her various properties to individual prostitutes. Rumors circulated that she was expanding her real estate portfolio to include properties in Muscatine, downriver from Davenport. In response, the *Muscatine Journal* editorialized, "stay away." That May, Mamie Magee married Leander Lawrence Beauchaine, a onetime traveling tobacco salesman from

Ohio who had become a saloon keeper in Davenport. In September 1892, she was arrested once again for keeping a house of ill-fame. This time she responded by suing Frank Kessler, the chief of police, and Charles Falkner, the same night captain she had once been suspected of bribing. Her suit asked for five thousand dollars in damages and charged the two men with a brutal beating and with conspiring "to impugn and harass" her. In her deposition, Beauchaine insisted that she had been in the neighborhood only to collect rent, not as the keeper of a brothel, and that she had been called into the house where she was arrested to see "a sick girl supposed to be dying." Weeks later, Beauchaine withdrew her suit, and the police immediately began arresting her tenants. She was brought to court on charges of renting buildings for immoral uses and found guilty. In March 1893, Beauchaine announced her intention to appeal the conviction, but the outcome of the appeal is unclear. That April, the election of a new city administration with a radically different policy toward prostitution may have made her case moot.[45]

Mamie Magee Beauchaine's readiness to sue the police chief reveals a woman of no little moxie, and it is not the only example of her legal sophistication. Mamie began accumulating property in Davenport well before she and Lee Beauchaine married, and even after their marriage, she continued to hold property in her own name. Indeed, while Mamie's holdings grew in number and value, Lee owned no property at all. Saloon keepers such as Beauchaine typically worked for breweries, which owned or leased the saloon site and furnished the accoutrements of the business. The discrepancy between his personal wealth and hers led the couple to take an unusual step. Before their marriage, Lee and Mamie drew up a prenuptial agreement. According to a newspaper report, the document permitted "the wife to convey any of the real estate which she might own without the consent of the husband." While Iowa law already gave married women the right to control their own property, such an agreement provided clear ground for Mamie Beauchaine to continue to manage her investments without her husband's assistance—or interference.[46]

Whether or not Mamie Magee Beauchaine chose prostitution as a career, her systematic approach to it allowed her to accumulate wealth and to remove herself from actual prostitution relatively early in her life. Within five years of her arrival, Mamie had turned herself from prostitute to landlady, an achievement matched by no one else in the business during the same period.

CONCLUSION

Looking at these six women together—placing Mamie Magee alongside Mattie Burke, for example—highlights how different their paths into prostitution could be and how diverse their experiences. Yet for all their differences, some patterns do emerge. If the ideal of the era was that a husband or father should provide for each woman, these women were living evidence of what could happen when the ideal failed and they were, as their contemporaries expressed it, "thrown on their own resources." Three women—Josie Mitchell, Emma Webb, and Kate Huber—entered prostitution after their marriages foundered. Minnie Hagan became a homeless child when her mother's marriage fell apart. And Mattie Burke was the product of slavery, a system that routinely destroyed marriages and apparently left her with no family at all. Mamie Magee's early history remains obscure, but if she chose to immigrate to North America, leaving her parents behind, she may have had little hope or expectation that her father could support her until a husband took over the job. Magee alone seems to have had a successful marriage, and she was the primary property holder in that partnership. Deprived of a breadwinner, these women had few resources on which to fall back, and they found in prostitution an alternative means of support. To legal authorities of the day, taking money for sex may not have been the essence of prostitution, but for these women, money really was at the heart of the matter.

Motherhood as well was turned on its ideological head. "Mother" was the most celebrated category of woman in the nineteenth century, the keeper of the sacred shrine of home and the guardian of virtue. Yet a mother's attachment to her children led Josie Mitchell, Emma Webb, and perhaps Kate Huber into the sex business. When their marriages failed, each struggled to earn a living for herself and her young children. The most common employment for women in this era, domestic service, was hardly an option for women with children (as Minnie Hagan's mother apparently found), and prostitution emerged as a more reliable option than laundry work or keeping boarders. Indeed, financial stability allowed these women to do more than support their children. Contrary to the assumptions of their middle-class contemporaries, these women were not shunned by their families. Minnie Hagan's mother rushed to Sioux City to nurse her, and, as chapter 9 will show, Josie Mitchell, Emma Webb, and Mamie Magee eventually supported siblings, nieces, and nephews through profits from the business. Entering the sex trade had some benefits, but it could have serious consequences for the next generation. Josie Mitchell's daughters followed her into the trade, as did at least one of the children who lived and worked in Mattie Burke's household.

Other patterns also appear. Two of the women, Josie Mitchell and Mattie Burke, were illiterate in a time and place where literacy was the norm, a situation that certainly limited their employment options and may have left them vulnerable to unscrupulous tradesmen. Trouble for Emma Webb and Josie Mitchell may have begun with marital strife over their sexuality. The conflict that resulted led their husbands to abandon and divorce them. In an era when even a worldly physician like William Sanger could write, "the full force of sexual desire is seldom known to a virtuous woman," women who expressed sexual desire outside the bonds of marriage put themselves at extraordinary risk.[47]

Finally, urban geography seems to have played a role in shaping the patterns of these lives. In 1919, a former prostitute who worked in the Mississippi Valley in the 1880s and 1890s remembered her first steps into prostitution, which had occurred after her family had fallen on hard times and moved onto a street where neighbors supplemented their income with prostitution. Their homes, she observed, seemed like "palaces" compared with hers. "Needless to say, I had an opportunity, and I heard many suggestions and learned many things that it is not well for a girl to know," she wrote. Like this prostitute, several of the six women examined in this chapter were pushed by poverty into the Davenport neighborhoods where prostitutes plied their trade. If they did not actively choose to imitate their neighbors, they may still have forfeited the chance to earn a living by respectable work. If they sought laundry work or sewing, their neighborhood associations could easily make them undesirable employees in the eyes of middle-class housekeepers. If they chose to keep boarders, they might find that their neighborhood attracted only boarders who left their landladies vulnerable to arrest for keeping of a house of ill-fame. Lacking the education and reputation of their neighbors in the Lend a Hand, these women's employment options were limited. With the example of neighbors nearby, when opportunity came knocking—perhaps literally—in the form of tipsy soldiers or commercial travelers, the decision to exploit an economic opportunity may have been no choice at all.

5

THE POLICE MATRON CAMPAIGN AND THE REFORM OF URBAN ENVIRONMENTS

There is a class of young girls that give us much anxious thought, where the antecedents are good; but obliged to take homes in bad neighborhoods for the sake of low rent, parents expose their children to the most demoralizing influences. . . . They drift into evil as if born to it, and run to ruin on our streets before our eyes.
—Dr. Sarah Devoll, Report on Police Matrons, 1881

IT WAS ALMOST FOUR O'CLOCK IN THE MORNING when police pulled two couples from rooms at the Ackley House and marched them through the icy January darkness to the police station. The foursome, who had taken rooms "as if they [were] married people," had become rowdy and wild, "defying the clerk when he begged them to keep quiet." Desperate, the beleaguered night clerk finally called the police, who charged the guests with disorderly conduct. On the face of it, the episode seems hardly unusual. The Ackley House, a "second class" hotel at the corner of Third and Perry, stood just a block and a half from the Chicago, Rock Island, & Pacific passenger depot and equally close to a dozen saloons and sites of prostitution. Tipsy and troublesome guests probably stumbled in often enough. But when the *Davenport Times* reported the arrests that afternoon, it provoked an outcry that launched local women's organizations into political action and exposed simmering conflicts in the community.[1]

What riveted public attention was the convergence of youth and sexual license. All four of those arrested were teenagers; the youngest, a girl named Ollie Kreps, was barely thirteen. Her youth made her a sympathetic figure in spite of her sexual improprieties, and she came to symbolize the vulnerability of young working

Perry Street, looking north, c. 1888. The center-left building, below the steeple, is the Ackley House hotel. (Courtesy of the Richardson-Sloane Special Collections Center, Davenport Public Library.)

women in the city. In the Ackley House arrests, organized women, including those of the Lend a Hand, saw the consequences of Davenport's policy of tolerated prostitution. The arrests became the vehicle through which these women addressed a problem women in Davenport faced every day: the presence of prostitutes and men seeking prostitutes along the streets where ordinary women lived and labored. As the winter of 1889 turned to spring, women in Davenport successfully campaigned for the appointment of Iowa's first police matron and for the establishment of a separate jail facility for women and children who came into police custody.

The campaign for a police matron evoked in microcosm the many ironies and tensions in women's efforts to shape public policy in this era. In a campaign waged largely by citizens without votes, women drew much of their authority to speak on a political issue from the insistence by nearly everyone involved that women's concerns were not political. As women organized to shape public policy affecting public space, leading men responded by defining the problem as private, a matter of failed family authority. Most significant, the campaign exposed the weakness of political efforts by those who could not vote. Organized women identified a problem and offered a solution, but as the police chief, newspaper editors, and other men in the community entered the debate, they transformed it. Choosing to see the problem of girls like Ollie Kreps as a private matter, they did not share the women's anxiety for safety in public. Partisan sniping focused instead on the role of the police in regulating saloons. The editors' polemics concerned not the women who worked and lived in the city center but middle-class girls who spent their leisure wandering the streets at night. Their fears revealed a profound discomfort with the changing urban geography of gender at the century's end.

FORGING AN ALLIANCE

In the days following the arrests, Davenport's organized women moved quickly to turn the incident into a political cause, carrying their concerns to both the city council and the county board of supervisors. The four teenagers appeared in police court on a Wednesday morning. By noon on the following Wednesday, the supervisors had granted to "the Charitable Alliance of the City of Davenport" the use of a courthouse annex for a house of detention. That evening, the city council received the alliance's petition for the appointment of a police matron. It took just days for the Charitable Alliance to move its campaign into high gear. A week earlier, the alliance had not existed.[2]

The confederation that sprang to life so quickly in those short winter days had roots in Davenport's intertwining networks of organized women and in a national reform campaign. Beginning with Portland, Maine, in 1878, cities across the Northeast and Midwest began employing police matrons in their station houses. The matron's duties varied considerably from city to city, but the core of her office was to shelter and protect women and children in police custody. As promoted in the professional literature of charities and corrections, a matron was always on duty when patrol officers brought women to the station house. She searched them for contraband, supervised their imprisonment, accompanied them to court, and, most important, offered assistance and encouragement to those who wished to reform. The national Woman's Christian Temperance Union (WCTU) was a major proponent of police matrons, considering them an effective way to intervene in the lives of women arrested for drunkenness or prostitution. In many cities, the local WCTU played the key role in persuading officials to employ a matron, sometimes even selecting the candidate and paying her salary. In Davenport, however, the WCTU was never more than a minor player.[3]

Instead, the ten organizations that came together to press for a matron called themselves the Charitable Alliance. They were a diverse group. Several were traditional charities: the venerable Ladies Industrial Relief Society (LIRS), the Friendly Visitors, the King's Daughters, and the American Educational Aid Association (AEAA), which sponsored a loan fund for young women students and found homes for orphaned children. Joining these was the Associated Charities, Davenport's charity organization society. Two more were religious organizations, the Ladies Catholic Union and the Hebrew Ladies Society. The Order of the Eastern Star was a Masonic women's auxiliary. The WCTU also took part, though it remained small and weak in Davenport, a victim of the local commitment to "personal liberty" and beer. (Indeed, local members complained that national WCTU organizers always left the city "with the same expression on their faces which we interpret, 'Can't do anything in Davenport.'") With its membership of self-supporting women, the Working Woman's Lend a Hand Club filled out the alliance. Catholic and Jew, Lutheran and Methodist, middle class and working class, the alliance members in some ways represented a cross-section of Davenport's citizenry. Still, it ignored significant sectors of the public. There were no representatives of the city's two African American churches or of the societies organized among black women. While women from Davenport's large German-speaking population were members of most of the organizations represented, none of these groups identified itself with the German community. Both the AEAA and the Associated Charities included men in their membership, and men represented these groups at alliance meetings, while the Hebrew Ladies' representative was Isaac Fall, their rabbi. Nonetheless, newspapers continually referred to the campaign as the work of Davenport's "charitable ladies," reflecting the cultural elision of charity and "women's work."[4]

The choice of the name Charitable Alliance suggests that right from the start, drawing together this coalition required compromises about the focus of the campaign and the work of the police matron. The name almost certainly reflected the organizers' familiarity with another group established a few months earlier, the Illinois Women's Alliance. Dr. Jennie McCowen always referred to the Davenport coalition by the name used in Illinois, as the "Women's" rather than the "Charitable" Alliance, suggesting that she had never privately accepted an amendment offered by others. This small alteration in the name hints at a larger difference in vision. As in Davenport, the Illinois Women's Alliance came together in response to a newspaper exposé. The catalyst in Chicago was a series of articles about women workers by a reporter who disguised herself as a job seeker and wrote under the pseudonym Nell Nelson. The Knights of Labor collected and republished the articles in a volume called *The White Slaves of Free America*. "White slaves," in this case, referred to the exploitation of women's labor, not their sexuality. Members of the Chicago Woman's Club, the Chicago Trade and Labor Assembly, and others shocked at Nelson's revelations came together as the Women's Alliance to urge factory inspections and the enforcement of school attendance laws. The primary interest of the Illinois Alliance—the condition of working women—was also the passionate concern of McCowen's life. In both Chicago and Davenport, some alliance organizations included men as members, but in Chicago the emphasis on class-bridging solidarity among women overrode the simple fact that the Trade and Labor Assembly was overwhelmingly men: theirs was a "Women's Alliance." In Davenport as well, gender accuracy was probably not at issue, since the papers insistently referred to the alliance members as "ladies" despite a nominal masculine presence. But describing the alliance as "charitable" rather than "women's" also announced a different ideal, assistance for the poor rather than shared interests among women. The first ideal emphasized class difference, the second cross-class solidarity. McCowen's reluctance to cede the name "Women's Alliance" marks her preference for an ideal of sisterhood but also retains the emphasis on working women associated with the Illinois group. This discrepancy colored the debates surrounding the campaign for months to come, offering subtle support to one faction's belief that the police matron's purpose was to deal with private failures rather than a public problem affecting working women.[5]

Whatever tensions may have lain beneath the surface during the campaign's first days, the Charitable Alliance moved swiftly and successfully, employing a blueprint tested in other communities and publicized in national journals. Mrs. J. K. Barney, head of the WCTU's division for jail, prison, and almshouse work, laid out the strategy in an 1887 issue of E. E. Hale's journal, *Lend a Hand*, which was readily available at the Lend a Hand club rooms and in McCowen's private library. "Ascertain facts; number of women arrested during previous years; accommodations provided, care furnished," urged Mrs. Barney. "Make a few unannounced visits to cells in Police Station and Police Court." Draw up a petition, she counseled, preferring "a few representative signatures" over "large numbers, miscellaneously signed." Public meetings, presentations by both men and women, and newspaper coverage were key. " 'Last but not least,' start for success and continue until it is assured."[6]

The alliance organizers in Davenport followed her recommendations point by point, beginning with the petitions. As Barney urged, they relied on "a few representative signatures." The petitions delivered to the city council and board of supervisors were signed not by individual women but by organizations. This was efficient, enabling the organizers to circulate their petitions in a matter of days. But it also played on the political symbolism that underlay the authority of the alliance, the proposition that women's organizations constituted a parallel public sphere.[7]

Local officials' responses sustained the fiction that women's organizations formed a separate, shadow representative body. When the county board of supervisors voted in favor of the women's petition, they voted *not* to establish a house of detention but to grant "unto the Charitable Alliance of the city of Davenport the use of the building . . . for the detention of women and girls." The alliance itself became responsible for establishing a separate jail for women. Similarly, when the city council voted to create and fund the position of police matron, it turned the matter of selecting the matron over to the alliance, then ratified the women's choice. Later, concerned about the security of the house of detention, the chief of police issued an order forbidding anyone except city officials and "the ladies who first interested themselves in the institution" from entering without a permit.[8]

Proponents of the national movement would have approved. "Always petition that the appointment of these matrons be only upon the written recommendation of a committee of women from the different organizations interested in the movement," admonished Mrs. Barney. "*This* is absolutely important, to remove it from personal and political hands." In Iowa, this stipulation became state law. "Ten women of good standing" in the community had to endorse any candidate for the position of police matron. Barney's insistence that women's concerns were not political says more about her perception of politics in the 1880s than about her perceptions of women. In men's "political" hands, appointment to a public office such as police matron was apt to become part of the patronage system that bound rank-and-file voters to party leaders. The *New York Times* warned that "in every case where the police matron reform was not successful," it failed because officials appointed a woman not for her "fitness" but "for political or other reasons." Women's organizations might constitute a separate public sphere, but it was supposed to be a rarefied sphere, free of personal ambition, self-interest, and most of all politics.[9]

Excluded from the male public sphere, the women of the alliance created a space where they could debate and formulate an oppositional interpretation of public issues. Political theorist Nancy Fraser has analyzed such strategies, observing that this kind of alternative public was "weak" and lacked the power of the male bourgeois public sphere. Women could debate all they wanted, but they were not part of a deliberative body empowered to make law. That was reserved for men. The paradox of women's political action in this era lay in the extent to which many women claimed a fitness for public life based in this very "weakness." The WCTU's Barney was hardly alone in insisting that giving women control over appointments removed them from "political hands." Paula Baker and others have argued that late-nineteenth-century women often staked their claim to political rights on the presumption that women's interests were not political, that women's distance from male political culture elevated them above its corruptions. "Weakness," however, was a relative matter. As Rebecca Edwards and Sarah Deutsch have argued, in the 1880s and early 1890s, the public efforts of organized women could make them serious players in political contests. In Boston, Deutsch found that elite men valued and supported organized women's social service activities in part because they competed with the social assistance provided by working-class political machines, thereby undermining the machines' power. Paradoxically, women's insistence on being nonpolitical, on keeping their public service projects out of patronage systems, gave women a degree of political clout. Excluded from government, their links to elite men placed them at the threshold of power.[10]

The women who emerged as leaders of Davenport's police matron campaign lacked the wealth undergirding Boston's leading women but represented a sector of

Davenport's population rich in other kinds of social capital. In fact, the timing of the campaign may reflect the women's sense of their own growing influence. The national movement to place police matrons in station houses had existed for almost a dozen years before women in Davenport dusted off Mrs. Barney's blueprint and began putting it in action. The decision to move forward was not solely the result of the Ackley House arrests. Though shocking, they were hardly unprecedented. A decade earlier, the thirteen-year-old prostitute Minnie Hagan, living in the woods at the edge of town, had drawn the attention of newspapers and organized women, as had other girls in years since. But concern about those girls had led to private efforts, not public campaigns. By 1889, however, a core group of women in Davenport played important roles not only in the separate public sphere of women's organizations but also in the networks created by Davenport's leading men. Significantly, much of the leadership of Davenport's matron campaign came from this group: self-supporting women who had chosen paths that took them out of domestic roles and into public life. Their familiarity with men's organizations encouraged these women to believe that they could make their voices heard by city aldermen and county supervisors, and their lives as working women made them keenly aware of the circumstances of downtown neighborhoods where prostitutes shared the sidewalks with clerks and cigar makers.

At the first reported meeting of the alliance, a man occupied the chair but women took the leading roles. As Seth Bryant, owner of a wholesale shoe business, wielded the gavel, three women dominated discussion: Dr. Jennie McCowen, Phebe Sudlow, and Martha Glaspell. In some ways, these women represent three strategies for gaining the kind of community standing that gave a woman a public voice. McCowen's history as a physician who organized working women through the Lend a Hand club is already familiar, but her activities in the community went far beyond a limited sphere of women's organizations. She had already served two terms as president of the Scott County Medical Society, whose virtually all-male membership included several of the city's most prominent men. In January 1889, two weeks before the Ackley House arrests, she was elected to lead the Davenport Academy of Natural Science, which had long since taken on the function of a social club, attracting prominent men with only an amateur interest in science. Its membership included newspapermen, bankers and capitalists, attorneys, physicians, and eleven men who had served as mayor. Jennie McCowen was their peer and their president.[11]

Phebe Sudlow had pursued a similar route to public prominence, though starting from the more conventional role of schoolteacher. She began teaching as a teenager in Ohio in the 1840s, then moved with her parents and siblings to Iowa in 1856. By 1860, the school district had promoted Sudlow to principal of one of Davenport's elementary schools, a job that enabled her to support her mother and sisters through the lean years of the Civil War. In 1874, the Davenport school board appointed Sudlow superintendent of schools, a position she refused until she won the same salary paid the man who preceded her. As superintendent, Sudlow administered a district of eight grammar schools, a high school, and a teacher training school. Her subordinates included some ninety teachers and principals, both men and women, and the school population increased from just over twenty-nine hundred students to nearly thirty-five hundred during her tenure. Members of the Iowa State Teachers Association elected Sudlow president in 1876, breaking precedent by choosing a woman for the office. She used her presidential address to issue a ringing call for women's higher education. Sudlow remained superintendent until 1878, when she accepted a professorship in English at the state university in Iowa City. By 1889, she had retired from teaching and become a partner in a downtown Davenport bookstore. While Sudlow was active in women's organizations like the LIRS and the Methodist missionary society, she also held membership in mixed-gender groups, including the Academy of Science and the AEAA. Through a career based in the feminized field of teaching, Sudlow had built a reputation as a capable administrator and public servant.[12]

The third woman to emerge as a leading figure in the alliance came from a background more typically associated with women's separate public sphere. Widowed just a year earlier, Martha Glaspell had a grown son and a daughter about twenty-one years old. Her husband, Barton Glaspell, had been a wholesale grain dealer, and both were longtime Davenport residents. In 1889, she lived with her daughter, Bertha, in the modest house left by her husband. As president of the local WCTU, Martha Glaspell was well acquainted with the national police matron movement, and as a widow whose children were grown, she controlled her own time and could devote herself to this public issue. Her standing in the community, however, came from her status as an established resident and the widow of a respected businessman. Unlike Sudlow and McCowen, Glaspell had no professional credentials that crossed gender lines.[13]

As the campaign unfolded, most of the other women who took active roles came from the same ranks of self-supporting women that produced Phebe Sudlow and Jennie McCowen. Among the thirteen women who were most prominent in the campaign—those who spoke at meetings, held offices, served on committees, signed letters, or gave public speeches—only two were married at the time. The others were single, divorced, or widowed, and nearly all were self-supporting. Ten of the thirteen were members of the Working Woman's Lend a Hand club or the King's Daughters or were otherwise close associates of Jennie McCowen.

For example, when the alliance chose a delegation to approach the city council, they named Jennie McCowen, Sarah Foote-Sheldon, and Mary L. D. Putnam. All three women were prominent in the Academy of Science. Foote-Sheldon was the foster daughter of a man who had been one of the academy's few active scientists, Professor David Sheldon. Following the deaths of Sheldon and his wife, Foote-Sheldon supported herself by working as the academy's secretary. Putnam was a wealthy widow whose fund-raising and organizational skills had turned the local Academy of Science into a respected regional center. She had preceded McCowen as the academy's president a decade earlier. Like Sudlow, Putnam had made a reputation as a skilled administrator among the city's leading men.[14]

Similar threads drew together other women in the alliance. Leading women included Anna McCrum, a cofounder of the Lend a Hand; Mary Welcher, a widow whose boarders included at least one member of the Lend a Hand; and Mrs. J. B. Edgar, whose husband, a Presbyterian minister, helped Jennie McCowen raise funds for the Lend a Hand. Another was WCTU member Victorine Boyle, who gave a speech during the campaign on "girls going astray." As a mother raising two teenage daughters, Dr. Boyle may have felt a particular interest in the topic, but as a divorced physician she was hardly the typical WCTU mother. Nettie Howard, employed as the secretary of the Associated Charities and representing them at alliance meetings, was also divorced and self-supporting. Her work, which involved directing applicants for aid to available resources, made her acutely aware of the struggles of poor women raising families on the pittance earned through laundry or sewing. The representative of the Ladies Catholic Union was Mrs. Margaret A. Thompson, a widow who worked as a U.S. revenue agent and belonged to the Lend a Hand. Among the most active women of the alliance, only Mrs. J. B. Young, wife of the superintendent of schools and representative of the LIRS, and Mrs. Sarah Osborne, a widow representing the Friendly Visitors, had no direct connection with the Lend a Hand or with Jennie McCowen, though Young certainly devoted a great deal of time to schoolteachers, even keeping some as boarders in her home.[15]

The women who led the alliance brought to the campaign a presumption that the issues raised by the Ackley House arrests were public issues, best addressed through public policy. Their city held threats as well as opportunities, some the direct result of policy choices. Since 1884, Iowa law had prohibited the manufacture or sale of all alcoholic beverages, including wine and beer. For five years, city administrators in Davenport had made a policy of ignoring the law, adopting a laissez-faire stance that allowed Davenport's saloons, beer gardens, and theaters to pursue business as usual. These businesses helped Davenport thrive as the entertainment center for that region of the Mississippi Valley, but they also attracted the clientele that supported prostitution. Whether they lived and worked in the city center or simply rode the streetcars down for meetings or shopping, the women of the alliance were well aware of the way prostitution permeated downtown streets. The most politically astute alliance members understood that this was the result of choices made by the men who led the city. The campaign for a police matron was not a radical step but a cautious strategy to claim downtown space for respectable women. Observing the conventional limits placed on women's public activity, they entered the campaign not on behalf of themselves and certainly not on behalf of prostitutes but on behalf of girls like Ollie Kreps, whom they saw as victims of the environment created by the policies in place.[16]

THE PROBLEM OF OLLIE KREPS

In the first days after the arrests, Ollie Kreps stood at the center of the controversy. Newspaper writers and city authorities probed her life, wondering who she was and how she had come to such a "condition of woe and wretchedness," as one article put it. From the beginning, reports strained to accommodate two opposing interpretations. Newspapers portrayed Kreps's parents as poor but honest. One described Ollie's father as "an industrious man, when he has work to do," and pitied her mother for having "no help at all in this period of great need and scant income." Yet all the papers agreed that when girls ended up as Kreps had, parents were to blame. Placing the blame within the family absolved the community of responsibility but also left unacknowledged a central fact of Ollie Kreps's life: she was a working girl whose life could not be confined to the domestic sphere and the supervision of her parents. As the debate unfolded, the girl arrested that bitter cold night was replaced by an icon, a girl-on-the-street who had little in common with Ollie Kreps. To understand how this happened, it is best to begin with Kreps herself.[17]

In 1888, twelve-year-old Ollie Kreps lived with her parents in a house on East Second Street in Davenport, just down the block from the homes and businesses passed by the shopper in chapter 1. She was the oldest child in a crowded, poverty-stricken home. Her parents, married thirteen years, had nine children. Ollie and her father were the family's sole wage earners. Albert Kreps worked as a laborer at the Davenport Lumber Company. His work, though poorly paid, was probably steady in the warm months, when river men floated huge rafts of logs down the Mississippi from the timberlands of Wisconsin for processing at riverside lumber mills. But in the winter months, when the central events of this story took place, the river froze and traffic dwindled to a standstill. Lumber milling and virtually all other work depending on the river came to a halt, and Albert Kreps joined hundreds of other seasonally unemployed men in Davenport, waiting for the spring thaw, when the river opened, the mills turned, and plowing and planting began again.[18]

Ollie was a domestic. The city directory does not say where she worked, but she lived at home, so it seems likely that her employer was somewhere in the neighborhood. This might have been the City Hotel down the block or the grocer, but a girl as young as Ollie was more likely hired by some neighbor as kitchen help. In Ollie's neighborhood, the kitchen probably belonged to a saloon or a brothel. The Kreps home was sandwiched between a boiler works and a saloon. Three more saloons stood directly across the street, and a fifth lay on the corner just opposite her home. In all, more than a dozen saloons operated within a one-block walk of the Kreps home, and several sites of prostitution lay nearby, including Mary Ford's "cigar store" just across the street. On that wedge of land between the railroad tracks, vice and poverty were Ollie Kreps's immediate neighbors. She knew which had money to pay a servant.[19]

Wherever Ollie worked, she would not have earned more than a dollar or two a week, though brothels did tend to pay servants better than other employers did. She too may have lost her job when the river froze and transient traffic dropped off. And somewhere, during that summer or fall, Ollie Kreps got a reputation. Perhaps a "friendly visitor" investigating the homes of poor families saw her hanging around her place of employment, or perhaps someone spotted her with shady friends from the neighborhood. One newspaper observed that Ollie had only "tough boys and tough girls in a tough community for playmates." However it happened, in late November or early December 1888, women active in Davenport's charitable organizations took an interest in her case. Ollie responded decisively to their attention. She fled.[20]

Six weeks later, Moline police arrested her in a brothel just across the river in Illinois. She probably worked as a domestic there as well, for in the days following her arrest, no one treated Kreps like a prostitute, who typically would have been fined and released or jailed if no one paid her fine. In Kreps's case, the Moline police chief returned her to the Davenport police chief, who returned her to her parents, who insisted that they had no idea of her activities during her extended absence. Once again, interested women began making plans for her. Her arrest must have alarmed them, for most middle-class women would have assumed that the step from brothel servant to brothel inmate was short—perhaps inevitable. This time the women arranged a district court hearing to send Kreps to the state-run Industrial School for Girls at Mitchellville. Her parents objected to this plan. They probably feared losing a beloved daughter, and they certainly could ill afford to lose her wages.[21]

Meanwhile, on 29 January 1889, the evening after her return from Moline, Ollie Kreps wandered out again in search of a good time. She hooked up with a fifteen-year-old girl and two teenage boys with money to spend, James Tomlin, a local boy of good family and a bad reputation, and George Mix, his friend from Omaha. Their night on the town ended at the Ackley House, where, around four A.M., police arrested Ollie Kreps and her companions. It was Ollie's second arrest in perhaps forty-eight hours. All four were charged with disorderly conduct, and all four paid their fines. James Tomlin and the other girl were apparently no strangers to the court, but the judge released them along with the boy from Omaha. Only Ollie remained in custody.[22]

No one considered the jail a fit place for a young girl, and authorities did not trust

The Reform of Urban Environments

her parents to cooperate with the plan to commit Ollie to Mitchellville. So, pending her hearing in the district court, an "interested lady" took custody of Ollie. At the lady's home, Ollie would get a glimpse of "intelligence and refinement," according to the papers. A few days later, Judge Charles Waterman committed her to the industrial school. On a final visit to her home, she shook hands with her parents, siblings, and neighbors, but declined to kiss them, declaring "she was not one of the kissing kind." Then, in the company of deputy sheriff Mary E. Welcher, a widow and alliance member who may have been appointed deputy for the express purpose of accompanying her young charge, Ollie Kreps traveled to Mitchellville, to remain until her eighteenth birthday or until her keepers judged she had reformed, whichever came first.[23]

The Ollie Kreps who emerges from this story is indeed a "tough girl" from a "tough community," but she also has a certain vitality and instinct for survival. Consider how she was able to resist the intervention of Davenport's interested ladies, or her decision to head out for an evening on the town only hours after her release from police custody. Consider too the circumstances of her arrest at the Ackley House. Just what could four teenagers have been doing to cause so much disruption that the night clerk would risk losing his job, as one newspaper implied, by calling in the police? Surely the disturbance was not merely the vocal expression of sexual pleasure, a common enough sound, one would think, in a "second class" hotel. One imagines instead drunken laughter, raucous singing, pillow fights, horseplay—not to mention wanton destruction of hotel property. Ollie Kreps was not, strictly speaking, a prostitute. She was what Kathy Peiss has called a "charity girl." She traded on her sexuality for entertainment and an escape from grinding poverty. She wanted to have fun.[24]

PRIVATE PROBLEM OR PUBLIC POLICY

To citizens of Davenport, Ollie Kreps symbolized something far more troubling than boisterous adolescence, however. Police chief Frank Kessler and Davenport's newspaper editors saw Kreps as a sign of the failure of family authority to cope with the temptations of the city. Kreps was one of the "young girls born in the city and allowed to have their own free way night and day because of poverty and many brothers and sisters in their home." Kessler claimed that he "could point out girls who were as sure to become inmates of brothels as they lived" but that when he had tried to warn parents of their daughters' certain fate, he had "received curses" and "made bitter enemies." The editor of the *Democrat-Gazette* concurred, describing the response of a "good man" long involved in Davenport philanthropy. "He was horrified when told that there are many homes like [Kreps's], and many girls as sure to be like her as they reach her age because of their homes and associates in the city." The editor of the *Tribune* was sure that these girls were aggressors: "Any one whose business requires them to be out at night" knew "there are a lot of young girls, ranging in age from 12 to 16 years, who can be found on the streets almost any evening, flirting and doing all in their power to attract boys of the same age who[,] by the way[,] will accept willingly any advances the girls may make."[25]

Among this chorus of agreement, one voice stood out. Roger O'Meara, city editor of the *Times*, typically pursued his themes with vivid rhetoric, and this was no exception. To O'Meara, Kreps was a "chippie," one of "hundreds" of girls between twelve and twenty-two who "wander the streets after nightfall. No man can insult them, because a vile proposal is solicited by their brazen deportment, and they either accompany the person who accosts them or dismiss him with a torrent of smart, new slang which gives her chewing gum a rest.... The 'chippie' is one whose father and mother does *not* 'know she is out,' or they imagine she is in decent company." He closed his essay with a challenge to neglectful parents: "It behooves some of the fathers and mothers of Davenport to begin to-night and investigate this question for themselves: 'Is there a daughter of mine running the streets to-night? But then, she couldn't be a-a-a "chippie."' Couldn't she? Follow her, and God grant you are not mistaken."[26]

Kessler and O'Meara may have agreed that parents deserved blame for girls like Ollie Kreps, but the police chief and the editor parted company on just about everything else, including how to address the problem. Kessler advocated private, individual intervention: "preventing of girls getting into the life that warrants their arrest." The *Democrat-Gazette*, which often seemed to act as the chief's voice on public issues, estimated that there were perhaps thirty or forty Davenport families where girls were "led into vice instead of away from it" and wondered, "How can their homes be made better? How can the course of their lives be changed?" Responding to Kessler's call for action, women from the LIRS held "earnest discussion" of how the society might reach "the young members of the families mentioned" and prevent "the daughters going astray."[27]

O'Meara agreed that parents failed to supervise their daughters but scorned the chief's call for private intervention, mocking him as "City Missionary Kessler." The problem was not one for private charity, O'Meara insisted, but for public policy. As police chief, Kessler chose to ignore saloons with private rooms where drinking led to debauchery. O'Meara published addresses for some of the "32 Curtained Sepulchres of Maiden Purity," challenging Kessler to clean up the city by ending the practice of admitting women to saloons through "ladies' entrances." Saloons with discreet doors and curtained rooms were nothing more than "traps" for foolish girls, "the back entrances to a life in a brothel, . . . which scores of our daughters have already blindly visited," he insisted. In these private rooms, a "precocious, prurient couple, son and daughter of good parents, heated with lust and aflame with drink,

Police chief Frank Kessler, c. 1900. (Collection of the author.)

draw the curtains . . . so that no stray individual can come in and discover them—drinking beer." O'Meara goaded Kessler unmercifully in print, hinting that he had become wealthy from illicit income, chiding him for his failure to enforce the law, even comparing him with a grave robber.[28]

O'Meara's quarrel with Kessler was part partisan politics, part an authentically different view of the role of government in addressing social problems. O'Meara was a Civil War veteran, a member of the Grand Army of the Republic, and a Republican who was still waving the bloody shirt in 1889. He accused Mayor Ernst Claussen, for example, of giving a city job to his own tenant so that the new immigrant could make rent payments, all the while denying a job to a needy old soldier simply because the Union veteran was a Republican and the mayor and his administration Democrats. To O'Meara, the Democratic city government was both corrupt and heartless.[29]

While O'Meara may have sounded at times like a temperance crusader, his quarrel was not with saloons. Like anyone in Davenport who hoped to shape public opinion, O'Meara did not attack that sacred institution. Indeed, he was a regular—some said too regular—participant in the masculine leisure culture built around saloons. Instead, O'Meara argued that preventing girls from following the path of Ollie Kreps required not keeping girls at home (the *Democrat-Gazette*, Kessler's mouthpiece, had urged a sunset curfew for those under fifteen) but reserving saloons for men: "no female, young or old, must be permitted to enter a drinking place," he insisted. Like Kessler, O'Meara believed that the gendered geography of the city was changing for the worse, that women were intruding where they did not belong, but he sought only to protect the saloon as masculine space. Respectable saloon keepers, claimed O'Meara, shared his view, and he quoted one at length. If a man wants to drink, said a Second Street saloon keeper, "let him go where they sell drink. If he wants to ruin a young girl let him take his chances of her father's or brother's bullet, but he can't use my house for that purpose. I sell drink but not the chance to ruin young girls. I've got girls of my own." According to O'Meara, Kessler's fault was in failing to use police power to regulate saloons. This was an especially loaded issue in Davenport, where all the saloons operated in open defiance of state law. O'Meara argued that Kessler ignored his duty, that he was more interested "in toadying to and protecting" saloon keepers than in making the city a safe place for women and girls. The Swiss-born Kessler, however, may simply have shared the German perspective that beer gardens and other drinking resorts need not be off-limits to women.[30]

If Kessler and O'Meara disagreed about how to address the problem embodied by Ollie Kreps, both men agreed about one other thing: the iconic girl on the street who really worried them was middle class. The *Democrat-Gazette*, summarizing Kessler's comments, reported, "The children he has seen on the road to ruin nights are not all children of the poor, by a good many. Parents of respectable standing do not know where their daughters and sons are evenings and nights, no more than parents who are in poverty, through drink, laziness or misfortune." The *Times* claimed that among the girls to be found in "curtained dives" where drinking and sexual promiscuity were winked at, "Not one tenth of them can plead poverty or parental abuse. They are of the middle classes—daughters, some of them, of our wealthy citizens." If Chief Kessler were to do his job and return these girls to their families with news of where he found them, "he will astonish many a well-to-do, Christian family, several Sunday school teachers, and our people generally."[31]

The newspaper editors' and the chief of police's insistence that the "chippies" who wandered Davenport's streets were daughters of middle-class families reveals these observers' underlying discomfort with the city's shifting gender boundaries. A half century earlier, flaneurs exploring the new urban metropolis had articulated the

The Reform of Urban Environments

Bird's Eye view of Davenport, c. 1888. This engraving, which appeared on business cards and commercial letterheads in the 1880s and 1890s, showed local pride in urbanization, but growth inspired fear as well as pride. (Collection of the author.)

cultural intersection of gender and geography. Those men divided urban space as they divided women, by distinguishing the chaste from the fallen, the vulnerable from the predatory. Sexuality defined the dangerous woman, who preyed on defenseless men. Though mapped onto urban geography, the distinction between the chaste woman and the predator was fundamentally one of class. As industrialization altered the urban landscape, severing the workplace from its roots in the household, men and women of the middle class increasingly agreed with Chief Kessler: respectable wives and daughters belonged at home, not on the streets or in the workplace. At midcentury, men might feel free to interpret any woman on the street without a male protector as a prostitute, but the women at greatest risk were those for whom the streets were places of work and sociability. For poor and working-class women, including African Americans, their unescorted presence in public marked them as sexually available. To more elite men, this justified men's sexual aggression. By the 1880s, however, the expanding urban workforce disrupted the old geography of gender and class. Middle-class girls and women now mixed on the streets with their working-class sisters, and their presence exposed the class assumptions behind the spatial codes of urban life: either working-class women had been unjustly sexualized by their presence in public, or middle-class women now cast doubts on their own chastity when they went unescorted into the streets.[32]

As Police Chief Kessler and city editor O'Meara sparred over meaning of the middle-class chippies supposedly crowding Davenport's streets at night, both men ignored a simple truth: the girl who started it all, Ollie Kreps, was clearly not "of the middle classes." She was not the daughter of a wealthy family seeking thrills by way of the ladies' entrance to a shady saloon or of depraved parents who "led [her] into vice instead of away from it." She was instead the working daughter of desperately poor parents who lived in a neighborhood where the opportunity to earn a more comfortable living readily presented itself. The choice to work in a brothel—whether as a servant or as an inmate—or to trade on her sexuality for a good meal, an evening's entertainment, and a bed in a steam-heated hotel may not have been difficult, especially on a January night in Iowa. For the leading men of the city to acknowledge these truths would have meant calling into question the policy under which Davenport protected illegal saloons and tolerated prostitution. Instead, critics focused on Kreps's home, refusing to distinguish between a poor home and a vicious one. If, as Kessler and the editors insisted, parents were to blame, then the only solution was to remove Ollie Kreps from her parents' care and make her a ward of the state.

Paradoxically, precisely because authorities could distinguish Ollie from a prostitute, they sent her to Mitchellville. She was, after all, not the only girl arrested that night. But it was she who became the center of controversy, she who lost her home. Beside Ollie Kreps, the second girl is a shadow. No newspaper reported her name, and the police and magistrate's court records for that period have been lost. For the historian, she exists solely in the news reports surrounding the arrests. But as those stories create her, she emerges as a foil to her companion, defining by opposition what made Ollie Kreps an object of public concern.

The difference between the two girls is not self-evident. At thirteen, Ollie was very young, but the second girl was only fourteen or fifteen. Writers acknowledged that the second girl was sexually active, but no one pretended Ollie was innocent. After all, police had arrested her in a brothel. But newspaper reports erased these apparent similarities. The *Morning Tribune*, for example, emphasized Ollie's youth, calling her "a mere child," but dismissed the second girl as "a woman of the demimonde and known as such." The *Democrat-Gazette* counterpoised their homes and upbringing, reminding readers that Ollie's father was "industrious" and her mother overwhelmed by household cares. The second girl, by contrast, "has not been free from wicked surroundings since babyhood. She has never lived in a pure home. She did not fall into vice—grew up in the middle of it, though not in penury's degradation." In short, Ollie was a child because she had respectable, if poor, parents; the second girl was a woman—and a fallen one—because her origins were not respectable. This is the closest the newspapers came to acknowledging that removing Ollie from her home was really about removing her from the temptations that attended poverty. The respectability of Ollie's home meant that she could be saved, yet her salvation lay in being separated from her home. The second girl did not face the temptations of poverty; her home was comfortable. But that comfort had been purchased at the price of "wicked surroundings." Sending Ollie to Mitchellville was about sending her away from such companions. The second girl was consigned to prostitution, a future beyond hope and help.[33]

THE OPPOSITION

As Davenport authorities cooperated to remove Ollie Kreps to Mitchellville, another group of citizens voiced its fears about prostitutes' penetration of their neighborhood. Within days after the board of supervisors consigned the courthouse annex to the Charitable Alliance as a house of detention, fifty-one men had signed and delivered a petition asking the city council to deny funding to the new facility. To the signers—mostly small businessmen whose homes or workplaces were scattered in the German neighborhood west of Brady Street in the blocks around the courthouse square—the house of detention itself posed a danger, because it would bring prostitutes (albeit as prisoners) into their neighborhood. The location, they insisted, was "too public." "Our wives and children," they argued, "will be subjected to such sights and sounds as will (or may) be of detrimental influence on them." Their complaints sounded much like those of the man who grumbled to police about the brothels north of the fairgrounds a decade earlier. Separated from the downtown blocks where prostitution was common by a short but clear distance, the men who signed the petition sought to protect their neighborhood from the intrusion of disorderly women brought to the house of detention. Such women, they asserted, belonged in a place "more secluded."[34]

Newspaper reports of the protest were quick to point out the ironies in the petition. "The county jail is only two hundred feet distant from the proposed house of detention," remarked the *Democrat-Gazette*. "Surely the sights at the latter will be pleasant to the eye in comparison with the most alarming spectacle that can be presented by the former." The *Tribune* made the same observation (but judged the distance to be only one hundred feet) and wondered, "Why is it that the residents in the neighborhood of the police station do not send in a formal protest on the same grounds?" The difference between the county jail, the police station, and the proposed house of detention was the way gender marked each. As long as police took women arrested to the police station along with men in custody, nothing flagged their numbers and presence. As long as the only jail cells available placed women alongside male prisoners, few women would be jailed. Establishing a separate jail for women forced the public's recognition of the prostitutes in their midst and raised the possibility that scores would now be arrested and jailed.[35]

Newspaper editors chided the petitioners for misunderstanding the purpose of the house of detention. Neighbors had nothing to fear, the editors argued, because the kind of women incarcerated there would pose no threat. "This proposed house of detention is not for lost and degraded females," explained the *Morning Tribune*, "but for young girls who are not yet steeped in sin." The *Democrat-Gazette* echoed this opinion, elaborating further, "Girls who can be warned, whose sense of pride and shame can be reached, are to be temporarily accommodated there." As they made their case against the petitioners, these editors aligned themselves with Police Chief Kessler in identifying the proper response to girls like Ollie Kreps: private intervention in individual lives. By excluding "lost and degraded females" (like Kreps's companion, for example), the newspapers implicitly admitted that prostitutes would remain part of Davenport's urban landscape.[36]

In claiming that only some women arrested would come under the purview of the matron and the house of detention, the editors were imagining a very different role for the matron than the one proposed by the alliance. The alliance petition specified "that every woman arrested should be given into [the matron's] hands to be searched and cared for" and that this care would "include all girls and women who would otherwise be committed to jail." Unlike Kessler, the newspaper editors, and the men opposing the house of detention, the alliance declined to write some women off as "lost." The alliance members did not share the opinion that prostitution was inevitable. In their view, every woman arrested should have the care of a matron because every woman stood in the same relation to male police, jailers, and prisoners. In the literature advocating employment of police matrons, writers played down the presumed distance between "good" and "fallen" women. The danger they mapped lay in a different place: in the physical intrusion of men on women. Respectable women who found themselves in the hands of the police faced the same dangers as common prostitutes. "The most innocent women, from sudden illness or other causes, may be at any moment brought to the station-houses," one writer explained. "Humanity, civilization, common decency demand that they shall not be exposed to frightful outrage; nor less do they require that the same protection shall be extended to other women, however degraded."[37]

For advocates of the police matron movement, "protection" meant preservation from both affronts to women's dignity and assaults on their persons. The same movement that argued for police matrons also called for separate jail facilities for women. In most cities, as in Davenport, the cells of male and female prisoners were not separated, which meant that women spent twenty-four hours a day in cells exposed to the view of male jailers and usually of male prisoners as well. Even where segregation existed, it did not always shield women from intrusion. A representative of the Women's Prison Association in New York City described a tour of the women's quarters led by a man who did not bother to alert the prisoners of his approach. "We entered, finding women in all conditions of undress." Her guide, she reported, was so accustomed to the sight that he took no notice. In contrast to this was the Tombs, which she praised for the privacy of its design and the vigilance of its matrons: "It is absolutely impossible for a man to obtain even a glimpse into the women's department of the prison." In Davenport, Mary Welcher urged that all women deserved the same physical privacy. "Lost to all shame as these our sister women may seem, they still must shrink from a male attendant," she argued. "It would be in every sense as appropriate that women, star on breast and club in hand[,] should garrison the west end of our station house as that men should guard the women."[38]

As advocates of the movement emphasized the need to protect jailed women from men, opponents insistently argued that good women needed protection from the vicious women in jail. In San Francisco, the chief of police prohibited the police matron from contact with "the most degraded," vowing that he would "allow no woman to be humiliated by such association." In New York, the prison association opposed matrons for similar reasons. One woman countered, "It is . . . true that a drunken and disorderly woman is a most depraved creature, but in what way she could demoralize a decent sober woman it is difficult to see." Indeed, advocates of police matrons were far more concerned about the indignities men in the police and court system could visit on the women in their custody. A New Hampshire police matron called her courtroom visits "one of the most humiliating things connected with the work" but believed them absolutely necessary. "I have every evidence to believe the presence of a true woman is a check, and the improper language that is sometimes used in police court, is not used when she is present," she explained. A "philanthropic lady" offered a similar experience. When she went to court to observe a young girl's trial, the judge urged her to leave the courtroom when the case was called. She refused, and afterward the judge admitted, "We were careful on you[r] account." "Didn't you ask all the questions that were necessary?" inquired the lady. "Yes; but if you had not been here, we might have got a little fun out of the case," admitted the judge. "Fun" that came at the cost of humiliating a young girl alone in a courtroom full of men was just what such women feared. Too often, they believed, men—whether police officers or judges—dismissed any troubled girl or woman as "lost" and therefore undeserving of respect or even safety. This philanthropic lady resolved never to permit another girl to go unaccompanied to court; other women organized to secure matrons for the same end.[39]

Advocates of police matrons were zealous in their desire to protect the dignity and reputation of women in the hands of police. They were certain that men judged women too quickly and failed to understand women's distinctive experience. A police matron could shield women from unjust prosecutions as well as from humiliating treatment, argued supporters. "There may be some mitigating circumstance concerning their arrest and imprisonment that would have occurred to a woman had she been in charge," argued one writer, "but which a man could not be expected to consider." The intimacy possible between a sympathetic matron and her jailed client could also give special insight. In court, a matron could give supporting testimony, proving "the condition of [a woman's] poor, bruised body." In private, she could ask the kinds of questions that, when asked by a man, would draw only miserable silence. Trust between women could elicit explanations from a woman "driven" to violence "to defend her unprotected honor."[40]

Jailed women, of course, had no means to protect their "honor." When police and other men assumed that "erring" women were beyond shame, they exposed prisoners to sexual assault. Mrs. Barney of the WCTU declined to be specific about certain "abuses" and "dastardly outrages" of which she knew but concluded, "The only wonder is that, under our present system, they have been so infrequent." Other writers were less circumspect. In an editorial advocating police matrons, *Harper's Weekly* cited the case of a New York police officer sentenced to prison for the attempted rape of a fifteen-year-old girl held at a station house, though it mourned not just the "fearful wrong" done the victim but also the "ruin of the life of the officer" who was placed in the way of such "temptation."[41]

If the petition offered by opponents of the house of detention is evidence, alliance members knew they had an uphill climb to persuade the city council that the women brought to Davenport's station house deserved the attention of a police matron and the shelter of a house of detention. The men who signed that petition sought to preserve the real and symbolic distance between "fallen women" and the women of the men's households. To counter these concerns, the alliance focused its campaign on raising public consciousness about girls like Ollie Kreps. Their strategy may even have contributed to the newspaper editors' erroneous claim that the house of detention would hold only girls "not yet steeped in sin." While many city aldermen may have supposed that prostitution itself was inescapable, the alliance argued that the "fall" of young girls was far from inevitable. Even more, they argued that the civic heedlessness that left poor girls to wander unhindered into prostitution had serious public consequences. Early in the campaign, the *Democrat-Gazette* printed an excerpt from an address given at the National Conference of Charities and Correction (NCCC): "No one doubts the propriety of large efforts to save a boy. A girl may do a much greater amount of harm in the world, hence political economy dictates that as great efforts should be made to rescue her." Girls, the speaker entreated, must be "redeemed from destruction and the power of destroying." The words belonged to Emma A. Hall, superintendent of the Michigan Industrial School for Girls. Her warning helped Davenport activists shape a local controversy in terms of a national debate. Through her words, the alliance sought to claim that rescuing girls was not a private act of charity but a matter of sound public policy, worthy of civic support.[42]

Hall's words found their way into the Davenport newspapers by Jennie McCowen's hand. Hall presented a paper on the "Reformation of Criminal Girls" at the 1883 NCCC meeting. That year, McCowen had been Iowa's official delegate to the NCCC, appointed by the governor. McCowen delivered her report at the same session during which Hall spoke. She also kept the NCCC *Proceedings* in her personal library. So it is easy to imagine McCowen returning to an especially memorable speech when she and other women began organizing in response to Ollie Kreps's arrest. Through the months that followed, Hall's words assumed a privileged position in the Davenport campaign. Excerpted in the *Democrat-Gazette*, they were also embedded in a letter circulated by the alliance seeking support for a police matron. What made Hall's language so compelling that McCowen returned to it nearly six years later? McCowen, after all, attended NCCC meetings throughout the 1880s, where she heard frequent discussions of "criminal girls." She also read widely on work with women and delinquents. Hall's words, however, appealed succinctly and persuasively to the prestige of science—to "political economy" and hereditarian thought. The city fathers might not dwell long on the concern of voteless women for the environment of downtown streets, but they might pay attention to arguments based in modern science.[43]

When Hall claimed that Americans were more willing to save boys than girls and when McCowen and the alliance chose to quote that passage, they invoked a complex of beliefs about gender and crime that shaped nineteenth-century social policy. American legal codes defined a number of offenses against chastity, but authorities rarely prosecuted men and boys for violating them. Police already knew James Tomlin, one of the boys arrested with Ollie Kreps, for his "high-handed capers," but no one contemplated incarcerating and reforming him, and his arrest provoked little comment about the dangers of middle-class boys wandering the streets. Men and boys did predominate, however, among those prosecuted for offenses against persons or property, crimes generally deemed more serious and worthy of strong public response. By the nineteenth century, public response included an optimistic commitment to "re-forming" criminals, to remaking them, through carefully prescribed penitentiary regimens, into useful citizens.[44]

Women and girls, in contrast, were far less likely than men to commit crimes against persons or property. While police certainly arrested women for larceny and assault, the women who crowded police courts—in Davenport, women nearly always outnumbered men—mostly faced charges related to prostitution. Throughout the nineteenth century, the "social evil" provoked bitter debate. As evangelicals launched increasingly fervent attacks on the vice trades, their movements encountered the inertia or opposition of those who took a laissez-faire stance, assuming prostitution to be inevitable, necessary, and for that matter, profitable. Prostitution was illegal, but many cities chose to tolerate or regulate it, and women convicted of prostitution-related offenses rarely faced severe penalties. Brothel prostitutes in Davenport generally paid their fines and went home, often without spending even an hour in jail (in part because there was no way to segregate so many women). Streetwalkers might face a thirty-day sentence, but a judge was likely to suspend it if the woman promised to leave town. These sentences reflected the twin assumptions that prostitution was a necessary evil and that prostitutes themselves were beyond reform. Authorities used arrests to manage the number and behavior of prostitutes, not to stamp out prostitution itself. Paradoxically, the handful of women who ended up in the prison system suffered horribly from this double standard. In the eyes of prison authorities, criminal women had strayed so far from the nature of womanhood that they had become utterly unnatural, which proved them unsuitable candidates for reclamation. The result was that women often languished in the worst, most neglected corners of the prison system. With no expectation of reforming these women, some prison wardens even put the women to work as prostitutes within the prison itself or ignored sexual exploitation by male guards.[45]

HEREDITARY DEGENERATION AND PUBLIC POLICY

By asserting that "a girl can do a much greater amount of harm in the world" than a boy, Hall and the alliance sought to challenge the system that accepted prostitution as inevitable and to establish crimes against chastity—girls' crimes—as a serious matter, worthy of strong public response. To do so, they linked girls' unchastity with contemporary arguments about the hereditarian origins of crime. The alliance deployed these complex, gender-specific arguments in a way that wove together Lamarckian genetics and Republican Motherhood and remained distinct from the eugenic theories of the Progressive Era. Their arguments defied those who dismissed prostitution as necessary and inevitable and, more important, opened the way to insist that the neighborhoods created by tolerated prostitution had terrible consequences, not just for those who lived in them but for the future of the nation.

Beginning in the 1850s, the concept of hereditary degeneration gained increasing influence in the emerging disciplines of psychiatry and anthropology, and in the decades following it shaped discussions of scientific charity as well. At its simplest, degeneration was the idea that an adverse environment (for example, poverty and overcrowding) or "vicious" behavior (for example, drunkenness) "weakened the hereditary endowment of subsequent generations," leading to a downward spiral of evolution in reverse. As an explanation for "pauperism" and hereditary criminals, degeneration contained seeds of hope absent from the similar concept of atavism. Most frequently associated with the work of Italian criminologist Cesare Lombroso, atavism proposed that criminals were evolutionary throwbacks, lawless savages born into civilization and therefore unreformable. Lombroso argued that criminal women were especially likely to be atavistic, which contributed to their general neglect in the prison system. Unlike atavism, hereditary degeneration rested within a Lamarckian framework, presuming that an individual would pass her responses to her environment on to her children and to theirs. Social investigator Richard Dugdale explained how heredity and environment reinforced each other. "The tendency of heredity is to produce an environment which perpetuates that heredity: thus, the licentious parent makes an example which greatly aids in fixing habits of debauchery in the child. The correction," he argued, "is change of environment." Just as pernicious influences could lead to degeneration, wholesome environment and behavior could forestall or even reverse the trend.[46]

For those who sought to apply such scientific advances to the agendas of organized women, the implications of hereditarian theories were heady. Antoinette Brown Blackwell used hereditarian arguments to rail against those who would deny women access to education and careers. "Defrauded womanhood," she wrote, "has been everywhere avenged for the system of arrogant repression under which she has always stifled hitherto." The human race was "forever retarding its own advancement" by oppressing women, who passed along stunted natures to boy and girl children impartially. In the mid-1870s, however, not Blackwell but medical conservatives such as E. H. Clarke and Henry Maudsley dominated the scientific discussions of heredity and woman's place. Clarke went so far as to propose that continued education and "advancement" for women would lead eventually to an evolutionary change "subtracting sex from woman" to create a third, unsexed sex, which he called "agenes."[47]

When Emma Hall and Davenport activists drew on hereditarian theories to support altering the circumstances of endangered young girls, these women were in the mainstream of social theory. In the mid-1870s, social researcher Elisha Harris published his finding that a single immoral woman, whom he called "Margaret, mother of criminals," living near the end of the eighteenth century, had been the progenitor of a family of paupers and criminals. Her descendants filled the jails, prisons, and poorhouses of several New York counties. Inspired by Harris's preliminary work, Richard Dugdale returned to the same locale for a more thorough investigation. He found that "Margaret," whom he called "Ada Juke," had four sisters and that these five women together had produced some twelve hundred descendants. Over seventy-five years, the Jukes had cost the state of New York more than $1.25 million in relief, jail and prison operation, and other expenses. Dugdale's 1877 study of the Jukes electrified the scientific charity movement, influencing those who sought to solve the problems of poverty and crime—or more properly, paupers and criminals—for nearly half a century. Even after the rediscovery of Mendelian genetics had rendered Dugdale's scientific framework outdated, social work experts continued to study and cite his research.[48]

Dugdale's study, which he described as "historico-biographical synthesis united to statistical analysis," teemed with detail. Charts traced branches of the Juke family; brief histories of each member and each spouse itemized their crimes, diseases, and dependencies. Dugdale gave special attention to the immoral tendencies of Juke women. More than half, he found, were "harlots," women who made "lapses through imprudence or even passion," though they may have "recovered themselves and led subsequently respectable lives." Harlotry, as Dugdale described it, was both sexual and racial. While the Jukes themselves were of old-stock Anglo-American ancestry (indeed, Bell Juke's legitimate descendants could have qualified for the Daughters of the American Revolution), Dugdale emphasized the way Juke women over generations repeatedly entered marriages and liaisons with African American men, both free and slave. Women's transgressive sexuality was so central to the concept of hereditary degeneration that both Dugdale and Harris constructed their studies matrilineally. It was "Margaret" who was the "mother of criminals," not her husband who was the father. The name "Juke" was given to "Ada," "Bell," their sisters, and their lineal descendants—spouses and sexual partners were designated only by the letter "X."[49]

Social theorists writing on hereditary degeneration recognized that both men and women bequeathed a legacy to their offspring, but the matrilineal focus persisted. New York charity administrator Josephine Shaw Lowell, proposing "One Means of Preventing Pauperism" to the NCCC in 1879, averred that her system was equally applicable to both men and women but declared that she would speak only of women "because they form the visible links in the direful chain of hereditary pauperism." At the same conference, Louise Rockwood Wardner of the Illinois girls' reformatory argued that "each unprincipled, impure girl left to grow up and become a mother, is likely to increase her kind three to five fold." The following year, Mrs. W. P. Lynde of Wisconsin criticized the Children's Aid Society of New York for its "orphan trains"—the practice of placing pauper children in midwestern homes. Doing so scattered "throughout the fertile West the baleful seeds that may speedily ripen into bitter fruit," she complained, arguing that New York City might better address crime and poverty by creating reformatories for "the four or five thousand mothers of these children." To support her position, she invoked the work of Elisha Harris. Henry Boles, writing of "unfortunate girls"—the seduced "innocent" as well as the common prostitute—asserted, "under present conditions they are not only condemned to the pauper criminal class themselves, but to a continual breeding of criminals and paupers."[50]

Discussions of hereditary degeneration continually shifted into matrilineal terms in part because nineteenth-century science had invested so much in discovering the differences and complementarities between the sexes and in identifying women primarily with their reproductive capacities. Men, of course, played a role in reproduction, but women were *about* reproduction. It was "as if the Almighty, in creating the female sex, had taken the uterus and built up a woman around it," one physician wrote in 1870. But the concern about women's illicit sexual behavior also drew on ancient fears of adultery and cuckoldry. If youthful "imprudence or even passion" made even the woman who reformed forever a "harlot," her early sexual experiences became part of the tainted legacy she passed along to future children. Roger O'Meara of the *Davenport Times* alluded to this fear when he wrote that the middle-class chippie was more dangerous than a confirmed prostitute because she would "some day dupe some good, honest, unsuspecting fellow into marrying a disguised trull for a virginal bride." Her sexual experience would inevitably poison the marriage, he wrote, because "her example is pestilential and contagious." This was the "power of destroying" of which Emma Hall warned.[51]

In contrast to this gloomy and deterministic vision of the role of women's illicit sexuality in hereditary degeneration, women activists consistently emphasized the implicit promise of Lamarckian genetics: that wholesome environment could curtail the dangers of flawed heredity. Girls could be "redeemed from destruction." Foregrounding environment in discussions of "unfortunate girls" had strategic advantages; it challenged the belief that some women were irretrievably "bad," reinventing them as victims rather than criminals. But it also left unresolved the ambiguity that haunted the alliance's efforts from its start: was their campaign about more effective charity for the poor or about altering public policy on behalf of women? Those making policy could construe "environment" broadly or narrowly, as urban neighborhood or as impoverished household.

The difference was significant. Police Chief Kessler, Davenport's editors, and some women of the LIRS saw the problem of Ollie Kreps as a failure of home. As a matter of family negligence, it required private intervention of the sort "friendly visitors" and "charitable ladies" could make, bringing middle-class virtues into poverty-stricken homes. This interpretation of "environment" highlighted the role women had been playing for much of the century as caretakers of environment: they maintained the home, provided moral instruction to children, and—especially in the case of girls—kept a watchful eye on their associations. In this model, a police matron became a conduit for established forms of charitable intervention. She played the role of liaison between the police and organized women, guiding the latter toward families where, as Chief Kessler put it, girls were "led into vice."

Where family intervention failed, the alternative was the one applied to Ollie Kreps: removal and confinement in a reformatory institution. The goal was to separate young girls from pernicious influences and place them in new, wholesome environments that would counteract the damaging effects of their upbringing. Josephine Shaw Lowell, for example, had urged the establishment of reformatories "to which all women under thirty, when arrested for misdemeanors, or upon the birth of a second illegitimate child should be committed for very long periods." Lengthy stays were crucial, argued Lowell, "since the very character of the women must be changed, and every good and healthy influence would be rendered useless without the one element of time." Some local activists in Davenport shared this perspective. In her report on the Mitchellville Girls' School, alliance member Mary Welcher urged her readers, "Remember these girls come, in most instances, from the lowest parentage—conceived in iniquity, having vicious heredity as their only heritage, victims of ante natal vices, surrounded by continuous degrading influences. So can it be expected that all tendency to sin and uncleanness will be eradicated in five or less years?" Jennie McCowen explicitly cited the example of "the New York 'Margaret' " in urging the state to establish a reformatory for women. By the Progressive Era, penologists recommended long prison sentences (or sterilization or even execution) to prevent criminals from reproducing, but these women placed such faith in reformatories that they expected the institutions to work not by preventing girls from becoming mothers but by turning them into Republican Mothers. As Sarah Keely argued in her presentation at the NCCC, "If it be true that, as the mothers are, so are the community, the State, the nation, what greater need can arise than the reformation of girls and women? If they are to be the mothers of future generations, they are in a measure to control public thought through the inheritance and training they give to their children."[52]

By associating endangered girls with their potential motherhood and motherhood with the formation of citizens, these women of the alliance successfully argued that the fate of young girls like Ollie Kreps was a matter for serious public concern. But those who wanted to push the campaign beyond traditional charity and to challenge established public policy toward prostitution faced a more difficult task. For them, private charity could never be enough. Any intervention on an individual level—like sending Ollie Kreps to Mitchellville—would remain a partial, stopgap measure. A judge could remove her, but the environment that produced her—the downtown neighborhood, with its second-class hotels, "cigar stores," strolling prostitutes, and tough saloons—remained, flourishing amid the working women and poor families whose homes were also there. Ollie Kreps's neighborhood was the result of the city government's policy choices—choices that had to change if the city valued protecting girls and women.

Jennie McCowen's contributions to the debate about environment and heredity made it clear that intervention in individual families would never be enough. Since the early 1880s, McCowen had organized Davenport's women physicians into an annual lecture series for girls and women. Her own contribution was often "Overcoming Evil Inheritance," in which she explained the difference between an inherited predisposition, an "underlying weakness or unbalance or taint," and disease itself. "If the inheritors of any special predisposing morbid elements knows [sic] of its existence they are thereby fortified with a weapon of resistance," she urged. They may then "keep it quiescent, hedge it about with precautions, dwarf it, smother it." In some environments, however, hedging weakness with precautions and smothering temptations was difficult indeed. Children, warned McCowen, were especially susceptible to "social conditions and occupations, effect of climate and locality."[53]

Even more significant to McCowen, however, was the way an environment where prostitution was tolerated jeopardized daughters yet unborn. In an article in the *Journal of Heredity*, published in 1886, McCowen shifted the focus of degeneration from mothers' "harlotry" to fathers' sexual dissipation. "Many a young girl, innocent of all evil intent, knowing nothing of the fatal inheritance lurking in her veins, is in an evil hour carried over the brink in a surge of passion, which she does not understand, but which is the legacy descended to her from the early wild oats of her now doting father," explained McCowen. Young men might patronize prostitutes with no apparent personal consequences, suggested McCowen, but their indulgence became a perilous legacy for the children they might father later in life. When society tolerated prostitution, men would visit prostitutes. "So long as women sow to the wind in marrying licentious men," wrote McCowen, "so long may they expect to reap the whirlwind in their children."[54]

When the arrest of Ollie Kreps brought endangered girlhood to the front pages of Davenport's papers, Jennie McCowen brought discussion of heredity and environment directly to Davenport audiences. Within two weeks, she announced that her next lecture at the Academy of Science would be "Shinbone Alley." Its subject drew comment from the local papers, which observed with interest that the topic was "not so much science . . . as a matter pertaining to social science, what can be done to rescue children from degraded and demoralizing environment, a subject apropos just now."[55]

Just as she had drawn on Emma Hall's NCCC speech to express the need for a matron, McCowen again returned to her library for inspiration. This lecture she based on a talk given two years earlier at the NCCC by Rev. R. W. Hill. In "The Children of 'Shinbone Alley,' " Hill described a particularly baleful slum neighborhood in a large city and the effects of the environment on the children who lived there. McCowen summarized and paraphrased Hill's talk, then linked it to the situation in Davenport. "The children in this wretched haunt," she observed, "necessarily reflected their surroundings and drifted to a life of crime, handicapped at birth and impelled by the force of circumstances which they had no power to control." Shinbone Alley, she admitted, was not in Davenport, but her home also had "plague spots." McCowen tallied up the millions spent each year by the state and counties, reflecting that taxpayers were already pouring money into the problems of such slums, "yet with all this lavish expenditure . . . causes are not disturbed." Spinning a metaphor to link urban blight with cultivated fields, McCowen offered the example of public policy brought to bear on a noxious weed, the Canada thistle. "The majesty of the commonwealth has interposed enactments with penalties etc., to protect the farmers from this weed," she reminded her readers. "Are human beings of less value than weeds? Is the spread of vice and crime beyond the reach of any preventive care?" The state did not abandon individual farmers to fight an invasive weed alone; it should not leave families to struggle alone against the "contamination" of children by urban "plague spots" left unchecked. "The body politic," she argued, was "one with many members." Citizens who ignored the Shinbone

Alleys in their midst did so at their peril, for the poisons allowed to fester there might injure their own families.[56]

When Jennie McCowen called on citizens of Davenport to address public policy to the larger environment of the neighborhood, she raised the stakes of the alliance campaign. Many women and most of the leading men who spoke publicly on the issue were willing to employ a police matron who would simply expand traditional charitable efforts to intervene in poor families with wayward daughters. But the larger challenge—the challenge to transform the downtown neighborhood by ending tolerated prostitution there—moved the campaign onto contested ground. As the opponents' petition and the arguments of supporters in the national campaign suggest, two dramatically different ideas about the source of social danger circulated in the 1880s. The men resisting the house of detention in Davenport and opponents of the police matron movement argued that encounters with prostitutes demoralized respectable women. The mere sight of arrested women would be a "detrimental influence" on otherwise virtuous wives and daughters, according to the men who signed the petition. In contrast, those who supported the campaign repeatedly asserted that prostitutes could not endanger "decent, sober" women. Instead, supporters feared that male police, jailers, and judges would destroy the self-respect and reputation of women in custody through humiliation, assaults on their modesty—or worse.

In arguing that prostitutes were essentially like other women, supporters of the police matron campaign reinterpreted the gendered geography of the city. Poor and working-class women were not temptresses whose sexuality defined the dangerous neighborhood; rather, men with money created danger wherever they felt secure in exploiting women's poverty by bargaining for sex. Ollie Kreps had not lured James Tomlin; James Tomlin had lured Ollie Kreps. Further, when Tomlin indulged his sexual desires with Ollie or another girl, his experiences tainted the legacy he would pass on to his future sons and daughters.

By reassigning responsibility to men, the women of the alliance implicitly asserted all women's right of access to the downtown streets. Frances Willard of the WCTU expressed their position succinctly: "It is not by the vain attempt to reintroduce the exploded harem method of secluding women that they are to be saved. It is rather by holding men to the same standard of morality" that men prescribed for women. When Chief Kessler, Roger O'Meara, and the other editors insisted that middle-class girls wandered the streets at night, brazenly soliciting attention, these men betrayed their discomfort with the way urban geography was changing. If a man chose to "have a little fun" with the girl walking down Second Street at nine in the evening, he might find an impoverished and willing partner like Kreps—or an insulted cash girl on her way home from Petersen's Department Store.

What disturbed Kessler and O'Meara most was the prospect of a cash girl who did not feel insulted.[57]

For those who expected the police matron to pursue traditional charity by intervening in individual families, the removal of Ollie Kreps from her home was a success story. From the time of her arrest in the Ackley House until her departure for Mitchellville, Kreps stayed not in the jail but in the home of one of the women who had interested herself in Kreps's case. The *Democrat-Gazette* reported that just a few days in an atmosphere of "intelligence and refinement" left Kreps "changed in demeanor, and softened in manner and language." If days could achieve so much, observed the editor, years in the industrial school would leave Kreps completely reformed, and she would "continue a virtuous life." Those like McCowen who insisted that such private intervention left the real causes of prostitution undisturbed might have felt vindicated—though hardly pleased—by Kreps's subsequent life. In 1894, Kreps turned eighteen, and the industrial school released her. That fall, her name turned up in grand jury proceedings in Davenport. A witness named Kreps as one of the "sporting women" whose presence proved that John McPartland's place was a house of ill-fame. Removal from her home and years in the "reforming" environment of Mitchellville had not produced the effect predicted. Where citizens permitted prostitution to flourish, girls would be drawn into the business.[58]

6

SPORTING MEN AND LITTLE GIRLS

Fish out of season are not fit to be eaten. Girls who have not reached the age of puberty are not fit even to be seduced. The law ought to be as strict about a live child as about a dead salmon.
—W. T. Stead, "The Maiden Tribute of Modern Babylon," 1885

ONE FRIDAY MORNING IN SEPTEMBER 1891, ten-year-old Ada Ammerman set off for school and disappeared. Or so it seemed to her mother, Lucy Matlock, as she recalled that day in courtroom testimony some weeks later. When Ada failed to come home for her midday meal, Mrs. Matlock hitched up the rig and went out to look for her daughter. As she drove to the school, she spotted two of Ada's playmates, Mamie Woods and Dolly Hamerly. Dolly, she thought, was wearing Ada's dress. At school, the teacher confirmed that Ada had not been there all day. Growing worried, Mrs. Matlock returned home to the saloon kept by her husband at the corner of Third and Iowa. Alarmed by her story, John Matlock reported his missing stepdaughter to the police and gave Chief Frank Kessler money to advertise for her. Then Matlock and his wife began to search. Because it was fair week, they drove out to the fairgrounds and continued looking until midnight. For the rest of the weekend, Mrs. Matlock spent her days searching and growing more and more frantic. Finally, on Monday afternoon, she found Ada, Mamie, and Dolly hiding in a shed only two blocks from Ada's home. After whipping Ada and putting her to bed, Mrs. Matlock drove Dolly home to her mother. Mamie she took to the house of detention.[1]

When Mrs. Matlock examined the clothes Ada had taken off, she felt overcome with revulsion: "They were all covered with slime and part of them looked so bad I would not let my husband see them." The slime, she reported, was semen. After questioning Ada, Lucy Matlock sent her husband to the police to swear out complaints against Henry Carpenter, Charles Lyon, and George Haikes. Carpenter, a dealer in race horses, had been a railroad engineer, an insurance agent, and a petty manufacturer before becoming one of the elders of a clique of sporting men who gambled on horses. Lyon worked as Carpenter's hostler. Haikes was the engineer on a local packet boat, the *Verne Swain*. The police arrested Carpenter and Lyon that night and Haikes the following day. They also picked up Dolly Hamerly and a fourteen-year-old named Della Wood implicated by Ada. Dolly and Della joined Mamie Woods at the house of detention. After Police Matron Annie Davis questioned the girls, the accusations first made by Ada quickly spiraled into eight rape charges filed against the three men.[2]

The subsequent trials and their aftermath illuminate a social world of men whose assumptions about sexuality could hardly differ more from those championed by the leaders of the police matron movement. Carpenter, Lyon, and Haikes—and for that matter, John Matlock—inhabited a masculine culture that assumed that male sexuality demanded not restraint but release. Sexual gratification with a willing girl or woman was a man's prerogative. Ideals like marital fidelity, personal chastity, or protection of the young belonged to a feminized culture that these men spurned, preferring the camaraderie of the saloon, racetrack, and gaming table. For most of his life, John Matlock moved comfortably in this world of men. He was a saloon keeper himself, and his stepson pursued a brief career as a prizefighter. Matlock certainly shared the resentment, even hostility, many men expressed toward the women who challenged their right to drink and socialize around the bar. But when some men exercised their sexual prerogatives with his stepdaughter, Matlock saw matters in a different light. He turned to the police, swearing out complaints for rape against the men Ada named. His decision, viewed by other men as a betrayal, nearly sent him to prison.[3]

More than one story emerges from the rape trials of 1891–92. The first is a tale of cultural conflict, pitting long-held beliefs about male sexuality, female nature, and age and gender hierarchies against values of restraint and protection newly enshrined in law. A second story is a tragedy: when harsh judgments dividing respectable women from prostitutes were imposed on little girls, the consequences shadowed the rest of their lives. The third is a conspiracy plot: men manipulated law and police power to protect the privileges of masculinity and to punish those who betrayed those privileges. Together, these stories suggest the futility of reform efforts meant to attack prostitution through law alone.

RAPE LAW AND THE CAMPAIGN AGAINST PROSTITUTION

Ada Ammerman's accusations placed three men in jeopardy of the law only because the law itself had recently changed. Women had lobbied Iowa's legislators to rewrite the state's rape law for the same reason that women had campaigned to bring a police matron to Davenport: to end prostitution. Certain that girls and women rarely entered prostitution by choice, women petitioned state legislatures across the nation for laws providing greater penalties against the men who created the demand for prostitutes. In 1884, for example, the Republican-controlled Iowa legislature passed a law directed in part at the sporting men who made the brothel a hub of their social world. The statute raised the maximum penalty imposed on both men and women found in a house of ill-fame from one year in the county jail to five years in the state penitentiary. The same session took aim at cigar stores and other businesses fronting for prostitution and strengthened laws against the recruitment of prostitutes. Legislators expanded the statute penalizing those who "inveigle or entice" girls into prostitution, extending its protection not only to girls previously "chaste" but also to reformed prostitutes.[4]

By the meeting of the next legislature in 1886, events far from Des Moines had helped swell the pressure for change. In the summer of 1885, a series of articles in London's *Pall Mall Gazette* shocked both Britain and America with evidence of a London market in child prostitutes. W. T. Stead's "The Maiden Tribute of Modern Babylon" claimed to reveal how easily "gentlemen" could purchase the virginity of girls "too young . . . to understand the nature of the crime of which they are the unwilling victims." Response to Stead in the United States was at first mixed. Ada H. Kepley, head of the Illinois Woman's Christian Temperance Union's (WCTU's) Department for the Suppression of Impure Literature, called on members to help stop advertisements for American sales of the *Pall Mall Gazette* and its "hideous disclosures." But Frances Willard, president of the WCTU, came to Stead's defense. "Mr. Stead, while we may not approve him in every detail of his methods, has earned the thanks of every thoughtful woman in the land." The WCTU's Department for the Promotion of Social Purity had been moribund for some time, so Willard, rocked by Stead's "moral earthquake," placed herself at its head and urged the WCTU's thousands of members and supporters to line up behind her. The department's new goals included "secur[ing] legislation of a character calculated to protect the honor and purity of women and girls, and render[ing] them safe from the depravity of brutal men."[5]

Stead's exposé dwelled with distaste on the fact that English law deemed girls of thirteen competent to consent to sexual intercourse, but the WCTU unsettled Americans by disclosing that in most of the United States, the age at which a girl's consent protected a man from a charge of rape was just ten. The legislative agenda of the newly revitalized Social Purity Department included revising laws relating to prostitution and seduction as well as rape, but the national campaign to raise the "age of consent" in rape statutes became the best known and most successful of these reforms. In its 1886 session, the Republican-dominated Iowa legislature responded to this new wave of activism by passing a single bill raising the "age of protection" in three criminal statutes. The law setting penalties for "decoying a child" away from her or his parents now covered children under fourteen rather than under twelve. In the statute prohibiting "inveigling" a girl into prostitution, the legislature raised the age from fifteen to eighteen. And in the rape statute, they raised the age of consent from ten to thirteen. By linking these three revisions, legislators confirmed their intent to make rape law a tool against prostitution.[6]

Supporters hoped that raising the age of consent would discourage men from seeking sex from girls by penalizing such encounters as rape. Girls, they believed, did not understand the lifelong consequences of consenting to sex, and men sought young girls out for that precise reason. Reformers working with prostitutes were certain that "it was not by accident that so many *little girls* entered the paths of sin." But the law that placed girls of ten off-limits as sexual partners ran counter to assumptions long held by men. Christine Stansell and Linda Gordon have documented the prevalence of juvenile prostitutes throughout the nineteenth century. While some men no doubt sought out girl partners to satisfy a sexual predilection for children, no evidence suggests that men generally thought sex with young girls was deviant. What George Chauncey has characterized as the "phallocentric presumption that a man's sexual satisfaction was more significant than the gender or character of the person who provided that satisfaction" governed men's interpretations of adult-child relations as well as male-male relations. As long as men did not violate the "complex social conventions of gender deference, inequality, and power," the choice of a partner did not jeopardize a man's understanding of himself as a normal, manly man. Most clients probably sought out girl prostitutes for practical reasons: they were easily available, inexpensive, and perhaps less likely to transmit disease. Girls who had not reached puberty were also unlikely to get pregnant. In a Davenport rape case involving Henry Albrecht and nine-year-old Lillie Boswell, a coworker testified that Albrecht "said little girls were better than big ones." He "told me I should go after them. Said I could f— any of them for 25¢." To men who shared this view, natural hierarchies of age and gender gave them sexual rights where girls were concerned.[7]

Sexuality itself also placed demands on men that justified their use of available partners, even girls. While middle-class writers of the day produced a wealth of prescriptive literature urging men to restrain their sexual urges in the interest of preserving their vital energy, their wives' health, and their families' economic resources, these ideals stood in stark contrast to another version of male sexuality based not on restraint but release. According to this view, a man who failed to satisfy regularly his sexual urges risked impotence, even illness. Folklore—and some physicians—drew an analogy between sexual continence and a healthy arm bound up in a sling. Just as the unused limb would gradually wither into uselessness, so, presumably, would a man's sexual power if deprived of regular exercise. Other writers went even further, asserting that men's sexual energy, if not safely channeled toward prostitutes, would lead to a frenzy of rape and sexual deviance.[8]

A man's needs did not, however, justify his exploitation of any girl. Stead's "Maiden Tribute" articles, grounded as they were in the icons of the English class system, tended to portray the "brute" who lusted after a child's virginity as a "gentleman" empowered by wealth and privilege to exploit poor country girls. Class figured in Davenport as well, but the boundary there was not drawn where Stead saw it. Working-class men were most likely to accept the sexuality of release—though the sheer, insistent volume of literature promoting restraint to the middle-class suggests that plenty of middle-class men continued to share that view. For both working-class and middle-class men, the important cultural boundary was not the line dividing elite men from poor girls but the one dividing respectable girls from those whose conduct was unseemly. Girls who played in the streets and alleys or who were not shocked by sexual overtures made themselves fair game. Even some evangelicals rejected the idea of innate childhood innocence, assuming that little girls could be "depraved and degraded" by nature. Of such girls, reformer Mason Long wrote, "These wretched outcasts are the creatures of the gutter and the pavement from birth. They are 'women of the town' from the beginning; what else is left for them?" Men seeking sexual partners divided girls who were available from those who were off-limits the same way they distinguished respectable women from prostitutes. The difference was that the new law of 1886 defied this "common sense" by establishing an arbitrary rule of age.[9]

The 1886 revision of Iowa's rape law may not have changed the way men interpreted their right of sexual access to young girls, but it altered dramatically the consequences of the accusations made by Ada Ammerman. Without the change, it is not likely that any of the men she named would have faced criminal charges. Ada was ten years old when the events in question took place, Mamie eleven, and Dolly twelve. Had these events taken place five years earlier, a ten-year-old victim's consent—however naive, reluctant, or frightened—would have shielded the men involved from prosecution for rape. But in September 1891 these girls' allegations, given new potency by women's political success, placed three men in jeopardy of spending life in prison.

THE PRESS

From the moment the newspapers broke the story, writers scrambled to assign blame. The *Times* attacked the men involved, calling them "grey-haired fiends" and "strong men who satisfy their lusts by ruining many children." Wielding the same high-octane rhetoric it had previously directed against the Democratic administration and the police department, the *Times* headlined another story, "Villains Entice the Darlings of Our Firesides . . . and Wreck Their Lives and Blight Their Parents' Future." Over the following days and weeks, the *Times* offered the most detailed coverage, even publishing an interview with Ada and Mamie. The *Democrat*'s reporting, in contrast, remained far briefer and more reticent. In assigning responsibility, the *Democrat* simply ignored the men involved. The writer expressed shock at the "depravity" of the girls but laid blame at the feet of their parents. "Children . . . whose parents allow them to run at large without restraint are not to be blamed for going astray. Other people are responsible for their fall." But those "people" were not the men who sought them out for sex, whom the writer never mentioned at all. Instead, the *Democrat* blamed the girls' parents. A third paper, the *Tribune*, also blamed the girls and their parents: "The total amount of depravity in all these cases is simply astonishing and any who has not heard the examination would hardly believe that little girls could be so bad morally. . . . It is perfectly evident . . . that the parents of these girls care but little what becomes of them. Had they the proper feeling for their children there would never have been any occasion for these trials."[10]

In refusing to censure the men, the *Democrat* and the *Tribune* might have insisted that they were simply reserving judgment about three men who were accused but not convicted of sexual assaults. Yet both newspapers took for granted the girls' sexual encounters with some men, if perhaps not the men accused. In declining to criticize these unnamed sexual partners, the *Democrat* and the *Tribune* naturalized a male sexuality that sought gratification from little girls while denouncing the girls and their parents as depraved and unnatural. While the law, urged by women and passed by men whose politics were hardly popular in Davenport, denied men access to girls of ten or twelve, the culture in which most men learned about sex drew different limits. Conduct, reputation, and class, not law and birthdays, separated acceptable partners from unacceptable ones. To the *Democrat* and the *Tribune*, the girls and especially their parents were to blame if men took advantage because men would not feel free to take advantage of girls who conducted themselves properly. Parents, of course, were a familiar target for both papers, which frequently decried the presence of girls on the streets but never acknowledged what made the streets unsafe for girls.[11]

The editor of the *Times* defiantly insisted on the culpability of men. From the beginning, the *Times* tried to maintain that sexual exploitation of girls was common. It reported that Ada had named several more men as partners, and it alleged that "a gentleman" had come forward with information about an "old man who had been abusing little children for about two years." The paper printed the names of other girl victims, including Nellie and Jessie Burns and a girl named Gildea, though the Burns sisters quickly insisted that they knew nothing of abuse. Mamie, Ada, and

Dolly the *Times* portrayed not as wretched urchins but as ordinary, even attractive, children. In its interview with Ada and Mamie, the paper described Ada as "a beautiful child" with a "fair complexion, blue eyes, and frank contenance [sic]." Her "neat figured dress" and black hat trimmed with white flowers and green leaves offered unspoken evidence that she was no neglected child. The writer cast Mamie as a Dickensian waif, a "little, thin, frail looking child" with a freckled face, "sunken chest," and consumptive cough, "more a child to be pitied rather than to be abused."[12]

Throughout the initial hearings, the *Times* published detailed accounts of the testimony. Comparing the *Times* with a few extant court transcripts documents the paper's accuracy. Indeed, a few readers found such accuracy indecent. The paper fended off critics by recording praise for its reports: "One of our ministers," the *Times* informed its readers, "said . . . the press exists for the purpose of telling the people what they have a right to know." The *Times* was perhaps disingenuous in portraying itself as the people's champion, battling forces that would "muzzle" the press. This was a scandal involving several men well known in the community, and the *Times* offered the only detailed coverage. Its lengthy columns on the trials no doubt boosted circulation—though some readers may have been reluctant to carry the paper home to the parlor table. But for all the benefit the paper may have gained from sometimes lurid reporting, the *Times* did not waver in its insistence that the sexual abuse of little girls was a matter for public concern.[13]

Some readers certainly agreed. At a "secret meeting," several "prominent ladies" discussed the trials and what they meant for the city. One of the ladies met with a *Times* reporter, telling him that a few women had at first "sharply censured" the paper "for giving the full details of the degrading trial, but that the verdict is now unanimous in favor of its publication." This lady affirmed "that the eyes of the good people had already been too long closed." The *Times* report is the only notice of this meeting, but its account rings true. The women's reaction to the *Times* coverage echoed responses to Stead's "Maiden Tribute": initial revulsion followed by a political awakening. Further, the girls' accusations raised precisely the kind of issue sure to draw the concern of Davenport's organized women. According to Jennie McCowen, the Women's Alliance (as she always called it) did not disband after winning the appointment of Davenport's police matron but continued to meet at least through 1896. If the arrest of Ollie Kreps had sounded an alarm about girls trading sex to teenage boys for food and entertainment, these charges two years later—that middle-aged men sought sex from girls of ten or twelve—evoked an even more disturbing image of male predation. While the Charitable Alliance did not launch a public campaign in response to these revelations, group members may have played an active role behind the scenes. A few weeks later the *Times* reported that "some of the foremost ladies of the city" were concerned that the defendants had more lawyers than the state and were seeking to enhance the number of prosecutors.[14]

THE TRIALS

Raising the age of consent may not have changed the way some men interpreted their sexual privileges, but the new law had important consequences in the courtroom. When the victim had passed the age of consent, prosecutors had to establish the identity of the assailant, the use of force, the victim's resistance, and her nonconsent. Prosecutors also had to corroborate the assault through evidence other than the victim's testimony. Defendants had every right to impeach a complaining witness's credibility by introducing evidence about her character and sexual history. And judges routinely warned juries that women lied about rape: "Rape is an accusation easily to be made and hard to be proved, and harder to be defended by the party accused, tho never so innocent," was the standard formula. Jurors may have believed this warning, but it was far from true. Women rarely made accusations of rape because the trial was so humiliating and the chance of conviction so slender. In Scott County, forty-seven victims brought charges of rape or "assault with intent to rape" between 1880 and 1910, but only seven of those victims were over the age of fifteen. Of the seven trials, just four ended in conviction. In one of those four cases, the state board of pardons suspended the sentences of the two convicted assailants even before they went to the penitentiary.[15]

When the victim was under the age of consent, proving rape in the courtroom became much simpler. Prosecutors had to establish only the age of the victim, the identity of the assailant, and the fact of vaginal penetration, however slight, by his penis. Resistance, the use of force, and the victim's consent became irrelevant, though the corroboration requirement and the warning to the jury remained in place. Physicians played a key role in child-rape cases. They acted as experts, testifying to the condition of the victim's genitals and the likelihood of penetration, and as witnesses to the victim's birth, verifying her age. When sexual contact involved something other than intercourse, juries could convict the assailant of a lesser charge such as assault with intent to rape.[16]

As the accusations made by Ada, Mamie, and Dolly moved into the courtroom, the prosecutors built their cases on the presumptions of rape law. They called physicians to establish that the girls had been abused and used other witnesses to corroborate the girls' testimony about their movements and their encounters with the accused men. Yet as the trials unfolded, a story emerged that disturbed most listeners. Instead of a melodrama of wicked men and innocent girls, some heard a pornographic tale of vicious girls and ordinary men.

The first evidence in the preliminary hearings came from physicians, who confirmed that all three girls had experienced recent sexual intercourse. Ada's mother had taken her to Dr. P. M. Bracelin, who saw her in his office on Wednesday, 16 September, two days after Ada first made her accusations. His examination verified that her genitals were "much inflamed" and in pain—evidence, he said, of her very recent "abuse." Bracelin then examined Mamie Woods and Dolly Hamerly at the house of detention, determining that they too had recently been abused. Of Mamie he testified that her sexual experience had left her in such a painful condition that he "could not make a very thorough examination without the use of opiates." A second physician, Dr. J. A. DeArmond, examined all three girls at the house of detention and reached a similar conclusion. DeArmond testified that the girls' bodies were sexually immature. Ada's body, he said, was "frail & slight" with the "beginning of hair on the mons." Mamie's development was "such as is found in children." Dolly was only slightly more developed.[17]

As witness followed witness to the stand, the events of that week gradually took shape. Mamie Woods was the first to run away, on Monday of fair week when her mother sent her to deliver a bundle of clean clothes to a fifteen-year-old sister who worked as a domestic. Anna Woods, searching for her missing daughter, heard that Mamie had ridden the *Verne Swain* upriver. Dolly Hamerly and her nine-year-old sister, Rosa, ran away to join Mamie on Thursday, and the three girls slept that night in a shed behind a fruit-and-candy store on Perry Street. On Friday morning, Ada met the girls on her way to school and decided to run away as well. That afternoon, about the time John Matlock was at the police station giving Chief Kessler money to advertise for Ada, his stepdaughter and her three companions were on the *Verne Swain* with George Haikes. Haikes took Mamie and Ada into the water closets on the boat and had sexual intercourse with them. The Matlocks were not the only ones out searching. Mary Hamerly, Dolly's and Rosa's mother, caught up with her daughters on the boat. "I first saw them downstairs near where Haikes was working and when they saw me they ran upstairs and hid in the water closets," she testified. "I told Haikes that I would make trouble for him if he kept bringing those girls down there. He only laughed at me." Mary Hamerly marched her daughters home, but two hours later, they slipped out again and joined Ada and Mamie. The four girls rode the streetcar out to the fairgrounds racetrack and climbed over a barbed-wire fence to get in. The Matlocks soon showed up, searching for Ada, so the girls fled to the barn and hid in one of Henry Carpenter's horse stalls. Carpenter told John Matlock he had not seen Ada. Thwarted, the Matlocks continued their search elsewhere, and the girls came out of hiding and climbed onto a wagon to watch the horse races. After dark, Zip Hamerly, Dolly's brother, found them and brought them home once again. The meeting was not cordial: Zip carried a stick and threatened to wallop the girls.[18]

Ada and Mamie rode back on the streetcar with the Hamerlys but did not go home. Instead, they wandered up Perry Street, mingling with the crowd outside the Burtis Opera House and stopping to rest on the steps of the old Baptist Church. As evening fell, they met Charles Lyon, who warned them that Ada's mother was out in her rig looking for them. The two girls asked if they could sleep that night in Henry

The *Verne Swain*. George Haikes was the engineer on this packet boat, where some of the rapes occurred. (Putnam Museum of History and Natural Science, Davenport, Iowa.)

Carpenter's horse barn, just up the street, where Lyon had a room in the loft. "Is there something in it to have you sleep there?" Mamie recalled his asking. He took them up to his room, where, as Mamie testified, "He took my drawers down, lifted my dress and stuck his 'pedee' into mine." Ada testified that he had intercourse with her as well. Lyon left them to return to the fairgrounds, where Carpenter had racehorses stabled overnight. He locked the barn behind him, and the two girls slept that night on Lyon's cot. Mamie testified that Carpenter came into the loft in the early morning, just after a heavy rain, and asked, "Who is here?" then saw them and said, "Oh! it is Ada." He had sex first with Ada, then with Mamie.[19]

Later that morning, Ada and Mamie wandered out once more. In the early afternoon, they met George Haikes again and rode the streetcar to Schuetzen Park. Haikes had intercourse with Ada in the park and gave her seventy-five cents, telling her to cut off her long hair. Dolly Hamerly spent the morning doing wash at home, but by afternoon she had run off with Ada and Mamie again and the three returned to Carpenter's barn. Around four o'clock, Lyon took the three up to his loft room. There on the cot, Dolly testified, "He took Ada on his lap. He opened her panties and opened his pants and then he put his pedie into hers." Dolly remembered

Perry street, looking south, c. 1884. Mamie and Ada were resting on the steps of the Baptist Church in the foreground when Charles Lyon invited them to sleep in Carpenter's barn. (Painting by Thomas G. Moses, collection of the author.)

laughing at Ada. "He put his hand on her back and commenced moving her up and down and then she jumped off." Ada laughed when he did the same to Dolly. Mamie did not laugh, and, probably already in pain from her injuries, she refused to be touched. "Then he went down stairs but would not pay us and we took his $1.25," Dolly reported. When Lyon detected the theft, the girls pretended to find the money in the straw and returned it to him.[20]

Afterwards, in the alley, they met Carpenter, who gave them a quarter. They took their riches to the candy store and then Ada went to a hairdresser and had her curls cut off. That night they returned to Carpenter's barn again, but it was locked, so they slept on a pile of straw in the barnyard. Around five in the morning, Lyon found them and chased them away. They spent Sunday playing in the river and slept that night in another barn. On Monday afternoon, Lucy Matlock finally caught up with them.[21]

Various witnesses corroborated the girls' stories. Dolly's mother had seen the girls with Haikes on the *Verne Swain* on Friday. Lena Kasch, whose husband rented the horse barn to Carpenter, saw Ada and Mamie at the barn on Friday evening and

Ada, Mamie, and Dolly there on Saturday afternoon. Her ten-year-old son and several other children reported seeing the three girls with Lyon at the barn on Saturday, when he was supposed to have taken them upstairs. A policeman confirmed sharing the streetcar with Ada, Mamie, and Haikes as they returned from Schuetzen Park on Saturday afternoon.[22]

From the distance of more than a century, evaluating the credibility of evidence is far from easy. Still, several elements of the girls' stories made them convincing. For example, Ada and Mamie knew that Lyon had not slept in Carpenter's barn on Friday night, something they probably would not have known unless they were in the barn when he left and locked it. The girls also reported that Carpenter came into the barn after a heavy rain, placing his arrival at around four in the morning. Both Carpenter and his wife testified that he rarely slept well in the later part of the night, and he admitted that it was his regular habit to leave his rooms at Third and Brady and stop at a saloon for a drink at about three or four A.M. before going to his barn. He simply insisted that he had not done so that particular Saturday morning. Finally, all of the girls, as they described how the men performed sexual acts, resisted the efforts of attorneys to impose a conventional "missionary position" on their experiences. For example, defense attorney George Gould asked Mamie, "Now about this cot that you tell about. Did he lay on top of the girls on it?" Mamie replied, "No sir, he took the girls and sat them on his lap." Gould persisted, "Didn't lay on top of you at all then?" "No sir." In spite of both prosecuting and defense attorneys' certainty that sex must take place lying down, the girls most often described the men as either seated or standing during sex. Had they been inventing their stories or responding to adult coaching, the girls would likely have adopted the adults' ideas about sexual positions.[23]

THE DEFENSE

Rape law offered several defense strategies to the accused men. They could show that the girls were all at least thirteen or provide alibis proving the men were elsewhere at the times of the alleged rapes. But in each case attorneys built their primary defense on something else entirely: impeaching the morals of the girls and their parents. The girls' reputation for chastity had no bearing on the charge of rape because all three were under the age of consent. The rules of evidence, however, permitted the defense to introduce evidence of "character" that might reflect on the girls' truthfulness. The girls were often the best witnesses for the defense. As the trials progressed, their testimony contributed to a growing impression that they had not been "ruined" in a single weekend by three "grey-haired fiends." Instead, each girl had been introduced to sexual activity months earlier, and they gave little evidence of being forced, coerced, or even unwilling. The men who sat in the jury box could hardly help making judgments about what they heard.[24]

Ada Ammerman testified that the previous spring, fourteen-year-old Della Wood had taken her to Carpenter's old stables behind the Ackley House hotel, where, as Ada watched, Della did "something bad" with Carpenter, for which she was paid a half dollar. During the races in July, Carpenter had asked Mrs. Matlock if he could take Ada riding out to the racetrack. Alone with Ada in the barn, he offered her a quarter to do "something bad" and had sexual contact with her. In her testimony, Mrs. Matlock recalled that when Ada came home, she "looked as if she had been crying," and the next day a man came to warn her, "Carpenter is the ruination of little girls. He is always giving them pennies and money and things." Ada testified that a week later, Carpenter took her to a house on Brady Street and again had intercourse. In August, Della Wood took Ada to see Lyon at Carpenter's barn. "He took me into a back stall and stood up and held me in his arms and had intercourse with me," said the formal language of Ada's deposition. Dolly testified that in late August, she accompanied Ada to the county courthouse, where they met George Haikes. Haikes took the girls up to the courthouse tower and had sex with Ada there.[25]

Mamie too had been introduced to Lyon by Della Wood. The previous spring, Mamie accompanied Della when the older girl wanted to earn some money for bells to wear to the Turner Hall masquerades. A fourteen-year-old like Della had few opportunities to earn spending money for small luxuries, but she had learned something men paid for. She may have brought her friends along to share her secret with them, because the men asked her to introduce them to other girls, or simply because she liked having company. In all the girls' testimony, only Ada ever mentioned going anywhere or doing anything without another girl companion. One consequence of this was that nearly every sex act had at least one eyewitness.[26]

The defense strategy focused not just on the girls' sexual experiences but on depicting the girls and their families in the worst possible light: vulgar, dishonest, even criminal. When Dolly took the witness stand, attorney Ruel Cook attacked even her appearance, attempting to show that the girl had been "rigged out for the occasion, and that the dressmaker had not yet been paid for her sewing." He prodded Dolly to use crude language, asking her if she had not called Mrs. Kasch a "son of a bitch." Dolly denied it, saying she had called Kasch "a chippie because she called us dirty brats." But Dolly hardly needed coaxing; the only language she knew for sex was far from refined. When defense attorney L. M. Fisher asked her about previous sexual experiences, even the sympathetic *Times* reported that Dolly's statement was "in such vile language as to cause even the oldest men to cast their eyes to the floor." Dolly testified to having sexual relations with several men over the course of the summer, including Haikes, a cook named Andy on the *Verne Swain*, and a man named Thomas Welcher. Attorney W. K. White, cross-examining Dolly's father, brought in John Hamerly's arrest record and a felony conviction and attempted to get him to admit having one of his children committed to the "house of correction."[27]

Ironically, the most electrifying testimony came when the defense attorneys did not expect it. During cross-examination, the defense attorney asked Dolly about the theft of $1.25 from Lyon's pocket in the barn, probably hoping to reinforce the jurors' perception that she was a thief. But her answers raised new questions.

> Q.—What did you mean Dollie, by saying that Lyon would not pay you?
> A.—Why, he was sitting us down and taking us on his lap, and then he would not pay us afterwards.
> Q.—Was he to pay you?
> A.—Yes.
> Q.—Did he say so?
> A.—No. He didn't tell us whether he would pay us or not. We never do anything that way for nothing. We wouldn't do it.

As the defense attorney pursued the matter, Dolly explained the arrangement the girls had worked out: "One time when we went to the fair ground he told us whenever he did anything, he would always pay us for it."[28]

The judge struck Dolly's testimony from the official record because it tended to incriminate her, but the message was lost on no one. Dolly's words meant that the girls were not innocent victims but prostitutes. For those whose understanding of prostitution was shaped by W. T. Stead's "Maiden Tribute," Dolly's explanation no doubt confirmed their worst fears about grown men who sought out little girls and led them into sin. But for others, Dolly's words simply established that these girls had long since crossed the line that separated good women from the fallen. Though only ten or twelve, they were already, as defense attorney George Gould called them, "strumpets."[29]

Redefining the girls as prostitutes was one strategy, but Gould and his fellow attorneys also strove to vilify the girls' families. Gould used his cross-examination of Lucy Matlock to raise questions about the death of Ada's father, trying to cast Lucy as a member of a criminal gang. As the *Times* reported it, Mrs. Matlock "broke down and cried" at the mention of Charles Ammerman's name. " 'You people have abused my child,' she said, 'but do not abuse my dead husband.' " Lucy Matlock's anguish stemmed from what must have been vivid, harrowing memories. Seven years earlier, Lucy had been seated next to Charles in an open rig when her sister's husband blasted a shotgun, at close range, into Charles's face. As the startled horses jerked her out of the line of fire, a second blast wounded Lucy's arm and side. The investigation revealed his motive. Lucy's brother-in-law, William Riddle, had burglarized a store. Charles and Lucy had discovered the crime and hidden some evidence, agreeing between themselves to keep the matter secret for the sake of Lucy's sister. When Riddle discovered that they knew and had kept evidence against him, he resolved to kill them both. Defense attorney Gould certainly wanted the jury to remember a notorious episode that linked Mrs. Matlock with a burglary, a murder, and a conspiracy to hide a crime, but his attempt may have backfired. The memory of a country road "bespattered" with her husband's "brains and pieces of skull bones" must have been devastating, and Lucy Matlock's tears were surely genuine.[30]

This was not the end of Gould's probing, however. He next attempted to get Mrs. Matlock to admit that her current husband was known as "Toboggan Jack" and that he had kept a saloon in Rock Island called the "Toboggan Slide" where a scandalous shooting involving a prostitute had taken place two years earlier. Mrs. Matlock vehemently insisted that she had never heard her husband called Toboggan Jack and that he never kept a saloon in Rock Island. Rock Island city directories, at least, support her in that.[31]

If Gould's first two attempts to smear the Matlock family had fallen short of their target, the third hit dead-on. Pressing Mrs. Matlock about her occupation in Rock Island before moving to Davenport, Gould asked if she had not kept a house "resorted to for purposes of prostitution." Mrs. Matlock replied, "I can say I had boarders. Very likely they didn't do just exactly right."

> Q.—You kept boarders that didn't do just right?
> A.—I suppose they were a little foxie like you are some times.
> Q.—What do you mean by being a "little foxy"?
> A.—Going out instead of attending to their own business.
> Q.—You mean by being "a little foxy," that they were on the order of prostitutes. Is that what you mean? You kept that sort of boarders?
> A.—I suppose they were that kind.[32]

Like many single mothers, the widowed Lucy Ammerman kept boarders to support her family. Her first husband had been a peddler, unlikely even to have insurance for his family. His murder left Lucy with two small children and a third on the way. As a struggling boardinghouse keeper, Lucy Ammerman could not afford to be choosy about her boarders, so like Josie Mitchell and Emma Webb, she took some boarders who were "a little foxy," accepting the risk to her own and her daughter's reputation. Lucy Ammerman was lucky in one thing, however. Among her boarders in Rock Island were John Matlock and his father. Matlock married his landlady, and the two combined their resources to open the saloon and boardinghouse in Davenport. Gould could not get Mrs. Matlock to admit that any of her current boarders were "a little foxy," but John Matlock's saloon stood at the corner of Third and Iowa, in the triangle known as Bucktown. If Mrs. Matlock did not have prostitutes boarding in her Davenport home, she certainly had them as neighbors.

Casting Mrs. Matlock as a criminal and a brothel keeper supported the defense effort to portray her daughter as a prostitute, but it furthered another strategy as well. Shortly after news of Ada's charges first broke in the papers, George Gould began telling the press that "he knew all about the case and that there was something behind it." He even predicted that the grand jury might not even bother to take up the case. He was wrong, of course, but throughout the trials, the defense attorneys strove to suggest that the girls' claims of rape were nothing more than an attempt to extort money from Henry Carpenter and George Haikes, cooked up by Mrs. Matlock and the parents of Dolly and Mamie. (No one claimed that the parents were demanding money from Charles Lyon, since everyone admitted he had none.)[33]

Based on their extortion theory, the defense raised questions about the role of the police matron. They repeatedly claimed that Matron Davis was exercising undue influence on Mamie and Dolly, who remained in Davis's custody at the house of detention throughout the preliminary hearings and the trials. Ruel Cook argued that if the girls were removed from police custody, "there would be an immediate change in the case."[34]

Testimony suggests that someone was indeed tampering with witnesses, but it was not Annie Davis. When fourteen-year-old Della Wood was called as a witness during the preliminary hearings, the newspapers agreed that she had nothing of significance to add to the case. "In fact," reported the *Tribune*, "there was apparently no reason for calling her." But two months later, when the first trial opened, Della had a stunning new story to tell. On the witness stand, Della reported that "Mamie Woods had told her that she was going to help Ada Ammerman send the men over the road, and that she was going to swear to a lot of lies when she was placed on the stand." Della further testified that "Mamie had told her that Miss Davis, the police matron, had told her what to testify to." Another girl, Florence Gale, reported that Dolly Hamerly had admitted that "her mother and others had a scheme to obtain money" from the defendants. When the attorney asked Dolly if she had said this, she "bristled up and replied, 'No! I'd box her ears if I had her here.'" Apparently feeling that her denial was not strong enough, Dolly slipped out after she left the witness stand and brought Florence back into the courtroom. "Squaring up before the jury," reported the *Democrat*, Dolly commanded Florence: "Now you just say that to the jury!"[35]

Neither Della Wood nor Florence Gale had testified about extortion schemes or perjury during the preliminary hearings, even though defense attorney George Gould was already suggesting these theories to the press. Their dramatic revelations two months later may shed more light on why Mamie and Dolly were confined in the house of detention for four months than on what either girl actually said. In the two years since Della Wood's family had moved to Davenport from Muscatine, she had lived, among other places, upstairs from a Bucktown saloon and in the seedy neighborhood along Front Street. Her stepfather, she testified, sold watermelons and "worked" for a living, but it was clearly not a very good living. Della had learned that sex could earn money for small pleasures, but the prosecutors suggested that her involvement in prostitution went further. They claimed that she supported her parents and that her parents had threatened to beat her if she told the police she had had sex with Thomas Welcher. Even if those claims were untrue, Della's destitution was such that friends of the defendants could easily have bribed her to tell a useful story on the witness stand. Florence Gale's identity is less easy to establish, but only two Gale households were listed in the Davenport city directory around that time. One was headed by Parker Gale, a traveling salesman who had previously lived in South Rock Island, where a "Miss Flora Gale" worked in the Graham Cotton Mill. If Florence Gale lived in the Parker Gale household, that placed her just a block down Front Street from Della Wood, in the same tough neighborhood and probably in equally straitened circumstances.[36]

The ease with which men with money could obtain sex—or perjury—from penniless girls helps explain why Mamie and Dolly stayed in the house of detention all those months. Matron Davis probably feared correctly that, if released, Mamie and Dolly would be subject to the same pressures that swayed the testimony of Della Wood and Florence Gale. *Ada's* mother, after all, had launched the entire process by sending her husband to swear out complaints for rape, and Ada awaited the trials at home with her family. Mrs. Hamerly certainly suspected what was going on, as her warning to Haikes suggests. "I would make trouble for him if he kept bringing those girls down there," is hardly the threat of a mother who supposes her daughters are just getting a riverboat ride. Mamie's mother had spent days looking for her own daughter before Ada ran away. Yet neither Mrs. Hamerly nor Mrs. Woods went to the police until after Mrs. Matlock had set the charges in motion.

Money may not have been the only motive shaping Della's and Florence's testimony. In other cases involving sex between men and girls, families resisted bringing charges against men in their social circle. For example, when Elsie Mae Hurto's mother sent her to fetch a pail of beer from a neighborhood saloon, bartender Buck Timothy pulled the eleven-year-old into a back room and raped her. Neighbors testified that Elsie's mother kept a house of assignation, frequented by known prostitutes and sporting men, including Buck Timothy. Though neighbors and physicians gave depositions, no one from Elsie's family cooperated in the case. Indeed, before it came to trial, Elsie's family spirited her across the river into Illinois, effectively halting the prosecution and protecting Timothy. If Della Wood's parents did threaten her, they may have been attempting to protect Thomas Welcher just as Hurto's mother protected Timothy. Dolly Hamerly also admitted to having sex with Welcher, but Welcher never faced a charge of rape in Scott County. Parents' motives in these cases are difficult to judge. Did they simply accept their daughters' sexual activity as inevitable or inconsequential? Did they feel loyalty toward the men accused? Or did they keep silent because they feared retaliation? Any of these factors may have made the Woods and Hamerly families unwilling to cooperate.[37]

THE VERDICTS

In the end, the justice system sided with those, like defense attorney Ruel Cook, who saw the girls as prostitutes, unnatural and undomestic creatures who "slept in the dirt piles in the several alleys" and "preferred the refuse of the stables for beds rather than to remain at home." Charles Lyon's trial for raping Dolly Hamerly was the first to end, and the jury returned a conviction not for rape but for simple assault, which carried a maximum penalty of thirty days in jail. Observers found this outcome perplexing. No one ever suggested that Lyon had beaten Dolly, for example, only that he was guilty of sexual contact which, given Dolly's age, could only be rape. The *Tribune* puzzled, "It is rather a queer verdict, . . . as the man is either guilty as he is charged or he is not guilty at all." The *Times* argued, "most certainly the girls were not to be believed in part, but fully or not at all. If the jury believed him as nearly innocent, then why impose [a] thirty-day imprisonment?" especially since Lyon, too poor to make bail, had already spent three months in jail.[38]

The second trial to conclude was of George Haikes. This jury returned a verdict of guilty and imposed a five-year penitentiary sentence. The defense immediately appealed the conviction, citing errors by the judge. Then John Streckfus, captain of the *Verne Swain*, came forward with ship's logs, which he said proved that Haikes was repairing machinery at the times he was alleged to be with the girls. Streckfus announced that he had "fifty men to conclusively prove the alibi," though neither the logs nor the witnesses had been introduced in the original trial.[39]

When the third trial ended in acquittal for Henry Carpenter, a reporter for the *Times* sought out a member of the jury, who explained that the girls' morals had settled the case. "The whole jury did not acquit him because they thought him innocent, but the character of the witnesses made the jurors feel like letting him go," the man explained. In the jury room, men were inclined to identify with the defendants and feel repelled by the girls. "Some of the jurors . . . have been a little wild themselves, and they were not anxious to convict him. [They] thought the girls were bad, which influenced them," reported the juror. After Lyon's conviction for assault, the judge moved his remaining trials to Muscatine on a change of venue. There, the local newspaper complained, "One would think that the county attorney would tire of nauseating the community with cases of this kind that are devoid of all decency when there appears to be so little in them." When Lyon was acquitted in the first of these trials, the state dropped all remaining charges against the men. Almost immediately, the *Tribune* editorialized, "it does seem as if Haikes should be released." The *Times* reported that a petition for the engineer's pardon would get support from nine members of the jury that convicted him, the county attorney, the judge, and "a large portion of the citizens." The report was apparently accurate; Haikes received his pardon just a few months later.[40]

Reformers had hoped to use rape law to cut off the recruitment of prostitutes and focus attention on predatory men as the source of social and sexual danger. But the jurors in these rape trials were inclined to view things differently. Mamie, Ada, and Dolly were already "bad," so men who took advantage of this were "a little wild"—sporting men, perhaps—but not criminally culpable in the sense that a charge of rape implied. This explains their decision to convict Lyon only of assault and the readiness of judge, jurors, and "citizens" to petition immediately for Haikes's pardon. The jurors, it seemed, believed that the men had done something wrong but also felt that the wrong was not serious because the girls were "bad." Iowa legislator C. H. Robinson, opposing an effort to raise the age of consent, expressed a view of child prostitutes these men clearly shared. "It is a fact as true as it is deplorable, that the majority of the inmates of houses of ill-fame have fallen long before they have arrived at that age," he declared. Changing the law "would render a man or boy liable to imprisonment for life for yielding to the solicitation of a prostitute[,] a punishment so enormous as compared with the offence that it needs no argument to condemn it." To this man, a girl "fell" not because some man pushed her but because of her character. For some girls, to fall was inevitable. Men should not be harshly punished for what was, after all, human nature.[41]

Sharing the view that prostitutes were naturally bad and that men's "venereal desires" could not be suppressed without risk to health or society, men like the jurors in these cases tended to be sympathetic toward those who "yielded" to a juvenile prostitute. Even the attorneys who lined up to defend Carpenter, Haikes, and Lyon continually affirmed that they had taken the cases because they believed the men wrongly accused. Lyon had no money to pay an attorney, but W. K. White told the papers that he and his fellow counsel were defending Lyon without pay "from principle's sake" because they believed him innocent. George Gould insisted that "he was absolutely positive in his own mind that Carpenter [was] perfectly innocent," hinting darkly of a conspiracy behind the charges. Attorneys, of course, have an obligation to speak in their clients' best interests, but these men may have been especially disposed to share their clients' point of view. Perhaps Mrs. Matlock was just lashing out at Gould for his harsh cross-examination, but when he asked if she "kept boarders that didn't do just right," her reply, "I suppose they were a little foxie *like you are some times*," certainly meant to imply that Gould's conduct was not above reproach. By taking her insinuation to mean that the boarders were "on the order of prostitutes," Gould seemed to confirm her innuendo. George Gould died suddenly in the interval between the preliminary hearings and the trials, and his place in the defense was filled by William Chamberlin, who had lampooned Belva Lockwood by portraying her in the garb of a prostitute. Chamberlin and Gould may have been eminently respectable attorneys, but they also participated in a male culture that scorned the politics of Prohibition and "protection." They may have shared, or at least found sympathetic, the sporting man's view of sexuality: that men were tempted and victimized by prostitutes, not the reverse.[42]

THE CONSPIRACY

Ada Ammerman's September 1891 charges ushered in a bitter season for the victims, the accused, and the city itself. Mamie and Dolly languished almost nineteen weeks in the house of detention, cut off from their families and from the liberty to roam the streets they had always taken for granted. Their parents watched them testify about the sordid details of sexual activities, then took the stand themselves, with humiliating consequences. Charles Lyon spent at least four months imprisoned at the county jail. George Haikes's employer considered the engineer so essential to operating the *Verne Swain* that Haikes awaited the trials in relative freedom and comfort, but his conviction sent him to the penitentiary for several months. Two years after a pardon unlocked the gates, police in Davenport accused him of keeping two young girls in a downtown room "for immoral purposes." Henry Carpenter had money enough for bail, and his jury returned a "not guilty" verdict, but he still anguished over whether "he would ever be respected again." Any of them might have felt anger at the Matlock family; any of them might have sought to settle the score. Henry Carpenter's friends did just that.[43]

In February 1892, less than three weeks after the last of the trials had ended, police arrested John Matlock on a charge of keeping a house of ill-fame. Adelbert DeMaranville, twenty-eight, swore out the complaint, and when the case came before Justice Bleik Peters, the primary witness was twenty-three-year-old Lafe Keller. Keller was the son and DeMaranville the son-in-law of brothel keeper Josie Mitchell. The *Times*, in its report, noted that DeMaranville was "not eligible for membership in the Y.M.C.A.," a wry understatement regarding a man who lived off his wife's earnings as a prostitute. Keller, the reporter observed, "to the shame of manhood ... was willing to testify to his own depravity." For sporting men such as Keller and DeMaranville, testifying against an alleged house of ill-fame was unheard of; complaints in such cases usually came from the police or from disgruntled neighbors. These men were neither. Already notorious, neither Keller nor DeMaranville had much credibility in court. That day, John Matlock went home.[44]

Three days later, police again arrested Matlock, this time on a charge of robbery. Henry Hass, the arresting officer, humiliated Matlock by marching him "through the business streets" of Davenport to the police station, where he was "imprisoned... for a considerable period of time." This was not the last time Matlock found himself in court. After yet another complaint—this time that Lucy Matlock kept a house of ill-fame—Matlock went on the offensive. He hired an attorney and sued Hass.[45]

Any of the charges against Matlock and his wife could have resulted in a penitentiary sentence, but none ended in conviction. No grand jury even issued a bill of indictment. Instead, Matlock claimed, all the arrests were part of a scheme of harassment led by Hass, who had "conspired and confederated" with others "to injure plaintiff and his family and to drive them from their home in this city, and to cause charges to be brought against plaintiff and his wife and to send them to the penitentiary." The conspirators were "one Henry Carpenter, one Demaranville, and one Joe." The motive, Matlock maintained, was retaliation.[46]

Matlock suspected his antagonists not just of harassment but of protecting his daughter's rapists. Hass, he said, "with three other policemen," was "very conspicuous in defense of said Carpenter." The policemen "have repeatedly testified against members of plaintiff's family, in the courts of this and Muscatine Counties." Further, "as peace officers" Hass and the other policemen "did all in their power to aid in the defense of said Carpenter and others charged with similar offenses." Matlock believed that Carpenter went free because police officers had schemed against Matlock, using their power to influence the outcome of the trials.[47]

Hass responded by hiring his own lawyer, William Chamberlin. The case of *Matlock v. Hass* never came to trial, and the police and justice court records for 1892 have been lost, so it is impossible to know exactly what evidence Matlock had for his claims. Yet circumstances suggest that Matlock's suspicions were reasonable. Della Wood and Florence Gale certainly changed their testimony to the benefit of Carpenter. More important, Henry Hass had a history of zealous, even reckless loyalty, and two years earlier, police officers had plotted with a brothel keeper to exact revenge against another thorn in their side.

In November and December 1889, the long-simmering feud between *Times* city editor R. W. O'Meara and Police Chief Frank Kessler had boiled over. Kessler ejected O'Meara from police court, and the editor responded by bringing a charge of assault and battery against the chief. Kessler was tried, found guilty, and fined. In the aftermath, policeman Henry Hass attempted to beat up a man who had publicly criticized Chief Kessler. The incident might have ended there, but when the *Times* reported it, O'Meara went on to allege that "Madam Van Ness," a well-known brothel keeper, received police protection "for favors granted." Four days later, police arrested O'Meara in the company of Van Ness and charged him as an inmate of a house of ill-fame. When O'Meara finally got out of jail, he responded in print. "For private revenge," he wrote, the two police officers "aided and abetted Madam Van Ness to entice" O'Meara into a known brothel so that he could be arrested.

Over the following weeks, police singled out O'Meara for arrest again and again, suggesting that the police were more than willing to use their power against a vicious critic. Within a few months, the police had literally banished O'Meara from town. According to the *Democrat*, officers "led [O'Meara] to this end of the bridge" and told him "to get to the other end of it and return no more." When John Matlock alleged that the police wanted to "drive [his family] from their home in this city," he had precedent for his claim.[48]

From the historian's perspective, other evidence suggests that Matlock's claims were true. The third conspirator named by Matlock, "Joe," was brothel keeper Josie Mitchell. (She was Josie Robison at the time, her fourth or fifth surname—no wonder Matlock stuck with the one name of which he was certain.) As chapter 4 discusses, Mitchell had drifted into brothel keeping in the 1880s as an illiterate divorced mother with five children to support. By the early 1890s, all of her children were old enough to work, and "feeble-minded" Lyman resided in a state home. She was in a position to get out of the brothel business, and indeed, she claimed to earn "an honest and competent living" running a boardinghouse and restaurant. She had certainly avoided arrest for more than seven months when suddenly, on 8 February 1892, police once again arrested her. Just ten days later, her son and son-in-law were in court testifying against John and Lucy Matlock. Was it coincidence, or were DeMaranville and Hass collaborating to force Mitchell and her son to cooperate in the campaign against Matlock? Just a few weeks later, about the time Matlock named her as a conspirator in his lawsuit, Josie Mitchell tried to kill herself. Her suicide attempt may have been a symptom of chronic depression—hardly unexpected, given her personal history. Still, Mitchell had apparently successfully reclaimed her life in recent months. A suicide attempt at that point might reflect the grim, growing recognition that others more powerful—Hass, DeMaranville, Carpenter—had wrenched the strings of her fate from her hands. Precarious as her financial condition was, to face the expense of hiring a lawyer and perhaps paying a judgment, knowing all the while that she could easily be forced into the same position again and again, may have been more than Mitchell could face.[49]

After her recovery from the suicide attempt, police arrested Mitchell twice more that spring as the grand jury heard evidence against Mrs. Matlock. Were the arrests to compel further testimony, perhaps from Mitchell herself? If Henry Hass and Adelbert DeMaranville did use police power to blackmail Josie Mitchell into cooperating, it would hardly be surprising. Josie Washburn, who kept a brothel in Lincoln, Nebraska, in the 1890s, reflected at length on the vulnerability of prostitutes to police blackmail. "Our women," she wrote, "must abide by whatever the police require, regardless of law or justice." Still, these coincidences may be just that, and Josie Mitchell may have simply drifted back into prostitution after Charles Robison left her. But after Matlock's lawsuit was withdrawn, Mitchell was not arrested again for more than a year, when Adelbert DeMaranville decided to contest

Mitchell's custody of his children in October 1893. Based on this evidence, John Matlock's suspicions look well founded, and Adelbert DeMaranville looks like a sporting man well set with the police.[50]

Finally, Ada's accusations and John Matlock's lawsuit had consequences for the city itself. While city counsel papers do not record debates or discussions, several fragments of information suggest that Matlock's claims of a police conspiracy caught the attention of the mayor and aldermen. In June 1892, the council specifically ordered Chief Kessler to enforce the rules for police conduct. Without a suspicion that some members of the force were flouting the rules, such an order would hardly seem necessary. Then in July, Henry Hass lost his job on the police force. The council papers are silent on the reason for Hass's departure, but the timing links it to Matlock's charges. Matlock, in turn, dropped his lawsuit during the next term of court, apparently satisfied that he had accomplished his purpose. If the mayor and aldermen took seriously Matlock's claim that police officers were conspiring with prostitutes and sporting men, the elected officials may have been ready to reconsider the long-standing policy of tolerating downtown brothels. When a new mayor took office the following spring, he immediately turned his attention to both the police force and the policy of toleration. The result of his efforts is the subject of the next chapter.[51]

THE CONSEQUENCES

In the years following the rape trials of 1891–92, Ada Ammerman stayed out of the house of detention and out of the public eye. Neither can be said for Dolly Hamerly and Mamie Woods. The trials turned both girls into public figures. Each subsequent arrest offered a new opportunity for the newspapers to remind readers of the girls' history and to evoke the social threat they embodied. When Dolly, Mamie, and Mrs. Hamerly were arrested as vagrants the following autumn, *The Democrat* called them a "batch of viragoes" and declared, "the sooner they are disposed of the sooner disturbance here will be reduced." A year later, the paper warned its readers that Dolly was "a graduate of the schools of vice. There is nothing now remaining for her to learn in their dark curriculum." Since her last appearance in the public eye, "she has gone hopelessly downward and has been the means of dragging with her more than one of the unguarded youths of the city." The transformation of Dolly Hamerly was complete. Where once reformers had seen a child in need of protection, now the public saw a vicious wanton who threatened young men.[52]

In truth, Dolly's chances were never very good. She probably learned as much about prostitution at home as from Charles Lyon or Della Wood. John Hamerly,

Dolly's father, was the son of old settlers, a skilled tradesman, and a Civil War veteran, attributes that might have made him a solidly respectable member of the community. But this was far from true. Perhaps his troubles began in the horror of the Confederate prison at Andersonville, where he suffered through the end of the Civil War. Certainly his marriage only added to his afflictions. Police arrested a drunken Mary Hamerly so often that the clerk, in disgust, gave up identifying her as a housewife and in the space for occupation wrote, "drinking beer." John Hamerly had his brushes with the law, but his record was minor compared with those accrued by his wife and family. Of nine children, at least seven spent time in police custody, including little Bennie, picked up for public drunkenness at the age of seven. Dolly's brother, Zip, served time in the penitentiary and eventually died of the effects of cocaine. His widow, Mabel, ran a brothel. Five years after the trials, Dolly's younger sister, Rosa, was arrested as a streetwalker. By 1915, both Mary Hamerly and Zip's widow lived in the asylum run by the Sisters of Mercy, confined as "insane."[53]

"Dysfunctional" does not begin to describe this family. For Dolly, prostitution may even have provided stability she did not find at home. In the summer following the rape trials, police arrested Dolly and Rosa as inmates of Mary Artelle's "resort," and the *Democrat* reported that Dolly had been dividing her time between home and the brothel for weeks. Then came her arrest with her mother and Mamie for vagrancy. Several efforts to send Dolly and Mamie to the State Industrial School for Girls at Mitchellville failed. Mamie eluded the plan by fleeing, probably across the river to Illinois. Errors in court documents freed Dolly, and her family promptly sent her to live with an uncle in Clinton, Iowa. But the following September, two years after Dolly first came into custody as a witness in the rape trials, the police finally found the evidence they needed to have her committed to Mitchellville. Dolly brought it to the police station herself: two notes, one from her father and a second from Eva Presley, a brothel keeper. Mrs. Presley's note read,

> September 2, 1893
> Chief Kessler, Sir: The bearer of this wishes to board with me as she is under age. will I have a right to take her with her parents consent. her mother tells her to go in a house and wont let her stay at home and as she is in no condition to do housework, that is heavy work[,] I would like to have her come[.] she will be taken care of and doctored, which she is badly in need of[.] she need not do business here unless she wishes to. her father gave me his written consent. I was told to see you.
> Respectfully, Mrs. E. Presley

Just fourteen, Dolly had wandered so far beyond the bounds of respectability that her own parents chose to consign her to a brothel. "I give my consent that Dolly shall stay with Mrs. Presley," her father wrote. Mrs. Presley's offer makes it clear why girls like Dolly may have seen the brothel as their best refuge: a place to stay, a promise that "she need not do business here unless she wishes to," and medical care for the syphilis that already wracked her young body. But the police intervened, and the district court judge committed Dolly Hamerly to the state industrial school for girls on 8 October 1893. Nine years later, Dolly was arrested again on the streets of Davenport, plying her trade as a prostitute.[54]

Mamie Woods avoided being sent to Mitchellville but, like Dolly, became a public figure and a symbol in Davenport. Her arrest in 1894 at the age of fourteen led the *Democrat* to ruminate on the need the "restrain" young girls like her, perhaps by creating a new institution that would remove girls from the street, a place "where wayward girls can be cared for as they should be." Instead, Mamie served several short terms in the house of detention as she pursued a career in prostitution. By 1903 she was a brothel keeper herself, paying the monthly fine that was the cost of doing business in Davenport. The size of her house ranged from one to five inmates.[55]

Ada Ammerman alone avoided arrest as a prostitute in Davenport. It was her brother who became a public figure, pursuing a brief career as a prizefighter, "Kid" Ammerman, in the sporting world that had rejected his stepfather. The Matlocks left the Tri Cities area until about 1899, when Lucy Matlock, once more a widow, returned to Rock Island with her daughter. That year, eighteen-year-old Ada married a railroad fireman, taking a new name that might have further shielded her from unwelcome memories and unwanted attention. But it would be wrong to assume that Ada had completely escaped the consequences of her encounters with Charles Lyon, Henry Carpenter, and George Haikes. One of the witnesses who signed her marriage certificate was Carrie Allars, a notorious Rock Island brothel keeper.[56]

The rape trials of 1891–92 evoked the conflict between two cultural views of sexuality in stark terms because the victims were children. Women reformers and the men who sympathized with them embraced the idea that all prostitutes were the victims of rape, but most men continued to believe that no one could rape a prostitute. Fallen women were "shameless," beyond caring who used their bodies. Since by nature male sexuality demanded release, good women could be protected from brutish men only if bad women met that need. Yet prostitutes as young as Dolly, Ada, and Mamie disquieted even some who believed prostitution to be a necessary evil. The fact that a new rape law now put men in jeopardy of prison for "yielding" to such girls further contributed to the sense that something was out of joint.

John Matlock's lawsuit also raised disturbing questions by exposing connections among brothel keepers, sporting men, and the policemen who were charged with maintaining public order. Tolerating illegal brothels created a situation ripe for corruption because prostitutes had no choice but to cooperate with the police. Whether, as editor R. W. O'Meara had charged, prostitutes were forced to buy "protection" from raids and random arrests by providing sex to police officers or whether, as John Matlock maintained, policemen colluded with sporting men and women to confound the justice system, tolerated brothels harbored a profound threat to the public order. All of these worries—about corruption, about children who wandered into prostitution, and about the danger to men who sought out girl prostitutes—led a new mayor to take a bold step in the spring of 1893.

7

MAKING THE CITY SAFE FOR WHITE MEN
Regulated Prostitution

The argument that a fornicator must be protected in his evil-doing against a young girl who offers to lead him astray, is the most cowardly instance of moral obliquity that can well be brought forward.
—Elizabeth Blackwell, *Right and Wrong Methods of Dealing With Social Evil*, 1883

THE NIGHT OF 16 APRIL 1893 WAS A LONG ONE for Police Matron Annie Davis. At 10:30 P.M., Police Chief Frank Kessler and night captain Charles Falkner brought in brothel keeper Myrtle Morrow along with three inmates from her house. According to established procedure, Davis would have searched them for contraband, then confined them in one of the three cells in the house of detention to await the morning session of police court. She usually recorded data about them for her docket: age, height, "complexion," occupation, and nationality. She would have spoken privately with each of the younger women before they left her custody, encouraging them to give up prostitution. But on this particular night, she had no time for confidential talks. Only a few minutes after Morrow arrived, police delivered Kittie Clarke with three girls from her house at 10:45. Then came Emma Webb and five inmates at 11 P.M. By 3 A.M., Annie Davis had recorded the names of fifty-eight women who worked in seventeen different brothels. Dressed in the wrappers, kimonos, and Mother Hubbards that were their working attire, the women crowded together, twenty or so to each cell meant for six. The luckiest found seats on the bare wooden shelves that served as bunks, but most had to make do with the floor. Raucous, uncomfortable, and angry, some drunk and some craving morphine, the women waited the hours until the magistrate gaveled police court into session. Since her room—her home—was just down the corridor from the women's cells, Annie Davis probably slept little that night. Unlike Kessler and Falkner, she could not retreat to a quiet haven when her shift ended. *Her* shift lasted twenty-four hours a day. In the morning, Davis accompanied the women to court and watched as the magistrate levied a uniform set of fines: Each of the keepers paid a fine of twenty-five dollars plus court costs; each of the inmates paid ten dollars plus costs. Miss Davis conscientiously recorded this in her docket as well.[1]

What she did not record was how she felt. As police matron, Annie Davis had been trained by the Chicago Woman's Christian Temperance Union (WCTU) and hired by Jennie McCowen and the women of Davenport's Charitable Alliance. Until that long April night, her job had always been to encourage girls and women to escape prostitution. Now, obeying the directives of a new mayor, Annie Davis found herself registering Davenport's sex workers as the city set up a system of licensed prostitution. No longer would Davenport merely tolerate downtown brothels. Beginning that April, the city embraced full-scale regulation, including registration, health certificates, and a monthly fine that operated as a license fee. To opponents of prostitution such as Davis, registration was the worst of all possible schemes. Not only did it give the state's imprimatur to sexual debauchery, but registration itself became a barrier to a woman's reform. "An unregistered woman who has fallen, has it in her power to recover herself, . . . but the difficulty after registration is increased a thousand fold," declared one opponent. Registration and reform were inconsistent goals, wrote another. "The same voice can scarcely say, 'Go and sin no more;' and 'Go, . . . return to your lawful trade.'" Annie Davis, no doubt fatigued by her long night's work, was surely angry as well—perhaps angry enough to protest to the mayor. At the next meeting of the city council, the aldermen debated but rejected a proposal to cut her salary from fifty dollars to thirty-five dollars a month, a reduction the mayor may have proposed as punishment.[2]

Five weeks later, on 24 and 26 May, Davis repeated the entire process, this time registering forty-nine women representing twelve brothels. She resigned the next day. Two days after that, she was on the train to Chicago. No record explains why Davis resigned, but one newspaper reported that "she has nothing in view in Chicago" and that the women who had organized to bring her as matron "keenly regret that she is going away." The archives do not contain her letter of resignation, but Annie Davis's reason for leaving is clear. She quit her job over the issue of licensed prostitution.[3]

At the end of the nineteenth century, European and American cities generally followed one of three policies regarding prostitution: regulation, toleration, or suppression. The last was strongly advocated by organized women in the United States and Great Britain—women like those of the Charitable Alliance, the WCTU, and, of course, Annie Davis. The first policy, regulation, predominated in Europe. To all appearances, most U.S. cities pursued the middle course, quietly accepting their brothels because they—like a St. Louis official in 1871—believed "toleration . . . inevitable, simply because there is so much licentiousness among men that law cannot restrain it." Historian Lawrence Friedman has suggested that toleration was part of the "Victorian compromise," successful because it was unacknowledged: "Covert, under-the-table recognition was one thing, *formal* recognition was another." Others, like Neil Larry Shumsky, have argued that tolerated districts were an early form of zoning, an effort to contain prostitution where respectable citizens could avoid knowing much about it and where it would not lower property values. Such under-the-table, "tacit acceptance" may have been the choice in some American cities, but it was not the only one available. Joel Best found that from 1865 to 1883, St. Paul, Minnesota, openly regulated brothel prostitution. Relying on a broad interpretation of police power, the city registered prostitutes, collected taxes in the form of fines, and kept the business out of respectable parts of town. The policy was regularly reported in the press and on several occasions became the subject of heated public debate. While not sanctioned by statute, St. Paul's system was certainly "formal" and hardly "covert." The evidence from Davenport shows that St. Paul was not alone in taking this approach and raises the possibility that to some, regulation could be the modern, progressive way of dealing with an "ancient evil."[4]

Winning office in the first city election after John Matlock's lawsuit raised fears of a conspiracy between police and brothel keepers, Mayor Henry Vollmer used his inaugural address to announce a new policy of regulated prostitution. "Since the beginning of history," Vollmer declared, "rulers have been decreeing and legislators enacting punishments much more severe than the mayor of Davenport can possibly inflict." In spite of this, "the scarlet woman walks the streets of every major metropolitan city." Confronted with such a record, "candid, thinking men will admit that the best method of dealing with these evils is rigid regulation and control." As his speech made clear, licensing also required a tight leash on the police department. "Police officers," the mayor warned, "should remember that they are servants of the law and not above it." He soon followed this admonition with revised rules for the police, including restrictions on the use of force and prohibitions against "maltreatment or abuse of a . . . citizen" and "immoral conduct, unbecoming a police officer." If Vollmer spoke directly of the rape trials or of the allegations of corruption that led to Henry Hass's departure from the police force, the historical record has not preserved his comments. Nevertheless, the mayor's licensing policy plainly responded to the concerns raised by the accusations, the trials, and the lawsuit.[5]

John Matlock's lawsuit against Hass had forced Davenport's leading men to recognize that tolerated brothels created a danger to civic order. When prostitutes lived outside the law, they could not expect its protection. Worse, when brothels conducted their business at the pleasure of the police, officers might yield to temptation, abusing their power over prostitutes to extract payments or other favors. In choosing to license brothels and register prostitutes, Davenport gave these women a degree of legitimacy that shielded them from some forms of exploitation. But the protection of brothel workers was a secondary effect. The policy's primary purpose was to safeguard men. When a woman registered as a prostitute, she eliminated all ambiguity about her status, ensuring that no man would be charged with rape for having sex with a prostitute, as jurors apparently believed had occurred in the cases of Charles Lyon and Henry Carpenter. A prostitute's health certificate promised to protect a man from venereal disease, and the threat of losing her license gave police a powerful tool to ensure that she did not pick a client's pockets while he slept. Finally, Mayor Vollmer expected the licensing system to protect him and his allies by deflecting political criticism. Davenport did not register prostitutes under eighteen, so no one could accuse city officials of encouraging girls like Ada, Mamie, and Dolly to enter the trade.[6]

The events of the previous year may have spurred Mayor Vollmer's decision, but the policy he initiated proved sturdy enough to continue through his four terms as mayor and beyond, lasting a total of sixteen years under both Republican and Democratic successors. Not until 1909, when a pioneering state malfeasance law made mayors and police chiefs culpable for failure to enforce state law, did opponents succeed in dismantling Davenport's policy of licensed prostitution. Vollmer's choice owed much to the political influence of German Americans in Davenport and to the trans-Atlantic debates about social policy that emerged in the decades after the Civil War. Vollmer's approach also reflected a view of "progressive" social policy strikingly different from that adopted by most American Progressives. The longevity of the policy, in turn, stemmed from its claims to be an honest and effective means of dealing with prostitution and from the financial windfall the city reaped as a men's entertainment district came to flourish around the brothels.[7]

THE "FRENCH SYSTEM" IN AMERICA

When Davenport chose "rigid regulation and control" over tacit toleration, the city took a bold step, but not an unprecedented one. In 1870, the Missouri legislature granted St. Louis the power to regulate as well as suppress houses of ill-fame, and the city responded with a four-year "experiment" in legalized prostitution. The experiment ended when antiregulation forces, including activist women, launched a successful campaign to change Missouri's law. Nevertheless, some American police and physicians continued to argue that regulation was the best way to preserve public health and promote public order. The American Public Health Association, for example, considered a model city ordinance proposed by Baltimore physician John Morris. He urged the registration of prostitutes, twice-monthly medical examinations, and the quarantine of those found to be infected. "The prostitute may very properly be ranked among the dangerous classes, and her personal conduct should be a matter of police supervision," argued Morris. In an 1878 article, J. B. McGaughey of Winona, Minnesota, went even further. He called for medical examinations for both brothel workers and "if possible, . . . those visiting such houses, for the protection of the inmates." Not until the 1890s did the American medical press regularly offer articles opposing regulation.[8]

Both regulationists and their opponents looked across the Atlantic for inspiration and support. Regulationists turned to European cities where registration and control of prostitutes was accepted practice, often known as the "French system." Their opponents forged an alliance with the British campaign to repeal the Contagious Diseases Acts. First passed in 1866 and subsequently expanded, these acts provided for the arrest, genital examination, and registration of women suspected of prostitution in towns with military garrisons. Outraged by what they considered assaults on the freedom of poor women and "instrumental rape," opponents led by Josephine Butler won the repeal of the Contagious Diseases Acts in 1886. In the United States, antiregulationists defeated similar laws in Chicago, Cincinnati, Philadelphia, San Francisco, and elsewhere.[9]

In England, the effort to regulate prostitution ignited a national women's movement. On the Continent, however, regulation had a long history and greater acceptance. In Paris, police had taken on the supervision of prostitutes by the early eighteenth century, and the work of social theorist Alexandre Parent-Duchâtelet in the early nineteenth century sanctioned and strengthened the practice. By the late nineteenth century, a woman in Paris could register with the police either as a resident of a *maison de tolérance* or on her own account. If the police arrested an unregistered woman, they could enroll her involuntarily after questioning her and compelling her to undergo a medical examination. Once registered, each woman was expected to submit to a medical check every other week. Elsewhere in France, even in small towns, similar systems prevailed. Prostitution was not legal in France, but police had more than a century of traditional authority behind them as well as an 1884 statute giving provincial mayors the right "to ordain local measures in respect to objects confided to [their] vigilance and authority," including "order" and "public health."[10]

The Napoleonic Wars helped extend the "French system" broadly throughout Europe. In German cities, as in France, police usually assumed the authority to regulate prostitution not on the basis of statute but through tradition and a "wide interpretation of the powers of the police." In Hamburg, an 1807 ordinance permitted brothel keeping and prostitution with certain restrictions, including registration with the police, medical examinations, and the maintenance of good order. French occupation only reinforced the practice, and as Hamburg grew with industrialization, so did the number of prostitutes. By 1820, civil authorities published an extensive code of regulations regarding prostitution, insisting all the while that prostitution, though tolerated, was not permitted. Most German cities had a corps of morals police (*Sittenpolizei*) whose primary duty was to compel compliance with local regulations, especially the confinement of prostitutes to sanctioned brothels along specified streets. With Germany's unification, however, the Imperial Criminal Code of 1871 made it a crime for anyone to aid and abet prostitution. Though intended to penalize pimps and brothel keepers, the law also forced cities throughout Germany to close their supervised brothels. Closing the brothels did not end surveillance. Cities simply inscribed prostitutes as individuals. The same code that outlawed state-run brothels also contained a provision authorizing the police to arrest any woman suspected of prostitution and force her to undergo a medical examination, and cities relied on this statute as legal cover for the regulatory work of the morals police. In Hamburg, however, authorities resisted efforts by the imperial government to close the brothels. There, brothel keepers continued to act as agents of police supervision through the end of the century.[11]

While American antiprostitution reformers insisted that the continental systems of regulation had failed, Europe's cities continued to draw the interest of American municipalities struggling with the growth of prostitution. As St. Louis embarked on its program of regulation in 1870, city officials sent a German American representative to Europe, "to familiarize himself with regulation laws there." Like Davenport, St. Louis had a sizable German immigrant population, undoubtedly familiar with the continental system of regulation. A St. Louis health officer ridiculed reformers' claims that the French system had failed. "It is indeed strange that in the light of that disastrous defeat, with misery, disease and depravity, increasing on every side," as opponents alleged, "the infamous and injurious law should be maintained in force," wrote William Barret, sarcastically wondering why the French people did not rise up as had "self-virtuous England after her short and imperfect trial." Barret insisted that regulation had not failed; further, it had "to some extent been adopted in every civilized country." Even Dr. Elizabeth Blackwell, an unyielding foe of regulation, warned that the repeal of the Contagious Diseases Acts had simply led English cities to imitate those on the Continent, undertaking "the insidious introduction of unjust municipal regulations," using police power rather than formal statute.[12]

While St. Louis was the only nineteenth-century American city to regulate prostitution under the authority of statute, tolerated districts quietly flourished. According to the 1890 federal census, among cities with a population over eight thousand, 166 (37 percent) admitted harboring houses of prostitution. Some of these cities unquestionably regulated their brothels. Antiprostitution reformers in the 1890s claimed that both Omaha and Cleveland maintained systems like Davenport's, and a number of historians have noted evidence of regulation in other cities. In truth, the model for Davenport's system was not St. Paul or even St. Louis. It was Hamburg. A cosmopolitan port city, Hamburg was one of just two major points of embarkation for German immigrants to North America, and it was the point of arrival for many German Americans returning to visit the homeland. Men departing and those returning could easily observe the registration system still operating in Hamburg, and some of those men were in a position to advise Mayor Vollmer.[13]

Though Vollmer was the son of German-born parents, his decision to turn to a German model was not a foregone conclusion. Both his parents had immigrated as children and grown up in the United States. His father trained as a printer in St. Louis and then moved to Davenport in 1861, a decade before St. Louis embarked on its famous "experiment." By 1879, the elder Vollmer had become partner in a prosperous rubber-stamp business. Young Henry was born and raised in Davenport, graduating from the public high school in 1885 and earning a law degree from the state university in Iowa City. He moved to Washington, D.C., where he worked as a distributing clerk for the U.S. Congress and attended lectures at Georgetown Law School. In 1889, Vollmer opened his own law practice in Davenport. He was just twenty-two, bilingual and bicultural, moving easily in Davenport's English- and German-speaking communities. In 1892, he secured his link to Anglo-Americans in Davenport by marrying his high school sweetheart, Jessie Peck, who could trace her ancestry straight back to the *Mayflower*.[14]

Vollmer was still several weeks short of his twenty-sixth birthday when he became mayor of Davenport. Like most German Democrats, he had a barely concealed scorn for moralists who attacked the saloon as the gateway to perdition. Locals dubbed him "the boy mayor of Davenport," and Vollmer's youth shaped his views on the touchy issue of prostitution. His skepticism toward Prohibition made him ill disposed to credit foes of regulated prostitution, since those who opposed the brothel also opposed the saloon. Vollmer had also a Progressive's faith in the authority of experts and a young man's arrogance toward those he judged less enlightened than himself. Though Vollmer had not, apparently, visited Europe, when he sought expert opinion on prostitution, he turned to reports from European cities with regulated brothels and found a model for Davenport.[15]

In contrast to American and English reformers, the European physicians Mayor Vollmer consulted considered regulated prostitution a moral and medical necessity. Belgian physician Jean Hubert Thiry, in a report cited by the mayor, warned that any effort to suppress prostitution would lead inevitably to an epidemic of syphilis. In addition, there would be "a growth, in frightening proportions, of seductions whose victims are poor girls, of illegitimate births and births resulting from adultery, of rapes, murders, and all the atrocious and abominable crimes committed by brutes in rut on women and unfortunate little girls." Regulated prostitution, by contrast, would limit debauchery and protect society from illness and excess. Vollmer also consulted a report by Moritz Kaposi, a Viennese specialist in syphilis and dermatology, who argued that marriage was no longer a sufficient social measure to contain

Mayor Henry Vollmer, c. 1900. (From *Picturesque Tri-Cities*, 1901.)

male sexuality. Prostitution, therefore, was natural and necessary though potentially dangerous to society and family. Only regulation could control the danger, Kaposi argued. Kaposi set forth a lengthy proposal for exactly how regulation should work, calling for large and small brothels dispersed through the city, medical examinations twice a week, and a ban on underage prostitutes. Given the vehemence of these experts' warnings, Vollmer may have felt regulation an urgent necessity. An older man might have hesitated, weighing the political costs of such a controversial move, but Vollmer put his plan for licensing into effect just ten days after his inauguration.[16]

REGULATION IN DAVENPORT

The late-night sweeps of brothels that kept Matron Davis at work until near dawn in April and May gave way by fall to a more systematic approach. After Davis resigned, the city immediately solicited applications for the matron's job, and by 24 July had appointed Mrs. Sarah Hill, a stonecutter's widow who had once worked at the state orphanage in Davenport. Like Davis, Hill had trained with the WCTU in Chicago. Unlike Davis, Sarah Hill acquiesced to the mayor's regulation regime and took up the task of registering prostitutes. By fall, once the brothel keepers understood what the police expected, notification supplanted arrest. On a designated day near the end of each month, the brothel keepers and their employees appeared in court and paid a standard fine. For keepers, the fine was $25 plus $2.85 in court costs; inmates paid $10 plus $2.85 in costs. Registered women who did not work in the brothels also paid $10 plus costs. In most months, between fifty and sixty women appeared, representing fifteen to seventeen brothels. That October, a new approach attempted to streamline the process. The police required only the keepers, not the inmates, to appear in court. Each keeper paid a fine based on the number of employees she had registered to her house, according to the same schedule of fines. One newspaper warned that the new system "may not work well," and apparently it did not. The following month, inmates appeared in court again. But police apparently adopted some version of this simplified system beginning in September 1895. That month and after, Matron Hill recorded only the names of brothel keepers in her docket, along with a figure indicating the number of employees in each house. The magistrate set the fine according to this number. Usually, the amount was $25 plus $5 for each inmate, and $2.85 in court costs.[17]

Monthly, standardized fines were only one element of Davenport's system of licensed prostitution. In addition, the police prohibited the presence of unregistered women in the brothels and enforced a minimum age of eighteen for prostitutes. In June 1894, for example, the newspapers reported that one brothel keeper was fined fifty dollars for "concealment of a young girl in her resort without the knowledge of the officers of the law." In this case, the keeper herself was only nineteen, but the girl in question was fourteen, too young to register. As police and prostitutes worked out the new system, the rules sometimes created confusion. In September 1893, just five months into the new regime, fourteen-year-old Dolly Hamerly showed up at Eva Presley's brothel with a note from her father giving her permission to stay with Mrs. Presley. Presley wrote to Police Chief Kessler for clarification. "As she is under age will I have a right to take her with her parents' consent[?]" Eva Presley's question may suggest she knew something about the law. According to the *Code of Iowa for 1873*, the consent of the parent or guardian was a bar to prosecution under the statute penalizing inveigling a girl into prostitution. When legislators revised the law in 1884, they removed the phrase about parental consent. But before that change, the

Police Matron Sarah Hill, c. 1900. (Putnam Museum of History and Natural Science, Davenport, Iowa.)

statute seemed to imply that parents had the right to put a fourteen-year-old daughter to work as a prostitute. Chief Kessler decided that under the new system, parental consent did not override the minimum-age rule. He initiated proceedings to have Dolly committed to the state reformatory. Girls sometimes lied about their age, of course. In such cases, being known to the police could quickly curtail a career as a prostitute. Police arrested Emma Krantz in 1902 as an accomplice in a bicycle theft. When a brothel keeper tried to register her as an inmate a year later, the chief recognized her name and launched an investigation. Confirming that Emma was just sixteen, he removed her from the brothel.[18]

The restriction on unregistered women in brothels applied not just to underage girls. On one occasion, Matron Hill reported receiving a note from a brothel keeper who had given overnight shelter to a homeless woman and her two-week-old infant. The note "begged" Mrs. Hill to find another place for the mother and child, for it was "against police regulations for her to take in any woman that way," and she feared being shut down. Since several of Davenport's brothel keepers had started out as impoverished mothers taking in boarders, the compulsion to register all residents as prostitutes undoubtedly created a crisis for some. Mayor Vollmer may have seen the end of ambiguity as a means of protecting men, but registration forced women to make a stark choice, to declare themselves prostitutes or not. For daughters living in their mother's home, the choice could be especially harsh, given that mothers often drifted into brothel keeping to maintain a home for children and grandchildren.[19]

That medical inspections were part of the licensing system in Davenport might have remained historically invisible had it not erupted into public controversy in December 1894. That month, when the licensing system had been in effect for a year and a half, the Scott County Medical Society devoted its monthly meeting to the question, "Does the medical profession uphold the licensing of prostitution for the prevention of disease?" Who suggested the topic is impossible to know, but the medical society, though predominantly male, was one place where Jennie McCowen wielded considerable influence. The discussion drew participation from all fifteen physicians present, including Dr. McCowen and Dr. Adella Nichol. According to the *Democrat*, one physician who had practiced in Davenport for more than twenty years "stated that to his knowledge venereal diseases had never been so prevalent in Davenport as at the present time, when the habitues of immoral resorts put their faith in the medical certificates held by the inmates." Another doctor "quoted one of his patients asking him if he could not recover damages from the doctor who signed a certificate which the experience of the patient had proved . . . erroneous." The *Times* reported that "the trend of the discussion was that the regulation of the social evil by license and medical supervision had been a failure wherever tried, and Davenport was no exception to the rule." After earnest discussion, the physicians voted unanimously in favor of a resolution offered by Dr. William Allen: "That it is the sense of this society that the licensing of prostitution does not limit or prevent the spread of venereal disease: that on the contrary, a false sense of security is the result and increase in disease."[20]

The *Democrat* printed its report of the meeting on an inside page of the morning edition. The mayor's angry response appeared on page 1 that afternoon. Sounding like the lawyer he was, Vollmer insisted that Davenport did not license prostitution: "no such contract, in fact no contract whatever is entered into with parties guilty of it." From a lawyer's perspective, he was right; the city's system was entirely extralegal. But the physicians had debated a matter of public health, not law. On that point, the mayor claimed that "a majority of the members of the Scott County Medical Society, who were present at yesterday's meeting, have come to me personally at one

Certificate of Health.

This is to Certify Davenport, Iowa, 7/23 1907.
That I have examined Jessie W. White
and find her free from any infectious disease.

Telephone 213-5. J. D. Chambers, M. D.

Prostitute's health certificate. This certificate was reproduced in the exposé *Hell at Midnight in Davenport*, but it is impossible to know if it is authentic. No one named Jessie White appears in the matron's docket. However, J. D. Chambers did practice medicine in Davenport. (From William Lloyd Clark, *Hell at Midnight in Davenport*, 1908.)

time or another and assured me that it was the best system that could be devised, and that they heartily approved of it from a medical standpoint." Not only did the doctors approve, insisted the mayor, but the debate and resolution "were inspired ultimately by a loss of inspection fees by certain medical gentlemen," the result of the city's decision to concentrate brothel inspection in the hands of the city physician. Until some physicians lost income, "there was not a murmur of disapproval from that direction," declared the mayor.[21]

Mayor Vollmer's accusation set off a rhetorical skirmish pitting the mayor against the physicians, with Dr. Jennings Crawford walking point for the medical society. "We are not willing to be represented as a set of professional vultures, watching for a carcass of human wretchedness, from which to exact a fee," asserted Dr. Crawford in a letter to the press. "There is not enough revenue in the city treasury . . . to induce the rank and file of the Scott County Medical society to sell their name on inspection certificates as a passport to safety through houses of wickedness, or to become a medical inspector to the prostitution wing of the municipality of Davenport." The physicians prominent in debate and the majority of members of the society had never signed certificates, he insisted. To this the mayor responded, "I have a list" of physicians signing health certificates, and he claimed that this list included more than half the medical society's members. Vollmer declined to share the list, however, bowing to what he called "the urgent request of several weak-kneed sisters of the fraternity."[22]

Going on the offensive, Vollmer then brandished the *Report of the Tenth Inter-*

national Congress of Surgeons, Berlin, 1890 in his next open letter. His wife's late father, Dr. W. F. Peck, had attended the conference, and the volume likely came into the mayor's hands through the agency of her brother, Robert Peck, also a physician. Vollmer listed by name the thirteen honorary presidents representing four continents and offered into evidence the reports on regulated prostitution by Jean Hubert Thiry of Brussels and Moritz Kaposi of Vienna published in the volume. Vollmer made a point of noting that the report had been issued "in three modern languages," but this claim was disingenuous. The tables of contents appeared in English, but Thiry's paper was entirely in French and Kaposi's was in German. Vollmer understood that few members of the medical society shared his linguistic skills, so wielding Thiry and Kaposi as his authorities reversed claims to expertise. Doctors who could not read German should defer on such matters to a mayor who did, especially when his authorities were "men presiding over the greatest universities of the Old World, and to whom thousands upon thousands of American young men go annually to sit at their knees and drink in the latest developments of medical science." With this hyperbolic flourish, Vollmer positioned himself as a participant in the modern, trans-Atlantic exchange of social policy ideas, in contrast to the backward, provincial members of the medical society. He concluded by repeating his claim that the physicians were motivated by the loss of fees but allowing that Dr. Crawford and "the female doctors" who had voted for the resolution "were merely used as cats-paws by somebody else."[23]

Crawford was not impressed by the mayor's grasp of language. His next letter castigated the "scholarly and dignified mayor" for employing "the sneering epithet 'female doctors,' which is equivalent to calling a colored man a nigger." He then declared himself honored to be placed in the "cat-paw combination" with "such splendid types of womanhood, who have been foremost and always right upon every subject affecting the public morals of this community." Since matters had started to get personal, Crawford added that the "lady physicians" had been moral leaders "from a time even before our youthful executive exfoliated his kilts" and wondered "how one who is so gallant a defender of the cause of women of the town, could be so rude and discourteous to these professional ladies, who possess the genius which makes them a factor in society transcending even his Honor's highest conception of himself." As to the mayor's invocation of the Berlin report with its thirteen honorary presidents—and his implied claim to superior knowledge—Crawford dismissed it as merely "names . . . which no man can number or pronounce."[24]

Crawford also undercut the mayor's claim regarding the list of physicians signing health certificates for prostitutes. Calling at the police station, Crawford asked to see the list, only to be told that no such list existed. The mayor's claim was based instead on "the memory and best recollection of the [police] chief and his associates." Presenting them with a membership roster for the medical society, Crawford asked Chief Kessler to check off the names of physicians who had signed certificates. The chief checked off nine of twenty-eight members and ventured that some of those checked "had not signed certificates . . . for a long time and had never made a practice of it." Meanwhile, another member of the society, J. W. H. Baker, challenged the mayor's assertion that a majority of the members present at the debate on licensed prostitution had privately advocated regulation. Polling the fifteen members who had attended, he found only three who admitted giving their approval to the mayor—Dr. Alonzo Cantwell, Dr. Lucius French, and Dr. John H. Kulp. A fourth was "not seen" by Baker but might also have voiced approval to the mayor: Dr. Robert Peck, the mayor's brother-in-law.[25]

On the plane of rhetoric, the mayor lost this argument, with the medical society demolishing his claims that the resolution against licensure was merely self-serving. On the plane of action, however, the mayor's position was never in danger. He remained certain that regulation was the correct policy, and the city physician continued to perform inspections of the prostitutes and their quarters. The following spring, voting men in Davenport returned Mayor Vollmer to a third term in office.

The debate between Jennings Crawford and Henry Vollmer reveals just how unsettled the question of gender in public life remained and suggests one reason why organized women did not speak out against regulated prostitution as they had during the matron campaign five years earlier. Vollmer, like his fellow attorney and Democrat William Chamberlin, considered the feminine unfit for the public sphere. Chamberlin made his point by lampooning Belva Lockwood. Vollmer made his by castigating the physicians he considered too timid to make public their private support for regulation as "weak-kneed sisters," associating femininity with moral cowardice. He assumed that the women physicians shrank from signing prostitutes' certificates out of ladylike delicacy rather than principle and that their votes against licensing proved them not morally vigorous but mentally weak. A "cat's paw," after all, is one whose vanity can be manipulated by a more clever—and greedy— colleague. Mayor Vollmer's basic position—that women could serve the public good as prostitutes but not by debating and shaping public policy—could hardly have been more offensive to Jennie McCowen and her colleagues.

Crawford saw matters differently. To him, Dr. McCowen and Dr. Nichol were "splendid types . . . who have been foremost and always right upon every subject affecting the public morals of this community." Indeed, they were the mayor's superiors. Vollmer and Crawford not only disagreed about the role of women in public life but also moved in professional worlds where gender figured in profoundly different ways. Crawford had attended the same medical school that graduated Abbie Cleaves and Jennie McCowen, had obtained his medical license in a state where women sat on the examining committees, belonged to professional societies (the Scott County Medical Society and the Iowa-Illinois Regional Medical Society) in which women were active members and officeholders, and succeeded in an occupation where women were a significant clientele. Since leaving high school, Vollmer's professional world had been exclusively masculine: his classmates in law school, his professors, the men who served in Congress, the judges before whom he argued cases, the attorneys who assisted or opposed him, and of course, the voters he courted as he ran for office. Even in Davenport, where women had successfully organized to shape public policy, men such as Vollmer could still see women as outsiders whose impertinent intrusions into public life merely hampered the efforts of "thinking men"—like himself. Vollmer's evident scorn for women in politics may have persuaded Davenport's organized women that taking a public stand would accomplish nothing. McCowen must have hoped the medical society could make the case for them, but Mayor Vollmer was not about to change his mind.[26]

ASSIGNATION HOUSES

The mayor's debate with the medical society was not the only controversy to emerge in 1894. Late on a Saturday night in September, two young men brought their companions, seventeen-year-old Grace Wilson and eighteen-year-old Maud Miller, to the Slate House Hotel and signed the register with their "wives." Early the next morning, police detective J. H. Jansen arrested Wilson and Miller, and the girls confessed that it was their second visit to the Slate House that week. Just days earlier, they had shared rooms with two other men. The *Democrat* reported that Grace Wilson was "a little wild" and "on the street too much at night" but "nothing worse." A city directory recorded Wilson as a laundress living in the tough neighborhood along Front Street. Maud Miller's residence and occupation were not listed, but the *Democrat* claimed she bore "a bad reputation." Neither one had registered as a prostitute with the police, and Wilson was too young, in any case. In Monday's police court, Magistrate John Ryan fined them ten dollars apiece. Then the two girls took the stand again, becoming the lead witnesses in the trial of Lee Lawrence Beauchaine for renting rooms "for immoral purposes."[27]

Ever since Lee Beauchaine and Mamie Magee had married, Mamie had been insisting that she was no longer in the prostitution business. Two years earlier, she had sued the police chief and the night captain for harassment when they arrested her. Now Lee and Mamie lived at the hotel, which she owned and he managed. The slate-shingled building housed a saloon and a wine room as well as several bedrooms. Located on Second Street at the foot of the Government Bridge, the Slate House was convenient for travelers arriving from Rock Island and was just blocks from the steamboat landing and the two railroad passenger depots. It also anchored one corner of the Bucktown district, making it equally convenient for couples like

Miller, Wilson, and their male companions who had been dancing and drinking in the nearby resorts.[28]

At Lee Beauchaine's trial, Wilson and Miller testified about sharing rooms with different men; Detective Jansen then swore to the reputation of the Slate House—"bad"—and named several "women of bad character" he had seen there. William Chamberlin, who seems to have specialized in defending men and women from Davenport's sporting world, called two Slate House lodgers and several other witnesses who testified that they had never seen evidence of immorality at the hotel. Chamberlin closed by insisting that the Beauchaines "had erred, but were now trying with all the earnestness of sincere repentance to follow the path of virtue, and to lead respectable lives." Whether or not Police Magistrate Ryan believed Chamberlin, Jansen's testimony may have settled the case. As discussed in chapter 1, in law, the presence of women with the reputation of prostitutes was sufficient to prove that the Slate House was a "house of ill-fame." Police Magistrate Ryan found the Beauchaines guilty and fined them twenty-five dollars.[29]

The Slate House case exposed one of the most troublesome challenges to any system of regulated prostitution: couples who sought opportunities for illicit sex outside the brothels. In the regulation system, women brothel keepers served as agents of the police by registering their inmates, paying the monthly fines, and cooperating with the health inspections of prostitutes and their quarters, but "bed houses" or assignation houses defied police control. In these places, unregistered prostitutes or unmarried lovers could rent private rooms for sexual trysts. Such activities confounded the mayor's fixed belief that regulation could control venereal disease. Assignation houses also blurred the line between "prostitute" and "lover," thwarting a primary goal of the regulation system. In these unregulated places, rules about age or efforts to control the recruitment of prostitutes came to nothing.

Within days of Beauchaine's trial, both Police Chief Kessler and Mayor Vollmer used the Slate House case to rail against Davenport's assignation houses while defending regulation. "I believe such places have a much worse effect upon the community than do the places that are rightly termed houses of ill fame," declared Kessler. "Fame, bad or good, implies general knowledge of the character of a place. A person who goes to such a house goes there with his, or her, eyes open." Places like the Slate House, where "the real nature of the place is concealed," are "ten times" worse "because they start young girls on the road to ruin." Having established secrecy as the source of social danger, Kessler blithely contradicted himself, calling the Slate House "a blaring advertisement for immorality." Its prominent location made ignoring it impossible. "It is right beneath the eyes of respectable mothers and daughters when they walk across the bridge on Sundays or other days, as so many do purely for recreation," grumbled Kessler. "Then everyone sees it who goes from Davenport to Rock Island or back, and it is the first place in town that a stranger strikes when coming here from Illinois." The real problem, of course, was not that the Slate House's nature was concealed but that it was well known yet not under direct police surveillance. Like Kessler, Mayor Vollmer worried about girls who might be tempted to visit the Slate House or a similar place: "The girl who thinks she is out for a lark, who 'catches on,' as the saying is, to some unprincipled fellow, who takes her into one of these wine rooms and 'fills her up,' is doomed. That is the end of the girl." But Vollmer was careful to say that saloons themselves were not the problem. "Public opinion will support them to a certain extent and I am convinced that the majority of them [are] decent and respectable," he averred.[30]

Prompted by the Slate House case, Vollmer ordered the police to investigate Davenport's houses of assignation. In November, they took their evidence to the grand jury, which issued indictments against four: the Metropolitan Hotel, operated by Mrs. M. E. May; William Porter's Turkish Bath establishment; a hotel kept by Mr. and Mrs. David Jacobsen; and Mr. and Mrs. John McPartland's place out by Central Park. The depositions prepared for the grand jury reveal an alternative sexual commerce that drew secret lovers, working women and their beaux, and casual prostitutes as well as some women from registered brothels. While the police described assignation houses as places "where a wink secures a room and no questions are asked," testimony revealed that some proprietors were far from mere silent partners in crime. Some actively encouraged—even recruited or coerced—women to provide sexual services for paying customers.[31]

The McPartland place most closely fit the model of winking accommodation suggested by the police, but it was also the most offensive to many because of its location at the southwest corner of Brady and Lombard Streets. Twenty years earlier, that neighborhood had bordered the old fairgrounds near the edge of town, and several brothels, including the Farm and the rowdy Black Hills, had flourished in the area. Most were shut down in the early 1880s, and in 1885, the city purchased the fairgrounds to become the new Central Park. When the fairgrounds moved to the western outskirts of town, it took one of the centers of male sporting culture, the racetrack, out of the neighborhood. Instead, the area attracted increasing numbers of affluent homeowners. The grounds of the Outing Club, a private park established by Davenport's elites, lay along the east side of Brady Street, and the newly landscaped Central Park contributed to the air of suburban serenity. In 1894, Jack McPartland's place, with its barroom, sitting room, and five bedrooms upstairs, stood on a corner opposite both the Outing Club and Central Park, the last holdout of Davenport's once bawdy fringe.

Neighbors were well aware of goings-on at the house. Attorney W. C. Putnam had lived nearby for seven years and believed McPartland's had been a house of assignation for all that time. John Temple, a florist, observed "a man and a woman taking off their clothes" in an upstairs bedroom around seven one evening. "Then I saw the woman close the shutters," he reported. Another often "heard people carousing upstairs." On steamy summer evenings when open windows provided the only ventilation for McPartland's bedrooms, near neighbors must have thought twice about taking lemonade on their front porches. Both neighbors and police noted traffic in hacks and carriages tied up outside the house at night, but McPartland's also benefited from its convenient location on the Brady Street car line. Patterson Hart, the motorman who drove the Brady Street route most evenings, had long since learned the reputation of the house that drew so many of his riders. John Temple testified that he had "often seen couples come up on the cars and get off at the street below" McPartland's. "The man would enter . . . by the Brady St. door, and the woman would go around the block and enter . . . by one of the Lombard St. doors. They would leave the house and go back to where they got on the cars in the same way." Sanford Ganson observed similar ruses by patrons using the streetcar line. One time, he saw a man and woman leave the house together and begin walking down Brady on opposite sides of the street. "The woman hailed a car and got on it and the man got on the same car and lifted his hat to the woman," he reported. The man's counterfeit greeting did not fool Ganson, and it may not have fooled anyone else. Such efforts at subterfuge suggest that these couples were not regular prostitutes and their clients. They may have been lovers carrying on adulterous affairs or even courting couples. The effort to disguise their purpose may also reflect one of the hardships created by regulation. To work within the system, a woman had to declare herself publicly a prostitute. Yet more than a few women who might choose to solve a temporary financial crisis by exchanging sex for money would still recoil from registering with the police and entering a brothel. For such women, McPartland's provided a way to evade the system.[32]

Down at the corner of Front and Main Streets, customers of the Metropolitan Hotel may have had a more difficult time disguising their destination. Not only was it at a busy intersection just opposite the ferry landing and a block from the Chicago, Milwaukee, & St. Paul passenger depot, but neighbors there were just as observant. Horace Birdsall, proprietor of the nearby St. James Hotel, reported that the Metropolitan had a "bad reputation" and recalled seeing "a couple of fast women making a spectacle of themselves on the street in front . . . with a man. They were sitting on the curbstone laughing and hugging each other." Hotel guests were sometimes so rowdy that neighbors notified the police. Detective Jansen recalled having to quiet a noisy crowd that was singing and drinking on the hotel's second floor.[33]

Depositions in this case suggest that Mrs. May's business catered more to casual prostitutes than to unmarried lovers. Seventeen-year-old Maggie Kohlsaat, for example, testified, "I have been there several times and have occupied rooms and beds with various gentlemen who have at such times paid the bartender for our use of the rooms." The fee was one dollar, and the bartenders obligingly entered false names on the hotel register. In language most likely concocted by the prosecutor, Kohlsaat confirmed, "I am not nor was I ever married to any of the gentlemen with whom I at such times occupied beds and rooms in said 'Metropolitan Hotel.' " Twenty-year-old Lou Perry worked as a cook in Ed Herrold's saloon four blocks up Front Street from the Metropolitan. At one time, she and a man had lived together at the hotel for about a year. Mrs. May, she reported, "knew that we occupied the room for purposes of prostitution and she received $3.50 per week for its use." Other women who testified before the grand jury about their visits to the hotel in the company of men said they did housework or kitchen work for a living. Of the six women who testified against Mrs. May, only one, May Diston, had ever been registered as a brothel prostitute. As a group, Mrs. May's customers appeared to be young, working-class women who visited the hotel with men for fun, to supplement their meager wages, or for some agreeable combination of the two.[34]

"Prof. William Porter" advertised his Turkish Baths as "a most healthful luxury," promising to "prevent Insomnia, Colds and Sickness." "Health is Wealth," his ad proclaimed. But the bath business brought Porter a more conventional kind of wealth, too. His customers paid to use the four assignation rooms in his establishment. Porter was also something of a prostitution entrepreneur. He not only made rooms available but recruited women to fill them. Lou Perry, the cook who admitted sharing rooms with men at the Metropolitan Hotel, also testified against William Porter. "Porter came for me once in the summer and said he wanted me to come down there, that there was a travelling man there who wanted to take a bath with me and there was good money in it," she reported. "I went down and had a bath there in said place with said travelling man and he and I occupied a bed together." That was not the only time Porter recruited her. "Once Annie Schwerdtfeger, myself, and two traveling men, another girl and another man, six of us without any clothing on, occupied the sweating room together," she reported. Minnie King and May Cummings also claimed Porter called them to provide sex to his male clients. As King explained, "When girls are wanted by the men either said Porter or one Johnson an employee of Porter, go out for girls." Porter also brought in beer and other drinks for his clients. "At one time," King recalled, "several sporting women roomed there."[35]

In contrast to McPartland's and the Metropolitan Hotel, the testimony against Porter's Turkish Baths indicated that a number of Davenport's brothel keepers and registered prostitutes also visited. Of course, the brothel prostitutes may have been attracted as much by the bathing facilities as by the assignation rooms. Not every public bathhouse would have welcomed prostitutes as clients, and Porter clearly did. Porter's sideline certainly shocked respectable Davenport. His Turkish Baths were not just on bustling Brady Street, they were in Hibernian Hall, a building that for thirty years had been the Christian Chapel, one of Davenport's oldest Protestant churches. Sold in 1888, by 1890 it had become the social hall of Davenport's Irish community, which rented space to Porter. Respectable Hibernians must have been mortified, and citizens who had worshipped in the building no doubt cringed at the thought of prostitutes plying their trade within those same walls.[36]

Just a block and a half from Hibernian Hall, David Jacobsen and his wife ran a hotel in their home on the corner of Fifth and Perry Streets, close to the Chicago, Rock Island, & Pacific passenger depot. At least, their license was for a hotel. But as Lou Perry, who had once worked for the Jacobsens, saw it, "The whole house is used for purposes of assignation." A sitting room doubled as a wine room, and the Jacobsens rented out rooms upstairs and downstairs for "assignation purposes." Like William Porter, the Jacobsens actively sought out women to provide their male clients with sex. Just weeks before the grand jury heard testimony, Mrs. Jacobsen came looking for Minnie Burmeister, a twenty-year-old domestic servant. "Mrs. Jacobsen came for me and told me there was some nice fellows in the wine room, and for me to come and drink with them that there was some money in them," testified Burmeister. "Afterwards I went to bed with one of them. He paid me two dollars, and he paid Mr. D[avid] Jacobsen a dollar for the use of the room." Lou Perry also reported being called to share a room with "travelling men." According to Perry, she had seen "a number of working girls who work up on the hill" (that is, as household servants employed in Davenport's residential neighborhoods) at the Jacobsens' "hotel." Jacobsen's recruiting sometimes verged on coercion. Perry recalled Jacobsen threatening to fire her and a girl named Annie "if we did not stay in the house and make money for him."[37]

The Jacobsens' hotel was adjacent to the small black business district that clustered around Linsey Pitts's saloon on Fifth Street. Perhaps as a result, some of the men who patronized the place were African American. Minnie Burmeister reported seeing Mamie Mills undressing and sharing a room with Wilson Patterson, who was black. "Mamie Mills is white," she affirmed in response to a prosecutor's question. The prosecutor may have been disturbed by the allegation of interracial sex, but Burmeister was probably not. She admitted being "in the habit of occupying a room" at the Jacobsens' with Al Woods, described by the *Times* as a "colored waiter." As a result of Burmeister's testimony, the grand jury indicted Woods for inveigling Burmeister into a house of ill-fame. When he came to trial, the *Democrat* predicted that he would "probably be placed where white girls will be free of his attentions for some time at least," but the jury acquitted him. In a decision that echoed the acquittals of Henry Carpenter and Charles Lyon, jurors declined to penalize even a black man for "inveigling" a girl who seemed unashamed of her own immorality.[38]

Against the four alleged houses of assignation, the grand jury returned two indictments each, one for keeping a house of ill-fame and another for maintaining a public nuisance. Prosecutors agreed to permit each of the defendants to plead guilty to the lesser offense, maintaining a public nuisance, and pay a fine of a thousand dollars. The alternative charge, keeping a house of ill-fame, was a felony for which the minimum sentence was six months in the penitentiary. The threat of penitentiary time proved an effective means of compulsion, and all four agreed to shut down their businesses. This spate of prosecutions in the winter of 1894 went unmatched through the history of Davenport's regulation system. Over the next fifteen years, only five more cases related to brothels or assignation houses entered the court system. The court dismissed two cases, and two men convicted in 1904 on misdemeanor charges in magistrate's court had their felony charges dismissed before they came to trial. The outcome of the fifth case is unclear, but it received no significant press coverage, suggesting that it too concluded in some fashion other than conviction.[39]

The campaign against assignation houses played out in the public press during the same weeks that the mayor publicly debated regulation with the medical society. This crackdown on illicit sex in places reserved for respectable activities—such as Hibernian Hall and the neighborhood around Central Park—must have satisfied those of the mayor's critics who were primarily concerned with their own neighborhoods. The brief campaign may also have reassured others who feared that regulation was simply a cover for abandoning all restrictions whatsoever. Coupled with the mayor's vigorous defense of the public health benefits of regulation, the assignation house cases seem to have satisfied matters for most voting men. The following April, Vollmer defeated a challenge from Republican attorney and temperance advocate Samuel F. Smith, winning with a comfortable 56 percent of the vote.[40]

RACE AND REGULATION

If the public debate between Henry Vollmer and the medical society exposed Davenport's use of medical examinations as part of its licensing regime, a profound silence masked another side of the policy: Davenport did not license brothels run by African Americans. No newspaper report or city council record announced this decision; no court document or police record alludes openly to such a policy. But careful examination of the records kept by the police matron reveals that every brothel keeper who paid a monthly assessment was white, and the black brothel keepers all but vanished from police records when registration became the rule. From June 1889, when the police matron's records began, through 15 April 1909, when the city closed down the brothels, police records show thirty-eight appearances by black brothel keepers. Seventeen of those incidents (45 percent) took place in the first four years, before Mayor Vollmer instituted regulation. During those years before regulation, police arrested at least four of the women more than once, indicating their ongoing presence as brothel keepers. In contrast, during sixteen years under the licensing system, the remaining twenty-one arrests of black brothel keepers were scattered among eighteen different women, only two of whom appeared more than once. Unlike the white brothel keepers, who appeared like clockwork at the end of each month to pay their assessments, some for years at a stretch, the irregular appearances by black brothel keepers demonstrate that they were excluded from the licensing regime. Their arrests most likely represented police efforts to control particularly disorderly houses.

The case of Mattie Burke illustrates the pattern. Burke had kept a brothel in Davenport since the late 1870s, and she appeared five times in the police matron's records before Mayor Vollmer implemented brothel regulation. Burke did not suddenly leave the business in 1893. She remained at the same address on Fifth Street, and her block retained its reputation for prostitution. In February 1901, almost eight years after Davenport adopted regulation, police again arrested Mattie Burke for keeping a house of ill-fame. That month, Burke paid a fine of fifty dollars (twice the usual tax) for keeping a house with one inmate. The inmate, Nora Haughs, was white. Instead of the usual fine assessed to women employed in white-run brothels, Haughs served three days in the house of detention. Haughs's presence and the challenge it represented to an emerging racial order was likely the sole reason for Mattie Burke's arrest.[41]

In the 1870s and 1880s, mixed-race brothels were, if not common, at least not unknown in Davenport. Mattie Burke and other black brothel keepers served both black and white customers, and a few white women worked in black-run brothels. By the 1890s, however, changing ideas about race relations began to affect the public perception of interracial sexual transactions. The police matron's record betrays the shift. Under Annie Davis, hired by the Charitable Alliance in 1889, black women's "nationality" was always listed as "American" or "Afro-American." When Sarah Hill took over in the summer of 1893, she relied on just one designation. In her dockets, the nationality of blacks was "coon." Hill also kept a pet dog named Nigger. Whites in Davenport clearly understood that "nigger" was an offensive term. Dr. Jennings Crawford relied on that knowledge when he invoked the word to criticize Mayor Vollmer's sneer at women physicians, for example. But Sarah Hill took over the police matron's job at a time when the standard of public civility toward African Americans was dropping to a new low. A generation of northern whites who had no personal memory of the racial crisis of the Civil War was more than willing to attribute expertise on matters of race to white southerners and to adopt what they considered southern ways of managing race relations, with grim consequences.[42]

Without this new racial context, the decision to single out black brothels for different treatment would seem an irrational twist in a policy defended as the triumph of manly, scientific reason over feminine sentiment. The mayor justified regulation on the grounds that it stemmed the spread of venereal disease and promoted public order. Yet choosing not to regulate black-run brothels undercut those goals. Only the racial science of the period makes sense of an otherwise paradoxical decision.

Since their earliest encounters with Africans, light-skinned Europeans had associated dark skin with hypersexuality. By the nineteenth century, medical writers had even developed an entire iconography of the black female body, "proving" the natural lasciviousness of black women. While scientists frequently proposed that white prostitutes were examples of atavism—throwbacks to an earlier stage of evolution before white Europeans had developed moral sensibilities and sexual restraint—no such explanation was required for black prostitutes. Indeed, ethnology presumed all women of African ancestry, whether prostitutes or not, to be savages, with a concomitant lack of moral discernment. In this model, all black women stood at the same moral threshold as the white women who worked as prostitutes. Attributing indiscriminate sexual desire to women of African ancestry, nineteenth-century science dismissed any need for black brothels. After all, public policy justified brothels on the grounds that they protected chaste women from rape by providing an outlet for men's irrepressible sexual urges. But if black women's sexual desires were indiscriminate, they could not be raped and needed no protection. Black men, by extension, required no special outlet for their sexuality since, presumably, they had no shortage of sexual partners among members of their own race. And while the law might insist that both prostitutes and black women could be legitimate victims of rape, in practice women of neither group expected to be heard in court.[43]

But what of the claim that regulation protected men from venereal disease? Just as nineteenth-century science associated black women with hypersexuality, contemporary anthropology and medicine also affirmed that syphilis was endemic among people of African descent. One physician wrote in 1886 that "at least half of all negro men" had syphilis but that it was "generally mild . . . running through its course without any treatment." Another argued that when the North's invasion of the South had freed the slaves, this laid the groundwork for the South's ultimate revenge: "an invasion of the North" by syphilitic black migrants. One popular theory of the period was that the disease was actually an African leprosy. As Keith Wailoo has pointed out, some physicians and policy makers predicted that, bereft of the health care supposedly provided by slave owners, emancipated blacks would gradually die off from diseases such as syphilis and tuberculosis. Given these assumptions, trying to protect black men from syphilis must have seemed as pointless as trying to police venereal disease in black prostitutes. Even more important, registering black-run brothels would have declared to white men that sex with black prostitutes was both safe and acceptable. In choosing not to include black-run brothels in the regulation system, city authorities for the first time drew the color line in Davenport's sex trade. They also declined to provide black citizens with the protections Mayor Vollmer insisted he was providing to whites.[44]

MUNICIPAL INCOME FROM REGULATED VICE

Only a year after Vollmer instituted regulation, Iowa's legislature produced a law one newspaper called "an instance of political acrobatism that is without parallel in history": the mulct law, a statute aimed directly at Davenport and similar cities. From 1884 to 1894, the Davenport city government had openly flouted the state Prohibition law, and it was hardly alone. In 1892–93, the federal government collected taxes from 6,599 liquor dealers in Iowa, in spite of state law prohibiting the sale or manufacture of alcoholic beverages. During same period, roughly two hundred saloons did business in Davenport, with the city collecting a quarterly license fee from each. Such open defiance of state law rankled many legislators. Unwilling to declare Prohibition a failure but concerned about the growing political power of those who favored "personal liberty," Prohibition moderates in the state legislature fashioned a compromise. Modeled on an Ohio law, Iowa's 1894 mulct law continued the ban on the sale or manufacture of alcoholic beverages. Prohibition remained in force. But the law also provided that in cities with a population over five thousand, when a majority of voters signed a statement of consent, liquor sellers could be assessed a tax of six hundred dollars, and payment of the tax would be a bar to prosecution under the Prohibition law. In other words, while the sale of liquor was illegal, saloon keepers in some urban places could operate openly without fear of prosecution. The mulct law set rigid standards for the location, conduct, and hours of these businesses: open no earlier than five A.M. and no later than ten P.M., for example, and closed on Sundays. The law also prohibited tables, chairs, screens, and side entrances; outlawed women employees; and banned the popular workman's free lunch. Davenport authorities were just as selective regarding the new statute as they had been with the old Prohibition law. The city collected the mulct tax, which was triple the old license fee, but ignored the rigid rules.[45]

In Davenport, the mulct law combined with the regulation system to turn the downtown sporting district into a money machine for the city. In 1891–92, before the mulct tax, Davenport collected almost twenty-three thousand dollars in license fees from saloons, about 25 percent of the city's general fund. In 1895–96, the city collected more than double that amount from the mulct tax plus another forty-four hundred dollars in (reduced) license fees—roughly 40 percent of the general fund. Although the city treasurers' records for 1892–93 through 1894–95 (the period when both the regulation system and the mulct law came into effect) have been lost, it seems clear that taxes on "illegal" saloons provided a burst of income for the city. Over the next several years, residents' property taxes dropped while city revenues climbed. By 1902, the city council had eliminated property taxes for the general fund altogether, a situation that continued for six years. The choice was not surprising. In 1902, the general fund closed with a surplus of more than seventy thousand dollars (almost half again the total expenses for that fund).[46]

Compared with the mulct tax, the income directly from fines on prostitutes was a drop in the bucket, amounting to about eighty-two hundred dollars in 1895–96. But in truth, licensed brothels contributed to the flow of wealth from saloons. The two businesses were complementary. By 1900, Davenport's city directory listed 146 saloons—down from the 200 or so operating from the mid-1880s to the early 1890s. The mulct tax was triple the old license fee, which no doubt pushed some of the smaller, neighborhood saloons—the kind run out of the back room of a corner grocery—out of business. Comparing the locations of saloons listed in the 1892–93 city directory with those listed in the 1900 directory reveals how the mulct law and the regulation regime affected the concentration of saloons. In 1892, 50 of 195 saloons (26 percent) lay in the Bucktown district (the area east of Brady Street from Front to Fifth Streets, bounded by the Chicago, Rock Island, & Pacific tracks, plus the first block of West Front Street facing the river). In 1900, 47 of 146 saloons (32 percent) lay in the same district. The loss of nearly a quarter of Davenport's saloons took place entirely outside Bucktown. Indeed, the concentration of saloons in Bucktown actually increased slightly, because by 1900, the city was reclaiming the first block of West Front Street for respectable businesses. In 1892, there had been 8 saloons in that single block; in 1900, there were just 2, and neither was operated by the proprietors who had done business there in 1892. Bucktown had become slightly smaller but even more densely devoted to drink. The brothels defined the district as a center of male leisure and entertainment, and the saloons crowded in to capitalize on the area's reputation. Far from creating predatory competition, the concentration proved profitable enough to ensure these saloons' survival even after they paid the high mulct tax.[47]

In Davenport, a local legend suggests that contemporaries may have grasped the way prostitution enhanced saloons' profitability. According to a story that has circulated since perhaps the 1920s, the city taxed prostitutes in the 1890s to pay for a new city hall. Behind the story is a core of truth: in the mid-1890s, in the depths of a national depression, Davenport built a ninety thousand dollar city hall without issuing bonds. Given that the fines and fees paid by prostitutes usually hovered around seven to nine thousand dollars a year, the city's quick retirement of the debt could not have been financed by prostitution alone. The mulct tax, however, provided just the shot of cash the city needed at just the right time. The substitution of prostitutes for saloons makes a juicier story but may also reflect a kind of metonymic memory. The saloons' profits were intensely linked to prostitution, so that the prostitutes, not the mulct tax, got the legendary credit for the city's financial boost.[48]

Although Davenport's business owners never spoke publicly about it, they may have believed that regulated prostitution had other economic benefits for the city as well. Spokane, Washington, businessmen repeatedly organized to oppose all efforts to suppress prostitution. One newspaper editorialized in 1895 that brothels "give the city an attractiveness it would not possess if they were closed, thereby attracting miners and others and making business for the merchants." Unlike Spokane, Davenport's hinterland did not harbor a large population of miners, lumbermen, or similar groups of unattached men. Yet testimony in court cases and reports in newspapers emphasized the presence of traveling salesmen, farmers, and other visitors to the city as patrons of prostitutes. If Davenport's businessmen thought like those in Spokane, it may help to explain the continuing support for regulation.[49]

Indeed, between the revenue generated by licensed prostitution and local support for saloons, Davenport's reform politicians had trouble finding a constituency. In October 1895, after losing his bid to unseat Mayor Vollmer the previous spring, S. F. Smith joined with a group of ministers and businessmen in an attempt to form a Citizens' League. Their avowed model was the Chicago Civic Federation, established just a year earlier. Citizens in Chicago had been electrified—and mortified—when "Maiden Tribute of Modern Babylon" author W. T. Stead turned his moral searchlight on their city, exposing its sordid secrets in *If Christ Came to Chicago*. In response, the Civic Federation brought together businessmen and reformers to address Chicago's social problems. In Davenport, the Citizens' League called for "civic purity" through the "enforcement of present laws and the enactment of such laws as are needed to accomplish that result." Focusing on gambling, prostitution, and Sunday hours for saloons as the most pressing concerns, the organizers arranged for Davenport's ministers to announce their meeting from the pulpits on Sunday. The response was underwhelming. Just twelve men, six of them ministers, came to the meeting. Disheartened, the would-be organizers shelved the project, but not before listening to one attorney express the source of their frustration. Faced with local grand juries that "chose to overlook" violations of state law, he called for the legislature to create an alternative general district court in Des Moines that could step in when local citizens ignored their duty. That way, he argued, "state law could be brought to bear upon houses of evil wherever located."[50]

No remedy of that sort could be expected from Des Moines, but another opportunity to reform Davenport's morals appeared the following spring. After four years in office, Vollmer declined to run again, and his departure eased the way for a Republican candidate. Smith won the nomination, and this time he won the election as well, becoming the city's first Republican mayor in fifteen years. Democrats held onto a slim majority in the city council, but another Republican, C. H. Hubbell, won the election for police magistrate.[51]

Smith's election put the fear of God into some denizens of Bucktown. The New England–born son of a Baptist minister, Smith had a reputation as a philanthropist, reformer, and temperance advocate, and he caught some reflected glow from his father, S. F. Smith Sr., the author of the patriotic hymn, "My Country, 'Tis of Thee." Unlike Vollmer, Mayor Smith made no inaugural address announcing new policies, though he did replace Police Chief Kessler with longtime Captain Henry Martens. Smith's silence on policy created "consternation throughout the tenderloin district." According to the *Democrat*, "the proprietors and inmates . . . are in daily expectancy of trouble at the hands of the authorities of the city, and a number of them are talking of closing their houses and moving out of town." Creating further confusion about the future of the licensing system, newly seated police magistrate Hubbell declared he would not continue the system of assessing fines against registered prostitutes without the formality of a trial. When a brothel keeper appears in court, "she will not make any stipulated monthly license payments to the city treasury through the police court," reported the *Democrat*. Or so everyone supposed.[52]

In spite of these warnings, on the "regular day" for brothel keepers to appear in police court and pay their fines, fifteen women showed up, money in hand. Hubbell collected the money. The papers warned that the women might be arrested and fined again at any time, but no such arrests followed. Matron Hill's records show the same pattern that had prevailed for the past four years: brothel keepers continued to appear and pay a "fine" at the end of each month, and arrests of brothel keepers at other times were rare. In spite of expectations that the reform Republican mayor would shut down the licensed brothels, the system remained intact. Indeed, the *Democrat* alleged that the number of prostitutes in town was higher than it had been at the end of Vollmer's term, as newly emboldened brothel keepers began registering new inmates from Chicago and elsewhere. Regulation had become so lucrative and so well established that even a reform Republican could not easily displace it.[53]

Members of the Charitable Alliance had campaigned for a police matron because they hoped she would be an instrument for ending prostitution, for aiding any woman whose victimization or destitution left her to see the brothel as her only alternative. In the hands of Mayor Vollmer, however, the matron's office became the hub of a system of regulated prostitution. Official policy now proclaimed that prostitution was inevitable and necessary, that women's work in brothels protected the health of men and the safety of women who remained at home—a blow to those who preferred to argue that prostitution was the result of men's predation or women's poverty. Defended as modern and scientific by the Democrat who installed the policy, it was retained as popular and profitable by the Republicans who succeeded him in office. Public criticism by the medical society did nothing to alter the city's policy, and no other criticism even found a public hearing—not even when a Citizens' League sought to create a forum where those appalled by the system could voice their ire.

The success of Davenport's system of regulated brothels suggests that, far from being a shameful urban secret, prostitution was in fact taken for granted by citizens or at least by voters. Davenport's approach rested on the assumption that prostitutes were not victims but wantons, women whose nature impelled them into sexual commerce. The nature of men and the nature of wantons could not be changed, so the question was not one of suppression but of management. Especially in a city where liquor laws had long been flouted, choosing to manage openly another illegal activity may not have seemed unreasonable, especially when it could be defended as protecting the health and liberty of the male citizenry.

8

PROTECTING MEN BY REFORMING GIRLS
Good Shepherd Homes

> On May 26th we received our first sheep, a child in years but mature in the knowledge of vice and wickedness. . . . The whole community assembled to receive our first child. Poor little Dolorosa looked so frightened on seeing the nuns in white but soon grew accustomed to us as well as her surroundings.
> —"Annals," Convent of the Good Shepherd, Dubuque, Iowa

ONE MIDNIGHT IN LATE JUNE 1894, police entered the home of Mrs. Mary Himes in Bucktown, arresting her along with her fourteen-year-old daughter, Eva, and a man named Tom Gaskey. The charge against Mrs. Himes was "disturbing the peace," but the newspapers agreed her real crime was keeping "a resort of improper character." Her daughter, the *Democrat* delicately reported, had been "associated with her." The police magistrate levied a fine of one hundred dollars. Unable to pay, Mary Himes served out a sentence in the house of detention. While incarcerated, she gave written consent for Eva, who was not a Catholic, to be placed in the care of the Sisters of the Good Shepherd, three hundred miles away in Omaha. Eva signed an agreement as well, promising to remain at the convent for three years. Eva more than kept her word. She stayed on for twenty-six years. In 1920, at the age of forty, Eva Himes died among the sisters with whom she had chosen to spend her life.[1]

When Eva Himes boarded the train for Omaha, she joined a growing stream of girls sent by public authorities in Davenport to private Catholic reformatories in several midwestern states. The policy of placing girls in reformatories called Good Shepherd Homes began in 1893 and expanded as a necessary adjunct to the system of regulated brothels. Between 1893 and 1910, city authorities placed at least 260 girls—and probably twice that number—in Good Shepherd Homes in Omaha, Peoria, Dubuque, and elsewhere. Like the system of brothel regulation, the use of Good Shepherd Homes was entirely extralegal. Indeed, it violated several state laws regarding the institutionalization of minors. Yet Good Shepherd Homes became the city's choice for dealing with girls on the streets.[2]

The decision to turn to private reformatories did not reflect a desire to accommodate the girls' or their parents' religion; two-thirds of those sent were not Catholic. Nor was this a case of a locally dominant group proselytizing for its faith. Davenport was not an especially Catholic city. In the 1895 census, only 13 percent of the population identified itself as Catholic, a figure slightly higher than the number of members reckoned by the local Catholic churches. Instead, the choice to use these private reformatories reflects the triumph of the view that girls became prostitutes because their homes were vicious, not because public policy legitimized prostitution as a form of employment. When Mayor Henry Vollmer announced that Davenport would move from tolerating its brothels to regulating them, he was responding in part to a wave of concern about girls on the streets that had been raised by the courtroom revelations of Dolly Hamerly, Mamie Woods, and Ada Ammerman. Jurors in those cases were reluctant to penalize men for breaking a law the jurors found unreasonable: the girls were prostitutes no matter what their age, and no man should face penitentiary time for soliciting a prostitute. Vollmer's new policy set out to clarify which women were sexually available and enforced a minimum age of eighteen for registered prostitutes. For younger girls, Good Shepherd Homes became the foundation of a second extralegal policy that operated in coordination with brothel regulation. Rather than defend against charges that regulation encouraged girls to become prostitutes, city authorities removed girls from their homes and placed them in private reformatories, thus demonstrating a commitment to saving girls from the brothel.[3]

STATE LAW AND PRIVATE REFORMATORIES

Davenport's reliance on Good Shepherd Homes reflects authorities' desire to find a flexible alternative to the reformatory available under the law, the Iowa Industrial School for Girls at Mitchellville. When city authorities began using Good Shepherd Homes, they stopped sending girls to the state institution. Davenport had never sent many girls to the reformatory—one or two a year at most from the 1870s to the early 1890s. But between police matron Sarah Hill's arrival in July 1893 and 1910, the matron's docket lists just one girl committed to Mitchellville. The state reports from Mitchellville confirm her records. While other Iowa counties with large urban populations continued to commit girls to Mitchellville throughout the 1890s and

1900s, authorities in Davenport substituted the private reformatories operated by the Sisters of the Good Shepherd. Scandals following an 1899 riot at Mitchellville no doubt provided support for the choice, but those revelations could only confirm a preference established six years earlier. Private reformatories and commitments arranged outside the legal system gave the city the flexibility to create an efficient system for controlling girls whose conduct marked them as potential prostitutes. As with brothel regulation, the hub of this system was the office of Matron Hill, who developed a range of strategies for removing girls from their homes and persuading families to cooperate. As she openly admitted, parents were often "coerced into it."[4]

Most of the hundreds of girls sent to Good Shepherd Homes would never have been removed from their homes if commitment to the state industrial school had been the only option. Between 1893 and 1906, state law permitted the district court to commit a girl to Mitchellville only if she were convicted of a crime or if a parent or guardian petitioned to have her declared incorrigible. A girl like Eva Himes, who had been convicted of nothing, would have been eligible for Mitchellville only if her mother employed an attorney and requested a hearing, and even then, a judge might decline the request. The juvenile court system established in Scott County in 1906 eased the process of commitment to Mitchellville and permitted almost anyone—not just a parent—to petition for a child to be declared incorrigible. But by 1906 reliance on Good Shepherd Homes was so well established that even the juvenile court used them, despite a provision of the law that explicitly barred the juvenile court from placing a child in an institution outside her or his home county, much less out of state.[5]

Other than commitment to the state industrial school, state law provided few tools for those seeking to intervene in a girl's home life. Under legislation dating from 1878, the courts could commit boys under twelve and girls under fourteen to "homes for the friendless" if the children's parents were dead, were habitual drunkards, were in prison for a crime, or had abandoned the family or if the mother were an inmate of a house of ill-fame. Few of the girls singled out as potential prostitutes fit this law, which was designed to give authorities the power to place children in orphanages. In 1902, a revision made a child in "circumstances tending to induce such child to lead a dissolute, immoral or vicious life" subject to commitment to a private institution, but many of the girls who attracted police attention in Davenport were over fourteen, too old for this provision. The maximum ages set for commitment to "homes for the friendless" derived from the historic practice of binding out indigent adolescents as poor-law apprentices. A girl of fourteen, the law proposed, should not be sent to a "home for the friendless" because she was old enough to earn her keep. But as far as Mrs. Hill and authorities in Davenport were concerned, such models did not fit the girls whose conduct earned them a reputation as wayward: "Private families are not open to them, and in a majority of cases cannot be expected to be, and there is no other place here that is open to them, except the house of shame." Faced with so many obstacles to legal intervention, Matron Hill and the police authorities in Davenport turned to the private sector and worked outside the law. They were not alone. Throughout the 1880s and 1890s, reformers increasingly promoted private institutions as the best way to deal with problem girls.[6]

When Mrs. Hill placed Eva Himes in the Omaha convent-reformatory, one woman publicly protested the decision to send the girl out of state. By 1894, "Mother" Lovina Benedict was one of Iowa's best-known crusaders on behalf of "erring girls." Thirteen years earlier, Mother Benedict, a minister for the Society of Friends, had launched a campaign to raise money and support for a private reformatory for girls and women under the auspices of the Woman's Christian Temperance Union (WCTU). The home opened in Des Moines in 1882, and Benedict, a gifted speaker and an effective lobbyist, won state funding for it as well. The home, which Benedict imagined as a refuge for girls and women who wished sincerely to leave the life of prostitution, remained under WCTU control.[7]

Mother Benedict brought an intense personalism to her crusade. The WCTU named the home in her honor, and she tended to treat it as an extension of herself, a pattern that inevitably led to conflict with the WCTU board. As she traveled the state speaking about the need for the home and soliciting donations, Mother Benedict also visited brothels to pray with the inmates. When she found a candidate for reform, she would bring the girl back to the home and insist on her admission. The board frequently felt that her candidates were inappropriate—young women with venereal disease, girls of good character who were, "through a single misstep," pregnant and wished only a brief stay to conceal their pregnancy, even small babies whose commitment to the home protected their unmarried mothers from scandal. Mother Benedict frequently favored compassionate efforts to protect a girl's reputation by hiding her "sin." The home's administrators preferred prostitutes who confessed their sin, repented, and stayed long enough to be reformed. In 1886, Mother Benedict resigned as the Benedict Home's financial agent and opened a second institution, the Retreat, in her own home in Decorah, which she could operate according to her own beliefs.[8]

Responding to Mother Benedict's complaint that Eva Himes should not have been sent out of the state, police matron Hill insisted that there were no real alternatives. Eva, she declared, "was not a candidate for Decorah or Des Moines," the two homes founded by Mother Benedict. She was not a prostitute in need of reforming or an otherwise respectable girl who had "misstepped" into pregnancy. She was instead a girl from a dangerous home who needed only "the restraint usually provided in any well regulated private family." Defending her decision to place Eva in a Catholic institution, Mrs. Hill argued, "the good sisters are the only people who (so far as I know) have established such homes and opened wide the doors."[9]

Mrs. Hill need not have explained Good Shepherd Homes to Mother Benedict. Before the opening of the Benedict Home in 1882, Mother Benedict had helped remove a sixteen-year-old girl from a brothel but then was at a loss about what to do. In desperation, she took the girl to the Good Shepherd Home in St. Paul. "I will never forget the humiliation that I felt as a Protestant" seeking help from the sisters, "whose religion I had always been taught was antagonistic to mine," she wrote in her memoirs. But she and her young charge were treated cordially, and the sisters invited her to join them in their morning devotions. After touring the home, Mother Benedict was mightily impressed. "I must confess I bowed to the cloister and said, 'Amen![']" she recalled. Having witnessed what the sisters were accomplishing, she pledged "to go and do likewise," modeling the WCTU Benedict Home in part on the Good Shepherd Home in St. Paul.[10]

Good Shepherd Homes may have been a revelation to Mother Benedict, but they were an international institution by the 1880s with foundations on nearly every continent. In the United States, five French sisters established an outpost in Louisville, Kentucky, in 1842, and over the next decades, the order spread west to the Mississippi Valley and east to New York, Boston, Philadelphia, and Baltimore. The St. Paul foundation, which eventually had jurisdiction over convent-reformatories in Iowa and Nebraska, began work in 1868. By the end of the century, a network of Good Shepherd Homes stretched across the country. The Peoria home, under the St. Louis province, was established in 1891, the Omaha home in 1894, and the two Iowa foundations, in Dubuque and Sioux City, in 1903. The example of the Good Shepherd Homes figured in the debates over the house of detention in 1889, and Chicago police matrons' use of the homes was almost certainly familiar to members of Davenport's Charitable Alliance, who investigated Chicago's matrons and eventually hired police matron Annie Davis from a Chicago precinct house. Sarah Hill also trained in Chicago, and her familiarity with the homes undoubtedly began there. One of the first Davenport girls she placed went to the Chicago Good Shepherd Home.[11]

By 1903, Davenport's citizens were organizing to bring a Good Shepherd Home to the city. A delegation of women, apparently led by Jessie Peck Vollmer, the wife of former mayor Henry Vollmer, went to meet with the sisters at their motherhouse and returned with a favorable report. As efforts unfolded over the following months, organizers in Davenport focused their hopes not on the Congregation of Our Lady of Charity of the Good Shepherd of Angers, which ran the homes in Dubuque, Peoria, and Omaha, but on a related order, the Sisters of Our Lady of Charity of Refuge. A group of sisters from Buffalo, New York, visited the city in January 1904. Both orders shared origins in the same seventeenth-century French convents founded by St. John Eudes, and both operated reformatories for girls, but the Sisters of Our Lady of Charity of Refuge maintained local autonomy rather than the centralized administration of the Sisters of the Good Shepherd. Since the Good Shepherds had just established homes in Dubuque and Sioux City, they may have been unwilling to consider Davenport's request for a third home in Iowa.[12]

The sisters from Buffalo met with citizens and with officials of the Davenport and Scott County governments. The newspapers expressed enthusiasm for the project, with the *Davenport Republican* praising the community show of support and calling the movement "worthy of encouragement." Both the city council and the county board of supervisors passed resolutions favoring the home, as did a meeting of citizens. At the meeting, every man and woman who spoke favored the establishment of the home, including Rev. Ned Lee, the evangelical clergyman who operated the People's Union Mission, and Jessie Peck Vollmer. Rabbi W. H. Fineschriber sounded the only mild note of dissent. He "expressed himself deeply in sympathy" with the project but thought it a bad precedent to appropriate tax funds for the home, as others were suggesting. The rabbi lost, and the resolution called for city and county appropriations. In spite of the local enthusiasm for the project, the sisters declined the offer, and Matron Hill remained dependent on distant reformatories.[13]

In many ways, Davenport's use of Good Shepherd Homes anticipated the juvenile court systems created by Progressive reformers a few years later. Just as juvenile courts sought to provide flexible intervention free of the rigid rules of criminal court, the system Davenport built around the police matron's office and the Good Shepherd Homes emphasized flexibility and informality. Indeed, Mrs. Hill's methods resemble the "unofficial" dockets of juvenile courts. David Rothman found that juvenile courts handled nearly half of their cases "unofficially," relying on probation officers rather than judges, with clients accepting "voluntary" probation rather than a court order. In the juvenile courts, the rhetorically assumed client was the delinquent boy, but Davenport's system addressed only girls and young women. Gender marked not only the clients but the authorities as well. Police matron Sarah Hill took the role of social worker and judge, and women operated the reformatory institution of choice. While it lacked both the uniformly male face of the criminal court and its inflexible procedures, Davenport's improvised alternative also lacked the legal protections such procedures could offer.[14]

Eva Himes entered this system when she and her mother were arrested—arrests that remain, for the historian, suffused with ambiguity. The newspapers reported that Mrs. Himes kept a brothel, and early articles hinted that Eva did business as an inmate. But Mrs. Himes had not registered as a brothel keeper, and Matron Hill's docket, which was never shy about such matters, listed Mrs. Himes's occupation merely as "housewife" and her offense as "disturbing the peace." The arrests had been prompted by a complaint from the wife of Tom Gaskey, the man arrested with Mary and Eva Himes. Judging from the city directory, Mrs. Himes and her husband were not living together: Eva's father resided about fifteen blocks away, in a respectable part of town. The *Democrat*, for its part, reported that Eva's father was "away from home all the time."[15]

One plausible explanation is that Eva's parents had separated and that her mother was keeping company with a married man. When his angry wife went to the police, their intervention revealed a home that violated community standards of respectable behavior. They exposed Mrs. Himes as an unfit parent, raising her daughter in an immoral atmosphere. A home in Bucktown, with registered brothels on every side, could only have increased the impression that Eva Himes was in danger. The *Democrat* quickly retreated from its earlier hint that Eva was a prostitute, suggesting instead that although it would "not do to leave her here with her mother," she was "thought not to have been influenced to the wrong to any serious extent." Mrs. Hill, the police matron, explained in a letter to the editor that Eva's "only crime [was] being found in bad company"—presumably, her mother's.[16]

Mrs. Himes's case also suggests one of the ways policing agents of Davenport—in this case the matron and the police magistrate—could cooperate to compel a parent to place her daughter in a Good Shepherd Home. Mrs. Himes's hundred dollar fine is key to this story. In 1894, a hundred dollars was an extraordinary fine: the usual penalty for disturbing the peace was five dollars. Even brothel keepers got off with less than Mrs. Himes. That same month, Minnie Hagan, with five prostitutes working in her house, paid a seventy-five dollar fine, the highest for any of Davenport's brothel keepers. The highest fine not related to brothel keeping that month was the single dollar assessed against several vagrant women. A fine so high Mrs. Himes could not possibly pay it ensured that she would be placed in the custody of Mrs. Hill for at least thirty days, permitting the matron to use various tactics of persuasion to achieve the goal of removing Eva from her home. As matron, Hill could offer the bribe of early release for a signed authorization or could spend a month describing the advantages Eva would gain in the care of the sisters. Whatever strategy she employed, in this case Mrs. Hill succeeded. She often did.[17]

THE GIRLS IN THE HOMES

Over the roughly seventeen years covered in this study, I have identified 127 Davenport girls sent to Good Shepherd Homes, and most of the girls were placed by the police matron. According to records kept by the convents, family members placed only 19 of the girls, and 3 girls placed themselves (one with the assistance of Mrs. Hill). Police matron Hill's records list 84 girls sent to Good Shepherd reformatories in Chicago, Milwaukee, St. Paul, Omaha, Peoria, and Dubuque, but she claimed to have placed more than 200 between 1893 and 1903 alone. The records kept by Good Shepherd Homes in Omaha and Dubuque and newspaper reports of Mrs. Hill's activities make it clear that Mrs. Hill did not record in her official docket every girl she placed.[18]

The differences between the records kept by Mrs. Hill and those kept by the convents suggest the role Mrs. Hill played in influencing families' decisions. For example, of twenty-four inmates listed in the records of the Dubuque institution as having been placed by Matron Hill, nine do not appear in Hill's records. Of forty-one who were placed by various authorities, including Mrs. Hill and the courts, seventeen do not appear in her records. Most (79 percent) of those listed by the convents as placed by members of their own families also appear in Mrs. Hill's dockets, suggesting that even when an arrest or other encounter with the police did not lead the police matron to place a girl, Mrs. Hill might still guide the family toward the Good Shepherd Homes.[19]

Most girls were in their mid-teens. Those placed by authorities averaged just over sixteen years old; those placed by their families were somewhat older, between seventeen and eighteen. The records kept by the convents also indicate whether the girls were Catholic when admitted. Half the girls placed by their families were Catholic, while half were not. Not surprisingly, families sent Catholic girls at a younger age, about sixteen. Non-Catholics placed by their families were significantly older, between eighteen and nineteen. Among those placed by the authorities, the reverse was true. More than 65 percent of those placed by the authorities were not Catholic, and their average age was between fourteen and fifteen. Catholics placed by the authorities had an average age of about nineteen.

These differences suggest balances being struck between family authority and state power, often to the detriment of families. The largest group of girls from Davenport were non-Catholics placed by the authorities, and these were also the youngest girls, averaging less than fifteen years old. One can imagine that families would be least willing to relinquish these youngest girls, to send them perhaps hundreds of miles away to an alien religious culture. Catholic girls placed by the authorities were older (and fewer) probably because Catholic families were more likely to take the initiative and place a young daughter in a Catholic reformatory. Among Catholics, only young women old enough to be beyond family control—about nineteen—found themselves arriving at the Good Shepherd Home at the behest of public authorities. The large proportion of non-Catholics placed by public authorities is notable because historians who have commented on the use of Good Shepherd Homes in juvenile corrections have tended to assume that they were used only for Catholic children, but such was clearly not the case.[20]

Adding another layer of information to these comparisons sheds even more light on how girls found their way to the homes. The police matron's official docket lists women and children who came into police custody. Most of those whose names appeared had been arrested, although some came asking for aid or lodging and parents brought a few others. Looking at which girls listed in the convent records had contact with the police department and which did not permits further conjectures about the matron's role in placing girls in these reformatories.

For example, all of the non-Catholics placed by their families appeared in the police matron's record as well. This suggests that when a Jewish or Protestant girl came to police attention, the matron could use the opportunity to acquaint her family with an institution that might otherwise be unfamiliar. Among Catholics placed by their families, two-thirds appeared in the matron's record. A daughter's arrest might alert a family of trouble brewing, but unlike non-Catholic families, Catholics could easily learn about Good Shepherd Homes from someone other than the police matron—a parish priest, for example, or the teaching sisters at parochial school. If Catholic parents believed their daughter had strayed, they could turn to the Good Shepherds for help before the girl wound up at the police station. More than 80 percent of Catholics placed by the authorities appeared in the matron's records; again, this is not surprising, because the matron was the authority most likely to place them. But only 53 percent of non-Catholics placed by the authorities appeared in the matron's record. However, the convents described nearly half of the remaining placements of non-Catholics by the authorities (another 22 percent) as being by the matron or at her suggestion. In other words, police matron Hill took or sent these non-Catholic girls to Good Shepherd Homes even though the girls had never been in police custody. This suggests that Mrs. Hill had a kind of outreach, a network that referred girls to her before arrests brought the girls to the police attention. The families of Catholic girls might be referred by a priest and willingly place a troublesome daughter in a Catholic reformatory. If the friendly visitor from the Relief Society identified a Jewish or Protestant girl as "endangered," her family might be skeptical about placing her with the Good Shepherd Sisters. Mrs. Hill, though a Protestant, was far from skeptical, and a referral begun outside police channels might end at the convent's reception room.[21]

These separate routes of referral may reflect class differences, but this question must remain unexplored. In spite of the fact that the convent records list not only each girl's name but those of both her parents, only about a third of families (25/73) appeared in city directories. This in itself may be significant, reflecting a high population of "women adrift," girls traveling to Davenport in search of employment and finding themselves in trouble instead. This was certainly Matron Hill's view of the matter. It may also reflect unstable families in which the primary wage earner was often unemployed and the family, as a consequence, often moved. Most of the girls whose family origins are clear came from economically marginal backgrounds.

One hundred eighteen girls committed to Good Shepherd Homes appear in either the matron's record or city directories or have their occupation identified in the newspapers: seventeen were prostitutes, nine appeared to be domestic servants, six held manufacturing positions, one worked in a saloon, one was a laundress, one a "shop girl," one a department store clerk, and one a bookkeeper (though Matron Hill listed her as a prostitute). No record specified an occupation for the others. Five fathers were laborers, five worked in factories, one was a tailor, one a driver, one a streetcar conductor, one a salesman, one a "magnetic healer," and one owned a factory. In addition, the obituary of another indicated he was a longtime resident of the county poorhouse. Seven girls appeared to live with siblings or widowed mothers. With some exceptions, these were not families or individuals with substantial resources. Some girls may have been the daughters of immigrants, but every girl listed in convent records was born in America.[22]

Of the girls sent to Good Shepherd Homes who passed through police custody, many passed silently, with no cause assigned to their presence in the station. Even before juvenile court laws sought to shield minors from intrusive public scrutiny, Mrs. Hill seems to have elected discretion in her record keeping when girls and young women were involved, and she actively—though not altogether successfully—discouraged the press from publishing the names of the girls she placed. Among those for whom she recorded a cause, 15 percent were merely "cared for." Police arrested fifteen others (18 percent) for vagrancy, five each for "leading an immoral life" and being "an inmate of a house of ill-fame," three each for larceny and disturbing the peace, two for public drunkenness, and one for assault. These fragments of information, while suggestive, convey little sense of what behaviors brought young women to the convent reception room. But if the police matron's record was often discreet, the newspapers—as in the case of Eva Himes—sometimes were not.[23]

For example, the district court sent the two daughters of Isaias Miller, aged fourteen and sixteen, to the Good Shepherd Home at Omaha after "he and his wife were run out of this city . . . as being too vile to live here." Like Eva Himes, public opinion deemed the Miller girls victims of unfit parents. However vile he may have been, Isaias Miller was not willing to relinquish his daughters. Following them to Omaha, he obtained a writ of habeas corpus securing their release. According to the *Democrat*, the cooperative judge was "an ardent member" of the anti-Catholic American Protective Association, only too willing to thwart the efforts of a Catholic institution and restore the girls "to the tender mercies of a father and mother who want them only to make merchandise of them." In making "merchandise" of their daughters, the Millers were not necessarily prostituting them. In the late nineteenth century, reformers considered children who performed in public abused, especially if the children were girls.[24]

Strikingly, this seems to have been the only moment when anti-Catholic sentiment entered public discussion of the city's use of Catholic reformatories, and no one in Davenport publicly took the protective association's side. Through most of this period, Iowa statutes prohibited placing minors in institutions not of their parents' faith, but this never deterred authorities in Davenport: two-thirds of the girls they placed were not Catholic. That Mrs. Hill's use of Good Shepherd Homes attracted no controversy reflects the new public image of Catholic sisters in the years following the Civil War, when sisters expanded their social services and developed a reputation as efficient institutional administrators. Good Shepherd Sisters in New

York, for example, traced their foundation there to the efforts of a Protestant woman who persuaded Archbishop John Joseph Hughes that New York desperately needed a reformatory institution for girls. Similarly, cities desiring a hospital often courted the Sisters of Mercy.[25]

POLICING SEXUAL CONDUCT

Most often, a girl found herself on the train to Dubuque or Peoria when someone in the community reported an illicit sexual relationship—or the appearance of a relationship—to the police, signaling that the girl was a potential prostitute. For example, neighbors observed that thirteen-year-old Dell was "in the habit of meeting" a fifty-year-old man near his place of work. Police arrested her, and Matron Hill sent her to Peoria in spite of Dell's claim that she was not a prostitute but the man's fiancée. In another case, Matron Hill heard reports of a white teenager named Maggie living with an African American man. Hill sought out the girl and tried to persuade her "that her conduct was very outré," but Maggie's parents resisted Mrs. Hill's intervention. Not until a neighbor complained about a loud, all-night party did police arrest Maggie, her parents, and their African American hosts for disorderly conduct. Maggie too went to Peoria. Sixteen-year-old Emma narrowly escaped being sent to a Good Shepherd Home when police arrested her for "leading an immoral life" with a Chinese man, but when a brothel keeper later sought to enroll Emma's name in the police register of prostitutes, her reprieve was over. She went to Dubuque. Girls may have attracted particular attention when their partners were of another race, but such relationships were no more illegal than others. Iowa had no miscegenation law.[26]

While some mothers and fathers resented the police matron's intrusion into what they considered family concerns, other parents turned to the police matron for help in controlling their daughters. One desperate mother brought her daughter to the station house, "saying she could do nothing with the child, who was going to the bad at a headlong rate." On another occasion, a mother swore out a warrant to have her daughter arrested for vagrancy. Police found the sixteen-year-old camping out on an island with five men and two other young women. Her father, the newspapers alleged, ran "a notorious resort" in Burlington, and her mother had left him. The girl agreed that she would rather go to a Good Shepherd Home than return to her father.[27]

Girls sometimes called attention to themselves by bringing charges against men. Seventeen-year-old Rachel took the first step toward a Good Shepherd Home when she swore out a warrant for seduction against "a prominent young fellow." When she met him in court, Rachel insisted he was not the right man, and the judge released him. She may have lost her nerve or been the victim of greater misrepresentation than she had suspected. But having revealed her own sexual indiscretion, she could not escape. Shortly after she made her accusation, police arrested Rachel for vagrancy "because of the evil life she was leading in a downtown block." One newspaper declared her a "victim of circumstances, her mother having died some years ago and her father having encouraged and assisted her moral ruin." Whatever the truth, the magistrate sentenced Rachel to thirty days in jail but permitted her instead to choose the Good Shepherd Home in Peoria. She went. With her on the train went another girl, placed by her father after she had publicly accused him of committing a murder.[28]

In some cases, the sexual crisis that caught the attention of authorities was rape. Lillie, for example, had just turned ten years old when she became the first girl placed in the newly opened Good Shepherd Home in Dubuque. She had the reputation of a troublemaker even before she accused a middle-aged man of rape. In the span of just two months, she was arrested for assault and picked up as a runaway in a nearby town. After her first arrest, newspapers reported that she used "words which would shock even a courtesan." In her deposition, Lillie testified that her assailant had dragged her into an outhouse and raped her, but he insisted that she had followed him and solicited sex. A young coworker accused them both, testifying that Lillie came into the shop and announced, "We had a good time out there & [he] gave me 50¢." These accusations and the fact that Lillie's older sister had been arrested at least twice for prostitution prompted Matron Hill to take Lillie to the Dubuque Home. Her assailant pled guilty to the lesser offense of assault, for which the usual sentence was thirty days in jail. Lillie remained at the Dubuque home for three years.[29]

Lillie's pattern of conduct and her sister's arrests no doubt led authorities to conclude that her home was unfit and that the Good Shepherd Home was a better alternative. But not every rape victim sent to a Good Shepherd reformatory came from a troubled home. When seven-year-old Isabelle developed gonorrhea, her anguished mother swore out a complaint for rape against two neighborhood young men. A jury convicted one, but in her deposition, Isabelle named at least five other men who had raped and sodomized her at different times. "They gave me a disease," she testified. "It hurts me." No one alleged that she had sought payment, and Isabelle's testimony made it clear that she was an unwilling victim. Describing how one man forced her to perform fellatio, she recalled, "I didn't want to, it almost made me vomit." Nevertheless, at the conclusion of the trial, a petition to the juvenile court argued that Isabelle's "vicious associations" had made her "very depraved and immoral" and recommended that she be placed in an institution where she could receive "proper moral training." The court sent Isabelle to the Good Shepherd Home in Dubuque, where she remained for more than eleven years.[30]

Perhaps because Isabelle did not report the assaults by neighborhood men until after her painful illness raised her mother's suspicions, authorities concluded that her parents were insufficiently watchful. Nevertheless, the petition did not focus on the shortcomings of her home but on her "depravity." Under the circumstances, the judge's decision to remove Isabelle from her home seems a heavy-handed exercise of discretionary power. She was, after all, the seven-year-old victim of a convicted rapist, a girl whose mother sought out and prosecuted the men who injured her. Yet by 1906, what happened to Isabelle was common practice. In the period examined in this study, at least 29 percent of the victims in sexual assault prosecutions ended up in Good Shepherd Homes. In some cases the sisters clearly provided a welcome refuge from a dangerous home. As often as not, however, the decision to remove a girl from her home seemed premised not on a desire to protect the girl but on the assumption that girls were complicit in their rapes and required "proper moral training."[31]

The most revealing of these cases involved Helena and her sisters. By the time the fifteen-year-old went to the Peoria home in March 1908, Helena had already gained a reputation for being "somewhat wayward." Three months earlier, she had been arrested for vagrancy; a year and a half before that, she had been "cared for" at the house of detention. So when her widowed father, Dan, called Helena "incorrigible" and sought to place her in a Good Shepherd Home, Mrs. Hill was ready to assist. Helena's two younger sisters accompanied her, entering the Peoria convent's separate boarding school. In the fall of 1909, after Helena and her sisters had been with the Good Shepherd Sisters for a year and a half, Helena's father wrote asking for Helena, now seventeen, to be returned so she could keep house for him at the new home he was building. The sisters responded that Helena had made such wonderful progress in reform that it would be best for him to take all three daughters and keep his family together. Dan agreed, and in early November he traveled to Peoria and brought the three girls back to the home he still shared with his eldest daughter, May, and her husband, Gus, who was in the process of buying the house from his father-in-law.[32]

Within two weeks, a tale that might have gone into Mrs. Hill's repertoire of success stories went grievously wrong. On the Sunday before Thanksgiving, Helena told her brother-in-law that an infant who had been placed with a foster family several years earlier—a child Gus had supposed to be the fifth born to Helena's and May's late mother—was actually May's child, the product of an incestuous assault by her own father. Worse, Helena revealed, she too had been "ruined" by their father, and she feared living with him again. Gus, distraught, sought help from County Attorney Fred Vollmer, who told him that Dan could not be prosecuted for the assaults on Helena and May because the crimes had been "outlawed"—that is, under the statute of limitations, the time for prosecution had expired. Gus then went to police matron Hill and the juvenile court probation officer, Henry Ditzen. Together, they visited the family home on Wednesday and obtained a confession from

Dan, but they agreed that they could do nothing because of the statute of limitations. They left, as did Gus, who spent the night at his mother's home because he feared violence at the hands of his father-in-law. On Thursday morning, Gus attended early Mass and arranged for the family's priest to call that afternoon. The effort at peacemaking did not go well. That Thanksgiving Day, in the presence of Helena, May, and the priest who had come to mediate, Gus shot and killed his father-in-law in a fit of rage.

To the newspaper editors, to Matron Hill, and to others caught up in this family's trauma, May's and Helena's dark secret came as shocking news, but historian Linda Gordon's work on family violence suggests that "domestic incest" followed a predictable pattern. Just as in the cases Gordon analyzed, Dan's sexual assaults on his eldest daughter began near the time of his wife's death, when she was no longer available as a sexual partner. The girls' mother, on her deathbed, begged May to take over for her to keep the family together. Dan, like other fathers studied by Gordon, turned May into a surrogate wife, compelling her to fulfill both domestic and sexual duties. Gordon found that daughters submitted because they feared and accepted their fathers' authority and felt duty toward their siblings. Their fathers also rationalized sexual exploitation as an assertion of paternal authority. At fourteen, May bore her father's child, but his assaults continued even after the baby's birth. At some point, Helena too became her father's victim. As the girls got older, they found ways to resist. May tried to protect her sister by checking the room and locking the door to their bedroom at night. One night, she opened the closet door and found her father, nearly naked, hiding inside. The girls forced him from the bedroom and locked the door. According to Helena's testimony, such occurrences were frequent: "each time we had to drive him out of our room."[33]

A year or so after May married, Dan conceived the idea of sending Helena to a Good Shepherd Home. In the eyes of Mrs. Hill, sending Helena to Peoria at her father's request must have seemed fairly routine. She had been in trouble with the police and then her father declared her incorrigible. It was an open-and-shut case. But Dan's assaults cast Helena's earlier troubles in a new light. She was just thirteen when Matron Hill noted in her docket that she had "cared for" Helena. Why was Helena at the house of detention? Had she sought Hill's protection but failed for some reason to obtain it? Her second appearance, a December 1907 arrest for vagrancy, occurred more than a year later. The conduct that attracted police attention that winter may have been Helena's way of acting out, expressing the pain and helplessness she felt as the victim of continuing sexual assaults. Helena's vagrancy arrest probably prompted Matron Hill to encourage Dan to place his daughter in a Good Shepherd Home, but after his history of sexual abuse came to light, the newspapers detected a sinister motive for his choice. Calling Dan "crafty," the *Democrat and Leader* argued, "it was not for purpose of obtaining for [his daughters] a moral and educational advancement, but was to outlaw the crimes which he knew would eventually prove his undoing." In other words, Dan sent Helena to the Peoria home to protect himself from her accusations. The conclusion is reasonable. With May's husband, Gus, now living in the home they all shared, Dan's access to Helena's bed was surely limited, and he may have feared that she would reveal the family secret. When the statute of limitations eliminated the chance that Dan would be prosecuted, he felt free to recall her as his housekeeper.[34]

Helena, of course, was terrified of being sent back to live with her father. She sought her brother-in-law's protection and set in motion the events that led to her father's death. After shooting Dan, Gus turned himself in to the police. In spite of overwhelming public sympathy for the devoted husband and hardworking young jeweler who shot the man who had raped his wife, Gus faced indictment for manslaughter. He stood trial the following March, but a few days into the proceedings, the prosecution moved for a dismissal, arguing that the evidence for both self-defense and temporary insanity in the case was overwhelming. The judge readily concurred, and Gus went free.[35]

After Gus shot Dan, the story of May's and Helena's suffering became mere background for the unfolding drama: would an exemplary young man such as Gus go to prison for defending his family's honor? Yet even before the shooting, public authorities' response to the crisis—especially the responses of the police matron and juvenile court officer Henry Ditzen—was limited in revealing ways. When Gus sought his help, Ditzen assured the man that "his connection with the case would be only so far as it affected the younger children," since Helena, at seventeen, was beyond the jurisdiction of the juvenile court. Yet even after Ditzen and Hill had confronted Dan and heard his confession, they took no action on behalf of the girls. Gus left the house, afraid of his father-in-law, but neither Mrs. Hill nor Officer Ditzen moved to take the youngest girls from the house of a confessed child rapist. There is also no evidence that Hill offered to shelter Helena or May in the midst of what must have been a terrifying situation for them all. The failure to offer help to Helena, May, and the younger girls suggests that Matron Hill's focus in such cases was not on protecting girls from the danger in their homes but on "reforming" those who became victims of rape. The Sisters had declared Helena reformed, and her little sisters were not yet victims, so there was no reason for the police matron to intervene.

Girls on the streets were another matter. After Bucktown began turning into a commercial entertainment district, Matron Hill and the police department began to focus more and more attention on the girls who went there for employment or for pleasure. Clara, for example, served drinks in a saloon on Iowa Street between Second and Third. When she asked for her pay, her employer suggested that she could earn more if she offered the customers something besides drinks. Clara's mother complained to the police, and the saloon keeper lost his license. Matron Hill, however, continued to keep an eye on Clara and a few months later took the girl to the Good Shepherd Home in Dubuque. Her mother secured her release eight months later. Nellie and Loretta, both about fifteen, also came to Bucktown hoping to work. The two "stage-struck girls" had signed up with an agent who promised them careers in musical comedy. They professed themselves "willing to begin in the back row carrying a spear." To Nellie, the stage seemed far better than working in a pearl button factory, which was her parents' plan for her. Loretta had worked much of her life in stage shows, though her previous experience primarily involved handling large snakes. Their agent sent them up to Davenport, promising to join them in a few days, but when police got wind of the two girls staying in a Bucktown hotel, they picked them up. Nellie never lost her preference for Bucktown over the button factory and a year or so later wound up before the new juvenile court. The petition argued that she "is incorrigible, runs the street late at night, and does not have proper parental care, and habitually is in such vicious, base, and corrupting surroundings as to bring her within the spirit of this juvenile law." The court dismissed the petition on the grounds that Nellie was sixteen and therefore was beyond the jurisdiction of the juvenile court. Nevertheless, Nellie arrived at the Dubuque convent, where the records indicate that she was sent by the court. Girls who went to Bucktown for a good time also risked being identified as endangered. Maude and Eugenie, fifteen and sixteen, were "constantly on the street as late as 10:30 o'clock at night" and attended "vaudeville theaters almost nightly." Matron Hill sent both girls to Good Shepherd Homes. Grace and Helen similarly spent too much time "on the East side." When police picked them up, Grace's father cooperated with Hill to send his daughter and her companion to a Good Shepherd Home.[36]

An anecdote Mrs. Hill shared with a newspaper reporter summed up her view of the lure of Bucktown and the danger it posed to ordinary working girls and women and to the community at large. A concerned employer questioned her servant: "'You are a good girl,' she said, 'why do you stay out so late?' You can imagine the lady's astonishment when the girl answered her somewhat to this effect: 'You are wrong, Mrs. _____, I am not a good girl.'" After a long, heart-to-heart talk, "the girl then made the startling statement that it is impossible for a girl who has once done wrong to reform in this city. She spoke of the many temptations besetting the young girl on all sides and insisted that it is impossible for the wayward girl to recover her self-respect here." The kindhearted employer persuaded her servant to go to a "refuge," and for good measure, the girl brought along "her most intimate girl companion." Mrs. Hill escorted them both to the Good Shepherd Home in Peoria. This was the paradox of the policy that supported Bucktown: the city posed temptations and danger that could even enter a the home of a "lady" in the guise of a girl who had "done wrong." The solution, however, was not to change the city but to remove the girl.[37]

Sometimes, for all its brevity, the police matron's record reveals a fuller story to the attentive reader. Nineteen-year-old Pearl was one of the few inmates identified in convent records as placing herself in the home. But in the eight months prior to her arrival in Omaha in August 1894, Pearl appeared eleven times in the matron's docket. Under Davenport's system of regulated brothels, Pearl was old enough to register, and she appeared nine times as an "inmate of a house of ill-fame" with brothel keeper Ruth Fairchild, so that Fairchild could be assessed the regular monthly fine. (Pearl was also arrested once, at 1:15 A.M., for stealing a dress, but that is almost certainly another story.) Curiously, Pearl's last arrest as an "inmate" did not link her to Fairchild or to any other registered brothel keeper, and her final arrest was for "vagrancy." Two possible explanations for this sequence suggest themselves. First, this may be a case of downward mobility. Perhaps Pearl had a falling out with Fairchild; perhaps she had become too obviously infected with venereal disease to serve in a brothel. Faced with the grim prospect of working the street, Pearl may have found the Good Shepherd Home an acceptable alternative. A second explanation emphasizes the agency of the police matron. Pearl's last three arrests took place in a single ten-day period. Matron Hill may have identified Pearl as a likely candidate for reform and asked the police department to make a point of bringing her in. Thus, having had her regular appearance with Ruth Fairchild on 28 July, Pearl was arrested on 1 August and yet again on 6 August. Two days later she was in Omaha.[38]

Pearl left the Omaha home almost exactly three years after she entered. Like Eva Himes, she probably signed an agreement promising to remain for that minimum. But Pearl's relationship with the home did not end with her departure in 1897. Three years later, she again committed herself to the home, this time staying five weeks. Seven months later she was back for a nine-day stay. Pearl's reasons for returning are among those secrets the past withholds from the present, but she clearly felt welcome to draw on the sisters' hospitality. Somewhat older than most of the girls placed by the police matron, Pearl was in a position to choose the home as a refuge when she needed it.[39]

Another girl who may have used the Good Shepherd Home to regain control of her life or who at least found it a useful refuge was Jessie, one of three children of a charismatic "magnetic healer." Like Pearl, Jessie was nineteen when she entered the Omaha home, placed by Matron Hill. Jessie, the matron later explained, had been "driven from home by inhuman parental treatment." At the time of her first encounter with the police, Jessie was living "adrift," working as a clerk in one of Davenport's department stores. In April 1899, she made her only appearance in the matron's docket: "taken to St. Luke's Hospital." The docket gives no hint why Jessie needed hospital care, but Hill later recalled that Jessie had been "driven to the point of despair" by the "treatment she had received at home and the temptations that confronted her after she left." Did Jessie collapse from nervous exhaustion? Did she attempt suicide? Was she suffering from venereal disease or a botched abortion? Perhaps she merely had the flu and no one to care for her. Matron Hill offered her recollections at a public meeting to support bringing a Good Shepherd Home to Davenport, so they may reflect her wish to make Jessie's "story" fit the conventional narrative of girls "adrift" in the city. Whatever the cause, a week after being taken to the hospital, Jessie entered the Good Shepherd Home in Omaha. Jessie stayed more than fifteen months, then left "of her own accord," according to convent records. Five months later, she "voluntarily" returned to the home and stayed for another six months. Two years later, she married a young optician from Seattle in her sister's home in Calhoun County, Iowa, far from Davenport. Jessie and her husband settled on the West Coast.[40]

Jessie's story suggests the complex role a Good Shepherd Home could play for a young woman in the turn-of-the-century city. Jessie may have had more resources at her disposal than most teenagers seeking to escape "inhuman parental treatment." (The parent was her father; her mother had been dead for many years.) Jessie's family, though unconventional, was not poor, and she had attended high school. But supporting herself on a clerk's wages was more than even she could manage. Jessie may have entered the home under pressure from Mrs. Hill, but her decision to return for a second stay was probably her own. For a girl struggling to survive in the city, the Good Shepherd Home could also be an open door, a refuge, and a place of rest and security.[41]

"The great and crying need of this town," declared Matron Hill, "is a place of refuge for these cases." Not only was immorality on the rise among local girls suffering from "fool in the head," but Davenport had become a magnet for vulnerable girlhood. "Young women are coming here all the time in search of work. They come from the country, from small villages or from cities at a distance.... Now what place of safety is there for a green country girl, or a girl from a little country village, or even a girl from a larger place, unless she has friends in this city? Where is she to go? Who is to take her in?" For the authorities in Davenport, especially Hill, Good Shepherd Homes were the answer. In the city evoked by Mrs. Hill, the convent stood as an alternative to the brothel, the cloistered sisterhood against the lost sisterhood. Matron Hill could tell more than one pitiful tale of an outcast girl wandering the streets at night only to be given refuge by a kindly prostitute who then begged the matron to take the girl away because the agreement under which brothels operated prohibited very young inmates.[42]

PENITENTS AND SISTERS

Once a girl entered a Good Shepherd Home, she lived a life designed as an antidote to the streets. To accomplish their work of reform, the sisters isolated girls entirely from their previous existences, regulated their lives through enclosure and surveillance, occupied them with labor, and instructed them in the Catholic faith. Much of the description of convent practice that follows is based on prescriptive materials produced by the order for its members' instruction. Hence, it represents an ideal, though perhaps not actual practice.[43]

In laying out the rules by which the homes operated, the order continually emphasized the distinction between "penitents" and sisters, urging that penitents not be asked to make the same sacrifices expected of religious. But the life created for the girls who entered the reformatories was modeled on that lived by the sisters. When a girl entered the home, she gave up her clothing, her possessions, her history, even her name. "Rings, papers, photographs, or other things which may be dangerous to her because of the souvenirs attached to them" the sisters locked away, and any "bad books or papers" they destroyed. "Mistresses," as the order called sisters who supervised the penitents, were instructed to learn what they could about a girl's religious training, baptism, and confirmation but never to "question the child herself on her past life nor let her suspect that we have received any information about her." The goal was to make the penitents "understand that the past is quite past, that with a new name they are to commence a new life, that they will be judged and esteemed only by their conduct in the house."[44]

Penitents also accepted an obligation to remain in the home. If a girl were a minor, her parents or guardian signed an agreement forfeiting "a sum of money" should she leave before reaching her majority. A girl who committed herself signed a similar agreement, generally promising to remain for at least two years. The order did not expect penitents to pay for their maintenance but did expect girls to work at convent industries.[45]

For young girls, especially those unfamiliar with Catholic sisters, immersion in convent life could be shocking. Ten-year-old Lillie, whose jaded language had appalled police and reporters when she was arrested for assault, arrived at the Dubuque home in handcuffs after an escape attempt en route. The whole community assembled to welcome its first penitent, but the sight of the sisters in their strange white veils and habits terrified "Dolorosa," as she was renamed. The sisters began their reform work by "teaching her her prayers also the alphabet; in both she was found quite deficient." (Indeed, the signature on Lillie's grand jury deposition confirms that she could not write her name.)[46]

The Good Shepherd Sisters themselves were a cloistered order. Sisters never left their convent or had contact with "the world" except under extraordinary circumstances. Soliciting charitable donations and other worldly business were performed by "tourieres," or outdoor sisters, who wore a distinctive habit and took no part in the reform work. In great measure, the girls who entered as penitents were cloistered as well. The change from the heterosocial world of the city streets must have been striking, but that was the point. In this regulated, enclosed new life, the sisters sought to teach their charges industry, modesty, and Catholicism.[47]

Good Shepherd Convent, Omaha, c. 1920. When built shortly after the turn of the century, the Omaha convent and reformatory lay at the western edge of the city, contributing to residents' sense of separation from the world. (Collection of the author.)

Admirers in Davenport praised Good Shepherd Homes for being self-supporting and for teaching girls to be self-supporting, but the grinding need for money to maintain both sisters and penitents sometimes led to exploitative conditions. In Omaha, the convent took in fine sewing from "ladies" and contracted with various merchants to make comforters; to crochet shawls, scarves, and vests; and to sew "men's shirts and jumpers" on power machines. In spite of the order's rule that penitents not be compelled "to sit up at night under the pretext that the work is pressing," girls at Omaha did exactly that. According to the manuscript "annals" kept by the convent, "It was difficult to support the number of children under the Sisters' care on their scanty earnings." The sister keeping the annals described all-night work sessions: "The children were willing and most generous and many times stayed up at night to finish some rush order for the store or some customer. By the faint light of coal oil lamps and tallow candles, they plied their needles till night paled into dawn, when they went to take their much-needed rest." Finding that some girls lacked the skills to do fine sewing, the convent took in laundry from churches, families, and Creighton College. The convent at first lacked any washing equipment, so "the washing and ironing had to be done by hand, which made the work of the children hard and laborious." In 1901, the laundry, now expanded into a steam laundry, became the source of a smallpox epidemic when one of the penitents contracted the disease from handling linen sent from a sickroom. More than forty residents fell ill, and the mother superior entreated the attending physician not to report the outbreak to public health authorities for fear that they would shut down the laundry.[48]

In Dubuque, the sisters at first faced difficulty in obtaining contracts. Local factory owners insisted that "they had never given out work and did not care to experiment in that line." Later, hard times affected the sisters as they did the rest of the city. In 1908, they reported, "most of the factories were closed and from early spring until September we had no machine work." The Dubuque convent also moved gradually into sewing, but resistance from factory owners was replaced with resistance from the girls. "We ... have experienced much difficulty in training them, so many are young and prone to idleness," wrote one sister in the convent's annals. Two years later, the convent upgraded from foot-powered to electric sewing machines, and the laundry expanded rapidly, "yet not without many difficulties." It was "only a repitition [sic] of our experience in training our children for the sewing, but victories are never gained without struggles." The perceived "idleness" of the girls in Dubuque raises questions about the alleged "willingness" of the "generous" girls of Omaha, who repeatedly sat up all night to meet contracts, though the difference may simply reflect the charisma of the mother superior in Omaha. Nearly a century later, elderly sisters in the order remembered the reputation of Mother Mary of St. Raphael—tough, and inspiring.[49]

Advocates of the homes claimed that the work performed by girls in the convents made both the homes and the girls self-supporting, but these two interests were at odds. The convents chose work suited to their unusual needs: piecework put out by merchants and manufacturers and low-skill laundry work. These industries were easily brought into a cloistered environment and at their beginning stages required little or no outlay of capital. The sisters did not teach skills with which girls could expect to support themselves when they returned to the world. Girls did not learn bookkeeping, shorthand, typesetting, millinery, or any of the skills by which a woman might earn a living wage. The sisters acknowledged that penitents were mostly "poor children" who would "have to gain their livelihood by honest labor," so mistresses sought to "form [girls] to work, and inspire in them a love of industry." But the order gave little or no thought to vocational training or to preparing girls for financial responsibilities. Penitents received no pay for their labor and were not permitted to handle money. The dime savings bank and passbooks of the Lend a Hand club had no counterpart in the Good Shepherd Homes.[50]

Training in modesty was the second element in the convents' program of reform. Modesty, as understood by the sisters, was a matter of self-presentation that reflected the inner soul, and mistresses were expected to provide an example of modesty to the penitents. For religious, modesty "supposes a certain gravity." To laugh loudly, to cry, to eat or drink in front of the penitents were forbidden, and sisters were encouraged to speak as little as possible: "We lose authority by speaking too much." On some subjects, the sisters were to speak not at all. "The Sisters . . . shall be very circumspect on this point [modesty], and take great care never to speak directly or indirectly, of the sin contrary to this virtue." Instead, "we should inspire horror of all that can wound it in any way without specifying the gravity of the fault." Sexuality was to be veiled in silence. Indeed, the ideal mistress would have little to say on the subject. The one "absolutely necessary qualification" for admission as a postulant was "an untarnished reputation for the individual herself and freedom from any moral stain on the immediate female relatives."[51]

Within the convent, the ideal of modesty reflected in part long-standing traditions of cloistered sisterhoods that emphasized blending of self into community and practices such as grand silence and "custody of the eyes." But this ideal had a useful congruity with late-nineteenth-century assumptions regarding respectable behavior in an urban setting. According to etiquette manuals of the period, women on the street were expected to draw around themselves a "mantle of reserve," that ideally protected them from the intrusive attentions of men. A "lady" was "unobtrusive, never talks loudly, or laughs boisterously, or does anything to attract the attention of the passers-by." She practiced a secular version of "custody of the eyes," keeping them averted from the faces of strangers. The business girls who increasingly populated urban streets could, etiquette writers insisted, draw their freedom of movement from the same dignified demeanor.[52]

This etiquette-book ideal of reserve, designed to contain and control heterosocial encounters in an urban world of strangers, stood in opposition to the street sociability, self-display, and flirtation characteristic of exuberant girl culture. To the police matron and her allies, "display in dress" and the desire to be "seen of men" were seeds of danger, too easily leading to sexual downfall. The discipline of a Good Shepherd Home taught girls to adopt a mantle of reserve. "Propriety and moderation" were the ideal even for recreation: "screaming, shouting, loud laughter, rough plays, course language, and in short, everything that savors of rudeness or vulgarity, should be severely suppressed," urged the order.[53]

To suppress undesirable behavior, the sisters relied on surveillance. Watching was so central to every part of the convents' reform program that sisters who worked directly with the girls were sometimes called "surveillantes." In their descriptions of the intimate transactions of power and the effectiveness of this method of discipline, the sisters often prefigure Foucault. They preferred not to punish girls: "the great point is not to punish but to foresee faults and prevent them, by surveillance." No girl was ever to be left alone, and even in the dormitory, the *surveillante*'s cell was arranged so that she could observe the entire dimly lit sleeping area at any time. In recreation time, when the sisters did not require penitents to maintain silence or to pray aloud, "there should be no corners in which some could hide from the eyes of the mistress. It is in such places the demon lies in wait." If she suspected some penitents of wrongdoing, the *surveillante* "should keep her eyes fixed" on them "until they change their conduct." Girls in Good Shepherd Homes may have been cloistered away and removed from public view, but they were on display at all times and learned to conduct themselves accordingly.[54]

Instruction in modesty, the presentation of the outward self, had its complement in the presentation of the inward self through the sacrament of confession. Instruction in the Catholic faith was fundamental to the sisters' reform work. The penitents "should be taught how to examine their conscience, excite themselves to contrition, and present themselves at the holy tribunal to accuse themselves of their sins." Penitents learned the catechism and prayed aloud while they worked. In the schoolroom they read sacred history and lives of saints. They attended daily Mass. But the heart of the reform work lay in bringing girls to the sacrament of confession. Girls made regular retreats, and in their histories, the sisters recorded many examples of remarkable conversions, especially those ending in a penitent's pious death.[55]

In Davenport, advocates of the Good Shepherd Homes repeatedly insisted that their work was "undenominational," claiming that "girls entering them were not questioned as to their religious beliefs." But the records kept by the convents carefully recorded each entering girl as either Catholic or "non-Catholic." The sisters accepted girls of any—or no—religious faith, but the order's mission undeniably included proselytizing. To the traditional vows of poverty, chastity, and obedience, the Good Shepherd Sisters added a fourth: zeal for souls. In practice, this meant laboring to bring wayward Catholics back to the sacraments and non-Catholics into the church. As late as 1930, one mother superior confirmed that the most important element of the sisters' reform work was "frequent confession and communion. . . . We do not force any girl to go to confession. We depend on our ability to convince her that it is the right thing."[56]

Girls subjected to this kind of pressure did not simply acquiesce. In fact, as the annals of the Dubuque convent attest, religion became a specific point of resistance for some. One girl who "positively refused to go to the Chapel where she would see that 'Catholic Priest' " required "a great deal of coaxing and maneuvering" on the part of the sisters before she would take part in a retreat. Another girl, placed in the home by her "respectable Catholic parents," refused "to perform any of the ceremonies of our Holy religion and absolutely [denied] that she was ever a Catholic." To impress on her "the awful danger of her condition," the superior led her to the sanctuary and forced her down on her knees before the crucifix. When a priest came to hold a retreat, "Carmelitta" refused to participate, but the sisters devised a ruse to bring the girl and the priest together. After a brief conversation with Carmelitta, the priest believed he had accomplished nothing, but later that day the girl reported to her mistress, "O Mother, I saw Father, he is awfully nice, he really talked to me!" and promised to "go first" at the next confession. Another girl was brought to the home in such an advanced state of disease that she died within a few weeks. The sound of voices "wafting heavenward in hymn and prayer ... rather annoyed than pleased her and she peevishly complained that they prayed too much here."[57]

Resistance came in secular forms as well, including escape. One group of girls slipped out during the night after "helping themselves to various articles of clothing they thought they might need" from the possessions of their sleeping companions. They planned to follow the railroad track to a small-town station "where they might board the train secretly and steal a ride" to Chicago, which their leader painted in enticing terms. They were caught when a station official, the brother of another penitent, suspected who they were and turned them in. A fourteen-year-old domestic from Davenport, placed in the home after her sexual relationship with her employer was discovered, succeeded in escaping for two days, but the Dubuque police returned her to the home.[58]

While some girls resisted, others came to find life in a Good Shepherd Home desirable. Eva Himes, for example, never left. Jessie and Pearl left but returned for additional visits of a few days or a few months. Records from both the Omaha and Dubuque convents reveal examples of other penitents who left only to return, sometimes repeatedly. About 14 percent of the penitents placed from Davenport returned voluntarily at least once after their initial release. For example, Isabelle, the seven-year-old victim of multiple rapes, stayed for eleven years. At eighteen, the sisters released her to the custody of an aunt, but within a week she returned to stay for another three years. Etta was only twelve when she first entered the Dubuque home in 1903. After three and a half years, the sisters returned her to her parents, but a little more than eighteen months later, she was back. After two years, she left again, this time to live with an aunt. But within six months, she returned yet again to the convent. This stay lasted several more months until Etta, now nineteen, found a home with her sister. During these years, Etta's mother spent repeated terms the house of detention for drunkenness and disorderly conduct, suggesting a powerful motive for Etta's attachment to the Good Shepherd Home.[59]

Pearl, Jessie, Eva, Isabelle, and Etta all first entered Good Shepherd Homes as non-Catholics. Of these, only Jessie remained outside the fold. Indeed, most of the girls coming back to the home after their initial release who had first entered as non-Catholics returned as Catholics. This is hardly surprising. Conversion of non-Catholics was one of the central missions of the order. But community life had its own satisfactions, and these were most readily available to penitents who embraced its spiritual dimension. Sodalities given to a particular devotion were open to penitents, and girls came to esteem wearing the badge of a sodality as a privilege. The sisters might permit girls whose piety was especially marked to become "consecrates," remaining among the penitents but taking a yearly vow to the Virgin and wearing a modified habit and veil. After a period of probation, the consecrate might renew her consecration "before Bishop or priest according to a very beautiful and impressive ceremonial, receiving at his hand first a lighted wax candle, and then . . . the girdle, the cord, and the rosary." Penitents who found a vocation in religious life could not join the Sisters of the Good Shepherd (it accepted only postulants "with untarnished reputation"), but the sisters maintained an affiliate order, the Sister Magdalenes. Magdalenes took no part in the reform work of the Good Shepherds but were instead contemplatives. Following the Carmelite Rule, they observed perpetual cloister, spending seven hours a day in prayer. At least one girl from Davenport, arrested for vagrancy in 1906, eventually entered the Sister Magdalenes. Her spiritual potential must have been evident from the first. Not long after she arrived at the Dubuque home, the sister keeping the annals made special note of the girl: "although not a catholic we expect very good results from her stay here."[60]

The existence of the Sister Magdalenes, the girls and young women who voluntarily returned to the convent homes, and those such as Eva Himes who stayed on as permanent members of the community point up one aspect of the Good Shepherd Homes that distinguished them from private Protestant reformatories being developed in the late nineteenth century. As Peggy Pascoe and Regina Kunzel have argued, Protestant rescue missions and homes for unwed mothers had as their primary goal the restoration of "erring" women and girls to an ideal of domesticity. For the client population, these homes defined successful reform as the formation of companionate, Christian marriages. As Kunzel found, "marriage to almost any man . . . was better than no marriage at all." The Good Shepherd Sisters certainly had no objection to successful marriages by their penitents. But the homes also posed an alternative possibility: girls were welcome to remain in the community of women for the rest of their lives or, having left, to return at any time. Indeed, the order viewed those who reentered "the world" with "sorrow" and urged, "We should make every effort to induce them to remain . . . where they are assured of the Grace of a happy death."[61]

THE GIRLS WHO LEFT

Most girls, of course, did not remain but left the Good Shepherd Home and returned to the world. Many did eventually marry: more than one in five either obtained a marriage license in Scott County or had her wedding announced in the local papers within a few years of her release. Some girls, however, returned to the same life from which the home was meant to deter them, even those whose time in the reformatory seemed at first to have great effect. As "Dolorosa," Lillie learned to read and to pray, and about two years after she entered the Dubuque home, Mrs. Hill reported that she had become "a fine young lady of consequence." Lillie spent more than three years with the sisters, yet less than two years after her release, the police arrested Lillie for streetwalking. Police matron Hill and other Davenport authorities may have believed that removing girls from vicious homes protected them from becoming prostitutes, but without marketable skills and support from the community, girls released back into "the world" were still likely to see prostitution as a viable economic option. In fact, nearly 8 percent of those who left the reformatories reappeared in the police matron's docket after being released from the homes.[62]

Davenport girls released from Good Shepherd Homes did not necessarily return to Scott County. Some no doubt purposely went elsewhere to start a new life, and many girls cannot be traced after they left the homes. For this reason, it is perhaps unwise to offer generalizations about the effect of time in a home on a girl's life. But a few specific cases offer cautions about what a historian can and cannot assume. For example, neither encounters with the police nor time in a Good Shepherd Home necessarily excluded a girl from respectable social circles. Rose, for example, had been arrested at seventeen for vagrancy and identified as a prostitute in the police matron's docket. She went to the Good Shepherd Home in Peoria. A few years later, her parents proudly announced that she and her brother would each take a spouse in a double wedding at Ehler's Hall before a "large company of relatives and friends." Helena, whose sexual exploitation at the hands of her own father earned front-page attention when her brother-in-law killed him, received society-page coverage when she married three years later. "The bride," reported the *Democrat and Leader* under the heading "Social Happenings," wore "a gown of cream colored voile and lace and . . . a white picture hat for the ceremony." Before her marriage, Helena had worked as a cigar maker. Both these women seemed to have married respectable, law-abiding men. Helena's husband owned his own home in Moline. The husband chosen by another young woman released from a Good Shepherd Home had a less promising background. He was the illegitimate son of Della Wood, born a few months after she became notorious as the fourteen-year-old "procuress" who taught Ada Ammerman, Dolly Hamerly, and Mamie Woods to be prostitutes.[63]

Convinced that the "girl problem" in Davenport was growing, police authorities turned to Good Shepherd reformatories to solve it. In doing so, they created an informal, extralegal system that in many ways anticipated the juvenile courts created nearly a decade later. This system was explicitly gendered, and its existence complicates some commonly accepted interpretations of the era. For example, Mary Odem, noting that girls came into juvenile courts primarily for status and sex offenses, has argued that before the creation of juvenile courts, these girls would probably not have been incarcerated. This may well be true if one looks only at formal, state legal structures. But in Davenport, many more girls entered reformatories through the informal system built around Good Shepherd Homes than through the formal structures of the district or juvenile courts. Systems like Davenport's probably existed in other cities as well. Lacking formal apparatus, they left no systematic records. But evidence suggests that the police matrons in Dubuque and Sioux City may have followed a similar policy. The hundreds of girls listed in Omaha and Dubuque convent records came from cities, towns, and rural areas all over the Midwest. Residents of the Omaha reformatory included African American girls from Omaha and Sioux girls from Rosebud and Pine Ridge, South Dakota. Even before the juvenile court, authorities removed sexually delinquent girls from their homes and from the streets and placed them in reformatories.[64]

As private reformatories, Good Shepherd Homes served multiple interests. Viewed from the perspective of police and reformers, the homes were institutions of social control. Girls whose flaw was their all-too-evident sexuality entered the care and custody of cloistered celibates, where they learned the skills of modesty and self-restraint valued in respectable bourgeois society. Even rape victims, sexualized against their will, came into the system. But to the sisters who operated the homes, the reformatories were the centers of their spiritual and community life. Returning girls to society was secondary to the sisters' avowed "zeal for souls," and they honored life consecrated to religious community above life in "the world." The primacy placed on community life meant whatever sustained it—including occasionally exploitative demands on the girls' labor—outweighed all other concerns. The girls had their own interests regarding Good Shepherd Homes. For some, the reformatories seemed no better than prisons. But for others, Good Shepherd Homes became authentic refuges, havens from a world in which employment, romantic encounters, and even their own homes could be sites of weary struggle or of danger.

In an irony that would certainly have disturbed the Sisters of the Good Shepherd, their reformatories helped protect men's access to prostitutes in Davenport. In 1889, the women who organized the police matron campaign had criticized the policy of tolerated prostitution, arguing that as long as brothels flourished, poor girls would end up staffing them. The police chief and his allies insisted that vicious families, not public policy, made girls go wrong. The sisters, in turn, promised to retrain wayward girls into industrious, sexually reticent young women. The reformatories ultimately shielded Davenport's regulated brothels from criticism by providing evidence that authorities were doing their best to save girls from "lives of shame," allowing officials to continue to insist that failed families, not public policy, caused prostitution.

WOMEN, MEN, AND THE BUSINESSES OF BUCKTOWN

If it is true that God has forsaken Chicago, then He has never even visited Davenport, Iowa.
—Anita Ray, *Hearst's Chicago American*, 1903

SOMETIME IN THE 1880S, folks in Davenport began to refer to the downtown blocks east of Brady Street as "Bucktown." The expression may have been a reference to the backroom poker games common in saloons, where gamblers "passed the buck" (buck knife) to indicate whose turn it was to deal. More likely, though, the bucks of Bucktown were the single young men who populated the hotels and boardinghouses and congregated in the saloons, cigar stores, and brothels scattered through the neighborhood. In 1894, Mayor Henry Vollmer looked back to the 1880s as the "classic days" of Bucktown, contrasting them with the new, more orderly era he had inaugurated with regulated prostitution. In truth, Bucktown's classic days were just beginning.[1]

Throughout the 1880s, the east end of downtown had been a mixed-use neighborhood, with a variety of households and businesses interspersed along its streets, including some devoted to sexual commerce. After 1893, regulated prostitution combined with the mulct law turned Bucktown into an institution. Saloons crowded into the neighborhood, and it rapidly grew to include dance halls, bawdy theaters, and gambling dens catering to the same male audience that visited the brothels. For the women of the Lend a Hand and the Charitable Alliance, the transformation laid bare a bitter irony. Not only had the police matron's office become the hub of the registration system, but at the very moment when Lend a Hand women were opening businesses and striving to claim the downtown streets as safe and respectable space for women to work, live, and socialize, the regulation policy reinscribed those streets as sexualized space—men's territory.

Another irony stalked city authorities. For all its claims to be modern and scientific, Davenport based its system of regulated brothels on a model of sexual commerce that was rapidly becoming obsolete. Brothels may have been the primary sites of sexual entertainments in the mid–nineteenth century, but increasingly, some saloon keepers recognized that the presence—and display—of women made their businesses more attractive to men. They transformed their saloons by adding dance floors and stages, openly exploiting what Peter Bailey has called "parasexuality"—that is, "sexuality that is deployed but contained, carefully channelled rather than fully discharged"—to attract male customers. These entrepreneurs hired singers, actresses, and chorus girls. They employed women to sell drinks and to drink with customers. And they encouraged the patronage of young women who embraced the "dance madness" of the era. Whether in brothels or in the new dance halls and saloon theaters, commerce in women's sexuality remained the key to Bucktown's profitability.[2]

In the 1880s, downtown workers had reluctantly shared the streets with prostitutes. Now, respectable girls and young women came to Bucktown willingly—to earn a living on the stage or simply to enjoy an evening of dancing and flirtation. In some ways, their presence challenged a gender system that tightly circumscribed respectable women's access to urban space, yet these women entered a space devoted to the entertainment of men on men's terms and usually for men's profits. Male customers patronized these businesses for the pleasure of looking at women, dancing with women, flirting with women, and perhaps taking women to nearby assignation houses. Whether the women were employees such as actresses or singers or simply young women out for a good time, their presence was as necessary to these Bucktown businesses as prostitutes were to brothels. Paradoxically, some of the women who accepted the system that consigned them to brothels found a measure of freedom they had never before experienced as well as profits of their own. But the growing tension over the presence in Bucktown of women who were not registered prostitutes precipitated a series of crises beginning in 1903, when the *Chicago American* pronounced Davenport "the wickedest city in America."[3]

PROSTITUTION UNDER REGULATION

The first women drawn to Bucktown were the ones Mayor Vollmer expected: brothel keepers and the women who worked for them. When he announced his plan for regulation, some citizens worried that it would make the city a magnet for prostitutes. They were probably right. Regulation almost certainly made Davenport a better workplace than many other cities. Josie Washburn, who ran a brothel in Lincoln, Nebraska, from 1895 to 1907, opposed regulation on principle because she believed passionately that prostitution degraded women, but she directed her most visceral anger at the city officials who manipulated prostitutes for financial or political gain. Late-night raids that piled women into wagons and crowded them into jail cells were, Washburn insisted, just crude shows for the public or weapons wielded to extort graft. In Davenport, regulation insulated prostitutes from the abuses that so outraged Washburn. Monthly fines replaced raids (or "protection" paid to the police), and the public character of the system shielded women from graft and blackmail.[4]

The police matron's records suggest that the number of prostitutes rose under regulation. In 1892, the year before regulation, Matron Annie Davis recorded 123 individual women arrested for brothel prostitution: 31 for "keeping a house of ill-fame" and 92 as inmates, a ratio of 3 prostitutes to each brothel keeper. In 1894, the first full year under the new system, Matron Sarah Hill registered 154 women as prostitutes. Thirty-three women appeared in her docket as brothel keepers, and 127 appeared as inmates (a ratio of almost 4 to 1). Six women appeared in both categories. The records for 1895 reveal a similar tally: 23 brothel keepers, 132 inmates, and 2 women in both categories, for a total of 153. The ratio in 1895 was almost 6 prostitutes to each registered brothel keeper.[5]

The jump from 123 in 1892 to 154 in 1894 may reflect an increase of 25 percent in the number of working prostitutes in the city. More likely, some portion of the increase was simply the effect of the new systematic effort to register prostitutes. Some women may have avoided arrest in 1892, but in 1894 the police would have compelled them to register. Whatever the level of real increase, the economy may have been as much a factor as the new system of regulation. The depression years of 1893–97 may have driven more women toward prostitution as they, their husbands, or other breadwinners lost legitimate employment.

After 1895, police matron Hill's practice of recording inmates only in aggregate per house rather than by name makes it much more difficult to determine how many women worked as prostitutes over the course of a year. Women moved from house to house, moved in and out of the business, and changed their status from brothel keeper to inmate and back again. Still, in 1902, after nearly a decade under the regulation system, the police recorded 111 women's names, which probably represented only a fraction of the total number of brothel prostitutes. Over the course of that year, 53 women registered as brothel keepers, more than twice the number who had registered in 1895. Calculating the 1894 ratio of 4 prostitutes to every brothel keeper suggests a figure of 265 women working in brothel prostitution in 1902. By 1902, however, a number of individual women operated brothels on multiple sites,

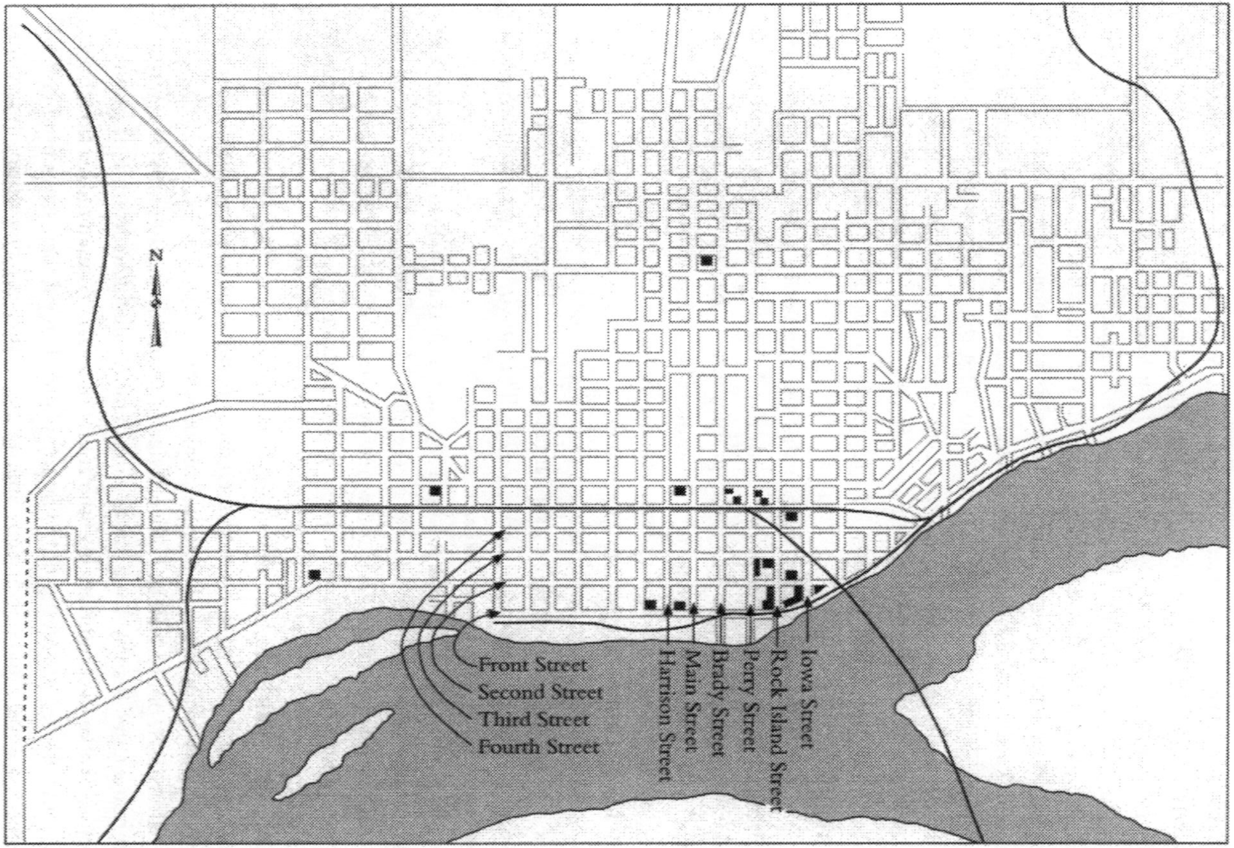

Map 3. Brothels, 1895

employing as many as 15 to 20 prostitutes apiece, so the typical ratio of 1894 may no longer have applied.[6]

In the first years of the system, the thoroughness of the matron's records provides an unusual opportunity to consider prostitution in the context of women's employments in Davenport. Comparing the matron's records with population data from the 1895 Iowa Census reveals that brothel prostitutes accounted for one in every forty-five women in Davenport between eighteen and forty-four years of age (2.2 percent). Comparing the number of brothel workers in 1895 with employment statistics from the 1900 U.S. Census gives an even more startling picture of the prevalence of prostitution: for every twenty-one women working in legitimate employments, one Davenport woman worked as a prostitute (almost 4 percent of the female workforce).[7]

Data from the 1897 Iowa Bureau of Labor report helps give a sense of the prevalence of prostitutes relative to women in other kinds of employments in Davenport. The city's 153 brothel workers in 1895 were nearly as common as women working as clerks in dry goods and department stores (165) or in all food-processing jobs combined (164). The 1900 federal census also provides useful comparisons, suggesting that prostitutes were almost as common as clerical workers. Women stenographers and typewriters that year numbered 78, and bookkeepers, accountants, and clerks together numbered 135. Even the single largest category of employment, domestic service (806 women, or about 25 percent of employed women) outnumbered brothel prostitutes only 5 to 1. The census columns on men's employment suggest that Davenport also had more prostitutes than barbers, bartenders, or butchers. Of course, not every woman who worked as a prostitute did so as her exclusive occupation or worked at it throughout the year, but the same could be said of many women employed in a wide range of occupations.[8]

In addition to altering the conditions under which brothel prostitutes labored and increasing their numbers, regulation reorganized the sexual geography of downtown Davenport. In 1889, when Jennie McCowen led other working women in their campaign for a police matron, at least fourteen brothels did business in the central business district, some even on Brady Street in the same block where McCowen had her home and offices. Others lay along the cross-streets immediately east and west of Brady, in the heart of downtown. After 1893, city authorities used the regulation system to concentrate sexual commerce into the periphery of downtown.

Map 3 shows the locations of thirty-five brothels recorded in police and court records and the newspapers during 1895. None did business on Brady Street or on the first blocks to the east and west of Brady below the Chicago, Rock Island, & Pacific (CRI&P) tracks. Instead, they were concentrated in three areas: in the grid formed where Perry, Rock Island, and Iowa Streets crossed Front, Second, and Third Streets; along west Front Street between Main and Ripley; and around the intersection of Fifth and Brady Streets, north of the tracks. That last cluster was very close to St. Anthony's Church and to the reputable businesses on Brady, but the CRI&P railroad tracks that ran along Fifth Street created a kind of barrier separating the more respectable blocks of Brady Street from the neighborhood just to the north, where Linsey Pitts's saloon anchored a small African American business district. The police recorded more than twice as many brothels in 1895 as in 1889, but these were far more concentrated spatially. For example, brothel sites in 1895 included six adjacent addresses on Rock Island Street and five adjacent addresses on East Front Street. Only two pairs of adjacent addresses appear in the 1889 tally. No longer were sites of prostitution scattered through a poor, mixed-use neighborhood. Increasingly, the city dedicated entire blocks of Bucktown to sexual commerce.

BROTHEL KEEPERS AS BUSINESSWOMEN

Within Bucktown, the women who ran the brothels found the conditions of their work transformed. No longer subject to random arrests, unpredictable expenses of bail and fines, or the hardship of the jail term, brothel keepers experienced an era of unprecedented stability. They also benefited from a new public image. Customers no longer feared arrest, exposure, and public humiliation, while the health certificates issued by the city reassured potential clients on the question of venereal disease. Given these new conditions, some women grasped the opportunity to capitalize on a form of labor that was reliably well compensated.[9]

While American folklore is filled with stories of women who became wealthy from prostitution, few are true. Most prostitution workers struggled just to support their dependents and pay their debts. But in some circumstances, prostitutes could do more than struggle. Historian Paula Petrik has documented the entrepreneurial success of the first generation of brothel keepers in Helena, Montana. There, a few women amassed enough property to rank among the city's largest taxpayers. But as Petrik argues, this opportunity was limited to Helena's "frontier" period, before merchants and other residents began to push for a more orderly city. By the 1890s, women no longer controlled the property in Helena's brothel district. In Davenport, some women found a comparable opportunity under regulation. Expanding their businesses and investing in real estate, some achieved financial competence for the first time in their lives. A return to the six women profiled in chapter 4 suggests both the opportunities regulation brought and the limits these women still faced.[10]

In the fall of 1893, when son-in-law Adelbert DeMaranville tried to keep Josie Mitchell from retaining custody of her grandchildren, Mitchell denied that she was keeping a house of ill-fame. She insisted that she and her daughter, Sevilla, "have been leading chaste and moral lives and are engaged in conducting a boarding house and restaurant and are making an honest and competent living." For several months thereafter, Mitchell kept out of police records. As other women registered brothels with the police, Mitchell and her daughters refrained from doing so in spite of the fact that under the regulation system, they would have faced no arrest, only a modest fine. This suggests they may indeed have been trying to run a legitimate business, but the following spring, Mitchell changed her mind. She registered as a brothel keeper, claiming three inmates for her house. It took less than two years for this decision to turn Mitchell into a property owner and a taxpayer for the first time in her life. About this time, she also learned to write her name. Over the next twelve years, Mitchell remained on the police list and gradually expanded both her business and her real estate holdings.[11]

No longer the illiterate, divorced mother who had struggled to support her family in the 1880s or the profoundly depressed woman who had attempted suicide in 1892, Mitchell used the stability created by regulation to become a modestly successful businesswoman. She made her first appearance in the tax records in 1898, but that year she owed just ninety-six cents, the total tax on fifteen dollars of personal property and one dog. She owned no real estate. A year later, her personal property had almost tripled in value, and she had acquired her first real property, a building she used as a brothel. Now married to saloon keeper W. W. Hovey, Josie Mitchell operated two brothels on Front Street that year. Her holdings reached their most extensive level in June 1904. That month, police records indicate that she paid the fine for six different brothel sites employing nineteen inmates. Between 1899 and 1903, she sold her Front Street properties and purchased three sites on East Second Street, still within the Bucktown district devoted to prostitution. Mitchell also invested in property in a respectable residential neighborhood around Ninth and Iowa Streets. During this same period, W. W. Hovey owned no property at all in Davenport.[12]

Mitchell had drifted into prostitution while laboring to provide a home for her children, and she continued to demonstrate a sense of family obligation in this new, more prosperous time in her life. She maintained a home for her "feeble-minded" son Lyman, now in his thirties. She adopted a girl born in 1901, perhaps her granddaughter or the daughter of one of her brothel inmates. Mitchell never became wealthy, but her businesses provided jobs for her husband and for sons Lafe and William, who ran saloons associated with her brothels. She even paid Lafe's gambling debts and complained publicly when the police did not shut down the gambling dens where he lost her money. Still, casting her lot with the sporting world had painful consequences for her children. Her daughters, Sevilla and Maggie, both worked at times as prostitutes, and her sons, Lafe and William, found wives among sporting women, with predictable results. Lafe married four times in ten years and came up before a grand jury in 1905 on a charge of "assault with intent to do great bodily injury" on his fourth wife, Ella Dunning Gross Keller. Both Lafe and Ella had been married to others when they began their relationship. Ella Keller and William's

W. W. Hovey's saloon business card. The front advertises "fragrant and soothing narcotic weeds"; the back features an off-color joke. (Collection of the author.)

wife, Birdie, continued the family business, running assignation houses in conjunction with their husbands' saloons.[13]

Josie Mitchell was not the only woman who decided that the regulation system made openly declaring herself a brothel keeper a reasonable choice. Minnie Hagan all but disappeared from Davenport's prostitution trade after recovering from a bullet wound to the head in 1883, keeping out of the police records and the newspapers for ten years. Given her connections to brothels in Sioux City, Council Bluffs, and Omaha, Hagan may simply have been doing business elsewhere. If so, Mayor Vollmer's policy proved attractive enough to lure her back to Davenport. In October 1893, just six months after Vollmer announced his plan to regulate brothel prostitution, Hagan registered a brothel with two inmates. Her business grew over the next year or two, and in 1895 and 1896, she paid for as many as nine or ten inmates each month. Unlike Mitchell and some other brothel keepers, Hagan did not invest in Davenport real estate.

Business may have been flourishing, but in August 1897, Hagan experienced the first of two blows that may have shaken her satisfaction with her trade. Jessie Gallagher, known in Bucktown as Edna Cook, had worked in Davenport brothels since 1893, when she was nineteen years old. After running a small brothel in the summer and fall of 1894, Gallagher became an inmate of Minnie Hagan's house at 224 and 226 East Front Street. The relationship seems to have been satisfactory, for Gallagher remained with Hagan for the next couple of years, moving with her to Mamie Beauchaine's building at 106 and 108 Rock Island Street. In the summer of 1897, however, Gallagher became despondent over the failure of a love affair with a young businessman named Abe Levy. Late one night, Gallagher checked into the Hotel Brunswick alone. She wrote two notes, one to Levy and one to her mother, then drank a bottle of carbolic acid. It was Minnie Hagan who collected Gallagher's belongings and sent them to her mother in Burlington, Hagan who paid for the girl's funeral, Hagan who felt "aggrieved" at accusations "that she was responsible for Jessie's career of shame." Having begun the year with six women working in her house, Hagan let the number of inmates dwindle after Gallagher's suicide, ending the year with just two women.[14]

Then in early February 1898, Hagan's house was the scene of yet more violence. Arriving on a Wednesday afternoon when the house was empty of customers, Zip Hamerly and Harry Toher raged through the rooms, breaking the plate-glass windows, ripping doors from their hinges, and smashing the furniture as they searched for Grace Jackson, one of Hagan's two remaining inmates. When Toher found her, he beat her savagely, breaking her nose and wrist and kicking her down the stairs. Searching for a weapon to redouble his attack, Toher grabbed a poker, but a quick-thinking cook used the brief delay to drag Jackson's senseless body out of sight. The interference was just long enough for the police to arrive and take Toher and Hamerly into custody.[15]

The suicide of one girl, the beating of another, and the destruction of her house may have been enough to drive Minnie Hagan from the business. Hagan, after all, surely carried physical and emotional scars from her traumatic encounter with Joseph Kiter fifteen years earlier. She never again registered a brothel with the police, though she apparently rented rooms for assignation purposes after 1907. Her choice highlights another difference between regulated brothels and illegal assignation houses. In a regulated brothel, the keeper acted as both manager and agent of the police. The emotional costs associated with this responsibility could be far higher than in an assignation house, where the proprietor accommodated customers but did not manage employees whose work put them in physical danger or caused them emotional anguish.

As Minnie Hagan's experience suggests, regulation did little to change the physical violence and psychic turmoil the ordinary inmate might face in her work. Within the trade, the benefits of regulation accrued primarily to the women who ran the brothels, not those who staffed them. Yet not every brothel keeper was able to exploit these benefits. African American Mattie Burke, shut out of the registration system that stabilized conditions for white brothel keepers, never earned enough money to purchase even the shabbiest piece of real estate. Suffering chronic dropsy, she died in May 1901, just months after her last arrest. She was only about forty-four years old.[16]

For Kate Huber, in contrast, the regulation system offered the opportunity to build economic stability for the first time since the departure of her husband.

Ironically, the German immigrant who had once been notorious for violence and neglect of her children was often known as "Mother" Huber, no doubt a reference to her age. By 1893, Huber was fifty-two, making her one of the oldest women in the brothel trade. Beginning in January 1894, Huber appeared consistently in the record of registered brothels, usually with three or four inmates in her house. The 1895 Iowa census taker recorded that she was providing a home for twenty-three-year-old Charles, her only son. Fifteen-year-old Clara did not live with her mother. Her presence would have raised questions for the police, but five young women aged nineteen to twenty-one did reside with Kate Huber.[17]

Tax records reveal that she was also buying real estate. In 1897, she owned property on Front Street just west of Iowa Avenue. A newspaper, reporting the property's later sale, described it as a "frame house given over to immorality, and the tumble down shacks adjoining it on the west." The buildings, the paper said, "date from Davenport's early history." Huber may have started with slum properties, but she quickly moved up. By 1899, the tax records show she had purchased a property at 212 Iowa Street, and she told the 1900 census taker that she owed no mortgage. By 1904 and 1905, Huber was paying assessments for as many as four brothel sites and up to fifteen inmates each month. After Davenport shut down its brothels in 1909, Huber may have continued to allow her property to be used as a saloon and house of assignation, though she claimed she was simply running a boardinghouse. Huber died in 1917 at the age of seventy-six, in the home she had purchased in 1899 with the profits of prostitution.[18]

Mamie Beauchaine withdrew from direct involvement in brothel keeping in 1892, but as the owner of several properties rented to prostitutes, she profited enormously when the regulation system began in 1893. Her wealth allowed her to provide for parents, siblings, and other relations on both sides of the Atlantic. Through the late 1890s, Mamie and Lee Beauchaine continued to reside at the Slate House Hotel. Their marriage was at times rocky. Lee was arrested at least once for beating Mamie and on another occasion for beating a domestic at the Slate House. Violence toward women did not hurt Lee's reputation as an affable saloon keeper and one of the leaders among Davenport's sporting men. He joined the Moose Lodge and gave generously to charities. In 1901, he even won a house and lot in a lottery run to benefit the Ladies Industrial Relief Society. One imagines Lee, wearing his diamond ring, diamond stickpin, and lion's head cufflinks, buying whole books of tickets to show his generosity—thus also increasing his odds of winning. That house and lot may well have been the only property Lee ever owned in Davenport.[19]

Mamie, meanwhile, owned plenty. She managed properties rented to prostitutes on Rock Island Street and Front Street, paying the mulct tax so her tenants, including Minnie Hagan, could sell beer to their customers. By the time Lee won his house and lot, Mamie owned the Slate House plus properties along Front Street,

Rock Island Street, Third Street, and LeClaire Street and near the intersection of Sixth and Perry Streets. All but the last she devoted to either saloon or prostitution businesses. Purchase of the Sixth Street house raised a "tempest and furor" among neighbors, who feared that Lee and Mamie planned to move out of the Slate House and into that respectable neighborhood. According to the *Democrat*, Mamie's purchase demonstrated that "the quarter to which it has been the announced policy of the city government to restrict people of her exclusive set has grown too small to hold them." For her part, Mamie insisted that the purchase was an investment and that she planned to convert the large house into flats and perhaps to build another set of flats at the rear of the lot.[20]

Mamie and Lee never moved to the Sixth Street house, continuing instead to dwell at the Slate House. During these years, Mamie's increasing wealth allowed her to become a benefactor to her extended family, spinning out a web of support that reached all the way back to Ireland. For example, Mamie's younger sister, Sabina, lived in the Beauchaine household in 1900, along with her husband, Edward Dolphin, and her two children, Mamie, seven, and Lee, five. In 1906 and 1907, Lee and Mamie Beauchaine made an extended visit to Ireland, where they purchased a home for Mamie's elderly parents and, according to one report, another for themselves. They dashed any hopes that they would stay in Ireland with the news that a spacious new house being built at the corner of Seventh and Brady Streets was theirs, but Lee and Mamie had another surprise for the citizens of Davenport: they announced that they had been caught up in a Catholic revival that swept through Ireland that year, perhaps part of the surge in Irish nationalism that culminated in the 1916 uprising. They returned to Davenport newly repentant and respectable, and in 1915 they completed their transformation by adopting a daughter. Marie Catherine Beauchaine, reared in comfort and given vocal and harp lessons and a convent school education, was the daughter—probably illegitimate—of Mamie Beauchaine's niece, Mamie Dolphin.[21]

The Beauchaines' declaration of conversion in 1907 may have been sincere, but their particular faith apparently accommodated loopholes. While the couple no longer lived at or operated the Slate House, Mamie Beauchaine still owned it. In 1915, the district attorney prosecuted her tenants for keeping a house of ill-fame, suggesting that Mamie still had no compunction about deriving high rents from the vice trade. She finally sold the property in 1922 for $30,000, a price one newspaper concluded "would not have approached its value" in the days before Prohibition, when it was a saloon and "resort." Mamie held onto her other properties, though. When Lee died in 1927, she gave him a lavish burial, including a requiem High Mass at St. Anthony's Church. Mamie's 1949 funeral was a more modest memorial Mass, and after a protracted trans-Atlantic court battle with Mamie's extended family, the adopted daughter, Marie, inherited an estate valued at about $111,000.[22]

For all Mamie Beauchaine's success, investing in real estate was no sure route to

The Beauchaine residence on Brady Street. Mamie and Lee Beauchaine pose with their house, cars, and chauffeur. They occupied this house after returning, reformed and repentant, from Ireland. (Courtesy of the Richardson-Sloane Special Collections Center, Davenport Public Library.)

affluence. The experience of Emma Webb suggests how even the profits earned under regulated prostitution could evaporate with bad choices—whether financial or romantic. Among the women profiled here, Emma Auerochs Webb was a latecomer to the prostitution business. A twenty-seven-year-old widow with an eight-year-old son to support, Emma Webb made her first appearance in police records in May 1891, just two years before regulation commenced in Davenport. In September 1892, she, like Minnie Hagan, was a tenant in one of Mamie Beauchaine's properties, and Davenport tax records show that Webb was assessed taxes on seventy-five dollars of personal property. Sometime that fall, however, Emma Webb moved her business to 312 and 316 East Front Street.[23]

When she registered her brothel, in keeping with the new policy instituted in April, Emma Webb had four young women, all aged nineteen or twenty, working for her, and she was in the process of buying the site of her Front Street business. Just around the corner on East Second Street, bartender Henry Clay Woodward paid taxes on just thirty-five dollars worth of personal property, but his prospects would soon improve. By February 1894, Emma Webb was helping him with his business, a saloon, giving surety on notes executed by Woodward to pay for shipments of liquor. That summer, Woodward rented a brick saloon building at 113–15 Brady Street from liquor wholesaler Ferd Roddewig and Sons. "The Brunswick," on bustling Brady Street, lay outside the Bucktown district, perhaps signaling Emma's and Clay's desire to move into a more respectable mode of life. That year, the city directory gave the Brunswick rather than the Front Street brothel as Emma Webb's residence. In June 1894, Emma Webb made her last appearance in police records as a registered brothel keeper. That September, a new brothel keeper took over the Front Street resort Webb owned. Maud Harris ran it for the next year and a half. The summer of 1894 may have been when Emma Webb and Clay Woodward married. They remained partners in both business and personal life until Clay's death in 1917.[24]

Becoming a landlord, marrying the keeper of a respectable saloon, and leaving the business of brothel keeping, Emma Webb Woodward seemed to be following Mamie Beauchaine's path to prosperity, but Emma would encounter far more difficulty in her journey. By early 1895, just months after opening Clay's new saloon, creditors were already suing Emma and Clay. Ferd Roddewig and Sons claimed that Clay had defaulted on both rent and debts for liquor, and another liquor wholesaler sought a lien against Emma's Front Street property. The Davenport Gas Light Company followed with its own suit to recover unpaid utility bills. It was not a good beginning.[25]

As partners, Clay and Emma were not as successful as Emma had been alone, though the reasons remain unclear. Perhaps maintaining a respectable Brady Street saloon required skills and a temperament Clay lacked. Perhaps Emma took a less active role in this enterprise and the business suffered from the loss of her organizational skills. Complaints made by Emma a few years later suggest another explanation, however. In 1905, Emma filed two lawsuits to recover money Clay had lost while gambling, asserting that he was drunk and therefore should not have been admitted to the card table. One of the defendants insisted in response, "Clay Woodward is known as an old-timer in gambling circles. He has both won and lost fortunes. . . . Now that he has lost it comes with poor grace for [his wife] to allege that he was beaten out of his money while intoxicated." Clay's long-established gambling habit may explain why his business debts and sometimes his employees went unpaid.[26]

Having lost the saloon on Brady Street, Emma and Clay returned to Bucktown, where Emma purchased a property on East Second Street that soon became known as the "Bridge House." In 1898, a newspaper report described it as "a near neighbor and close cousin of the Slate House," the saloon and hotel operated by the Beauchaines. Indeed, the Bridge House stood directly across Second Street from the Slate House. Emma and Clay, however, had other plans for their Bucktown property. By 1901 they had transformed the Bridge House into the Iowa Theater, a vaudeville stage, saloon, and dance hall. Their advertisement promised "High class vaudeville every evening and Sunday matinee.... Entire change of program every week. Free dance after the show. Bar attached stocked with the choicest line of Wines, Liqueurs, and Cigars." Like Josie Mitchell and Mamie Beauchaine, Emma Webb Woodward used this business to support her extended family. Her brother, David Auerochs, no longer a railroad brakeman, worked as a bartender, and nephew Henry Auerochs, orphaned by the death of his mother, Mary Cullivan, in 1898, also worked at the theater. Eddie Webb, Emma's son, began as a doorkeeper at the theater.[27]

Emma's and Clay's foray into theater management lasted only a few years. In what seemed to be a recurring theme in their business ventures, Clay and Emma could not pay their creditors. They mortgaged Emma's property to the Davenport Malting Company, and when they defaulted on the mortgage, the Malting Company took possession. The company agreed to sell the property back to the Woodwards on contract for twelve thousand dollars, but again, Clay and Emma were unable to make their payments. In August 1904, newspapers reported that Clay had relinquished the property and that the Malting Company was looking for a new tenant.[28]

Clay's gambling may have been one source of their financial troubles, but by 1903 and 1904, the Woodwards had other problems as well. In January 1903, a scandal erupted involving one of the performers at their theater, and reformers focused their wrath on Clay Woodward. Almost two years later, in December 1904, city authorities were still unwilling to issue him a license for a new saloon and dance hall. In spite of these setbacks, Clay and Emma Woodward managed to hold onto some of their property, and when the 1915 census taker called on the retired couple, Clay reported that he owned their four thousand dollar house free and clear. Emma Webb Woodward never achieved wealth comparable to Mamie Beauchaine's, but if the measure of success was to climb out of poverty and provide for a family, Woodward clearly succeeded. Her son, Eddie Webb, eventually attended two years of college and became a union stage hand.[29]

DANCE HALLS, THEATERS, AND CONCERT SALOONS

Clay and Emma Woodward's venture with the Iowa Theater represented one of the ways Bucktown changed as it prospered under regulated prostitution and the mulct law. New sites of commercial entertainment joined brothels and saloons along the blocks east of Brady Street, inviting a new kind of mixing between women who worked at legitimate employments and those who worked as prostitutes. By police order, brothels were off-limits to unregistered women. State law barred women from saloons as well, but as with so many mulct-law regulations, the ban went unenforced in Davenport. Some kinds of drinking resorts had always drawn the patronage of respectable women in Davenport. Before the mulct law, corner groceries throughout the city sold beer by the bucket for home consumption, and some sold it by the glass as well, attracting neighborhood housewives. The German community introduced Davenport to the beer garden, where families gathered to listen to a brass band on Sunday afternoons and friends or couples sipped beer at outdoor tables on warm summer nights, enjoying the strains of a violin, squeeze box, or even a small orchestra.[30]

But downtown saloons were different. Women who entered those saloons entered a gendered space where women's presence marked them as prostitutes. Some saloons accommodated women with "ladies' entrances" that led directly to wine rooms in the basement or back room, where curtained booths or stalls with doors further protected patrons' privacy. Although these were structurally similar to the "ladies' entrances" to hotels, which permitted women to reach their rooms without navigating the masculine territory of the lobby (which often included a bar), the association of drink with debauchery meant that ladies' entrances and wine rooms were never really respectable. Indeed, some historians have suggested that only prostitutes and their clients patronized wine rooms, but observers at the time were quite sure that wine rooms attracted women and girls from respectable families who foolishly put their reputations at risk.[31]

The high cost of the mulct tax—fifty dollars a month, the equivalent of an ordinary workingman's wages—drove most corner groceries out of the beer business after 1894 and made saloon keepers more conscious of the need to attract patrons and keep sales volumes high. Some Bucktown proprietors realized that the presence of women made their businesses more attractive to men. While many saloon keepers believed that the barroom should be reserved for men only, others had no qualms about using women to attract customers. These proprietors began to reinvent their saloons, adding stages and dance floors.

The theaters and dance halls that sprang up in Bucktown at the turn of the century differed from their predecessors in several ways. Dancing, of course, had always been a popular form of recreation. Davenport's German immigrants in particular delighted in music, and bands and orchestras flourished. Turner Hall had sponsored Sunday night dances for decades, as had Lahrman's Hall. Both were on the west side, in the heart of the German neighborhood. On warm summer evenings, commercial parks such as Black Hawk's Watch Tower in Illinois and Offerman's Island in midriver featured bands in breezy dance pavilions. An 1887 announcement in the *Gazette* was typical: "The fast favorite steamer *Verne Swain* with barge, will make hourly trips to Offerman's Island, from 1 until 11 P.M., Sunday Aug. 14, Bleuer's Band will be in attendance. Dancing and a general good time for all. Round trip 25 cents. Ladies 10 cents. Good order on the grounds." These park pavilion dances and those sponsored by the Turners or the Harugari, another German social club, had been weekly or semiweekly events at best, but the new commercial dance halls of Bucktown were open every night. Their orchestras often played until three or four o'clock in the morning. Even more important, these proprietors did not distinguish theaters from dance halls, frequently combining both attractions in a single venue.[32]

Like dancing, theaters had a long history in Davenport. But the variety theaters that sprang up in Bucktown owed more to the concert saloon than to legitimate theaters such as the Burtis Opera House and the German Theater. Through most of the 1880s, the two-thousand-seat Burtis Opera House on Perry Street and the smaller German Theater at the corner of Third and Scott streets were the sole venues for professional theater companies. Both catered to the respectable—and respectful—audiences increasingly sought by theater managers in the last half of the nineteenth century. Opera House patrons in Davenport enjoyed touring companies of New York City hits, concerts of classical music, and even opera. The German Theater featured a similar bill, with productions in both German and English. Only occasionally did more bawdy fare find a stage in Davenport. The Olympic Theater operated for a while in the mid-1880s, specializing in minstrel shows and working-class entertainments. When "Amy Stanley's Female Minstrels" performed in 1887, the show's coarseness drew police criticism. Such performances attracted a "hard crowd," insisted one officer, and were likely to "start young men on the way to the brothel." Police disapproval was not a good thing for a theater. Although the Olympic advertised its shows in 1886 and 1887, it did not survive long enough for a city directory to record its presence.[33]

By the mid-1890s, more bawdy fare began to appear on Davenport stages. On New Year's night in 1894, for example, the Grand Opera House, located in the west-side building formerly occupied by the German Theater, advertised "Fanny Hill with her 40 English Blondes" in a burlesque, "Sin-a-Bad, Sailor." As if the pun on "Sinbad" and the invocation of John Cleland's "woman of pleasure" were not enough to promise a ribald evening with plenty of "leg business," the newspaper ad concluded with a promise of "Living Models," indicating that the show would feature tableaux posed by women in drapery designed to evoke, well, a lack of drapery. The Fanny Hill show was not the typical fare at the Grand, however. That same week it featured a German dialect comedian, Gus Williams; a French Revolution drama, *Paul Kauvar*; and Bartley Campbell's sentimental "Southern idyll," *The White Slave*.[34]

In contrast to the edifying, middlebrow entertainments offered by the Burtis Opera House or even by the Grand Opera House on most nights, the Bucktown saloon theaters aimed for a lower brow. They modeled themselves on the concert saloons that first became popular in the 1850s. In the 1860s and 1870s, just as theater owners were attempting to attract respectable women by expelling prostitutes from their traditional haunt in the "guilty third tier," the concert saloon reinscribed sexuality, even prostitution, on the performance space. Taking root in cities around the country, these establishments combined saloons with variety shows and sometimes dance halls, relying on the spectacle of the woman's body to lure male audiences. All saloon theaters hired women as variety acts for the stage, and the larger establishments employed a "ballet corps" to dance in abbreviated costumes. Concert saloons with dance floors often employed women to dance with customers, and many also featured "waiter girls" who served (and pushed) drinks, flirted with customers, and sometimes sang and danced as well. Most observers assumed that waiter girls worked as prostitutes on the side.[35]

BUCKTOWN'S SALOON THEATERS AND DANCE HALLS

In spite of their widespread popularity, the concert saloon model did not arrive in Davenport before the end of the century, an absence perhaps explained by the dominance of German immigrant culture in the saloon business. With the beer garden filling the niche for a drinking resort with musical performances and tolerated brothels providing sexual entertainment, the market for the concert saloon may not have been great enough to overcome local resistance to women's presence in downtown "men's" saloons. But after the mulct tax imposed new financial pressures on saloons, a handful of saloon keepers recognized an opportunity and expanded their businesses to take advantage of Bucktown's growing regional reputation as an entertainment district for men.

At least five saloon theaters and dance halls opened in Davenport between 1900 and 1902, all in Bucktown. Four stood along East Second Street, between Perry Street and the CRI&P tracks, and one more was just around the corner on Perry Street. Nearly all of the owners had histories connecting them to Davenport's sporting culture, which may explain what distinguished these saloon keepers from neighbors who continued to exclude respectable women. Emma Woodward and her husband, Clay, purchased and expanded the Iowa Theater on East Second Street with profits from her brothel businesses. John McPartland, who had closed his assignation house out by Central Park under threat of a prison sentence, was part owner of the Hobson Vaudeville Theater on Perry Street, soon renamed the Orpheon. Harry "Jock" Manwaring's occupation as a hack driver "brought him into contact with the seamy side of the ill-woven web of Davenport's demimonde life," according to the *Democrat*. He was "known as a thoroughbred sport" who kept racehorses. James "Brick" Munro also worked as a hack driver in the 1890s before expanding his businesses to include the Pavilion at the corner of Second and Rock Island Streets. Perl Galvin alone had no discernible personal link to the community of sporting men, but the site he chose for his Summer Garden, 218 East Second Street, had been known as a brothel since at least 1883 and would continue to have that reputation until at least 1911, suggesting that Galvin was no stranger to Bucktown.[36]

Top: Second Street, looking east from Harrison Street, c. 1902. Bottom: Second Street, looking west from Brady Street, c. 1907. Intended as postcards, these two images reveal photographers' strategies to mask the parts of urban space considered less than respectable. Looking east from Harrison Street puts Second Street department stores in the foreground and Bucktown businesses such as Brick Munro's four blocks distant, out of view. Looking west from Brady Street puts Bucktown behind the photographer's back. (Putnam Museum of History and Natural Science, Davenport, Iowa.)

In all of these places, the line between parasexuality deployed as a marketing strategy and outright prostitution could be perilously fine. At the Orpheon, for example, the actresses roomed above the theater. The Orpheon served drinks in private boxes, and most actresses earned seven dollars a week for a job that included working in the boxes to "encourage the sale of drinks between the acts." On some occasions the boxes became so lively that the audience began "paying more attention to the boxes than to the stage," even though, according to one newspaper, the featured vaudeville performance was generally "far from being conducive to cleaner thoughts." When Mamie Nathan came from Chicago to sing at the Orpheon, she professed herself "mortified" the moment she entered. "When I saw the theater I was horrified," she explained. "No white woman would enter such a place in Chicago, I believe." Required to lodge upstairs with her wages held until she had paid the booking agent's fee and her room rent, Nathan felt trapped and was more than happy to return to Chicago with her brother, who had traced her to Davenport. Charles Nathan, in turn, threatened criminal prosecution: Mamie was only fifteen.[37]

On the small stage at the rear of Jock Manwaring's saloon, a girl who called herself "Fatima" performed a "danse du ventre." Better known as the hoochie-coochie or just cooch, the dance was first popularized at the 1893 World's Columbian Exposition in Chicago. There, "Little Egypt" and other dancers in the Middle Eastern theaters on the Midway Plaisance shocked some and thrilled many with dancing described as "sensuous" and "lascivious." Soon, American-born Fatimas and Odalisques were dancing cooch at carnivals, amusement parks, and saloon theaters all over the country. Manwaring's stage also offered "a living pictures affair said to have been a very warm number." His dance hall, upstairs from the saloon, played host to masquerade balls popular with prostitutes and sporting men and provided entertainment for working men and women. Like the dances at the Woodwards' Iowa Theater, admission to Manwaring's dance hall was free. He expected to make his money off liquor sales.[38]

Perl Galvin opened his Summer Garden saloon and dance hall around 1902, expanding it and renaming it the Standard Theater in 1904. The building where Galvin started out had been a brothel for decades. The shopper strolling Second Street in chapter 1 would have seen Ella Teller's cigar store and brothel at that site in 1885, and the place clearly continued its reputation under Galvin's management. In 1904, for example, Rock Island police arrested Carrie Allars for enticing Mabel Benson to work as a prostitute. Allars's attorneys offered evidence that a police officer had some weeks earlier seen Benson at Perl Galvin's place, "sitting down hatless and alone watching the revelers in the dance." Benson's lack of a hat was significant: it showed she resided at Galvin's, since a woman leaving her home would wear a hat. The attorneys meant for the evidence to prove that Allars was guiltless, since any resident of Galvin's must already have been a prostitute. Later that year,

Galvin installed boxes in his theater so that his patrons could drink with the actresses, and police arrested the "daughter of an eminently respectable family" for drunkenness and "leading an immoral life" in his theater.[39]

In the spring of 1905, Perl Galvin acquired the Iowa Theater, built and lost by Emma and Clay Woodward. He transferred the name Standard Theater to his new property and sold the old Standard to Jack McPartland, once the keeper of an assignation house and then partner in the Orpheon, who renamed it the Bijou. As the Bijou, it quickly acquired a reputation as the toughest of the theaters. One visitor described a barroom "blazoned with lewd pictures" and populated by "half drunk, half dressed prostitutes." Behind the barroom was "a long gloomy hall with a rough stage at the farther end" where "half-dressed women and pimply men" delivered songs and jokes "so low and vile that they are beyond the comprehension of respectable people. Obscene does not express it." In 1906, police officers arrested an especially provocative cooch dancer at the Bijou. In this case, the perception of lewdness was certainly increased by the fact that the dancer was a man in drag. One of the arresting officers testified that "he had seen many exhibitions" of the *danse du ventre*. This one, he said, was the "best," calling it "very indecent." (A newspaper reported that the dancer professed to be highly complimented by the officer's review of the performance.)[40]

"WHY PEOPLE GO TO BRICK MUNRO'S"

If Jack McPartland's Bijou stood at the bottom of the scale of Bucktown saloon theaters and dance halls, Brick Munro's Pavilion stood at the top. A newspaper reporter in 1905 called it "one of the sights" of Davenport. "It is over 100 feet long and when filled with dancers with as many more people seated at the tables around the sides, hundreds of lights blazing and the orchestra playing, it presents a sight to be long remembered." Another writer asserted, "When a drummer from Des Moines, a farmer from Blue Grass, or a theological student from Kalamazoo comes into town, the first thing he asks after he has got a shave and a shine, is the whereabouts of Brick Munro's." Admission to Brick's was ten cents, which may have channeled the poorest clients to Manwaring's or the other dance halls that charged nothing. Once inside Brick's Pavilion, patrons could mingle at tables "roofed by a trellis of vines" ringing the dance floor, order beer or cocktails from the bar, and dance to the rhythms of the orchestra seated on a small platform. It was "said to be the only place of its kind in the state."[41]

Not just drummers, farmers, and students went to Brick Munro's. At the opening of the twentieth century, dance halls like Brick's Pavilion became one of the most popular forms of recreation for girls and young women. The appeal of dance

Advertisement for Brick Munro's Pavilion. (*From Stone's Davenport City Directory, 1902–1903.*)

halls transcended divisions of region, class, and race. Rural midwestern women, Manhattan working girls, and African American domestics in the South all preferred dancing to almost any other form of amusement. Dance halls also increasingly became a source of concern for reformers, who saw them as sites of sexual danger. When these fears were couched in such titles as *From Dance Hall to White Slavery: The World's Greatest Tragedy* and *From the Ballroom to Hell: Facts about Dancing, a Dancing Masters Experience*, it is easy to dismiss these fears as exaggerated expressions of moral panic, as some historians have. Yet the circumstances of the Bucktown dance halls suggest that these concerns had a real foundation.[42]

Joan Jensen has delineated two kinds of dance cultures that existed in the late nineteenth century, one based in family and neighborhood and the other based in the sporting world, where brothel inmates' parlor performances of the hoochie-coochie or burlesque styles often culminated in steamy couple dances. At the opening of the new century, a third dance culture emerged, the commercial dance hall, where "youth of both sexes . . . could dance and negotiate various types of relationships." But Jensen also found and puzzled over authorities' increasing "efforts to restrain young women from frequenting dance halls." Kathy Peiss's classic study of "dance madness" among New York City's working women similarly emphasized a division between dancing practiced in traditional immigrant settings such as weddings and lodges, where family and community supervised, and an emerging culture of commercial halls. The latter were largely segregated by age, attracting youth but not their parents.[43]

Some historians have suggested that authorities' concern about the sexual dangers girls faced in dance halls was the result of misperception and class prejudice, pointing out that middle-class investigators who tried to "pick up" girls in dance halls generally failed. Working-class youth, these writers argue, had codes of conduct, and working-class girls felt comfortable in places where they understood these codes. But the example of Bucktown suggests the limits of this interpretation. First, the sexual geography established by police authority in Davenport meant that girls and women who went to Bucktown to dance entered an urban space literally set apart for prostitution. Second, the dance halls—especially Brick Munro's Pavilion—were not merely places where working-class men and women mingled in the context of shared culture and codes of conduct. These dance halls also attracted more elite men who brought their own interpretation of gender and class relations into an atmosphere heady with drink, flirtation, and sexual competition.[44]

In the new commercial dance halls, young women enjoyed the sensuality of dance and the pleasures of flirtation in a largely unsupervised setting. But as Peiss made clear, sensuality and flirtation were not merely forms of self-expression. They were a kind of currency. In dance halls, girls and young women did not meet men—even men of their own social class—on terms of equality. Girls might go to the dance halls in groups, and management might offer a reduced ticket price for unescorted women. But once inside, girls depended on winning the attention of men who would pay for their drinks and perhaps even their carfare home. The culture of "treating" required girls to mold their appearance and behavior to appeal to men by drinking cocktails, smoking cigarettes, participating in kissing games, and providing sexual favors, all the while negotiating the fine line between being "game" and being "promiscuous."[45]

Dance halls like Brick's Pavilion complicated these negotiations by introducing the element of class difference. Brick's was not only the most spectacular of the Bucktown dance halls, it was also the most respectable, attracting a clientele that included middle-class and elite men. A teenage Floyd Dell visited Brick's in 1906 and reported his observations in an essay published in the *Tri-City Worker's Magazine*,

"Why People Go to Brick Munro's." The son of a butcher who never quite managed to keep his family out of poverty, Dell was an aspiring writer and a recent convert to socialism when he visited Brick's. He did not like what he saw. To Dell, Brick's was no center of working-class sociability. Few working-class men patronized the place, he insisted, because "the men pay; the women don't." Working-class women, however, did go to Brick's. At the tables around the dance floor, Dell saw "department store clerks, servant girls, stenographers, tobacco and candy factory workers, and many others, dressed for the most part attractively and quietly," as well as "girls from the red-light district . . . arrayed in cool kimonas." At Brick's, working-class women became "the prey of the men of the business and professional classes" who purchased drinks and expected something in return. At least some of those quietly dressed workers, Dell believed, would eventually "graduate into the red-light district," joining their kimona-clad sisters.[46]

Dell's reading of the class dynamics of Brick's undoubtedly reflected his youthful enthusiasm for the socialism he was learning from local Germans. But his insistence that Brick's attracted primarily working-class women and middle-class men found support in unexpected corners. F. Leslie Clendenen, the author of several books on stage and ballroom dancing, had for years taught ballroom skills to Davenport's children and youth. His business included running respectable dances where no liquor was served. As Brick's Pavilion prospered, Clendenen's dances dwindled. Disturbed by the loss of business, Clendenen made his own investigation, visiting the commercial dance halls some weeks after Dell published his essay. During one visit, "I counted 164 young men, over 100 of whom hold tickets entitling them to admission to respectable dancing functions, and who come from our 'best families,' and many of them from families prominent in the churches," he reported. As Clendenen saw it, young men no longer attended respectable dances like his because they preferred places like Brick's, "where they could sit vis a vis at the drinking table with the young woman of loose morals or bad character, or touch elbows with her at the bar between dances."[47]

Like Dell, Clendenen was no disinterested observer. Whether the women Clendenen saw were truly of "bad character" or merely working girls and women being sociable according to their codes of behavior is an open question. Clendenen made his report to the Davenport Ministerial Association, seeking its support for his respectable dances, so he had reason to emphasize the immorality of places such as Brick's. But registered prostitutes certainly visited Brick's. A year before Clendenen's visit, Brick's Pavilion hosted a masquerade ball and awarded the prize for prettiest costume to Jennie York, who dressed as a jockey and who had been running a brothel in Davenport for about five years. The young women whose attractions lured Clendenen's customers away may have been brothel inmates, or they may have been cigar makers and salesgirls. It was this confusion and the sexual exchange behind the practice of treating that disturbed middle-class observers.[48]

Just as important, Brick's and the other dance halls employed women to drink with customers. Munro paid his girls five dollars a week for "selling drinks for the house and . . . boosting the trade along." At the Davenport Theater, chorus girls earned five dollars a week plus board for similar duties. Joanne Meyerowitz has suggested that women in the "sexual service sector"—including chorus girls, taxi dancers, and other women who marketed parasexuality, as well as prostitutes—earned more than other working women because employers did not pay them as "dependent daughters" whose primary support came from a breadwinner father. While this may have been the case in Chicago, the pay scales reported for Bucktown businesses do not follow this pattern. At five to seven dollars a week, chorus girls, drink boosters, and minor actresses earned less than many clerks, and the stage performers had to provide their own costumes, cosmetics, and jewelry. Employers may not have viewed these women as dependent daughters but may well have assumed that "treating" or casual prostitution would make up the difference between low wages and the cost of living.[49]

The road from the dance hall to the brothel may not have been as direct as sensational titles of the day proposed, but those who saw a connection were not simply misinterpreting a culture they did not understand. Brothel prostitution was real and represented one employment option for young working women, though by most standards, it was not an especially desirable option. Nevertheless, scores of women worked in Davenport's brothels, and their example was readily visible both in and around the city's dance halls. Brothel prostitutes almost certainly earned more than the women engaged in parasexual commerce as stage performers and waiter girls pushing drinks.

While most of the young women who flocked to the dance halls for entertainment would have vehemently repulsed any suggestion that they were veering toward prostitution, their self-perception was not always shared by the men who sought their company. Especially when complicated by class difference, girls' flirtatious efforts to attract attention and treats from men undermined their claims to sexual respectability and personal safety. Josie Washburn was a great fan of social dancing, considering it "wholesome, beneficial, and rejuvenating for the tired body," yet even she, with her clearheaded, insider's knowledge of brothel prostitution, felt that dance halls posed a special danger to girls who depended on "chance acquaintances for their entertainment." The danger lay not in the dancing but in the drinking urged by men "who go to pick up girls if they can." Secure that they could "act as they please" without jeopardizing their social standing, Washburn believed that men felt free to "attack the innocent girl" after dampening her resistance with drink. Given Washburn's bitter experience in prostitution, her view of men's motives may have been especially harsh. But since some working women certainly visited assignation houses like the Slate House, Jacobsen's, or the Metropolitan Hotel with their partners, many men may have expected or even insisted on the same privilege with the women who accepted their treats. This was certainly Clendenen's meaning when he complained of young men from the "best families" preferring to mingle with "young woman of loose morals." The consequences of misunderstanding could be grave. A young woman who drank and flirted with strangers could not expect the sympathy of police or jurors if she tried to bring a charge of rape.[50]

Those who feared the consequences of Bucktown's dance halls might have joined with the women of the Lend a Hand club to improve work opportunities and pay for women. Eliminating the economic disparity between men and women would have made treating unnecessary and would have rendered brothel prostitution far less attractive as a work option. Instead, when a scandal turned public attention on the dangers of Bucktown's saloon theaters and dance halls, city fathers closed ranks to protect men's prerogatives by attempting to bar working women from Bucktown.

"THE WICKEDEST CITY IN AMERICA"

In January 1903, Clay and Emma Woodward booked a girl with a "sweet soprano voice" to sing at their Iowa Theater. Eighteen-year-old Anita Ray, "slender, flaxen haired and blue eyed," came to Davenport hoping to start a new life. She had earned seven dollars a week as a clerk at Marshall Field's department store in Chicago, but this was not enough for a "comfortable living." So she quit her job and applied to a theatrical agency, hoping for a career as an actress and a salary of fifteen dollars a week. After a few engagements in Chicago, her agent sent her to the Iowa Theater. She sang and acted in a small comic role, and her pretty face attracted the attention of men seated in a private box. They sent a note to the theater's manager requesting that Miss Ray join them. The manager, Clay Woodward, instructed her "to go up into the boxes with the men" and "drum up trade for the bar." At first she refused, but when he threatened to turn her out into the bitter cold January night, she complied. She had spent her last five dollars for a dress, leaving her with no money for other lodgings or a ticket home. The *Democrat* described her assignment bluntly: "She was to barter smiles for drinks and drink with all the men until their thirst gave out or she was under the table." The men, noted the writer, had a "practically limitless" capacity "for both lingering and drinking." After four days of working in the boxes, often until three or four in the morning, Anita Ray quit, leaving the theater and turning to Davenport's police matron for assistance. Sarah Hill gave the singer a night's lodging and persuaded the owner of the Burtis Opera House to buy the girl a ticket back to Chicago.[51]

At first, Davenport's newspapers paid little attention to the story. On an inside page, under the headline "White Slavery in Davenport," the *Leader* reported, "Pretty and Attractive She Is Engaged at One of the Local Variety Theaters and Started upon a Life Which Would Soon Have Led to Shame and Ruination," casting the episode as yet another example of Mrs. Hill's laudable efforts on behalf of endangered girls. But when Anita Ray got back to Chicago, the Hearst papers smelled a good story and quickly trumpeted Davenport as "the wickedest city in America." An article appearing under Ray's byline taunted, "If it is true that God has forsaken Chicago, then He has never even visited Davenport, Iowa."[52]

Anita Ray did not set out to become a prostitute, but that may have mattered little to Clay Woodward or the men who sought her company. Without friends or resources in Davenport, she had to live at the theater, subject to "all the regulations of the place," including the one that required her to drink with customers in their private boxes. Like struggling women before her, Ray also faced the legal consequences of her associations. The Iowa Theater operated in a prostitution district, across the street from a notorious assignation house, and the theater owner was Emma Woodward, who had a well-known history of brothel keeping. Patrons devoted the hours after the stage show to drinking and couple dances with the performers, very much like the dance culture characteristic of brothels, where prostitutes' performances of the *danse du ventre* led to seductive turns in the arms of customers. The neighborhood, the space, and the activities all blurred the distinction between brothel and saloon theater. In such a setting, a young woman who spent hours every night drinking herself "under the table" with strangers who paid for her companionship became an easy target for rape. Men might easily presume that any woman living at the Woodwards' dance hall and conducting herself as Ray did must be a prostitute. Because law asserted that any woman found in a place associated with prostitution was herself a prostitute, she could hardly expect police or jurors to sympathize if she brought a charge of rape against an assailant.[53]

When newspapers invoked the term "white slavery" in 1903, they no longer meant the exploitation of women's labor. As discussed in chapter 5, fifteen years earlier, Nell Nelson's exposé of white slavery had detailed not sexual exploitation but the "sufferings, privations and hardships" endured by working women. She inspired Chicago women to organize a Women's Alliance to improve conditions for these workers. But in 1903, white slavery had taken on a new meaning, and newspapers in both Davenport and Chicago shaped Anita Ray's story to fit the tropes of the white slave narrative: she was ambitious, naive, imprisoned, and deceived by a trusted woman. As reported in the papers, a "lady friend, . . . daughter of a Methodist clergyman," had been performing at the Iowa Theater and vouched for its respectability. Rescued by the police matron, Ray escaped "shame and ruination" by accepting restoration to her home, yet her rescue left the root problem untouched: long hours and hard work at Marshall Field's still paid only seven dollars a week. In the terms of the white slave narrative, danger came to Anita Ray because of her independence and bad judgment, not because of low pay or public policy that valued men's pleasures over women's safety.[54]

Wrested from the trappings of the white slave narrative, what remains of Anita Ray's story parallels those of thousands of other young women at the end of the nineteenth century and the beginning of the twentieth. Like Minnie Brennicke or Lettie Meacham, Anita Ray traveled far from home in search of an opportunity to earn a better living. Indeed, about the time Anita Ray quit her job as a Chicago store clerk and came to Davenport, a Davenport store clerk was in Chicago improving her own opportunities. The contrast between their lives is instructive. Meta Wittig had come of age among the women of the Lend a Hand club, and she relied on the club as she moved from cigar factory to dry goods store to the McCowen Oral School for the Deaf, where she worked and studied in 1902–3. With practical assistance—the educational loan fund and a network of sisters and friends in Davenport and Chicago—the Lend a Hand club supported Wittig's ambition for independence. Anita Ray, with far fewer resources at her disposal, turned to the parasexual commerce of the theater and its promise of higher wages and found herself alone and unable to control the terms of her employment.

"WOMEN MUST KEEP OFF THE STREETS"

Like Ollie Kreps before her, Anita Ray figured in Davenport newspapers for only a few days. Local response at first seemed limited to skepticism or to amusement that Chicago, of all places, dared criticize Davenport's morals. But the Catholic bishop of Davenport, Henry Cosgrove, took advantage of the publicity generated by the Hearst papers' accusations to launch a crusade against vice. By most standards, it was a mild crusade. The bishop raised no objection to saloons or to drinking. Wine and beer, he declared, "are things . . . God has given us to use." Of the brothel, he complained only that it "flaunts itself a little too boldly in this city." Instead, the bishop focused his criticism on late nights, Sunday hours, and gambling, elements of saloon culture that posed a particular threat to homes and families because they kept men away and drained their money. Bishop Cosgrove also singled out Bucktown businesses where women worked and socialized as a special danger. From hack drivers and "others who are in a position to know," the bishop reported hearing "tales of young women of good families and good names, frequenting . . . wine-rooms with men," where they drank so much "that they are hardly able to stagger."[55]

Complaints made by Chicago newspapers could be ignored or ridiculed, but complaints from the local Catholic bishop were another matter altogether. The *Democrat* quickly joined in calling for reform but insisted that moderation should be the watchword. "People are Reasonable," the paper proclaimed. They understand that saloons, gambling, and prostitution "will be here for a long time to come, no matter what the efforts to extirpate them." Citizens of Davenport, the paper editorialized, "want matters regulated.... They don't want a puritan city, and they don't want the impossible attempted. They want an ordinarily decent and clean city." While the bishop had called for shorter hours and Sunday closing, the *Democrat* focused on the wine room and its women customers as "worst of all" and called for its suppression.[56]

In an effort to deflect attention from the bishop's call for more comprehensive reform, Mayor Waldo Becker took aim at the presence of unregistered women in Bucktown. He ordered the dance halls closed, banned dance music from saloons, and called for the removal of doors and curtains from saloon wine rooms. When these efforts failed to silence criticism, he barred women from theater boxes. The bishop would not be deterred. He insisted that saloons must close at midnight. At first, Mayor Becker resisted, arguing that removing women would be enough. Music, he proposed, was "one of the attractions that tend to draw girls and women into the saloons and winerooms." Ridding saloons of music and women "will be a powerful agent in effecting the closing of the saloons at midnight." Becker implicitly endorsed what dance hall and theater owners believed: women were the magnet that drew men to Bucktown and made them linger and drink into the night.[57]

The mayor's efforts did not satisfy the bishop. Smarting from continued criticism, Becker capitulated and ordered all saloons closed at midnight. Finally, he declared Bucktown itself off-limits to unregistered women. Department store clerks and cigar makers who sought to shake off the weariness of the day in a whirling polka or Cuban grind now found themselves subject to arrest. "Young ladies who are in the habit of flaunting themselves before the public had better beware," warned the *Times*. "Many of them can be seen whisking along the streets and in and out of restaurants and other public places and the order has gone out to bring all of these in." The *Leader* headlined its report, "Women Must Keep off the Streets." Although the writer invoked the common-law formula for vagrancy, "on the streets with no visible means of support," he made it clear the rule was not aimed at beggars or streetwalkers. The objects of the regulation were working women, "girls . . . employed . . . in factories or as domestic[s]."[58]

Becker's efforts to protect men's access to saloons—even all-night saloons—by banning women echoed the debate that followed the arrest of Ollie Kreps in 1889. Then, one faction had advocated a public policy eliminating wine rooms and banning women from saloons, while another considered the problem a private one, blaming parents who failed to keep their daughters home. In 1903, no one mentioned parents. The existence of Bucktown was so clearly a matter of public policy that the debate focused only on public solutions, but removing wine-room doors proved no solution at all for the mayor's critics.

When Bucktown's saloon theaters and dance halls turned ordinary working women into profit-enhancing sexual commodities, these businesses participated in a cultural shift that can be traced in turn-of-the-century amusement parks, movies, and vaudeville as well. But as women entered Bucktown, they precipitated a local crisis. Ten years earlier, Davenport had solved the conundrum of preserving men's access to prostitutes in the face of new laws regulating sexual conduct by consigning "fallen" women to regulated brothels. Now, with unregistered girls and women "whisking along the streets" and mingling in saloons where once only prostitutes ventured, the spatial segregation was crumbling. The only solution seemed to be to exclude unregistered women forcibly from saloons, from dance halls, from the streets themselves.[59]

Such draconian measures proved impossible to enforce. Indeed, it is far from clear that Mayor Becker ever intended to enforce them. Women made Bucktown dance halls and saloon theaters profitable, and Bucktown profits filled city coffers. Within weeks of the announced ban, dance halls reopened, women returned to theater boxes, saloon keepers replaced wine room doors, and working women whisked back into Bucktown. A frustrated Bishop Cosgrove sent his secretary, Rev. George Giglinger, to pressure the mayor, with no effect. Giglinger took his complaints to the grand jury but failed to secure indictments in September and again in November. Jurors listened to the evidence but declined to issue indictments, a sign, perhaps, of the general consensus on Bucktown held by voting men in Davenport. A furious Giglinger raged to the press, "It seems that the devil has such a firm hold on Bucktown that even the grand jury bends its knees to him and shirks its duty." Frustrated by the failure of the mayor, the grand jury, and "moral suasion" to secure early closing, Giglinger promised, "the fort will be taken by hammering and battering it down." He hired lawyers.[60]

The first blow of Giglinger's hammer fell on 4 December. His attorneys filed petitions with the district court, seeking injunctions against seven saloons for violating the mulct law. Of all the possible targets in Bucktown, Giglinger focused first on spaces where working women mingled with men: Harry Manwaring's saloon theater and dance hall, Clay and Emma Woodward's Iowa Theater, Jack McPartland's Orpheon, Brick Munro's dance hall, and Mamie Beauchaine's Slate House, along with two other Bucktown saloons. Giglinger's conditions for withdrawing his petitions were simple: no wine rooms, suppression of the "low dance hall" (which did not include traditional ethnic spaces such as Turner Hall or any other sites outside Bucktown), and midnight closing. Brick's Palace Hotel, where the bedrooms "have not been above reproach," fell to Giglinger's hammer as well. While some saloon keepers grumbled, the fear of mulct-law penalties, which included a lifetime ban on saloon keeping for violators, quieted resistance. Over the next weeks, Giglinger's attorneys filed more petitions, and saloon keepers lined up to sign consent agreements. On 22 December, eleven months after Anita Ray fled the Iowa Theater, Giglinger announced that his campaign was over. Working through the courts, Giglinger had achieved what Mayor Becker refused to enforce, but the change would prove only temporary.[61]

The return of spring brought the usual increase in traffic through Davenport, and some businessmen began to feel less cooperative than they had back in December, when cold weather made for slow business. In April, Brick Munro decided that his dance hall had been closed long enough. He unlocked the doors and turned on the lights. According to the *Democrat and Leader*, word of its opening "spread like wild fire" and "attracted a large crowd of pleasure seekers." Promptly at 11:55, he turned out the lights, and by midnight, the closing hour set for saloons in Giglinger's consent agreements, the dance hall was deserted. His manager explained that Munro believed that if he abided by the regulations set for saloon keepers, he was "entitled to the same consideration. . . . No immorality or indecent dances will be admitted about the place, and I cannot see where the public can reasonably have cause for complaint."[62]

The public may not have complained, but Giglinger did. This time, however, his attorneys balked at seeking an injunction against Munro, apparently feeling that midnight closing was restriction enough on Brick's Pavilion. Giglinger found new lawyers who forced Munro to shut down again. Meanwhile, city elections that month put a Republican, Harry Phillips, in the mayor's office. After an interview with the new mayor, Giglinger declared himself satisfied that "the honorable mayor stands for midnight closing and proper regulation" and ended the crusade. Six days later, Brick Munro opened his doors again. This time, both he and Jock Manwaring had the new mayor's blessing. They agreed to bar "girls under twenty" and "indecent dances" in their dance halls, to hire a special police officer to keep order, and to close at midnight. They also promised their patrons to be "open every night in the year" from then on.[63]

In the long run, Bishop Cosgrove's crusade had little effect on Bucktown. Brick's and the other dance halls agreed to close at midnight but remained open on Sundays, and the bans on women's presence—on the street, in saloons, in wine rooms—went unenforced. Despite all the promises of good order, prostitutes continued to patronize both establishments. Gambling too escaped suppression. In fact, by the fall of 1904, Mayor Phillips had decided to regulate gambling according to the model used for brothels. Fines were set at twenty-five dollars for a poker game and thirty dollars for craps, faro, and roulette. As long as the games were honest and the fines paid monthly, police did not interfere. During the first year, fines on Bucktown gambling brought an additional ten thousand dollars in revenue into city coffers. The district remained a lucrative site for entertainment businesses. In 1906, Brick Munro purchased the property where his saloon and dance hall stood and announced his plan to expand and remodel the entire property to add a "first class cafe and restaurant, where meals and short orders will be served at all hours." He promised the "finest" restaurant in the Tri Cities. Munro had even greater ambitions, however. Commenting on concerns about the future of Bucktown, he announced, "They will not find me a stumbling block to the building up of the East End. Moreover I will conduct nothing but a first-class amusement place. I may later on decide to put in a skating rink and vaudeville theater, in addition to my dance and music hall but they too will be strictly first-class affairs and conducted in such a manner than no one can complain of them." Brick Munro staked his fortune on Bucktown's future as commercial amusement district and on the continuing profitability of parasexual entertainments.[64]

The choice by Mayor Henry Vollmer and his successors to establish and maintain a system of regulated brothels created a kind of urban enterprise zone for sexual commerce. During the same years when women of the Lend a Hand—their sights on economic and political independence—were struggling to launch legitimate businesses such as restaurant and dressmaking establishments, brothel keepers found a different route to economic mobility. Some became successful businesswomen, investing in real estate and expanding into multiple brothel sites with a combined total of fifteen or twenty inmates. Their success symbolized the tenacity of the gender system that emerged under industrial capitalism. In spite of decades of advocacy for self-supporting women by the Association for the Advancement of Women, the Lend a Hand club, and suffrage organizations, few women succeeded in legitimate businesses, and public policy did little to support them. Most men continued to believe that respectable women belonged at home. In Davenport, the regulation regime rested on the belief that "fallen" women could provide a valuable public service. By furnishing an outlet for irrepressible male sexuality, they protected good women from rape and preserved a long-established form of male leisure. For most of the women who worked at brothel keeping in Davenport, the prospects for financial success were probably no better than those of milliners and dressmakers, 60 percent of whom failed within five years. But given that these were women with little education and no capital, brothel keeping under regulation was a far more lucrative and stable choice than the most common alternatives, sewing or laundry work. For ordinary inmates, prostitution remained a physically and emotionally battering form of employment.

The same zone that supported prostitutes also incubated new businesses capitalizing on Bucktown's reputation as an entertainment district for men. Gambling and various forms of parasexual commerce took root in Bucktown. Dance halls and saloon theaters, operated by men and women with close ties to the brothel trade, relied on young women—both patrons and employees—to attract men and their billfolds. While most of the girls and young women who flocked to these Bucktown businesses for entertainment or employment did not consider themselves prostitutes, the men who joined them may have seen things differently. Bucktown had been set apart to draw a clear line between girls and women who were sexually available and those who were not, and most men still subscribed to the belief that respectable girls and women did not belong in saloons and dance halls. In a neighborhood thick with brothels and assignation houses, young women who drank and flirted risked being treated as prostitutes by the men who paid for their company. Some observers worried that this confusion staffed the brothels, but efforts to ban unregistered women from Bucktown theaters, dance halls, and streets failed. The presence of unregistered women was as necessary to Bucktown profits as prostitutes were to the brothels.

CONCLUSION:
THE POPULAR YOUNG LADY
IN BUSINESS LIFE

ON ELECTION DAY 1900, as men in Davenport headed to the polls, the working women of the Lend a Hand club held their own rally and mock election. Members took the parts of Republicans, Democrats, Socialists, Prohibitionists, and several minor parties, with a representative of each delivering a speech on her party's platform. (By agreement, no one could make a speech for the party she really supported.) A writer from the *Democrat* reported that as the returns began to come in, "the wildest excitement prevailed." The women cheered and clapped as one candidate or another pulled ahead, "the only failure being in the inability of the ladies to imitate the shrill whistle of the small boy." When the election judges posted the final tally, William McKinley had won, but Socialist Eugene Debs came in second and William Jennings Bryan trailed dead last, collecting just four votes. Some working women of the Lend a Hand clearly shared the anti-Prohibition sentiments of Davenport, and many endorsed the working-class idealism that drew so many into Debs's camp.[1]

As a performance of gender-role reversal, the Lend a Hand mock election had nothing on the torchlight parade of the Belva Lockwood club twelve years earlier, and the election's purpose could not have been more different. The men who marched in 1888 were protesting the intrusion of women into public life. The women who voted in the Lend a Hand rooms were rehearsing for the day when they would shoulder the obligations of citizenship. Their mock election came at the culmination of a three-year course of study in political science. In 1897, when the National American Woman Suffrage Association (NAWSA) held its annual convention in Des Moines, the Lend a Hand launched its study program with a visit from NAWSA lecturer Emma Smith DeVoe. The club's first reading was John Stuart Mill's *The Subjection of Women*.[2]

Jennie McCowen had long been a suffragist, yet for most of the twenty years that Davenport had been her home, she directed her public efforts not toward winning the vote but toward assisting women like her who earned their own living. From her earliest years as a working woman, she also understood that employment and suffrage were linked. As a young woman, she heard in the discourse of free labor the connection drawn between woman's "dependence" and her exclusion from the polls. As Dr. McCowen strove to support herself, voting men shaped her opportunities at every turn. When she was a schoolteacher, an elected official set her salary. Elected men established the public medical school she attended and appointed the state hospital administrator who hired her for his staff. Even in Davenport, where she was a physician in private practice, McCowen felt the effects of voting men's choices every day. From her office, a short walk north on Brady Street to the library or south to shops or the Lend a Hand rooms reminded her that elected officials accepted brothels in her neighborhood, acknowledging by implication that prostitution was one employment option for women.

In 1889, Jennie McCowen drew on the political tools available to women to challenge this policy. Through speeches, articles, petitions, and personal lobbying, she organized women to enter public life and change public policy. They succeeded in persuading the city to open a separate jail for women and to employ a police matron who could protect women in custody and help them leave prostitution. Yet barely four years after McCowen and the Charitable Alliance won their campaign, the matron became the registrar of licensed prostitutes. Davenport committed itself openly to a policy of regulated prostitution, forcefully reinscribing gender on downtown streets. In 1889, McCowen and the women who joined her had believed that they stood on the threshold of political influence, but the events of 1893 taught them that without votes, women's vaunted "influence" meant nothing. Unlike their counterparts in Boston and Chicago, Davenport's organized women had neither the wealth nor the alliances with powerful men that might have enabled them to wield real political influence. When the medical society's criticism failed to alter the policy of regulating prostitution, McCowen and the Lend a Hand publicly embraced suffrage.

Every Iowa legislature since the end of the Civil War had considered woman suffrage. An amendment to the constitution passed both houses in 1870, only to fail in the Senate when the measure came up for the required second vote in 1872. This pattern of passing but then defeating the suffrage amendment repeated itself regularly for the rest of the century. Meanwhile, the legislature debated several proposals for partial suffrage—for school directors, for municipal candidates, for presidential electors, for bond issues. All went down in defeat until 1894, when the Iowa Assembly passed a bill granting women the vote in school and municipal referenda where bond issues or tax increases were at stake.[3]

Even this innovation ran aground at the local level. In Davenport, an 1895 referendum on a tax levy for a new railroad bridge raised the possibility that women might vote, and County Attorney William Chamberlin (the same man who had played Belva Lockwood in 1888) cautiously sought an opinion from the state attorney general as to whether the suffrage statute applied. The answer was yes, but Chamberlin nevertheless announced that he would not permit women to vote because they had not registered. Not until 1897 did Davenport women have the chance to exercise their new right, this time on a proposition to raise taxes for a new school building. The state attorney general eased their way by ruling that the law did not require voters to register for school elections.[4]

In September 1897, the Lend a Hand Club sponsored a suffrage convention in Davenport. The guest speakers were Rev. Henrietta Moore of Ohio and Rev. Anna Howard Shaw, president of the NAWSA. From Davenport, Maria Purdy Peck, whose daughter Jessie was married to ex-mayor Henry Vollmer, answered the question "Does the Tax-Paying Woman Need It?" in the affirmative, and Dr. Jennie McCowen addressed the question "Does the Professional Woman Need It?" with equal certainty. Representatives from the Illinois cities spoke to the needs of the wife, the mother, and the single woman for the right to vote.[5]

The convention met in Library Hall on Brady Street, just north of the Fifth Street tracks and only a couple of blocks from streets set apart for prostitution. If the newspaper reports are accurate, only one speaker addressed the issue that must have been on many minds: regulated prostitution. Rev. G. S. Rollins was on the program merely as a "discussion leader," but when his time on the platform came, he rose and declared himself a "recent convert" to the cause of equal suffrage. He then spoke briefly and directly about the need for women's votes in municipal elections. "If women were given the ballot," he argued, "the morality of the towns would be elevated." He did not mean this in a vague and general way but spoke specifically of "municipal officials" who failed to "bring about certain reforms" because, they claimed, "they would not have the support of the majority of voters." If women could vote, argued Rev. Rollins, these officials would have the support they needed to move forward. With equal suffrage, "many of the evils in our cities would be expurgated, and the morals of men and women alike would be elevated."[6]

Rollins did not name S. F. Smith but was certainly thinking of the Republican mayor elected five months earlier. When voters put Smith in office, many had expected him to end Vollmer's regulation system. By September, when the suffrage convention met, it was already clear that the police were pursuing business as usual and that the system of licensed prostitution remained in place. Whatever Smith may have intended when he and like-minded men attempted to oppose brothel regulation through a Citizens' League, as mayor he found he had the support neither of voters nor the city council when it came to changing the regulation system. Rollins was probably not alone in his views. While no paper reported the details of Maria Purdy Peck's convention speech, the *Davenport Democrat* published her prosuffrage letter to the editor. Opposition to woman suffrage, she wrote, came primarily from "party bosses, gamblers, prize-fighters, wreckers of homes, despoilers of women's virtue, the frail sisterhood, criminals and law breakers of all sorts," a veritable catalog of the sporting element that profited from regulation in Davenport.[7]

Davenport's organized women may have turned away from direct challenges to public policy on prostitution, but in 1907 Bucktown came under assault from another direction. Just as in 1903, this new attack focused not on the brothels but on the saloons. The offensive began in August 1907, when two men sought injunctions against the owner and operator of every saloon and liquor wholesaler in all of Scott County—about 240 businesses. The two, Theodor H. Kemmerer and attorney C. W. Neal, were both American-born sons of American-born parents, and almost immediately, saloon keepers, other businessmen, and the German community began claiming that the campaign was anti-German and bad for business. Neal insisted that the goal was not to compel compliance with the mulct law but simply to "force" saloons "to eliminate the[ir] objectionable features," including wine rooms, the presence of women and children, Sunday hours, and the workman's free lunch. The elements selected for criticism by Kemmerer and Neal share specific characteristics: they reveal the saloon as more than just a place for men to drink, and two—Sunday hours and the presence of women and children—were typical of German immigrant culture.[8]

Within a week, German Americans organized a "monster demonstration" against Sunday closing and the mulct law. Led by a volunteer band and six hundred members of the Turner Society, the parade struck out to the tune of "Stars and Stripes Forever," staking claim to their identity as not just Germans but German Americans. At least twenty-seven organizations joined the Turners, some displaying banners with Iowa's state motto, "Our liberties we prize, our rights we will maintain." Estimates numbered the marchers at five thousand. At Washington Square, speakers in German and English decried the injunctions. The president of the German-American Central Association denounced the "microscopic minority" trampling the rights of thousands, and C. A. Ficke urged civil disobedience, comparing the mulct law with the Fugitive Slave Law: "disobedience to this law was deemed more creditable than obedience to it." Indeed, the use of the term "personal liberty" to characterize the right to drink beer echoed the "personal liberty" laws passed by states in the 1850s to encourage resistance to the Fugitive Slave Law.[9]

In spite of the protests, on 25 August most saloon keepers accepted a consent decree banning wine rooms, free food, women and children, and Sunday morning hours and imposing other restrictions. The penalty for violating the agreement was six months in jail or a thousand dollar fine. Each saloon keeper also paid Neal's fee of twenty-five dollars per case. With 240 or so saloons in the county, Neal's take was about six thousand dollars. Some observers immediately surmised that the prosecutions were mere extortion, a suspicion many felt confirmed when Kemmerer and Neal declined a suggestion to turn the money over to the Associated Charities. By mid-September, tempers ran so hot that when *Der Demokrat* editor August Richter encountered Kemmerer on a downtown street, their chance meeting ended with the sixty-four-year-old Richter caning Kemmerer, who was a decade younger, until his stick broke. At Richter's assault trial the following month, the courtroom audience quickly raised enough money to replace Richter's broken cane with a new gold-headed stick. The crowd then turned its anger on Neal, Kemmerer's attorney. Out on the streets, they mocked and threatened, offering to toss him in the river or to tar and feather him. Neal brandished a revolver to protect himself, only to be arrested for carrying a weapon. That night, a torchlight rally ended with Neal hanged in effigy. The next morning, when Neal showed up for his police-court trial, the crowd returned as well, heckling and jeering. When his trial concluded and he had paid his five dollar fine, Neal demanded police protection until he could take the afternoon train for Des Moines. At the depot, Bucktown musicians mustered an impromptu band and saluted Neal's departing train with a funeral dirge.[10]

To Prohibition supporters around the state, the anti-mulct-law protests in Davenport simply proved the lawlessness and hypocrisy of the proliquor factions. Prohibitionists considered the mulct law a concession to the liquor interests. Opponents saw its restrictions as a draconian infringement of their liberties. The different perspectives on the mulct law reflect radically different understandings of the relationship between manliness and the saloon. For Prohibitionists, the saloon was about liquor, and all the things banned by the mulct law—tables and chairs, privacy, women, food—were merely traps to seduce men into taking a drink. Once he succumbed, the drinker was sure to forfeit self-control and shirk responsibility—to become less than a man. To the saloon's defenders, liquor was just one part of the social space where men could most readily affirm their manhood. Through the rituals of treating, competition, and bawdy talk, men built reputations in the eyes of their peers. The mulct-law rules reduced the saloon from the hub of men's social lives to a mere liquor dispensary. Depending on one's perspective, the saloon was either the source of manly identity or the greatest threat to it.[11]

Conclusion

In December 1907, Governor Albert Cummins, speaking to a mass meeting at Davenport's First Presbyterian Church, brought the voice of the state's Prohibition voters to Davenport. He criticized the consent decrees accepted first by Giglinger and then by Kemmerer and Neal. "I don't recognize the right of any civic league or ministerial association to agree that a part of the law shall be obeyed and a part violated," he declared, warning that he had asked the state legislature for the power to remove from office any local public official who refused to enforce the law. Cummins called on citizens of Davenport to uphold the entire mulct law—that is, to enforce provisions ignored in the previous consent decrees, such as ten o'clock closing, the ban on tables and chairs, and the requirement that saloons have permission from property owners within fifty feet of their businesses.[12]

In response, ninety Davenport saloon keepers signed an "iron-clad agreement" to abide by almost all of the restrictions, though the proprietors held out for an eleven o'clock closing time and the Sunday afternoon hours so dear to German families. Nevertheless, Iowa's attorney general ordered the Scott County attorney to prosecute violators of the mulct law, resulting in what the *Democrat* described as the "first dry Sunday in the history of Davenport." Almost immediately, the papers began reporting the negative effects. Sunday crowds crossed over to Illinois to spend their leisure time and leisure dollars. Turner Hall announced that it might close to all but members. Some saloon keepers declared that they were closing their doors, while others reported that neighbors were using the fifty foot rule for extortion, demanding payments of between one hundred and five hundred dollars in return for permission.[13]

Beginning in March 1908, a new Davenport Civic Federation entered the fray. In a letter signed by Presbyterian minister W. H. Blanke and sent to every saloon keeper in Davenport, the federation threatened injunctions for violating any portion of the mulct law. Over the following months, the group forced dozens of saloons into compliance and others out of business. Businessmen complained of the campaign's effect on the commercial climate. One cigar maker laid off eighty employees, and the butchers and grocers who had once supplied the "free lunch" complained of a loss of business. Some of Bucktown's landmarks closed as well. Brick Munro sold his famous Pavilion to make way for a grocery wholesale house, and Harry "Jock" Manwaring relocated to Illinois, closing his dance hall theater and opening a saloon in Peoria. According to the *Democrat*, everyone from architects to department stores to musicians reported a falling off in business, and city tax revenues dropped off as well.[14]

The campaign in Davenport to enforce the mulct law took its strength from small-town and rural voters around the state and from their representatives in Des Moines. In 1909, the state assembly passed several new laws designed to shut down Bucktown and its counterparts in other river cities. One of these was a pioneering "red-light abatement" act. No longer would local authorities alone decide whether to prosecute brothel keepers, nor would juries alone have the power to decide guilt. Instead, any citizen could bring an action in equity court in the name of the state of Iowa, and if evidence established that a place was a house of ill-fame, the law required the court to issue a permanent injunction closing down the business. Any violation of the injunction required a summary trial, and the law made it all but impossible to dismiss a case once it had been initiated. Davenport might have continued business as usual, waiting for the Civic Federation to spend time and money on lawyers to force compliance, but a second new law passed that season hauled local officials up short. Governor Cummins did not win the right to remove recalcitrant local officials, but he got something just as good. Whenever five citizens signed a complaint against a mayor, county attorney, or police chief for failure to enforce the law, that official could be tried for malfeasance and removed from office. Had Mayor G. W. Scott declined to enforce existing laws against brothels, the Civic Federation would have been ready with five citizens and a complaint.[15]

The new red-light abatement law certainly would have transformed Davenport's regulation system, but it was the malfeasance statute that created crisis and panic in Bucktown. On 15 April 1909, local newspapers published Mayor Scott's announcement that the brothels would have to close by the Fourth of July, when most new statutes took effect. But sometime on 15 April, Scott discovered that the malfeasance law took effect upon publication, meaning immediately. The new abatement law might not have been in effect, but Mayor Scott was already vulnerable for failing to enforce existing statutes prohibiting houses of ill-fame. He moved quickly to protect himself. As police officers went out on their beats at six that evening, Mayor Scott issued new instructions: brothels must close immediately.[16]

Most women could not believe what they were hearing. These, after all, were not streetwalkers or casual prostitutes. They were women who had agreed to abide by the rules of brothel regulation, who had come to rely on the stability created by the system. These women had only just grasped the idea that they had less than three months to settle their affairs and find new work. Suddenly, many were literally on the streets. Most of the ordinary brothel workers owed money to downtown merchants for clothing and personal items, and creditors streamed into Bucktown to claim what they could before the women left town. Many women ended up with nothing but the clothes on their backs—their working apparel, which was hardly suited for street wear. A writer for the *Democrat and Leader* reported seeing women "scurrying all over the east end endeavoring to borrow some suitable clothes." Other women ended up without shoes or hats. Mayor Scott's rush to protect himself created other hardships as well. Dozens of brothel workers went to the house of detention, hoping that police matron Sarah Hill would assist them, but Mrs. Hill was out of town, visiting a friend in Kansas. She returned ten days later to find "a pack of letters several inches high" from "ladies" in Davenport and surrounding towns. "They were beautiful letters," Mrs. Hill said, explaining that most made the same offer: "If you know of any of these women who are sincerely in earnest in desiring to lead a new life, my home is open to them." But by the time Matron Hill read the letters, most of the women these offers might have helped were gone.[17]

Some women tried to arrange to work in Rock Island brothels, but the police force of that city rounded them up and "marched them back to Davenport." One girl driven back across the bridge was so distraught that she threatened suicide and began walking to the riverbank, but "some of the other unfortunates overtook her and led her away." The *Democrat and Leader* reported that the "moral element of the city" was not living up to promises to help the women. One girl, described as a former employee of one of the city's hospitals who had been a brothel inmate only a short while, sought employment from a local minister. He hired her as a household servant, but from there, stories diverge. She claimed that when she explained her recent past and admitted she had no references, he withdrew his promise of employment. He insisted that he fired her because she had lied about her recent past. Wherever the truth lay, the story suggests the difficulties a woman from the brothels faced when she sought legitimate employment: was it better to lie or to tell the truth? The wrong choice could be costly. The women suddenly cut off from their livelihood faced other hard choices as well. While newspaper writers assumed that brothel prostitutes were outcasts, the women expressed attachment to their home and community. "I was born in Davenport, and have been here all my life," explained one woman, uncertain of her next step. "I do not know where to turn," she worried. "I have not a dollar to my name. I am heavily in debt. Everything I have in the world is on my back. I do not know where my next meal is coming from." For women with few choices, one more had just vanished.[18]

The April 1909 crisis reveals the extent to which some long-standing ideas about prostitution and woman's nature continued to shape responses to the problem. Mayor G. W. Scott never considered the consequences of his order for the women who worked in Davenport's brothels. To him, the women were simply inconsequential, outcasts whose well-being concerned no one. Similarly, the governor and legislators in Des Moines who devised the malfeasance law were more concerned with punishing defiant local officials than with the law's effect on brothel workers. To the women who wrote to Matron Hill and asked for opportunities to help, the brothel workers were far from inconsequential. Like the women of the Charitable Alliance twenty years earlier, these women began with the presumption that prostitutes were victims, not wantons, and stepped forward with offers of help. It is impossible to know what might have happened if Hill had not been out of town, if a bleached blonde with a jones for nicotine—or morphine—had tried to start a new life in the kitchen of a farm wife in Blue Grass. The letters were probably more sincere than realistic, yet they reveal that some women were still reluctant to draw the bright line separating prostitutes from other women.

As Bucktown flourished, Davenport's organized women stayed aloof from the mulct-law controversies. But the changes wrought in downtown space prompted the Lend a Hand club to adopt new programs that gradually led to a change in the club itself. A membership roster from 1897 indicates one trend in the club after ten years' presence in the city. Teachers, clerks, and office workers had grown to account for more than half of all members, while servants, factory hands, and seamstresses dropped from one-third to one-fifth of the membership. Two printers, both union members and both employees of the *Davenport Times*, had also joined.

Occupations of Lend a Hand Members, 1896–97

Schoolteachers	11
Bookkeepers/stenographers	7
Domestic servants	5
Clerks	4
Factory hands	3
Printers	2
Music teachers	2
Social service workers	2
Milliner in department store	1
Nurse	1
Proprietor, shoe store	1
Seamstress	1

While nearly all members still worked downtown (the exceptions were primarily teachers and domestic servants), only eight out of the fifty whose homes could be traced still lived within five blocks of the club's downtown rooms. The shift of residences away from downtown probably reflects two kinds of changes. First, schoolteachers, who made up a larger proportion of members, naturally would have gravitated toward the neighborhood schools where they taught. The second kind of change was spatial. The rise of Bucktown meant that rooms downtown were less desirable for single women, and the expanding network of electric streetcar lines made transportation for those who worked downtown more convenient although still rather expensive for most self-supporting women.

The Lend a Hand responded to the reconfiguration of downtown space with new programs and a new location. After years of occupying rooms in various buildings along Brady Street, the Lend a Hand club moved west in 1902 to the intersection of Second and Ripley. The new location put the club closer to the city's large department stores, where many women worked (and shopped), but also put distance between the club rooms and the dance halls and bawdy theaters of Bucktown. Two new programs also addressed the changes in downtown. The first expanded on the kitchen facilities that were an early feature of the club rooms: the Noon Rest, a lunchroom for women, opened in May 1900. The second was a boarding home for women workers. McCowen Hall opened in July 1901. Both projects represented important shifts in the club's vision of itself and its mission.[19]

In contrast to the Home Cooking Company, which had opened in 1893, the Noon Rest was never intended as a profitable business that could combine public service with an opportunity for women to support themselves. From the beginning, the Noon Rest relied on the labor of volunteers to subsidize its operations. Located in the Lend a Hand rooms, the lunchroom employed a cook—Carrie Heinz, sister of former mayor Fred Heinz—but used a staff of middle-class volunteers to serve lunch to club members and other women, who paid about thirteen cents for a meal that included meat, bread, vegetables, and coffee, tea, or milk. Given that so many downtown workers now relied on the streetcar to travel to and from homes in outlying residential neighborhoods, the lunchroom provided a valuable service. Because the Noon Rest was not a commercial enterprise, a woman who carried lunch from home could still enjoy a sociable meal with friends, purchasing just coffee or individual items from the menu or nothing at all. During the first few months, the Noon Rest served between eighty and a hundred lunches a day, six days a week. Ten years later, it was serving some two hundred lunches daily plus supper on Saturdays, and it continued as a Davenport institution through much of the twentieth century, eventually serving not just working women but shoppers visiting from small towns and rural areas as well as from Davenport's residential areas.[20]

The boarding home, McCowen Hall, was not as enduring. At a public meeting in May 1901, Jennie McCowen spoke about the problems facing young women coming to the city to earn a living and the need for inexpensive but congenial rooms. In a nod to the Bucktown dance halls, she urged the need for "wholesome company and entertainment, instead of the questionable article to which they must in so many cases turn." Women immediately formed a committee, raised money, and searched for a suitable site. The home opened in a rented house at 708 Brady Street in July, and the committee christened the home McCowen Hall.[21]

As with the Noon Rest, McCowen Hall relied heavily on subsidies from middle-class patrons. The *Democrat* reported what the sponsors may have hoped: "There is no element of charity in this home," insisting, "the home is to be self-supporting. It is to pay its help. Its inmates are not living on the bounty of others, but are to pay for what they get." In fact, from the start, the home relied on donations. The Daughters of the American Revolution and women's groups from Methodist, Congregational, and Episcopal churches each adopted a room and provided the furniture. Almost immediately, the boarding home committee knew that the house was too small. The home had four times as many applicants as beds, even after expanding the number of spaces from thirteen to seventeen by squeezing more beds into the attic. According to the committee chair, "They come and plead to be taken in and are willing to sleep on a couch anywhere." The crowding publicized what McCowen and her colleagues already knew: many Davenport boardinghouses simply refused to take women—"some cases of refusal... have been positively brutal"—and most were too expensive for working women. McCowen Hall charged $2.50 a week for room and board in a dormitory bed and $5 for a shared room. The matron of McCowen Hall tried to assist the women she turned away but was often unsuccessful. One girl reported trying "25 places to secure board before anything at all suitable was found, so many boarding houses taking men only." The home's small size also precluded economies of scale, and operating costs overran the budget. Committed to keeping room charges within the means of working women, sponsors relied heavily on donations of food, bedding, and cash. Still, the home lost money from the start and never recovered. Efforts to raise money for a larger building fell short. After just over four years, McCowen Hall shut its doors.[22]

Both the Noon Rest and McCowen Hall reflected a shift away from the ethos of the early Lend a Hand. Far more than earlier projects, these required the initiative and management of affluent patrons whose time was not taken up by hours on the job. In response, the Lend a Hand altered its organizational structure to create a board of five vice presidents who oversaw the club's projects and operations. Unlike the early leadership—the presidents of the "tens" who had played the central role in governance and the members of the King's Daughters—the new vice presidents were not working women. Their involvement shifted the Lend a Hand away from its ethos of mutual assistance toward a view of working women as objects of charity, the perspective typical of more conventional class-bridging organizations such as Young Women's Christian Associations (YWCAs) and working girls' clubs. Indeed, the Lend a Hand's new leadership changed the organization so much that in 1907 it opened a Woman's Exchange, embracing the charity designed to hide the fact that women worked for pay.[23]

A quarter century earlier, the Lend a Hand club had been born out of the experiences and expectations of a small circle of self-supporting women. Their lives had taught them to rely on networks of sisters and friends to make their way in the world, and they shared with members of the Association for the Advancement of Women a faith that paid employment was key to women's social and political equality. At the same time, these women confronted a culture that censured paid employment as contrary to woman's mission in the home, as an assault on men's status as breadwinners, and as a step on the downward path that led to the brothel. In creating the Lend a Hand club, they sought to provide practical aid to women workers by helping them move into better-paying positions, to create space for working women in the city center, and to assert their respectability. Sharing downtown streets with prostitutes, these women also came to see tolerated brothels as a threat to all women but especially to women who needed to earn a living. For desperate women with few resources, prostitution could indeed seem a well-paid and readily available alternative to legitimate work. As long as the city tolerated brothels, some young women would end up staffing them.

By 1910, much had changed about both the cultural and spatial geography working women occupied. They were still ill paid, but young women who worked for pay no longer faced the same censure. Indeed, that summer, the *Davenport Democrat and Leader* ran a series of articles celebrating the skill and glamour of the city's "Representative Salesladies" and "Popular Young Ladies in Business Life." Accompanying the articles were photographic portraits of more than a score of working women, including Miss Gretchen Schramm, a stenographer at the county attorney's office; Miss Clara Rosenkranz, an assistant in a physician's office; and Miss Fannie Stapleton, who worked at a cigar stand. Another article profiled Louise Mooney, who had gone to work at the age of thirteen to help support her widowed mother and younger brothers, taking a job delivering telegrams. As she bicycled through the streets of Davenport, carrying messages to offices and factories, Mooney's work continually brought her into contact with strangers, yet the writer affirmed that "she has emerged . . . unsullied and untainted." The profile of Mooney, like the earlier articles, accompanied photographs depicting her "rare beauty." According to the profile, "every photographer of prominence in the city asked the little messenger girl to favor them with a pose," bewitched by her "lustrous eyes" and the "piquancy" of her features. For its part, the telegraph company, impressed with Mooney as a "remarkable business woman," promoted her to bookkeeper.[24]

This was a very different view of working women than had prevailed in the 1880s. Then, writers warned women to be subdued and modest to protect themselves from "impertinent intrusion" and worried that businesswomen "unsexed" themselves. A quarter century later, the newspaper published photographs of respectable working women flirting for the camera, a skill they learned from the movies. Film actresses also helped popularize cosmetics, and sexuality became one of the assets a young woman brought to her job. The new respectability of paid employment came, however, with a condition: these glamorous businesswomen were young because they were temporary sojourners in the world of commerce. For them, employment was not an alternative to subordination in marriage but a prelude to it. They did not work for independence and self-reliance; they were the helpmeets of the office, preparing to be wives and helpmeets at home.[25]

Just as the image of working women changed, so did the perception of the danger signified by prostitution. In the 1880s, when organized women called for laws to curtail the entry of girls into brothels, those laws expressed the belief that danger lay in male aggression, in rape, seduction, and the abuse of women in police custody.

Cast out by family and society, the "ruined" girl faced a stark choice: "die, or do worse." This view of prostitution held a critique of both male power and capitalism, for what sent girls to the brothel was not rape alone but the resulting poverty. Prostitution may have been a fate worse than death, but it was a kind of choice, a determination to survive. In 1909, as part of the same program of reform that created the red-light abatement law and the malfeasance statute, the Iowa legislature passed one more new law aimed at prostitution. It established penalties for "confining any girl or woman against her will for the purposes of prostitution." Popularly known as the "white slave traffic" law, it signaled a new interpretation of prostitution. The "white slave" was not a rape victim who chose the brothel over poverty or death but a literal prisoner, a victim of conspiracy. No longer did danger permeate society in the form of male aggression. Instead, it dwelled specifically in an underworld of foreigners and criminal conspirators, some of whom might even be women. "White slavery" also transformed the economic meaning of prostitution by proposing that it was not paid employment itself that corrupted gender relations and endangered girls, nor was it poverty, nor even women's sexuality. It was independence. Even a poor girl faced danger only when she flouted the protection of fathers or brothers—or YWCAs and working girls' clubs. The "white slave" was a sexual innocent enslaved by force, and her existence made the "popular young lady in business life" possible. Louise Mooney, the beautiful telegram girl, could ride the streets and work among men yet remain "unsullied and untainted" because danger no longer lay in the promiscuous mixing of men and women in the workplace and city streets. If Louise Mooney became a prostitute, it would not be because she was raped, seduced, or poor but because Mooney, innocence intact, became a slave.[26]

The federal White Slave Traffic Act, passed in 1910, carried the denial of women's capacity to an even greater extreme. That law, commonly called the Mann Act, deemed even an adult woman who chose to cross a state line for an "immoral purpose" a victim. And in a particularly perverse twist, she could be convicted as a coconspirator in her own exploitation. The new white slaves were not workers impoverished by industrial capitalism; they were stolen property. A wise young woman did not work to be independent and self-reliant. Instead, she served the man who employed her, ornamented his office, and accepted protection until she was safely wed.[27]

Jennie McCowen was born before Seneca Falls hosted the first Woman's Rights Convention in 1848, and she lived long enough to see women cast votes in the election of 1920. When she died in 1924, her body lay in state in the recently completed Lend a Hand building. For hours, hundred of mourners—the babies she had delivered, the patients she had healed, the women she had led in public life, the medical colleagues whose respect she had won, and members of the Lend a Hand club from its nearly forty years of service—filed through the spacious parlors over-

Conclusion

looking the Mississippi River to say a last farewell. For many of these visitors, the Lend a Hand building was a triumph, the culmination of a dream: a place for working women in the heart of the city. Like many YWCAs, the new facility provided rooms for ninety residents, a movie theater, a swimming pool, a gymnasium, and a spacious dining room and kitchen for the Noon Rest cafeteria. It stood at the foot of Brady Street, on land reclaimed by Prohibition from the seedy, ramshackle neighborhood of Front Street. But the Lend a Hand building also represented a compromise. The home was built and financed only by turning away from an ideal of independence, political equality, and mutual assistance for working women and toward a view of working girls as dependents in need of charity. McCowen might not have minded. Women had won the right to vote, and if their opportunities still needed improving, they had a new political tool that might change everything.[28]

Dr. McCowen was buried in one of a pair of plots purchased by her beloved companion of almost thirty years, Clara Craine. Craine no doubt expected to occupy the plot next to McCowen, but when Craine retired from the Visiting Nurses, she moved to Portland, Oregon, to be near a niece. At her death in 1953, Clara Craine's family did not return her to Jennie's side. Perhaps they never knew a place was waiting for her. McCowen's simple stone is carved with a large Maltese cross, the emblem of the King's Daughters, but she lies alone among hundreds in Oakdale cemetery. Just over the hill and out of sight, in a family plot marked by a tall, elegant monument, brothel keeper Belle Walker rests near her partner, Charles, paired for eternity. Even in death, they defy expectations.

NOTES

Abbreviations

AAW	Association for the Advancement of Women
ADI	Annals of the Dubuque, Iowa, Home of the Good Shepherd, Sisters of the Good Shepherd Provincial Archives, St. Paul, Minnesota
AO	Annals of the Convent of the Good Shepherd, Omaha, Sisters of the Good Shepherd Provincial Archives, St. Paul, Minnesota
BED	Book of Entrances and Departures, Omaha Home of the Good Shepherd, Sisters of the Good Shepherd Provincial Archives, St. Paul, Minnesota
DCCP	Davenport City Council Papers, DPL
DCD	*Davenport City Directory*
DD	*Davenport Democrat*
DG	*Davenport Gazette*
DD-G	*Davenport Democrat-Gazette*
DD&L	*Davenport Democrat and Leader*
DDL	*Davenport Daily Leader*
DDT	*Davenport Daily Tribune*
DMT	*Davenport Morning Tribune*
DPL	Richardson-Sloane Special Collections Center, Davenport Public Library, Davenport, Iowa
DR	*Davenport Republican*
DT	*Davenport Times*
DWL	*Davenport Weekly Leader*
PMR	Police Matron's Record, Police Department Records, DPL
RP	Record of the Penitents of the Convent of the Good Shepherd, Dubuque, Iowa, Sisters of the Good Shepherd Provincial Archives, St. Paul, Minnesota
SCTR	Scott County Tax Records, DPL
SHSI	State Historical Society of Iowa, Iowa City
WCHSM	Warren County Historical Society Museum, Lebanon, Ohio

Introduction

1. *DD-G*, 25 October 1888, 3; *DDT*, 25 October 1888, 4; Downer, *History*, 2:499–500; *DD&L*, 8 March 1908, 11.
2. Dan Elbert Clark, "History," 539–41, 561–63; *DD*, 3 December 1884, 1; 29 May 1892, 1; 3 March 1884, 1; Acton, "Remarkable Immigrant," 99.
3. Richter, *Geschichte*, 6; Acton, "Remarkable Immigrant," 88, 99.
4. Edwards, *Angels*, 43; *Des Moines Leader*, 16 May 1888, 4. Foster is perhaps best known for rejecting the WCTU's endorsement of the Prohibition and Home Protection Party. As a committed Republican, Foster refused to follow Frances Willard into the new party. Foster broke with Willard and became the head of the new Non-Partisan (i.e., Republican) WCTU.
5. *Biographical History and Portrait Gallery*, 463; Downer, *History*, 2:500.
6. Gardner, "Battle," 353; Robinson, "Age."
7. *DD*, 24 October 1891, 1.
8. Blanchard, "Boundaries," 25–31; *DD*, 14 August 1884, 1.
9. *DDT*, 25 October 1888, 4.
10. Gilmore, *Gender and Jim Crow*, 82–89; Bederman, *Manliness*, 46–53, 75–76.
11. *DDT*, 25 October 1888, 4; *Des Moines Iowa State Register*, 22 April 1888, 9.
12. Ryan, *Civic Wars*, 230–31.
13. Buck-Morss, "Flâneur"; Rabinovitz, *For the Love*, 6–10; Walkowitz, *City*, 50–52, 127–29; 220–28. On planned feminine spaces in the city, see Peter C. Baldwin, *Domesticating*, 25–26.
14. Dall, *"Woman's Right,"* 6–7; Penny, *Employments*; Alcott, *Work*, 431.
15. Kessler-Harris, *In Pursuit*, 8.
16. Roediger, *Wages*; Nelson, *White Slaves*; Stanley, *From Bondage*, 86.
17. Thornton, *Women*; Yellin, *Women*; Tong, *Unsubmissive Women*; Bristow, *Prostitution*; Guy, *Sex*.
18. U.S. Department of the Interior, Census Office, *Statistics*, xxx.
19. Rabinovitz, *For the Love*; Peiss, *Cheap Amusements*; Meyerowitz, *Women Adrift*; Deutsch, *Women*; Stansell, *City*; Polacheck, *I Came*, 60.
20. Peiss, *Cheap Amusements*.
21. Twain, *Life*, 336–37.
22. U.S. Department of the Interior, Census Office, *Report on the Social Statistics*, 721; *DMT*, 10 July 1889, 3.
23. Espenshade, "Urban Development," 69–79; Roba, *River*, 75–76, 103; Mahoney, "Down."
24. Hildegard Binder Johnson, "Adjustment," 68–69; Espenshade, "Urban Development," 82–84; U.S. Department of the Interior, Census Office, *Report on the Social Statistics*, 723–24, 543; *Morrissey and Bunn's DCD*, 275–311.
25. *DD*, 3 August 1891, 4; Juhl, "J. P. Doremus."
26. Meyerowitz, *Women Adrift*, 9; U.S. Department of the Interior, Census Office, *Report on the Social Statistics*, 719; U.S. Department of the Interior, Census Office, *Statistics*, xxxiv; Iowa General Assembly, *Report of the Bureau of Labor*, 47–48. For examples of women coming to Davenport for abortions, see *DD*, 31 May 1880, 1; 10 December 1895, 1; for abandoning infants at baby farms, see *DD*, 6 May 1881, 1; 27 December 1883, 1. Tales of girls and women coming to work in brothels are a staple of news reports in this period; for two examples, see *DD*, 9 April 1880, 1; 27 May 1893, 1.
27. Noë, "Romantic"; Svendsen, Pfiffner, and Bowers, *Where*, 14-1–2; U.S. Department of the Interior, Census Office, *Report on the Social Statistics*, 722; Bateman, "Albert B. Cummins." On the leisure culture of Germans, see Ross, *Workers*. The lawsuit that overturned Iowa's 1882 Prohibition amendment was brought by Davenport brewers and saloonkeepers; in 1887, after another Prohibition law had been passed, local authorities responded to the governor's inquiry about its enforcement by pleading ignorance (Dan Elbert Clark, "History," esp. 527–37, 561–63).

28. *DD*, 21 April 1877, 1; 3 May 1877, 1; 26 June 1877, 1; 4 May 1877, 1; 1 May 1879, 1; 19 July 1879, 1; 28 July 1880, 1; 26 July 1880, 1; 16 August 1880, 1; 17 August 1881, 1; 7 September 1881, 1.

29. Ginzburg, *Clues, Myths*.

Chapter One

1. *DD*, 28 July 1880, 1.

2. Ibid., 27 August 1883, 1; SCTR (Davenport), 1882, 2:2, DPL.

3. *DD*, 15 March 1879, 1; 27 August 1883, 1.

4. Mitchell, "Plea," 3; Warren, *Thirty Years' Battle*, 78, 95–96; Bushnell, *Woman Condemned*, 10.

5. *DT*, 30 January 1889, 4.

6. "Work for Women," 219; AAW, *Report*, 20; McEnnis quoted in Nelson, *White Slaves*, 17; Mitchell, "Plea," 3; *The Revolution*, 7 January 1869, 1; Wegars, "'Inmates,'" 25; Best, *Controlling*, 22; "cozy room" quoted from an 1876 exposé of Dun and Company, in Gamber, *Female Economy*, 162; see also Gihon, "On the Protection," 58; Reitano, *Tariff Question*.

7. *DD*, 26 July 1880, 1; 28 July 1880, 1.

8. Ibid., 26 July 1880, 1; Bowers and Svendsen, *Davenport*, 1–5; *State of Iowa v. Claude Merrill*.

9. *DD*, 21 April 1877, 1; 23 April 1877, 1; 3 May 1877, 1.

10. This paragraph and those following are based on reports, including testimony from the coroner's inquest, appearing in *DD*, 21 April 1877, 1; 23 April 1877, 1; 3 May 1877, 1.

11. *American Heritage Dictionary of the English Language*, 3d ed. (New York: Houghton-Mifflin, 1992); *State v. Clark* (emphasis added); *State v. Rice*. Just as an individual woman need not charge money to be identified as a prostitute, the keeper of a house of ill-fame need not pursue the business for pecuniary gain (*State v. Lee*; Mackey, "Red Lights Out," 42–43).

12. *State v. Lee*, 82–83; *State v. Toombs*; Iowa, *Annotated Code*, chap. 9, sec. 4944; see also Novak, *People's Welfare*, 158, 167–69.

13. Davenport, *Charter*, 112; U.S. Manuscript Census, Murphysboro, Jackson County, Illinois, 1880, 141.

14. *DD*, 17 July 1879, 1; *State v. Evans* (quoted in *State v. Gill et al.*); *State v. Marvin*; *State of Iowa v. Charles Smith and Maggie Smith*.

15. *DD*, 19 July 1879, 1; 8 March 1877, 1; Schmidt and Jacobsen's *DCD*, 301; H. Pfabe's *DCD*, 1885–86, 321. Joel Best noted cigar-store prostitutes working in St. Paul in 1878 (*Controlling*, 22).

16. Mackey, "Red Lights Out," 30, 32–35; *Andre v. State*; *DD*, 31 July 1901, 6; Novak, *People's Welfare*, 167.

17. Iowa Manuscript Census, Scott County, 1885; Davenport, Iowa (map); H. Pfabe's *DCD*, 1885–86.

18. On mixed-use urban neighborhoods, see Kwolek-Folland, "Customers and Neighbors," 131–32, 134–35.

19. Of the neighborhood's 292 households, 64 (22 percent) were headed by women. Of 59 Davenport's woman-run businesses, 25 were in this neighborhood. I exclude from this calculation dressmakers, who often worked out of their homes and were widely dispersed in the residential sections of the city.

20. *DD*, 5 February 1882, 1.

21. *State of Iowa v. Lizzie Woods*; *DDT*, 8 November 1889, 4; 11 November 1889, 4; *Stone's DCD*, 1890–91, 183; *DD*, 3 March 1887, 1; *DG*, 18 November 1882, 2.

22. *DD-G*, 8 April 1888, 1; 25 July 1888, 1; 7 August 1888, 1; *DMT*, 26 July 1889, 3.

23. PMR, book 1. Between June and December 1889, fifty-four arrests took place between 7 A.M. and 10 P.M., while twenty-three arrests occurred during the remaining hours.

Chapter Two

1. Penny, *Employments*, v; Hartt, *How to Make Money*; Croly, *Thrown*; Alcott, *Work*, 1. For other examples, see Church, *Money Making*; Manson, *Work*; Rayne, *What Can a Woman Do*; Aguirre, *Women*; Willard, *Occupations*; Mossell, *Work*.

2. *DG*, 16 September 1883, 7.

3. Alcott, *Work*, 431.

4. Levine, *Labor's True Woman*, 111; Katzman, *Seven Days*, 284; Kessler-Harris, *Out to Work*, 84–85; Kennedy, *If All We Did*, 74; Philip S. Foner, *Women*, 160.

5. U.S. Department of the Interior, Census Office, *Report on the Social Statistics*, 724; U.S. Bureau of the Census, *Eleventh Annual Census*, 182–85; *DG*, 15 November 1882, 4; *Cigar Makers Official Journal*, 15 January 1882, 5; 15 December 1882, 15; 15 January 1883, 5.

6. *DD*, 14 November 1882, 1; 15 November 1882, 1; 21 November 1882, 1; 6 December 1882, 4; 29 December 1882, 1; *DG*, 15 November 1882, 4.

7. U.S. Bureau of Labor, *Third Annual Report*, 1408, 1449; *Cigar Makers Official Journal*, 15 September 1883, 7–8.

8. *DD*, 15 November 1885, 1; 23 November 1885, 1; 28 November 1885, 1; Kessler-Harris, "Where"; Mill quoted in Kessler-Harris, *Woman's Wage*, 10; see also 16–17, 86–87.

9. On class-bridging organizations, see Deutsch, "Learning." On gender-based moral authority, see Pascoe, *Relations*; Ginzberg, *Women*, 202–3. For other examples of women's class-bridging organizations, see Scott, *Natural Allies*, 104–10; Peiss, *Cheap Amusements*, 164–84; Murolo, *Common Ground*; Reitano, "Working Girls Unite"; Kessler-Harris, *Out to Work*; Sander, *Business*.

10. Meyerowitz, *Women Adrift*, 46–55 (quotation 53), 80–91; Scott, *Natural Allies*, 104–5.

11. Reitano, "Working Girls Unite," 116, 119; Peiss, *Cheap Amusements*, 170, 171; Murolo, *Common Ground*, 1; Kessler-Harris, *Out to Work*, 92. On middle-class clubwomen and self-improvement, see Martin, *Sound*.

12. Murolo, *Common Ground*, 17–18, 44–45; Peiss, *Cheap Amusements*, 170–71.

13. Deutsch, "Learning," 388–97; Sklar, *Florence Kelley*, 75.

14. Bristol, "Present Phase," 95; *Des Moines Iowa State Register* (morning), 11 October 1885, 1. In addition to Bristol's paper, those dealing with women's labor included Wolcott, "Work"; Avery, "Plea"; Smith, "Need"; French, "Comparative Effect"; Sweet, "Ministry"; McCowen, "Women Physicians."

15. Eric Foner, *Free Soil*, esp. 13–19; Kessler-Harris, "Law and a Living," 90–92.

16. Kessler-Harris, "Law and a Living," 90; Fraser and Gordon, "Genealogy," 315; see also Roediger, *Wages*, 65–87.

17. Carey quoted in Eric Foner, *Free Soil*, 19; Kessler-Harris, "Law and a Living," 90–91; Fraser and Gordon, "Genealogy," 314–19; Boydston, *Home and Work*, 44. Fink has argued that in the 1870s and 1880s, the link between economic independence and citizenship was displaced by "a more individualistic emphasis on the rights of property," including the worker's ownership of his labor and, most importantly, of his leisure ("From Autonomy," 126–28).

18. Fraser and Gordon, "Genealogy," 317–18; Kessler-Harris, "Law and a Living," 90; Glickman, *Living Wage*, 3–4, 44; Boydston, *Home and Work*, 146.

19. Fraser and Gordon, "Genealogy," 318–19; Pascoe, *Relations*, xiii–xxiii; Deacon, "Politicizing," 9; Kerber, *Women*, 283–88.

20. Fuller, *Laura Clay*, 3–6, 16; Boyer, "Laura Clay," 346–48; Anderson, *Pioneer Courts*, 97–98; Rayne, *What Can a Woman Do*, 100–102; Watson, *Physicians and Surgeons*, 729–30.

21. Buhle and Buhle, *Concise History*, 97.

22. Avery, "Plea," 34–35, 37; Smith, "Need," 47; Sweet, "Ministry," 72–73.

23. Sweet, "Ministry," 72, 73; Clay, "Right," xi; Antoinette Brown Blackwell, "Women's Industrial Position," 66.

24. DuBois, *Woman Suffrage*, 73–74.
25. Avery, "Plea," 38; Smith, "Need," 47.
26. Lapham, "Women," 12; AAW, *Report*, 20; Smith, "Need," 48–49; Bristol, "Present Phase," 104.
27. Fales, "Women's Industrial Position," 69.
28. Lapham, "Women," 9; Antoinette Brown Blackwell, "Women's Industrial Position," 66.
29. Wolcott, "Work," 12; Antoinette Brown Blackwell, "Women's Industrial Position"; Fales, "Women's Industrial Position"; Chapin, "Women's Industrial Position," 63–72. My reading of the AAW papers and themes differs from Karen Blair's. In *Clubwoman*, Blair argues that the AAW was essentially conservative, the bastion of what she calls "domestic feminists" who eschewed public activity that could not be made consistent with woman's role in the domestic sphere. In this interpretation, Blair is joined by Degler, *At Odds*, 326.
30. Bristol, "Present Phase," 96, 97, 100–101.
31. AAW, *Historical Account*, 5, 9; AAW, *Thirteenth Annual Report*, 5–11; AAW, *Annual Report*, 12–17. There were 452 members (and 2 honorary members) in 1885, for example.
32. Watson, *Physicians and Surgeons*, 729–30; AAW, *Eleventh Annual Report*, 32, 46–47; AAW, *Twelfth Annual Report*, 38–47.
33. AAW, *Twelfth Annual Report*, 38–47 (quotations 41).
34. McCowen, "Women in Iowa," 97–98; Clay, "Right," xii.
35. *DG*, 2 February 1883, 1; *Woman's Tribune*, 1 July 1884, 2.
36. AAW, *Eleventh Annual Report*, 32; McCowen, "Women in Iowa," 102.
37. *Trident*, 4 February 1905, 11; Iowa Bureau of Labor, *Second Biennial Report*, 190–95 (quotation 191).
38. Iowa Bureau of Labor, *Second Biennial Report*, 194–95.
39. Ibid., 193. On the typical woman wage earner of the period, see Peiss, *Cheap Amusements*, 4–5; Kessler-Harris, *Out to Work*, 123–28; Kessler-Harris, "Where," 92–93.
40. Howe, "Opening Address," 10–11.
41. *New York World*, 12 June 1869, 5, quoted in Blair, *Clubwoman*, 40; Howe, *Reminiscences*, 386; Freedman, "Separatism." On women's organizations as women's public sphere, see Ginzberg, *Women*, 174–213; Higginbotham, *Righteous Discontent*; Paula Baker, "Domestication," 631–32; Deacon, "Politicizing," 8–11; Sklar, *Florence Kelley*.

Chapter Three

1. *DD&L*, 26 December 1886, 1; *DG*, 25 December 1886, 4.
2. McCowen, "History of the Lend a Hand Club," DPL; Watson, *Physicians and Surgeons*, 729; U.S. Manuscript Census, Washington County, Iowa, 1870, 232; Peck, "Davenport," 167. On the transformation of Christmas in the nineteenth century, see Nissenbaum, *Battle*, esp. 49–89, 176–218; Restad, *Christmas*, esp. 42–74.
3. Quotation from *DG*, 26 December 1886, 1; *DG*, 1 December 1882, 4; Peck, "Davenport," 175–76; *Biographical History and Portrait Gallery*, 530–31. Of the fourteen elderly women who resided there on census day in 1885, six were born in Europe, and none was born in Iowa (Iowa Manuscript Census, Scott County, 1885, 282). Cook's insistence that the home be open to both white and African American women was unusual, but the women who administered the home lived up to her directive. At least one African American, Maria Buckner, lived at the home as a resident in the 1880s and 1890s (Record of Transient Admissions, 27 July 1885, Clarissa C. Cook Home for the Friendless, Davenport, Iowa).
4. Sara Mullin Baldwin, *Who's Who*, 119; McCowen, "History of the Lend a Hand Club," DPL; Iowa Manuscript Census, 1885, 282; Dodge, "Working Girls' Societies," 225; *DD-G* (evening), 15 January 1888, 1.

5. *DD-G*, 5 August 1887, 1; 16 September 1887, 1; *Stone's DCD, 1888*, 1.
6. *DD-G*, 16 September 1887, 3; 12 October 1887, 1.
7. *Stone's DCD, 1888*, 422–26; Ryon, "Craftsmen's Union Halls," 217–18, 221.
8. Purcell, *Them*, 153–55; Duis, *Saloon*, 55–56, 187; Chudacoff, *Age*, 109–10.
9. Chudacoff, *Age*, 35, 108.
10. U.S. Department of the Interior, Census Office, *Statistics*, xxx; Lofland, *World*.
11. The phrase "cartography of gender" is from Ryan, *Women*, 68–76; see also Stansell, *City*, 86–97; Srebnick, *Mysterious Death*, 8–9; Halttunen, *Confidence Men*, 114–16; Rabinovitz, *For the Love*, 5.
12. Ryan, *Women*, 77–78; Benson, *Counter Cultures*, 75–85; Abelson, *When Ladies Go*, 20–21, 54–55; Peter C. Baldwin, *Domesticating*, 26.
13. Wells, *Manners*, 39, 330, 129; Szuberla, "Ladies," 77.
14. Murolo, *Common Ground*, 16–18, 38.
15. U.S. Manuscript Census, Savoy, Berkshire County, Massachusetts, 1850, 99; U.S. Manuscript Census, Adams, Berkshire County, Massachusetts, 1860, 313; *Trident*, 17 March 1906.
16. Massachusetts, Secretary of the Commonwealth, Division of Vital Statistics, Massachusetts Vital Records: Registration of Marriages, New England Historical Genealogical Society, Boston, 69:75, 99:22, 171:27, 180:36; Abbie O. Craton Pension File, National Archives and Records Administration, Washington, D.C.
17. Livermore, *What Shall We Do*, 138–39.
18. Craton Pension File; U.S. Manuscript Census, Albany, Whiteside County, Illinois, 1870, 2; *DD&L*, 7 December 1905, 11. According to the census taker, Lettie's occupation was "housework." Since adult women in neighboring households were designated simply as "at home," the descriptor for Lettie almost certainly refers to domestic service.
19. Iowa General Assembly, *Report of the Joint Committee Appointed to Visit the Hospital for the Insane*, 16; Iowa General Assembly, *Tenth Biennial Report*, 143; U.S. Manuscript Census, Lyndon, Whiteside County, Illinois, 1880, 156B.
20. "Jennie McCowen," 531; Downer, *History*, 2:1026.
21. *Encyclopedia*, 5:533; Index of Marriage Records, Warren County Genealogical Society, Lebanon, Ohio; John McCowen Probate File, Warren County Probate Court Archives, Lebanon, Ohio; James Boggs, B.P., to John McCowen, 29 July 1837, and Maria McCowen to John McCowen, 15 April [1846?], WCHSM; Public Domain Land Tract Record Sales, Havana Public Library, Havana, Illinois; U.S. Manuscript Census, Havana Township, Mason County, Illinois, 1850, 369; Illinois Manuscript Census, Havana Township, Mason County, 1855, 47; Haines, *Genealogy*, 219b–d; *Combination Atlas Map*, 21. In 1846, the opening of the Mississippi and Illinois Canal promised a boom in land values around Mason County.
22. *Official Roster*, 369; Downer, *History*; Haines, *Genealogy*. Jennie and Israel left at the outbreak of the war; Mary and Susan left as soon as they were of age, first to live with Jennie and then to strike out on their own. Sarah married Edward Janney and emigrated to the Kansas frontier.
23. National Normal University Card File, WCHSM; U.S. Manuscript Census, Massie Township, Warren County, Ohio, 1860, 346; James Boggs, B.P., to John McCowen, 29 July 1837, WCHSM; "Medicine," Warren County Genealogical Society, Lebanon, Ohio; McCowen Probate File; *Western Star*, 4 January 1866; 11 January 1866; 8 November 1866. According to the 1860 census, John McCowen owned real estate valued at $11,000 and a personal estate of $9,000.
24. U.S. Manuscript Census, Oakfield Township, Audubon County, Iowa, 1860, 704; *Encyclopedia*, 5:471.
25. "Jennie McCowen," 531; Downer, *History*, 2:1026; *W. A. Lloyd's Southern Steamboat and Railroad Guide*, January 1861, 4; *Official Roster*, 369. Polly Welts Kaufman suggests that many schoolteachers who migrated to the West were, like McCowen, elder daughters in disrupted

families and that many were adventuresome, innovative spirits. By McCowen's era, they were also likely to use teaching as a route to other professions (*Women Teachers*, xx–xxii, 15, 38).

26. McCowen remembered the year as 1869—the same year Mitchell ran and won—but Audubon County records confirm that McCowen was a candidate in 1871 (*Biographical History of Shelby and Audubon*, 653; H. P. Andrews, *History of Audubon*, 239; Watson, *Physicians and Surgeons*, 729; Gallaher, *Legal and Political Status*, 228–29; Noun, *Strong-Minded Women*, 140–41). The year before McCowen ran for office, the U.S. Census counted only 302 eligible voters in Audubon County out of a population of just over 1,200 (U.S. Department of the Interior, Census Office, *Ninth Census*, 629).

27. Iowa, *Fourteenth Biennial Report*, 101–3; AAW, *Twelfth Annual Report*, 40.

28. *History of Scott County*, 879. The 1870 census credits Jennie McCowen with a personal estate of $125 (U.S. Manuscript Census, Oakfield Township, Audubon County, Iowa, 1870, 583). While it is unlikely that Jennie McCowen studied medicine in her father's library, she may have had access to another physician's books. Samuel Ballard, who may have been her aunt's brother-in-law, was both a wealthy land speculator and a physician in Audubon County (U.S. Manuscript Census, Oakfield Township, Audubon County, Iowa, 1860, 704; 1870, 587). Mary and Susan McCowen, like Jennie, earned teaching diplomas from the normal school in Lebanon. Mary entered the pedagogy program at the State University of Iowa in 1869, then moved to Nebraska, where she worked in deaf education. In 1883 she opened a school for the deaf in Chicago, and John Dewey became one of its trustees. In 1896, Mary McCowen was recruited to superintend deaf education in the Chicago public schools, and she taught deaf education at the Chicago Normal School. Susan also worked for a time in Iowa and then emigrated to California, where her career was cut short by an early death from "nervous exhaustion" (State University, *Bulletin*; *Wolfe's Omaha City Directory*, 201; *History of the State*, 733; McCowen Oral School, *Circular*; Currey, *Chicago*, 298–99. DD-G, 5 August 1887, 1; *DD*, 19 June 1890, 1).

29. Willard and Livermore, *Woman*, 181–82; Cleaves, *Autobiography*, 27–29. Martha Ranney, Mark Ranney's wife, was also a member of the AAW (AAW, *Twelfth Annual Report*, 16).

30. Gilmore, "Gender and Jim Crow," 70; Sklar, *Florence Kelley*, 62. Historians who have proposed that women's colleges nurtured feminists include Horowitz, *Alma Mater*; Smith-Rosenberg, *Disorderly Conduct*, 245–54; Freedman, "Separatism," 517–18.

31. Morantz-Sanchez, *Sympathy*, 70–71; Mary H. Baker, "Jennie C. McCowen," 108.

32. Willard and Livermore, *Woman*, 181–72; Cleaves, "Mental Peculiarities"; *DD*, 10 April 1877, 3; 28 July 1880, 1; Cleaves, "Memorial." In the East, women struggled well into the 1800s simply to be admitted to medical societies; see Moldow, *Women Doctors*, 106–10; Morantz-Sanchez, *Sympathy*, 179; Walsh, *Doctors Wanted*, 153–62; Martin Kaufman, "Admission of Women."

33. *DG*, 1 December 1882, 4; record book A, 82, Clarissa C. Cook Home for the Friendless, Davenport, Iowa; Peck, "Davenport," 175–76.

34. U.S. Manuscript Census, Concord, Merrimack County, New Hampshire, 1880, 225; *Manchester Directory*, 35; *DG*, 1 December 1882, 4; Hurd, *History*, 118; Woman's Medical School, *Woman's Medical School*, 148; *Manchester Union Leader*, 2 January 1890, 5; *DD*, 13 October 1885, 1; DD-G, 26 October 1887, 3. In the nineteenth century, an engineer was someone who operated a steam engine. A locomotive engine moved trains, while a stationary engine powered equipment, as in a factory or workshop.

35. On gendered barriers to travel in the mid–nineteenth century, see Cohen, "Women."

36. U.S. Manuscript Census, Louisa County, Iowa, 1860, 860; U.S. Manuscript Census, Washington County, Iowa, 1870, 232; *DD&L*, 2 September 1921, 11; SCTR, 1883, 117, DPL; U.S. Manuscript Census, Scott County, Iowa, 1900, E.D. 136, sheet 134; 1920, E.D. 122, sheet 14.

37. Other young adults in the blacksmith's household where Santry lived included two more seamstresses and a young man and a young woman who worked as printers (Iowa Manuscript

Census, Scott County, 1885, 226, 282; U.S. Manuscript Census, Sangamon County, Illinois, 1900, E.D. 99, sheet 24).

38. Adams, *Edward Everett Hale*, 1–5, 59–62.

39. Hale, *Ten Times One*, 3, 16.

40. Ibid., 58–60, 53, 93, 100.

41. Ibid., 105, 33.

42. "Wadsworth Club"; *DD&L*, 21 June 1909, 21.

43. Gugle, *History*, 22, 268–69; *DD-G*, 26 October 1887, 3. In addition to raising funds for the Lend a Hand, the King's Daughters in its first year collected sickroom equipment for use by poor families and collaborated with the Association of Collegiate Alumnae to study "the effects of school life upon the health of young girls," a project intended to debunk Harvard medical professor E. H. Clarke's claim that the rigorous college curriculum pursued by young men would overtax young women's brains and bodies, leaving them infertile (*DD*, 15 June 1892, 1; Clarke, *Sex*).

44. *DD-G*, 15 January 1888, 1; *DD*, 12 October 1887, 3; *DD-G*, 15 January 1888, 1. Martha A. Cooke, A.M., resigned as "lady principal" of Monmouth College in December 1893 (Monmouth College, *Thirty-eighth Annual Catalogue*, 8).

45. Iowa Bureau of Labor, *Fifth Biennial Report*, 245, 306–7. If the Lend a Hand did indeed attract more clerical workers and teachers, it resembled some of the class-bridging organizations in eastern cities; see Deutsch, "Learning," 381, n. 10; Murolo, *Common Ground*; Reitano, "Working Girls Unite."

46. Lend a Hand Club, *Fifteenth Annual Report*, 17; on the need to rest at lunchtime, see also *Trident*, 19 March 1904, 7; on the difficulty women faced finding respectable lunches downtown, see Duis, *Saloon*, 186. An episode related in the *Times* reported that in cold weather, men waited for the streetcar in a saloon, while women were forced to stand in the cold and then to board a car with no fire in the stove. The women retaliated by bringing firewood and lighting the stove themselves (*DT*, 12 November 1904, 4).

47. *DD-G*, 26 October 1887, 1; "Auswannerer," 27. William Bauer had several daughters who worked as clerks. Whether the one who recited the poem was Antonia, Cecilia, or Hannah cannot be determined.

48. *DD-G*, 15 November 1888, 1; *DD*, 19 October 1886, 1.

49. Lend a Hand Club, *Dime Savings Agency*; Lend a Hand Club, *Protective Circular*; Lend a Hand Club, *C[hautauqua] L[iterary] S[ociety] C[ircle] Program*; *DD-G*, 15 February 1888, 1; Fink, *Workingman's Democracy*, 10–13 (quotation 12).

50. *DD-G* (evening edition), 17 April 1888, 3.

51. Antoinette Brown Blackwell, "Women's Industrial Position," 66.

52. *DMT*, 15 September 1889, 5. The dressmaking establishment operated for only a couple of years and may have closed when Santry married and moved to Springfield, Illinois; see Lend a Hand Club, *Tenth Annual Report*, 20. On dressmaking, see Gamber, *Female Economy*.

53. Miller, "Artistic," 3.

54. *DD-G*, 15 September 1889, sec. 2, p. 1; *DMT*, 15 September 1889, 5; *DD&L*, 10 March 1912, 13.

55. Sander, *Business*, 2–3, 109.

56. *DMT*, 4 April 1889, 3.

57. Ibid., 17 March 1889, 5; 21 March 1889, 3; 4 April 1889, 3; 3 May 1889, 3; Reverby, *Ordered*, 3, 15–16; Melosh, *"Physician's Hand,"* 30; *DD*, 4 October 1895, 1.

58. *DD*, 1 September 1893, 1; 15 March 1894, 1.

59. Ibid., 15 March 1894, 1; 15 January 1895, 1; 8 October 1896, 1; 17 February 1897, 1; Lend a Hand Club, *Tenth Annual Report*, 20; Hayden, *Grand Domestic Revolution*, 215–27; Stone's *DCD*, 1894–95.

60. *DMT*, 19 July 1891, 4; *DD*, 14 January 1893, 1.

61. Lend a Hand Club, *Tenth Annual Report*, 25; *DD*, 14 January 1893, 1; U.S. Manuscript Census, Denver County, Colorado, vol. 4, E.D. 104, sheet 1.

62. *DD*, 12 September 1901, 7; 20 February 1902, 4.

63. Stone's *DCD*, *1892*, 117; Stone's *DCD*, *1894*, 119; Stone's *DCD*, *1898*, 131; *DD&L*, 19 September 1935, 2; *Portland Oregonian*, 10 May 1953, 37.

64. *DDT*, 3 March 1911, 5; *DD&L*, 3 March 1911, 12; Stone's *DCD*, *1888–89*, 340; Stone's *DCD*, *1896–97*, 463; Employee Card File, University of Iowa Library Archives, Iowa City; Stone's *DCD*, *1890–91*, 180, 140; Stone's *DCD*, *1892–93*, 185; Stone, *Ancestry*, 49.

65. *DG* (evening), 15 January 1888, 1.

66. "Jennie McCowen," 533.

67. Gamber, *Female Economy*, 36–37; Deutsch, *Women*, 5. The R. G. Dun and Company records, which provide useful credit information for many cities, extend no later than the 1870s for Davenport.

68. McCowen, "Women in Iowa," 98.

Chapter Four

1. On New York City, see Stansell, *City*; Gilfoyle, *City*; Cohen, *Murder*; Marilynn Wood Hill, *Their Sisters' Keepers*. On the West, see Nichols, *Prostitution*; Goldman, *Gold Diggers*; Butler, *Daughters*; Petrik, "Capitalists"; Diffendahl, "Prostitution"; Chalfant, "Down"; Sylvester, "Avenues."

2. Sanger, *History*, 488.

3. Historians who have turned to Sanger include Rosen, *Lost Sisterhood*, 139–44, 162–66; Marilynn Wood Hill, *Their Sisters' Keepers*, 69–81; Stansell, *City*, 176–77; Gilfoyle, *City*, 69–79.

4. Scott County Iowa Genealogical Society, *Early Marriages*, n.p.; U.S. Manuscript Census, Scott County, Iowa, 1870, 499.

5. Scott County Iowa Genealogical Society, *Marriage Records*, 108; U.S. Manuscript Census, Scott County, Iowa, 1870, 494; Historical U.S. Census Browser (http://fisher.lib.virginia.edu/census).

6. *In the Matter of the Estate of Josephine Hovey*; Owen's *DCD*; *William H. Keller v. Naomia [sic] J. Keller*.

7. U.S. Manuscript Census, Scott County, Iowa, 1880, E.D. 277, sheet 19; *Josephine Mitchell v. Frank Mitchell*.

8. Holland's *Directory*, 157; *DD*, 27 December 1883, 1; *In the Matter of the Estate of Josephine Hovey*. Between September 1883 and November 1887, Josie Mitchell appeared sixteen times in the reports of the Overseer of the Poor, three times for receiving relief and the rest for care of the sick or providing board and lodging; see, for example, *DD*, 11 September 1883, 3; 18 December 1883, 3; 6 November 1886, 2; 4 November 1887, 2.

9. *DD*, 27 December 1883, 1; *DT*, 11 February 1889, 4; Iowa Manuscript Census, Scott County, 1885, 434; *DD*, 22 September 1885, 1; 19 July 1877, 1; 27 March 1892, sec. 2, p. 1; PMR, book 1, 27 June 1889.

10. *State v. Toombs*, 79 Iowa 743.

11. Scott County Clerk of Court, *Marriage Record*, Charles Robison to Josephine Sheridan, 7 April 1888; William Ray Hawkins to Josephine Wiley, 29 December 1892; *Josephine Robinson v. Charles Robinson [sic]*; *DDT*, 18 November 1892, 4; *DD*, 30 August 1896, 1. Josie used the surname Sheridan when she married Robison, but I have located no record of a marriage, death, or divorce relating to a spouse with that name. "Sheridan" is, however, the name of the township where Josie lived before moving to Davenport. She told the clerk that she was marrying for the second time when she married Robison and made the same claim when she married Hawkins. Using false

surnames (she claimed Wiley as her name when she married Hawkins) may have been a way to hide the fact that these were in fact her third and fourth marriages and that she was a decade older than she claimed.

12. Blackhawk Genealogical Society, *Index*, 108; U.S. Manuscript Census, Scott County, Iowa, 1880, 536A; *Adelbert W. DeMaranville v. Josephine Hawkins*; *DD*, 17 December 1893, 1; 26 December 1893, 1.

13. *DT*, 16 March 1892, 3.

14. PMR, book 1, 16 June 1891, 8 February 1892, 1 May 1892, 14 September 1892, 2 October 1893, 28 November 1893, 19 May 1894; *DD*, 16 March 1892, 1.

15. *DD&L*, 16 May 1917, 15; Iowa Manuscript Census, Scott County, 1915, card D945; *Owen's DCD*, 296; *Morrissey and Bunn's DCD*, 113. In 1915, Kate Huber reported that she had been in Iowa for thirty-six years, which corresponds with Ernst's first appearance in the Davenport directory in 1878. However, the 1880 census shows ten-year-old son Carl as an Iowa native, which would put their arrival in Iowa somewhat earlier.

16. *State of Iowa v. Catherine Uber*.

17. Ibid.

18. U.S. Manuscript Census, Scott County, Iowa, 1880, E.D. 133, sheet 22; *DD*, 27 December 1883, 1; *Holland's Directory*, 211; *H. Pfabe's DCD, 1884–85*, 294; Iowa Manuscript Census, Scott County, 1885, 436; *Stone's DCD, 1890*, 414.

19. *State of Iowa v. Mary Ortell*; PMR, book 1, 27 June 1892.

20. *Rock Island Union*, quoted in *DD*, 23 April 1878, 1; *DD*, 9 June 1877, 1.

21. Muscatine County, *Marriage Register*, 21 July 1869, no. 92; U.S. Manuscript Census, Muscatine County, Iowa, 1870, 292; U.S. Manuscript Census, Washington County, Iowa, 1870, 113.

22. *Emma J. Hagan v. Andrew J. Hagan*; *DD*, 22 March 1877, 1; 24 May 1877, 1; 26 May 1877, 1; 9 June 1877, 1; 23 April 1878, 1.

23. Emma signed her divorce papers with an "X" (*Hagan v. Hagan*). In late August 1877, a woman named Jennie Snyder rented a horse and light carriage from a livery stable for an hour, then, instead of returning them, drove to Andalusia, Illinois, where she picked up Emma Hagan and proceeded to drive to Council Bluffs, a journey that took two weeks. Snyder was indicted as a horse thief, but Emma persuaded officials that she had not known about the plan and had repeatedly urged Snyder to return the horse and carriage. Unlike Snyder, Emma Hagan was not "notorious." Her protestations were accepted and she was released without facing charges (*DD*, 27 August 1877, 1; 15 September 1877, 1; 17 September 1877, 1; 18 September 1877, 1; 19 September 1877, 1).

24. *Minnie Murdoch v. Ezra Murdoch*; *DD*, 11 January 1879, 1; 14 January 1879, 1; *Sioux City Daily Journal*, 8 July 1883, 5.

25. *Sioux City Daily Journal*, 8 July 1883, 5; 12 July 1883, 3; *Sioux City Daily Times*, 7 July 1883, 1; 8 July 1883, 5; 10 July 1883, 3; 12 July 1883, 4.

26. *Sioux City Daily Times*, 7 July 1883, 1; 9 July 1883, 4; *Sioux City Daily Journal*, 8 July 1883, 5; *DD*, 9 July 1883, 1.

27. *Sioux City Daily Times*, 9 July 1883, 4; *Sioux City Daily Journal*, 12 July 1883, 3; 12 July 1883, 3; *DD*, 12 July 1883, 1; 13 July 1883, 1.

28. *Murdoch v. Murdoch*.

29. *Stone's DCD, 1888–89*, 156; PMR, book 1, 30 October 1893.

30. U.S. Manuscript Census, Scott County, Iowa, 1870, 346; *E. Coy's Twin Cities Directory*, 33.

31. U.S. Manuscript Census, Scott County, Iowa, 1880, E.D. 275, sheet 28; E.D. 277, sheet 20; *DD*, 17 October 1882, 1; *Holland's Directory*, 215; Scott County Clerk of Court, *Birth Returns*, Edward Webb, no. 10177; *Stone's DCD, 1888–89*, 354; *Stone's DCD, 1890–91*, 425; Iowa Manuscript Census, Scott County, 1915, card H285.

32. *Stone's DCD, 1888–89*, 354; *Stone's DCD, 1890–91*, 59, 425; *Stone's DCD, 1892–93*, 442.

33. *Stone's DCD, 1888–89*, 57; *Fannie Auerochs v. Chicago, Rock Island, and Pacific Railroad Co.*; Stromquist, *Generation*, 109; *Stone's DCD, 1902–3*, 117.

34. *Mary A. Auerochs v. Theodore Auerochs*; *Stone's DCD, 1902–3*, 117.

35. PMR, book 1, 27 May 1891, 21 October 1891, 15 November 1891, 16 April 1892, 29 April 1892, 10 September 1892, 5 October 1892.

36. *DD*, 17 July 1879, 1; 16 August 1880, 1; *State of Iowa v. Mattie Burke*.

37. Iowa Manuscript Census, Scott County, 1885, 413; U.S. Manuscript Census, Scott County, Iowa, 1880, 591B; 1900, 35A.

38. U.S. Manuscript Census, Rock Island County, Illinois, 1880, 426; U.S. Manuscript Census, Scott County, Iowa, 1900, 263A; PMR, books 1–3. Eliza's first reported arrest was in June 1889.

39. *Schmidt and Jacobsen's DCD*, 195; *H. Pfabe's DCD, 1885–86*, 237; *DD&L*, 31 December 1913, 13; SCTR (Davenport), 1889, 2:3; 1890, 2:51; 1891, 2:61.

40. *Stone's DCD, 1888–89*, 85; SCTR (Davenport), 1891, 1:36; 1892, 1:27.

41. *DD&L*, 2 October 1949, 12.

42. The 1901 Irish Census for County Sligo is abstracted at http://www.rootsweb.com/~irlsli/kilmacshalgancensus1901part2.htm; U.S. Manuscript Census, Scott County, Iowa, 1900, E.D. 134, sheet 17; Iowa Manuscript Census, Scott County, 1915, card B8; *DD-G*, 16 January 1888, 1.

43. PMR, 25 January 1890, 2 May 1890, 26 June 1890, 15 July 1890, 25 January 1891, 15 March 1891, 14 June 1891, 18 October 1891, 14 November 1891; SCTR (Davenport), 1890, 2:19; 1891, 2:22; 1893, 2:10; 1894, 1:15, 2:11, DPL.

44. *DT*, 27 January 1890, 4; *Davenport Weekly Times*, 15 February 1890, 4; DCCP, June–July 1894; *DD*, 12 May 1891, 1; 17 May 1891, 1.

45. *DD*, 11 May 1892, 1; *DD&L*, 9 February 1927, 15; *Marie Beauchaine v. Frank Kessler et al.*; *DD*, 27 January 1893, 1; 7 February 1893, 1; 17 February 1893, 1; 19 February 1893, 1; 23 February 1893, 1; 2 March 1893, 1; 17 March 1893, 1.

46. *DD*, 23 May 1902, 6; Davenport tax records for the 1890s reveal no property owned by Lee Beauchaine (SCTR).

47. Sanger, *History*, 489.

Chapter Five

1. *DD-G* (morning), 31 January 1889, 4; 1 February 1889, 4; *DT*, 30 January 1889, 4.

2. *DD-G* (morning), 6 February 1889, 4; 7 February 1889, 4; *DMT*, 7 February 1889, 3.

3. Devoll, "Results"; Kennard, "Progress"; Hobbs, "Police Matrons."

4. *DMT*, 12 February 1889, 3; McCowen, "Shinbone Alley," 9; *Union Signal*, 13 December 1883, 11.

5. *DMT*, 10 February 1889, 3; *DD-G* (morning), 10 February 1889, 1; 12 February 1889, 3; Sklar, *Florence Kelley*, 211. Nelson's articles began appearing in the *Chicago Times* on 30 July 1888; they were reprinted by the Knights of Labor in *White Slaves*.

6. Barney, "Police Matrons."

7. Ibid., 474; DCCP, February 1889.

8. *DD-G* (morning), 7 February 1889, 4; 21 June 1889, 4; *DMT*, 21 June 1889, 3; 27 November 1889, 3.

9. Barney, "Police Matrons," 474; Wilson, *Legal Status*, 80; *New York Times*, 23 March 1890, 20. Similar concerns motivated the women of Hull House a decade later when they chose to pay the first juvenile court officers from private funds rather than have the officers become yet another cog in Chicago's political machine (Addams, *Twenty Years*, 227).

10. Fraser called this alternative public sphere a "subaltern counterpublic" ("Rethinking"; see also Paula Baker, "Domestication," 620–47). Ginzberg discusses the partial integration of women

into certain kinds of governmental activity in the postwar years in *Women*, 174–213; see also Edwards, *Angels*, 8; Deutsch, "Learning," 391–92.

11. *DMT*, 17 January 1889, 3; Goldstein, "Midwestern Naturalists," 159, 170, 184–85.

12. Report of the Superintendent, School Board Minutes, 8 July 1878, Davenport Public Schools, Davenport, Iowa; "Miss P. W. Sudlow"; Iowa State Teachers' Association, *Proceedings*, 2–10; Barnhart, "Phoebe W. Sudlow"; Phebe Sudlow [niece] to Myrtle Dunlap, 21 February 1936, Phebe Sudlow Collection, SHSI.

13. *DD*, 5 February 1888, 1; *In the Matter of the Estate of Martha Glaspell*.

14. *DD-G*, 10 February 1889, 1; *DMT*, 10 February 1889, 3; *DT*, 11 February 1889, 4; *DD&L*, 6 June 1886, 1; *Biographical History and Portrait Gallery*, 122–27.

15. *DMT*, 10 February 1889, 3; *DD-G* (morning), 10 February 1889, 1; 14 February 1889, 4; 27 June 1889, 4.

16. Dan Elbert Clark, "History," 539–41.

17. *DD-G* (morning), 31 January 1889, 4.

18. Stone's *DCD, 1888*, 207; *DD-G* (morning), 31 January 1889, 4.

19. Stone's *DCD, 1888*, 207; *Davenport, Iowa* (map); *Insurance Maps*; Stone's *DCD, 1890–91*, 152.

20. *DD-G* (morning), 31 January 1889, 4. My estimate of Kreps's wages is extrapolated from Katzman's discussion of servants' pay in *Seven Days*, 304–9.

21. *DD-G* (morning), 31 January 1889, 4; 7 February 1889, 4. Gordon has suggested that impoverished parents, wittingly or not, sometimes encouraged their daughters' entry into the sexual marketplace (*Heroes*, 243); Odem argues that mothers were more likely to contact juvenile authorities over the loss of a daughter's labor or wages than over her sexual misconduct ("Single Mothers").

22. *DMT*, 31 January 1889, 3; *DT*, 30 January 1889, 4.

23. *DD-G* (morning), 7 February 1889, 4; *DD-G* (evening), 4 February 1889, 1; 11 February 1889, 1; *Der Demokrat*, 7 February 1889, 6.

24. *DD-G* (morning), 1 February 1889, 4; Peiss, "'Charity Girls.'"

25. *DD-G* (morning), 31 January 1889, 4; 1 February 1889, 4; 6 February 1889, 4; *DMT*, 6 February 1889, 3.

26. *DT*, 30 January 1889, 4.

27. *DD-G* (morning), 6 February 1889, 4; 1 February 1889, 4; 10 February 1889, 1.

28. *DT*, 5 February 1889, 4; 1 February 1889, 4; 4 February 1889, 4; 5 February 1889, 4; 11 February 1889, 4.

29. Ibid., 27 January 1890, 4; 2 December 1889, 4.

30. *DD-G* (morning), 1 February 1889, 4; *DT*, 5 February 1889, 4; 6 February 1889, 4.

31. *DD-G* (morning), 1 February 1889, 4; *DT*, 6 February 1889, 4.

32. Ryan, *Women*, 58–94; Ryan, *Cradle*; Stansell, *City*, 76–101; Best, *Controlling*; Cohen, *Murder*; Boydston, *Home and Work*.

33. *DMT*, 31 January 1889, 3; *DD-G* (morning), 31 January 1889, 4.

34. Petition, DCCP, 1889.

35. *DD-G* (morning), 9 February 1889, 4; *DMT*, 9 February 1889, 4.

36. *DMT*, 9 February 1889, 4; *DD-G* (morning), 9 February 1889, 4.

37. Petition, DCCP, 1889; "Police Matrons," 675.

38. "Police Matron's Bill"; *DD* (evening), 20 August 1890, 2.

39. Kennard, "Progress," 182; "Police Matron's Bill," 165; *Union Signal*, 12 November 1885, 6; *New York Times*, 23 March 1890, 20.

40. *New York Times*, 23 March 1890, 20; Dawes, "Experiment," 130.

41. "Police Matrons," 675; Barney, "Police Matrons," 475.

42. *DD-G* (morning), 20 February 1889, 3; Hall, "Reformation," 188–89.

43. *DG*, 5 December 1886, 4; *DMT*, 23 July 1889, 3.

44. On gender difference and criminal prosecution, see Freedman, *Their Sisters' Keepers*, 10–14; Schlossman, *Love*, 197, 151–53; Brenzel, *Daughters*, 123–25; Pisciotta, "Race." According to the records kept by Davenport's police matron, in the period 1889–1912, at least 24 percent of girls seventeen and under who came into custody were arrested for sex offenses. No boys were (*DMT*, 31 January 1889, 3; Rothman, *Discovery*, 79–85).

45. Shumsky, "Tacit Acceptance"; Gilfoyle, *City*, chaps. 6, 12; Rosen, *Lost Sisterhood*, 5–7; Pivar, *Purity Crusade*, 24–30, 131–40; Freedman, *Their Sisters' Keepers*, 14–21; Butler, *Gendered Justice*, 183–84, 211.

46. Russett, *Sexual Science*, 67–68; Dugdale, *Jukes*, 65.

47. Antoinette Brown Blackwell, *Sexes*, 117–18; Clarke, *Sex*, 93–94.

48. Dugdale, *Jukes*, esp. 70 and the introduction by Franklin Giddings.

49. Ibid., 15, 18, chart III. In another study, McCulloch, "Tribe," 155–56, the seeds of degeneration come from "the wandering blood" of a "half-breed mother" and "the poison and passion that probably came with her."

50. Lowell, "One Means," 195; Wardner, "Girls," 188; Lynde, "Treatment"; Boles, *Prisoners*, 210–11.

51. M. L. Holbrook, quoted in Smith-Rosenberg and Rosenberg, "Female Animal," 56; for the scientific investment in sexual difference, see Russett, *Sexual Science*, esp. chap. 5.

52. Lowell, "One Means," 197; *DD-G* (evening), 11 February 1889, 1; Wright, "Presidential Address," 5; *DD*, 21 February 1886, 1; Keely, "Reform Work," 180; Kerber, *Women*, 11.

53. *DD-G*, 20 January 1887, 4.

54. McCowen, "Heredity," 49.

55. *DMT*, 12 February 1889, 3.

56. R. W. Hill, "Children," 229–39; *DD-G* (morning) 28 February 1889, 4; McCowen, "Shinbone Alley."

57. *Union Signal*, 19 November 1885, 6.

58. *DD-G* (morning), 7 February 1889, 4; *State of Iowa v. John McPartland and Mrs. John McPartland*.

Chapter Six

1. Summary based on typescript of testimony given by Mrs. Lucy Matlock, *State of Iowa v. Charles Lyon*, case file no. 1201.

2. *State of Iowa v. Charles Lyon*, case file no. 1201; *DT*, 16 September 1891, 4; *State of Iowa v. Henry Carpenter*; *State of Iowa v. George Haikes*.

3. Rosenberg, "Sexuality," 140–41; Rotundo, *American Manhood*, 122–24; Chudacoff, *Age*, 38, 68; Gilfoyle, *City*, 92–116; see also Cohen, *Murder*; Gorn, *Manly Art*, 192–94.

4. Iowa General Assembly, *Acts and Resolutions . . . Twentieth General Assembly*, 145–46. One of the best discussions of the social purity movement appears in Odem, *Delinquent Daughters*, 8–37; see also Bordin, *Woman*; Ginzberg, *Women*; Pivar, *Purity Crusade*.

5. *Maiden Tribute*, 2; *Union Signal*, 10 September 1885, 12; 25 February 1886, 13; 28 January 1886, 12.

6. *Maiden Tribute*, 5; Mark, "Age," 4; Mark, "Morality," 4–5; Iowa General Assembly, *Acts and Resolutions . . . Twenty-first General Assembly*, 136.

7. "Modern Moloch," 3; Stansell, *City*, 180–85; Gordon, *Heroes*, 242–45; Chauncey, *Gay New York*, 85, 81; *State of Iowa v. Henry Albrecht*. Sexual intercourse with a virgin was a folk remedy for syphilis, and some historians have suggested this as an explanation for why men sought child partners. However, child prostitutes are another matter. Since they had multiple partners, and men knew this fact, it seems unlikely that men believed such girls were virgins; see Gilfoyle, *City*, 69.

8. Chauncey, *Gay New York*, 83; Shannon, *Self-Knowledge*, 205, 313–15; Gerrish, *Duties*, 12; for

a summary of the argument that prostitution protects women from rape, see Washburn, *Underworld*, 19–20.

9. Long, *Save the Girls*, 134–35.

10. *DT*, 15 September 1891, 4; 16 September 1891, 4; *DD*, 18 September 1891, 1; *DMT*, 30 September 1891, 4.

11. A number of studies of rape in the United States from the late eighteenth through the nineteenth century have observed that young girls made up a significant proportion of the victims, suggesting that men's presumption of access to girls had a long history; see Arnold, " 'Life of a Citizen,' " 42–47; Stansell, *City*, 182; Gilfoyle, *City*, 349–50 n. 34.

12. *DT*, 18 September 1891, 4; 16 September 1891, 4; 17 September 1891, 4.

13. *State of Iowa v. Charles Lyon*, case file no. 1201; *DT*, 23 September 1891, 4.

14. *DT*, 29 September 1891, 4; 24 November 1891, 4; Watson, *Physicians and Surgeons*, 729.

15. Robinette, "History," 9–11, 16–23; Bourque, *Defining*, 97–99; Iowa General Assembly, *Report of Pardons*, 46. Information on age of victims in rape cases compiled from complaints for "rape" and "assault with intent to rape" in the Criminal Causes Appearance Docket, books 1–3 (1880–1909), fee book and judgment docket, docket A (1909–10), District Court of Scott County, Iowa, Davenport, supplemented by information taken from case files, the manuscript censuses, and newspaper reports.

16. Mohr, *Doctors*, 72–73; Mills, "One Hundred Years," 42–43; see, for example, the summary of the judge's charge to the jury in *State of Iowa v. Charles Lyon*, in *DT*, 5 December 1891, 4.

17. *DT*, 19 September 1891, 4; 26 September 1891, 4; *State of Iowa v. Charles Lyon*, case file no. 1201; *DDT*, 23 September 1891, 4.

18. *DT*, 16 September 1891, 4; *State of Iowa v. Charles Lyon*, case file no. 1201.

19. *State of Iowa v. Charles Lyon*, case file no. 1201.

20. Ibid.; *DT*, 16 September 1891, 4.

21. *State of Iowa v. Charles Lyon*, case file no. 1201; *DT*, 19 September 1891, 4.

22. *DT*, 19 September 1891, 4; 25 September 1891, 4; 28 September 1891, 4; *DDT*, 30 September 1891, 4.

23. *DT*, 24 September 1891, 4; *State of Iowa v. Charles Lyon*, case file no. 1201.

24. Nemeth, "Character Evidence."

25. *State of Iowa v. Henry Carpenter*, case file no. 1190; *State of Iowa v. Charles Lyon*, case file no. 1201; *DDT*, 30 September 1891, 4; 9 December 1891, 4.

26. *State of Iowa v. Charles Lyon*, case file no. 1201.

27. Ibid.; *DT*, 1 December 1891, 4; 2 December 1891, 4.

28. *State of Iowa v. Charles Lyon*, case file no. 1201; *DT*, 2 December 1891, 4.

29. *DT*, 24 September 1891, 4.

30. Ibid., 28 September 1891, 4; *Wilton Review*, 14 August 1884, 2; *Tipton Advertiser*, 14 August 1884, 2; 21 August 1884, 2.

31. *Rock Island City Directory, 1888–91*, 137. In that episode, Lucius Dimick's wife suspected that her husband was having an affair, took a gun, and went searching for him. Lizzie Dimick found Lucius at the Toboggan Slide in the company of a prostitute. She fired the gun, perhaps aiming at the prostitute, and shot her husband dead (*DMT*, 30 July 1889, 3).

32. *State of Iowa v. Charles Lyon*, case file no. 1201.

33. *DT*, 25 September 1891, 4; 1 December 1891, 4; 4 December 1891, 4.

34. Ibid., 26 September 1891, 4.

35. *DMT*, 29 September 1891, 2; *DT*, 28 September 1891, 4; 4 December 1891, 4; *DD*, 10 December 1891, 1; *DMT*, 10 December 1891, 6.

36. *State of Iowa v. Charles Lyon*, case file no. 1201; *DT*, 4 December 1891, 4; *Stone's DCD, 1892–93*, 164; *Stone's Rock Island City Directory, 1891–92*, 111.

37. *State of Iowa v. Buck Timothy*; *DD*, 13 April 1894, 1.

38. *DT*, 1 December 1891, 4; *DMT*, 6 December 1891, 4; *DT*, 7 December 1891, 4.

39. *DT*, 9 January 1892, 4.

40. Ibid.; *DMT*, 28 January 1892, 4 (reprinted from the *Muscatine Journal*); 27 January 1892, 4; Criminal Causes, Appearance Docket, book 2, p. 166, District Court of Scott County, Iowa.

41. Robinson, "Age."

42. Gerrish, *Duties*, 12; *DT*, 26 September 1891, 4; 25 September 1891, 4; *State of Iowa v. Charles Lyon*, case file no. 1201 (emphasis added); *DD*, 13 November 1891, 1.

43. *DD*, 29 October 1894, 1; *DT*, 25 September 1891, 4. One of the girls Haikes was accused of keeping in 1894 was Nellie Burns, whom the *Times* had named as a rape victim in 1891.

44. *DT*, 19 February 1892, 4; *Stone's DCD, 1890–91*, 124; *Stone's DCD, 1892–93*, 62.

45. *John Matlock v. Henry Hass*; *DT*, 22 February 1892, 4; *State of Iowa v. Lucy Matlock*.

46. *John Matlock v. Henry Hass*.

47. Ibid.

48. *DT*, 26 November 1889, 4; *DMT*, 26 November 1889, 3; *DD*, 26 November 1889, 1, 4; 7 December 1889, 1; 8 December 1889, 1; 26 January 1890, 1; 22 June 1890, 1; 11 January 1891, 1; *DT*, 27 November 1889, 3; 2 December 1889, 4; 11 December 1889, 4; 27 January 1890, 4; 3 February 1890, 4; 9 February 1890, 4. In the same article, the *Democrat* claimed that a Roger O'Meara who had been just been indicted as a horse thief in Chicago was R. W. O'Meara.

49. PMR, book 1, 8 February 1892.

50. Ibid., book 1, 16 April 1892, 1 May 1892, 14 September 1892; *DT*, 16 March 1892, 3; Washburn, *Underworld*, 33. Historians who have documented police coercion of prostitutes include Selcer, *Hell's Half-Acre*, 180–81; Gilfoyle, *City*, 251–53.

51. DCCP, June–December 1892; record book 28, District Court of Scott County, Iowa, Davenport, 59; Hass's name appears on the July police payroll but does not appear in August or any subsequent month.

52. *DD*, 17 October 1892, 1; 7 September 1893, 1.

53. Ibid., 30 June 1902, 4; 13 February 1887, 1; 17 October 1892, 1; 13 December 1893, 1; PMR, book 2, 3 August 1899, 9 August 1896; *DD&L*, 21 December 1904, 12; 9 January 1906, 9; 2 January 1910, 11; Iowa Manuscript Census, Scott County, 1915, cards J947, J928.

54. PMR, book 1, 12 July 1892; *DD*, 13 July 1892, 1; 2 August 1892, 1; 4 August 1892, 1; 17 October 1892, 1; 15 December 1892, 1; *DT*, 5 December 1892, 4; *State of Iowa v. Dollie Hammerly* [sic] (note from Mrs. Presley is identified as "State's Exhibit A"); PMR, book 2, 2 September 1902.

55. *DD*, 19 June 1894, 1; PMR, books 1–3. Mamie Woods's arrests for keeping a house of ill-fame occurred between January 1903 and December 1904.

56. *DD&L*, 13 September 1905, 15; 20 May 1904, 3; *Shaffer, Bleuer, and Schlemmer's Rock Island City Directory*, 181; Scott County Clerk of Court, *Marriage Record*, vols. 10–11, Jule Banker and Ada Ammerman, 6 April 1899.

Chapter Seven

1. PMR, book 1, April 1893.

2. Eliot, *Practical Discussion*, 4 (first quotation attributed to John Chapman); DCCP, 3 May 1893.

3. *DD*, 28 May 1893, 1.

4. Edmund Andrews, *Prostitution*, 21; Friedman, *Crime*, 225; Shumsky, "Tacit Acceptance"; Mackey, *Red Lights Out*, 263; Hobson, *Uneasy Virtue*, 148; Best, *Controlling*, 3–5, 19, 25–27. The literature on tolerated districts is extensive; see, for example, Humphrey, "Prostitution"; Diffendahl, "Prostitution"; Adler, "Streetwalkers," 741–42; Chalfant, "Down"; Butler, *Daughters*, 100–103; Sylvester, "Avenues," 298; Peter C. Baldwin, *Domesticating*, 68–69, 72–74; Petrik, "Capitalists," 32. Another early example of licensing comes from the Civil War. U.S. military authorities issued licenses to prostitutes in Nashville; see Jones, "Municipal Vice."

5. *DD*, 6 April 1893, 2; 28 April 1893, 1.

6. On police exploitation of prostitutes, see also Selcer, *Hell's Half-Acre*, 180–81; Gilfoyle, *City*, 251–53; Butler, *Daughters*, 100–103. For an example of organized women's defense of suppression, see Elizabeth Blackwell, *Right and Wrong*.

7. Iowa's abatement law became the model for other states and reformers' tool of choice against vice districts in the early twentieth century (Rosen, *Lost Sisterhood*, 28–30; Mackey, *Red Lights Out*; *DD*, 22 March 1893, 1; 6 April 1893, 2; 16 April 1909, 14). On the trans-Atlantic intellectual exchange, see Rodgers, *Atlantic Crossings*.

8. Pivar, *Purity Crusade*, 52–62; Burnham, "Social Evil"; Brandt, *No Magic Bullet*, 35; Rosen, *Lost Sisterhood*, 10; Hobson, *Uneasy Virtue*, 147–48; "Additional Report"; McGaughey, "Importance." For other American physicians supporting regulation, see Swayze, "Protection"; Beardsley, "Chartered Brothels"; Gihon, "On the Protection"; Carrow, "Prostitution"; Rohé, "State Regulation."

9. Walkowitz, *Prostitution*; D'Emilio and Freedman, *Intimate Matters*, 148–50; Connelly, *Response*, 81.

10. Walkowitz, *Prostitution*; Sanger, *History*, 121; Corbin, *Women*, 30–32, 88–89; Flexner, *Prostitution*, 139.

11. Evans, "Prostitution," 110–11; Sanger, *History*, 193–97.

12. Powell, *State Regulation*, 63; Barret, *Prostitution*, 7; "Municipal Regulation of Vice," 4.

13. U.S. Department of the Interior, Census Office, *Report on Crime*, 1024–35; "Municipal Regulation of Vice," 4–5. Rosen names Detroit, Minneapolis, San Francisco, and Douglas, Arizona (*Lost Sisterhood*, 10); see also, Ripp-Schucha, "'This Naughty, Naughty City,'" 51–52.

14. Downer, *History*, 2:35–36; *History of Scott County*, 887; *Annals of Iowa* 17 (1930): 477–78; obituary, 26 August 1930, Henry Vollmer Clippings File, SHSI; Reeves, *Blue Book*, 105–6.

15. Obituary, Henry Vollmer Clippings File, SHSI; Roba, "What Would You Do?," 3–4.

16. Thiry, "Dangers," 3, translation by the author: "on verrait aussi s'accroître, dans des proportions effrayantes, les séductions dont sont victimes des filles pauvres, les naissances illégitimes, adultérines, les viols, les assassinats et tous les crimes atroces et abominables commis par des brutes, en rut, sur des femmes at de malheureuses petites filles"; Kaposi, "Gefahren," 16, 18–19. Moritz Kaposi is the same physician for whom Kaposi's sarcoma, early associated with AIDS, was named.

17. *DD*, 24 July 1893, 1; "Municipal Regulation in Davenport," 5; *DD*, 30 October 1893, 1. An illustration in Rettmann, "Business," 79, offers evidence that the practice of recording only brothel keepers by name was not limited to Davenport. A page reproduced from the Spokane, Washington, "Register of City Prison" for 1897 shows some brothel keepers' names followed by a numeral, with the amount of the fine calculated accordingly.

18. *DD*, 7 June 1894, 1; *State of Iowa v. Dolly Hammerly* [sic]; Iowa, *Code*, sec. 3865; *DD*, 21 June 1903, 5.

19. *DD*, 12 October 1895, 1.

20. *DD* (morning), 7 December 1894, 4; *DT*, 7 December 1894, 4; *DDL*, 7 December 1894, 4.

21. *DD* (evening), 7 December 1894, 1.

22. *DD*, 9 December 1894, 1; 10 December 1894, 1.

23. *DD* (evening), 10 December 1894, 1; *Biographical History and Portrait Gallery*, 43.

24. *DD* (evening), 12 December 1894, 1.

25. *DD*, 12 December 1894, 1; 11 December 1894, 1.

26. Watson, *Physicians and Surgeons*, 734–35; Willard and Livermore, *Woman*, 181–82; State University of Iowa, *Twenty-second Commencement*; State University of Iowa, *Catalogue*.

27. *DD*, 17 September 1894, 1; *Davenport Morning Democrat*, 18 September 1894, 4; PMR, book 1; *Stone's DCD, 1896–97*, 496.

28. Scott County Tax List, 1894, 1:15; 1893, 2:11, DPL.

29. *Davenport Morning Democrat*, 18 September 1894, 4; 19 September 1894, 4.

30. *DD*, 21 September 1894, 1; 23 September 1894, 1.

31. Ibid., 17 September 1894, 1; *State of Iowa v. D. Jacobsen and Mrs. D. Jacobsen*; *State of Iowa v. William Porter*; *State of Iowa v. John McPartland and Mrs. John McPartland*; *State of Iowa v. Mrs. M. E. May*.

32. *State of Iowa v. John McPartland and Mrs. John McPartland*.

33. *State of Iowa v. Mrs. M. E. May*.

34. Ibid.; PMR, book 1, January 1894.

35. *State of Iowa v. William Porter*.

36. Ibid.

37. *State of Iowa v. D. Jacobsen and Mrs. D. Jacobsen*.

38. Ibid.; *DT*, 1 December 1894, 4; *DD*, 6 December 1894, 1; *State of Iowa v. Al Woods*.

39. *DT*, 1 December 1894, 4; 3 December 1894, 4; 7 December 1894, 4; *DD*, 2 December 1894, 1; 6 December 1894, 1; 27 December 1894, 1; *DDL*, 2 December 1894, 4; *State of Iowa v. D. Jacobsen and Mrs. D. Jacobsen*; *State of Iowa v. William Porter*; *State of Iowa v. John McPartland and Mrs. John McPartland*; *State of Iowa v. Mrs. M. E. May*. On later cases, see *State of Iowa v. Clay Woodward and Emma Woodward*; *State of Iowa v. Henrietta Sears*; *State of Iowa v. Josephine Hovey*; *City of Davenport v. Peter Schaum*.

40. *DD*, 7 April 1895, 1; *Biographical History and Portrait Gallery*, 75.

41. PMR, book 2, 10 February 1901.

42. Bergmann, *Negro*, 44–45; for "coon," see PMR, book 1, August 1893, and thereafter.

43. Jordan, *White over Black*, 35, 150–51; Gilman, "Black Bodies," 231, 237; Russett, *Sexual Science*; Hine, "Rape."

44. Tipton, "Negro Problem," 572; Gilman, "Black Bodies," 231; Wailoo, *Dying*, 14.

45. Dan Elbert Clark, "History," 595, 598–99; *DD*, 29 May 1892, 1; Briggs, *History*, 140–41; quotation from *Des Moines Weekly Leader*, 29 March 1894, in Dan Elbert Clark, "History," 600.

46. DCCP, Treasurer's Annual Report, 1 March 1891–1 March 1892; Davenport, *Annual Reports*, (1896) 1591–92, (1897) 11–15, (1898) 9–16, (1899) 32–35, (1900) 30–33, (1901) 12–15, (1903) 10–11, (1904) 10–11, (1905) 18–19, (1906) 10–11, (1907) 10–11, DPL; *Twentieth Century Edition*, 469–71.

47. PMR, book 1, March 1895–February 1896; *Stone's DCD, 1892–93*, 638–44; *Twentieth Century Edition*, 469–71.

48. For versions of this legend, see *Quad-City Times*, 10 June 1981, 6; Roba, *River*, 106. The city had managed to pay only about half the debt before the mulct tax revenues began to accrue; see Davenport, *Annual Report* (1896) 1591, DPL. I have often wondered whether the disappearance of the city treasurer's records from 1892–93 through 1894–95 is the result of a local sleuth's efforts to verify the truth of the legend.

49. Rettmann, "Business," 82.

50. *DD*, 1 October 1895, 1; 22 October 1895, 1.

51. Ibid., 4 April 1897, 1.

52. Ibid., 27 April 1897, 1; 18 April 1897, 1; 28 April 1897, 1; *Biographical History and Portrait Gallery*, 72–73.

53. *DD*, 19 June 1897, 1; PMR, book 2, April–December 1897. Another possible explanation exists for S. F. Smith's leniency. In 1904, Smith was arrested for embezzling more than sixty-five thousand dollars from estates and trusts under his control. He was convicted and served several years in the penitentiary before being released in 1909 because of his ill health. He died two days later. While there was apparently no investigation of graft at the time, Smith was certainly ripe for temptation (*DT*, 27 April 1904, 6; *DR*, 23 June 1904, 6; *DD*, 23 June 1904, 8; *DD&L*, 9 August 1909, 8; see also Roba, *River*, 105).

Chapter Eight

1. *DD* (evening), 25 June 1894, 1; PMR, book 1, 25 June 1894; *DD* (evening), 27 June 1894, 1; *DMT*, 28 June 1894, 4; BED.

2. PMR, book 1, 28 November 1893. In March 1905, Sarah Hill told a newspaper reporter she had sent "over 200 girls" to Good Shepherd Homes. I have identified at least sixty more sent after that statement, but they probably reflect only a fraction of the total. Of the two hundred sent before March 1905, I have identified only fifty-one. In July 1904, Mrs. Hill mentioned having thirty girls at that time in the Peoria home, but I have identified only thirteen (*DD&L*, 20 March 1905, 7; 24 July 1904, 10).

3. On Davenport's Catholic population, see Iowa, *Census*, 432–33.

4. During the same seventeen-year period, the state reports record one girl from Scott County committed in 1903, one in 1907, and two in 1908. According to court records, the 1907 commitment removed a girl from the state orphanage in Scott County and placed her in the industrial school, an institutional transfer that would not have involved city authorities. The other Scott County girls may easily have come from rural areas or small towns, not Davenport (Iowa General Assembly, *Biennial Report . . . Iowa Reform School*, [1880] 4:55, [1882] 4:71, [1884] 4:58; Iowa General Assembly, *Biennial Report . . . Iowa Industrial School for Girls*, [1886] 4:63, [1888] 3:50, [1890] 3:15, [1892] 3:29, [1894] 4:28, [1896] 4:38, [1898] 4:19; Iowa General Assembly, *Report of the State Board of Control*, [1900] 6:361, [1901] 5:191, [1904] 8:168, [1906] 4:187, [1907] 2:197, [1909] 2:231, [1911] 2:242; PMR, books 1–3; *State of Iowa v. Hazel Johnson*; Wood, "Savage Girls"; *DD*, 12 October 1895, 1).

5. Iowa, *Annotated Code*, chap. 8, secs. 3255–60; Iowa, *McClain's Annotated Code*, chap. 6, sec. 2301; Briggs, *History*, 97.

6. Iowa, *Supplement*, chap. 8-A, sec. 3260-d; Grossberg, *Governing*, 263–68; *DD*, 12 October 1895, 1; Mennel, *Thorns*, 114–15; Briggs, *History*, 227. A home for prostitutes opened in Davenport in the late 1870s but quickly closed after the inmates ransacked the building and stole the furnishings. In the 1890s, Miss Jennie Barnes traveled the state to raise money for a refuge to be sponsored by the "Woman's Home Association of Iowa," but it was never built. The Salvation Army established a Rescue Home in Des Moines in 1901. When the People's Union Mission of Davenport planned a new building in 1902, the original proposal included a floor devoted to "friendless" girls, but organizers abandoned this design as a result of lack of funds. By 1904, Sioux City had a Women's and Babies' Home and Dubuque a Salvation Army Rescue Home (*DD*, 1 February 1889, 4; 7 November 1895, 1; 25 June 1896, 1; 26 August 1899, 6; 1 August 1897, 1; 2 April 1900, 4; 8 March 1900, 4; 9 April 1902, 7; 28 January 1904, 6; Iowa General Assembly, *Legislative Documents: Report of the State Board* (1904), 8:524–27. On rescue homes nationally, see Kunzel, *Fallen Women*; Pascoe, *Relations*.

7. *DD*, 13 November 1881, 1; 25 July 1886, 1; Benedict, *Woman's Work*, 86, 122; Iowa General Assembly, *Report of the Joint Committee Appointed to Visit the Benedict Home* (1886), 2:3–5; Briggs, *History*, 205.

8. Benedict, *Woman's Work*, 167–75. The precipitating event for Benedict's resignation as financial agent was her perception that funds she had raised for the home were being misappropriated to other WCTU activities. The position taken by Benedict Homes administrators resembles the mission adopted by the Salvation Army and Crittenton Homes as they shifted from working for the reform of prostitutes to taking in unwed mothers; see Kunzel, *Fallen Women*, 17–18.

9. *DD* (evening), 7 July 1894, 1; 15 July 1894, 1. The Des Moines Benedict Home had proved an unreliable resource. During the 1880s and 1890s, administrators repeatedly rejected applications to place Davenport girls in the home, pleading lack of space, a situation that irked Scott County residents who calculated the tax revenues from Davenport that subsidized the home (*DD*, 22 October 1883, 1; 29 October 1883, 1; 7 January 1897, 1; 14 January 1897, 1).

10. Benedict, *Woman's Work*, 46–47.

11. Forlitti, "First Thirty Years," 8; *DD*, 17 February 1900, 7; AO. The Congregation of Our Lady of Charity of the Good Shepherd of Angers, more commonly called the Sisters of the Good Shepherd, had its origins in seventeenth-century France. For nearly two hundred years, the order existed as several autonomous communities of women, each operating a refuge for the reform of prostitutes. In the 1830s, under the leadership of Mary of St. Euphrasia Pelletier, the order underwent a complete transformation. She drew the handful of existing convents together under a central administration and embarked on a worldwide missionary effort, establishing, by the time of her death in 1868, more than a hundred convents for the reformation of prostitutes and wayward girls; see Dehey, *Religious Orders*, 144–50; Andreoli, "Sisters." A girl removed from a Davenport brothel in 1882 was apparently sent to the Good Shepherd Home in St. Paul; see *DD*, 1 June 1882, 1. See also *DD-G*, 15 March 1889, 3; *Chicago Sunday Herald*, 29 September 1889, 30; PMR, book 1, 14 May 1894.

12. *DT*, 27 January 1903, 8; O'Grady, *Catholic Charities*, 173.

13. *Davenport Republican*, 22 January 1904, 4; 21 January 1904, 7, 8; *DD* (evening), 12 October 1895, 1; *DD*, 19 January 1904, 8; 21 January 1904, 6; 28 January 1904, 6.

14. Rothman, *Conscience*, 249–51; *DD*, 12 October 1895, 1. On the creation of juvenile courts, see Rothman, *Conscience*, 205–35; Schlossman, *Love*, 124–41; Mennel, *Thorns*, 124–57.

15. *DD* (evening), 25 June 1894, 1; 27 June 1894, 1; *Stone's DCD, 1894–95*, 216.

16. *DD* (evening), 27 June 1894, 1; 15 July 1894, 1.

17. PMR, book 1, 28 June 1894.

18. The analysis that follows is based on several sets of data about girls placed in Good Shepherd Homes. These sources provide different information, so it seems important to clarify the distinctions among them. The police matron's docket lists 84 girls sent to six different Good Shepherd Homes but primarily to Omaha, Peoria, and Dubuque. Records for the Peoria home are apparently not extant; therefore, a second set of data reflects only the records of the Omaha and Dubuque homes. For the period under consideration, the total number of girls identified by these two homes as being from Davenport was 73.

When these two lists (the matron's and the convents') are collated, they provide a total of 110 girls. This is by no means the whole number from Davenport, since for ten years the Peoria Home was Mrs. Hill's favorite, and its records were not available. The total of 127 given above comes from adding an additional 17 girls mentioned in newspaper reports who appeared in neither Mrs. Hill's records nor the records kept by the convents. Nearly all of these newspaper reports indicated that the girls in question went to Peoria.

19. PMR, books 1–3; BED; RP. Looking only at the girls listed in the records of the homes in Omaha and Dubuque, family members—parents, stepparents, or siblings—placed just over a quarter (26 percent) of the girls. Two-thirds (67 percent) came at the behest of "authorities"—the matron, the courts, agents of child-saving organizations, or just "the authorities of Davenport." A handful placed themselves, and unidentifiable individuals placed the others. These figures and those in the paragraphs following are based on a study of the seventy-three names drawn from the BED and RP. These girls were all identified in convent records as coming from Davenport.

20. Schlossman, *Love*, 140; Hoy, "Caring," 266–67.

21. Sarah Hill is identified as Protestant in ADI, 8.

22. *DD*, 13 May 1903, 7; *DD&L*, 22 July 1904, 6; 26 September 1904, 5; 28 June 1905, 6; 19 October 1905, 8; 13 November 1908, 6; 19 September 1909, 15.

23. *DT*, 13 July 1904, 10.

24. *DD*, 24 June 1894, 1; see also Mennel, *Thorns*, 131; Gordon, *Heroes*, 40–41.

25. Conniff, *Good Shepherd*, 78–79; Thompson, "Discovering," 286. Dr. W. F. Peck, for example, worked to recruit the Sisters of Mercy to establish hospitals in both Davenport and Iowa City (Peck, "Davenport," 77–78). For examples of Protestants' favorable impressions of Catholic sisters,

see Livermore, *What Shall We Do*, 177; Dall, *"Woman's Right,"* 105. Protestant Deaconess orders were created specifically to emulate the successes of Catholic sisters; see Dougherty, "Methodist Deaconess." William Lloyd Clark, an evangelist and rabble-rouser from Illinois, sharply criticized the police matron and city authorities in Davenport for using Good Shepherd Homes, but there is no reason to see his views as anything other than a radical fringe. Indeed, on one visit to the city, he was jailed after delivering an anti-immigrant harangue (Clark, *Hell*; *DDT*, 25 May 1895, 2).

26. *State of Iowa v. William Ryland*; *DDL*, 10 May 1904, 8; 3 May 1904, 6; 20 May 1904, 6; *DD*, 2 April 1903, 5.

27. *DD*, 17 February 1900, 7; 23 June 1901, 4.

28. Ibid., 7 March 1900, 4; *DR*, 6 March 1900, 8; 8 March 1900, 6; PMR, book 2, 3 March 1900.

29. *DD*, 3 January 1903, 6; *State of Iowa v. Henry Albrecht*; *DR*, 15 February 1903, 8; PMR, book 2, 3 February 1903, 25 February 1903; *DDL*, 4 February 1903.

30. *State of Iowa v. Ed Lindblom and Alden Bennett*; *DD&L*, 8 March 1906, 10; 13 March 1906, 10; RP.

31. Figures were obtained by comparing names of prosecuting witnesses in rape, assault with intent to rape, and lewdness with a child cases listed in Criminal Causes, Appearance Docket, books 1-3 (1880-1909), and fee book and judgment docket, docket A (1909-10), District Court of Scott County, Iowa, Davenport, with names of girls sent to Good Shepherd Homes listed in PMR, BED, RP, and newspaper reports. See also *DD*, 14 May 1903, 6.

32. This paragraph and those following are based on reports appearing in *DD&L*, 26 November 1909, 10; 28 November 1909, 13; *DT*, 26 November 1909, 1, 7; PMR, book 3, 31 August 1906, 18 August 1907. In addition to reformatories, many Good Shepherd Homes also operated a "preservation" or "protectorate" class, a kind of boarding school or orphanage; see Dehey, *Religious Orders*, 145; Delaney, "Catholic Reformatory Agencies."

33. Gordon, *Heroes*, 227-49; *DD&L*, 31 March 1910, 10.

34. *DD&L*, 22 March 10, 8.

35. Ibid., 1 April 1910, 1; 3 April 1910, 8.

36. *DD*, 13 May 1903, 7; RP; *DD&L*, 15 November 1908, 6; *DT*, 13 November 1908, 6; *State v. Nellie Edgington*; *DD&L*, 27 April 1905, 7; 24 October 1904, 9.

37. *DD&L*, 28 June 1905, 6.

38. Pearl's arrests took place between 7 December 1893 and 6 August 1894 (PMR, book 1; BED).

39. BED.

40. PMR, book 2, 10 April 1899, 17 April 1899; BED; *DD*, 21 January 1904, 6; 19 February 1903, 6; Calhoun County Recorder's Office, *Marriage Record*, 16 February 1903; Palmer, *Three Generations*, 5; *Stone's DCD, 1894-95*, 345; *Stone's DCD, 1898-99*, 384-85.

41. Scott County Clerk of Court, *Marriage Record*, vols. 12-13, 15 October 1895.

42. *DD* (evening), 12 October 1895, 1; 26 July 1899, 5; 17 February 1900, 7.

43. *Practical Rules*. The publication date for this handbook is 1943, but the introduction is dated 1897, and it includes the assertion, "This book has not been undertaken to propose new practices, but to assure the observance of those which have been transmitted, for more than sixty years, in our Congregation." For this reason, I have accepted it as a reliable source for the ideals pursued by the Good Shepherd Sisters in the period 1890-1910.

44. Ibid., 174-78.

45. Ibid., 177. The sisters acknowledged that the contracts were probably unenforceable but required them because they "may have the effect of restraining certain persons who would not wish to violate such a promise."

46. ADI, 8-9; *State of Iowa v. Henry Albrecht*.

47. *Dubuque Catholic Tribune*, 4 June 1903, 8.

48. AO, 4, 12–15; *Practical Rules*, 126.
49. ADI, 11, 18–19, 37; *Bulletin of the Congregation of the Good Shepherd of Angers* 17 (1909): 80.
50. *Practical Rules*, 118, 121, 178.
51. Ibid., 88, 19; *Dubuque Catholic Tribune*, 4 June 1903, 8.
52. Szuberla, "Ladies," 170–72, 177.
53. *Sioux City Journal*, 16 May 1903, 4; *DD*, 5 November 1896, 1; *Practical Rules*, 140. On working-class girls and self-display, see Peiss, *Cheap Amusements*, 62–67.
54. *Practical Rules*, 155, 110, 136–38. Unlike the prisoners in Bentham's panopticon, girls in the convent were not isolated from each other, nor were they unable to tell when they were being observed, but the technique of creating internalized restraints through surveillance described by Foucault has parallels in the sisters' practice; see Foucault, *Discipline and Punish*, 195–228.
55. *Practical Rules*, 13–26, 30, 42; ADI, 14–16, 56, 71–75; on the use of the Catholic confessional to elaborate and contain discourses of sexuality, see Foucault, *History*, 58–62.
56. *DD*, 28 January 1904, 6; Forlitti, "First Thirty Years," 7; O'Grady, *Catholic Charities*, 175.
57. ADI, 21–22, 45–51, 56.
58. Ibid., 45–51; *State of Iowa v. William Spence*; RP.
59. BED; RP; PMR, book 2, 27 April 1901, 24 November 1905.
60. *Practical Rules*, 118–19; *Dubuque Catholic Tribune*, 4 June 1903, 8; Forlitti, "First Thirty Years," 60–62; Conway, *In the Footprints*, 203–5; Dehey, *Religious Orders*, 146–47; AO, 1314; RP; ADI, 37; PMR, book 3, 12 May 1906.
61. Pascoe, *Relations*, 149; Kunzel, *Fallen Women*, 32; *Practical Rules*, 182.
62. *DD&L*, 20 March 1905, 7; PMR, book 3, 17 February 1906, 31 January 1908, 1 February 1908, 12 April 1908; *State of Iowa v. John Burke*; *DD*, 12 July 1912, 15. Statistics for marriage and rearrest are based on a list of 104 girls sent to various convents drawn from the PMR, the BED, and the RP. I excluded girls who did not return to "the world" (i.e., died or remained in the convent community) and those who clearly relocated to someplace other than Davenport after their release.

Neither marriage nor rearrest precluded the other. Lena, who first came to public attention at the age of eight when she brought a rape charge against two neighbors, went to the Good Shepherd Home in Peoria after being arrested in a brothel at sixteen. At least twice after her release, police arrested her as a prostitute. Four years later, she obtained a license to marry.

63. PMR, book 3, 20 July 1904; *DD*, 24 February 1907, 9; 3 March 1907, 6; *DD&L*, 7 July 1912, 6; Marriage Register, Scott County, Iowa, 27 May 1914.
64. Odem, "Delinquent Daughters," 191.

Chapter Nine

1. Mayor's report on Falkner investigation, DCCP, July 1894.
2. Bailey, "Parasexuality."
3. *Hearst's Chicago American*, 28 January 1903, 5.
4. Washburn, *Underworld*, 16–18, 28–40; for an interesting but unverifiable letter purporting to be from a brothel keeper praising the effects of the regulation system in St. Louis, see Rohé, "State Regulation," 85–86.
5. PMR, book 1, 1892, 1895. Month-by-month comparisons for 1893 are not useful because the number of women working as prostitutes varied according to the season. Far more were arrested or registered in the summer and early fall than in December, January, and February.
6. PMR, book 2, 1902. The minimum of 111 individual prostitutes was obtained by adding the registrations by brothel keepers (53) and new inmates (40) and subtracting the number of women who appeared on both lists (5). To this I added the aggregate for January but subtracted the 2 new registrations for that month—the difference being the number of prostitutes continuing in January

who had registered the previous year (23). Because registered prostitutes did not necessarily work every month and January was always a slow month, this total is likely a low estimate.

7. Iowa, *Census*, 147. The 1895 Iowa census tables do not break down age cohorts over twenty-one; however the U.S. censuses for 1890 and 1900 do. For 1890, the cohort of women forty-five and over made up 19.6 percent of the female population. For 1900, that cohort constituted 19.5 percent of the female population. Given the consistency over a decade, I used the figure of 19.5 percent to adjust the total from the Iowa census for 1895, providing an estimate of the cohort aged eighteen to forty-four. Since Davenport's overall female population increased 15 percent between 1895 and 1900, the true ratio in 1895 may have shown prostitutes even more prevalent (U.S. Department of the Interior, Census Office, *Report on Population*, 118; U.S. Bureau of the Census, *Census Reports*, 127).

8. Iowa Bureau of Labor, *Eighth Biennial Report*, 51–52; U.S. Bureau of the Census, *Census Reports*, 559–61.

9. Porsild found that when authorities in the Yukon stopped issuing health certificates for prostitutes, the women recognized that the certificates had been good for business. They arranged for an alternative certificate from local physicians (*Gamblers*, 102).

10. Petrik, "Capitalists."

11. *Adelbert W. DeMaranville v. Josephine Hawkins*.

12. SCTR (Davenport), 1898, 1:121; 1899, 1:202; 1903, 1:194, DPL; *DD*, 25 June 1899, 6; 9 July 1899, 6; 11 July 1899, 6; 12 July 1899, 4; *In the Matter of the Estate of Josephine Hovey*.

13. U.S. Manuscript Census, Scott County, Iowa, 1900, vol. 69, E.D. 133, sheet 22; *Twentieth Century Edition*, 226; *DD*, 3 January 1904, 7; Felony Docket, 24 November 1905, Police Department Records, DPL; *DD&L*, 2 January 1910, 11; 17 October 1910, 10.

14. PMR, book 1, July–November 1894; *Stone's DCD 1894–95*, 191; *DD*, 14 August 1895, 3; 9 August 1897, 1; 10 August 1897, 1; 11 August 1897, 1; 15 August 1897, sec. 2, p. 1; PMR, book 2, January–December 1897.

15. *DD*, 3 February 1898, 1.

16. Ibid., 30 May 1901, 4.

17. *DD&L*, 9 April 1905, 7; PMR, book 1, January 1894–December 1895; book 2, January 1896–July 1900, August 1902, November–December 1903, January–December 1904, December 1905; book 3, November 1906, September 1907; Iowa Manuscript Census, Scott County, 1895, 220; *DD*, 1 June 1899, 5.

18. SCTR (Davenport), 1897, 1:177; 1898, 2:201; 1899, 2:206, DPL; U.S. Manuscript Census, Scott County, Iowa, 1900, vol. 69, E.D. 133, sheet 22; *DD&L*, 9 April 1905, 7; 2 January 1910, 11; 15 July 1910, 8; *DDL*, 16 May 1917, 15.

19. *DD&L*, 9 February 1927, 15; *DD*, 28 Aug 1896, 1; 27 November 1898, 1; 22 February 1901, 4.

20. SCTR (Davenport), 1899, 1:19; 1903, 1:19, DPL.

21. U.S. Manuscript Census, Scott County, Iowa, 1900, vol. 69, E.D. 134, sheet 17; *DD*, 5 February 1907, 7; *DD&L*, 14 July 1907, 12; *DDL*, 3 April 1950, 11; 18 April 1951, 15.

22. *State of Iowa v. Thomas O. Waggener and Folsom Waggener*; *DD&L*, 20 September 1922, 15; 9 February 1927, 15; *DDL*, 18 April 1951, 15.

23. PMR, book 1, May 1891; *DD*, 11 September 1892, 1; SCTR (Davenport), 1892, 2:144, DPL; *Stone's DCD, 1892–93*, 442.

24. PMR, book 1, 16 April 1893; SCTR (Davenport), 1893, 2:144, DPL; *D. Sachs and Sons v. H. C. Woodward and Emma Woodward*; *Ira Tabor v. H. C. Woodward and Emma Woodward*; *Stone's DCD, 1894–95*, 462; *DT*, 27 April 1917, 5.

25. *D. Sachs and Sons v. H. C. Woodward and Emma Woodward*; *Ira Tabor v. H. C. Woodward and Emma Woodward*; *Davenport Gas Light Co. v. Emma Woodward and H. C. Woodward*.

26. *DD&L*, 5 May 1905, 8; 21 February 1905, 7; *Davenport Daily Republican*, 17 August 1904, 7.

27. *DD*, 20 January 1898, 1; *Stone's DCD, 1901–2*, 686, 630; *Stone's DCD, 1902–3*, index page J, 117.

28. *Davenport Daily Republican*, 17 August 1904, 7; *DD&L*, 16 August 1904, 6.

29. *DD*, 12 January 1903, 1; 13 December 1903, 5; *DD&L*, 19 December 1904, 9; Iowa Manuscript Census, Scott County, 1915, card A284.

30. Purcell, *Them*, 157.

31. Duis, *Saloon*, 254; Deutsch, *Women*, 85–86.

32. *DG*, 11 August 1887, 1; 13 September 1889, 4; *DD*, 9 May 1894, 1; 17 December 1877, 1; 19 June 1894, 2; *DDT*, 16 January 1905, 6.

33. Allen, *Horrible Prettiness*, 62–71; *DG*, 28 November 1887, 1; *DD*, 5 September 1886, 1; 20 February 1887, 1; 3 March 1887, 1. Allen argues that while male, blackface minstrels catered to a family audience, female minstrels, who generally wore blonde wigs but eschewed blackface, used elements of burlesque to attract a predominantly male audience (*Horrible Prettiness*, 165–66).

34. *DD*, 1 January 1894, 1; Wills, "Olive Logan," 37–38; Gilfoyle, *City*, 127.

35. Zellers, "Cradle"; Claudia D. Johnson, "That Guilty Third Tier"; Allen, *Horrible Prettiness*, 65; Nasaw, *Going Out*, 13–14.

36. *Twentieth Century Edition*, 470; *DD*, 16 July 1902, 7; 18 July 1883, 1; *DD&L*, 18 December 1904, 25; 10 January 1911, 18; *Stone's DCD, 1900–1901*, 453.

37. *Stone's DCD, 1900*, 470; *DD*, 4 November 1903, 5; 7 April 1903, 6; *DT*, 31 January 1903, 5; *DD&L*, 5 February 1905, 14.

38. *DD*, 30 June 1902, 5; 16 July 1902, 7; 9 December 1903, 5.

39. *DL*, 20 May 1904, 3; *DD&L*, 18 December 1904, 25; 7 April 1905, 10.

40. *DD&L*, 25 April 1905, 9; 6 February 1906, 11; 22 February 1906, 7; William Lloyd Clark, *Hell*, 35–36.

41. *DDT*, 16 January 1905, 6; *DD&L*, 1 May 1904, 6; Thersites, "Why People Go," 1.

42. Jensen, " 'I'd Rather Be Dancing' "; Peiss, *Cheap Amusements*, 88; Hunter, *To 'Joy*, 168; Lytle and Dillon, *From Dance Hall*; Faulkner, *From the Ballroom*; Nasaw, *Going Out*, 111–13.

43. Jensen, " 'I'd Rather Be Dancing,' " 9, 13; Peiss, *Cheap Amusements*, 90–97.

44. Nasaw, *Going Out*, 11–13; Peiss, *Cheap Amusements*, 98–99, 113–14.

45. Peiss, *Cheap Amusements*, 105–11; Meyerowitz, *Women Adrift*, 101–6.

46. Thersites, "Why People Go."

47. *DD&L*, 17 December 1906, 11.

48. Ibid., 24 November 1905, 6.

49. Ibid., 10 September 1905, 16; 2 January 1905, 10; Meyerowitz, *Women Adrift*, 40; *DD*, 4 November 1903, 5.

50. Washburn, *First Drink*, 38, 8–10.

51. *DDL*, 11 January 1903, 7; *DWL*, 23 January 1903, 8.

52. *DWL*, 23 January 1903, 8; *Hearst's Chicago American*, 28 January 1903, 5.

53. Nelson, *White Slaves*; *DD*, 12 January 1903, 7.

54. On the "white slave narrative," see Connelly, *Response*, 114–16; deYoung, "Help"; Langum, *Crossing Over*, 15–47; Meyerowitz, *Women Adrift*, 62–64.

55. *DDL*, 22 January 1903, 6; *DD*, 19 January 1903, 6.

56. *DD*, 20 January 1903, 6; 23 January 1903, 7.

57. *DDL*, 21 January 1903, 5; *DD*, 21 January 1903, 6; 23 January 1903, 7.

58. *DT*, 2 February 1903, 5; 30 January 1903, 9; *DWL*, 3 February 1903, 6.

59. Rabinovitz, *For the Love*, 45–46; Kibler, *Rank Ladies*.

60. *DD*, 22 March 1903, 7; 29 March 1903, 7; 1 April 1903, 6; 7 April 1903, 6; 3 August 1903, 6; 13 September 1903, 5.

61. Ibid., 2 December 1903, 7; 4 December 1903, 5, 6; 6 December 1903, 6, 13; 9 December 1903, 6; 13 December 1903, 5; 14 December 1903, 6; 10 December 1903, 6; 16 December 1903, 6; 22 December 1903, 6.

62. *DD&L*, 17 April 1904, 3.

63. Ibid., 24 April 1904, 6; 1 May 1904, 6.

64. Ibid., 30 November 1904, 21; 5 July 1906, 7; City Treasurer's Reports, DCCP, 1904, 1905.

Conclusion

1. *DD*, 8 November 1900, 4.

2. *DR*, 14 January 1897, 7.

3. Gallaher, *Legal and Political Status*, 186, 202.

4. *DD*, 5 April 1895, 1; 6 March 1897, 1.

5. *DDL*, 17 September 1897, 1; *DD*, 19 September 1897, 1.

6. *DR*, 24 September 1897, 7.

7. *DD*, 23 April 1900, 5.

8. *DD&L*, 4 August 1907, 14; 5 August 1907, 10; 6 August 1907, 10; 7 August 1907, 12; 11 August 1907, 14; 12 August 1907, 8; *DT*, 2 August 1907, 6; U.S. Manuscript Census, Scott County, Iowa, 1870, 264A; 1900, 52. Kemmerer's surname is of German origin, but he was probably three generations removed from the old country. Before emigrating to Iowa, his parents resided in Northampton County, Pennsylvania (U.S. Manuscript Census, Forks Township, Northampton County, Pennsylvania, 1850, 71). Kemmerers had lived there since the mid-eighteenth century.

9. *DD&L*, 16 August 1907, 7; *DT*, 16 August 1907, 4.

10. *DD&L*, 16 September 1907, 10; 17 October 1907, 9; 18 October 1907, 10, 14, 15; 21 October 1907, 8, 10; *DT*, 16 October 1907, 1; 17 October 1907, 1; 21 October 1907, 12; Bateman, "Albert B. Cummins."

11. Gorn, *Manly Art*, 142; Taillon, "'What We Want'"; Parsons, "Risky Business."

12. *DD&L*, 2 December 1907, 10.

13. Ibid., 4 December 1907, 11; 15 December 1907, 1; 16 December 1907, 7; 30 December 1907, 9.

14. Ibid., 10 March 1908, 6; 12 March 1908, 11; 15 March 1908, 10; 26 March 1908, 10; 29 March 1908, 11; 31 March 1908, 8; 17 July 1908, 14; 21 July 1908, 7; 3 October 1909, 14; 10 October 1909, 12.

15. *DT*, 14 April 1909, 10; 15 April 1909, 12; *DD&L*, 15 April 1909, 10. A third law passed that session was known as the Moon law. It limited the number of saloons in any city to one for every thousand residents, though any saloon already operating within the law could continue in business. The Civic Federation campaign had reduced the number of saloons in Davenport from about 200 to about 160, but strict enforcement of the Moon law would have permitted only about 45.

16. *DT*, 15 April 1909, 12; 16 April 1909, 1; *DD&L*, 16 April 1909, 14.

17. *DT*, 16 April 1909, 1; *DD&L*, 16 April 1909, 14; 18 April 1909, 15; 25 April 1909, 11.

18. *DD&L*, 18 April 1909, 15; 16 April 1909, 14.

19. *DD*, 11 May 1902, 7.

20. Ibid., 5 May 1900, 4; 25 July 1901, 4; *DT*, 1 October 1907, 14; Lend a Hand Club, *Fifteenth Annual Report*; *DD&L*, 22 March 1909, 7; 16 October 1910, 5; *DD*, 23 March 1903, 6.

21. *DD*, 5 May 1900, 4; 26 May 1901, 4; 2 June 1901, 4; 9 June 1901, 5; 25 July 1901, 4.

22. Ibid., 28 March 1904, 7; 25 July 1901, 4; 7 April 1902, 4; *DD&L*, 13 October 1905, 11; 3 April 1904, 5; *DT*, 27 March 1905, 4; 14 October 1905, 10.

23. *DD*, 18 September 1899, 7.

24. *DD&L*, 10 July 1910, 9; 31 July 1910, 8; 7 August 1910, 14.

25. For a perceptive analysis of the figure of the "flirt" in the American city, see Rabinovitz, *For the Love*, esp. 22–28.

26. The phrase "die, or do worse" is borrowed from Dall's formulation of a poor girl's economic options: "Marry, stitch, die, or do worse" (*"Woman's Right"*, 104). See also Briggs, *History*, 335; *Davenport Weekly Democrat*, 15 April 1909, 1. For examples of the "white slave" narrative summarized here, see Bell, *Fighting*; Lytle and Dillon, *From Dance Hall*. The narrative has been the focus of much study by historians and literary scholars; see, for example, Rosen, *Lost Sisterhood*, 112–35; Meyerowitz, *Women Adrift*, 62–65; Hobson, *Uneasy Virtue*, 141–47; Haag, *Consent*, 64–65; Guy, *Sex*; Hapke, *Girls*.

27. On the federal White Slave Traffic Act, see Langum, *Crossing Over*; Haag, *Consent*, 61–72.

28. *DT*, 30 July 1924.

BIBLIOGRAPHY

Archival Sources

Boston
  New England Historical Genealogical Society
    Massachusetts. Secretary of the Commonwealth. Division of Vital Statistics.
    Massachusetts Vital Records: Registration of Births, Marriages, Deaths, 1841–1910.
Davenport, Iowa
  Clarissa C. Cook Home for the Friendless
    Record Book A.
    Record of Transient Admissions.
  District Court of Scott County, Iowa
    Civil Actions Case Files
      Fannie Auerochs v. Chicago, Rock Island, & Pacific Railroad Co. (April 1894), case file no. 3254.
      Marie Beauchaine v. Frank Kessler et al. (September 1892), case file no. 2503.
      Davenport Gas Light Co. v. Emma Woodward and H. C. Woodward (November 1896), case file no. 4151.
      Adelbert W. DeMaranville v. Josephine Hawkins (December 1893), case file no. 3103.
      John Matlock v. Henry Hass (April 1892), case file no. 2249.
      D. Sachs and Sons v. H. C. Woodward and Emma Woodward (February 1895), case file no. 3454.
      Ira Tabor v. H. C. Woodward and Emma Woodward (January 1895), case file no. 3571.
    Criminal Causes, Appearance Docket
      Books 1–3 (1880–1909).
      Fee Book and Judgment Docket, Docket A (1909–10).
    Criminal Proceedings Case Files
      City of Davenport v. Peter Schaum (September 1904), case file no. 2295; (December 1904), case file no. 2360.
      State of Iowa v. Henry Albrecht (February 1903), case file no. 2137.
      State of Iowa v. John Burke (July 1898), case file no. 1758.
      State of Iowa v. Mattie Burke (October 1883), case file no. 457.
      State of Iowa v. Henry Carpenter (October 1891), case files nos. 1190, 1197.
      State of Iowa v. George Haikes (October 1891), case files nos. 1193, 1203.
      State of Iowa v. Dollie Hammerly [sic] (September 1893), case files nos. 1351, 1352.
      State of Iowa v. Josephine Hovey (July 1899), case file no. 1828.
      State of Iowa v. D. Jacobsen and Mrs. D. Jacobsen (November 1894), case files nos. 1479, 1480.

Bibliography

> *State of Iowa v. Hazel Johnson* (June 1907), case file no. 2623.
> *State of Iowa v. Ed Lindblom and Alden Bennett* (January 1906), case file no. 2487.
> *State of Iowa v. Charles Lyon* (October 1891), case files nos. 1198, 1199, 1200, 1201.
> *State of Iowa v. Lucy Matlock* (April 1892), case file no. 1236.
> *State of Iowa v. Mrs. M. E. May* (December 1894), case files nos. 1488, 1489.
> *State of Iowa v. John McPartland and Mrs. John McPartland* (December 1894), case files nos. 1486, 1487.
> *State of Iowa v. Claude Merrill* (November 1880), case file no. 177.
> *State of Iowa v. Mary Ortell* [sic] (September 1887), case file no. 832.
> *State of Iowa v. William Porter* (December 1894), case files nos. 1485, 1486.
> *State of Iowa v. William Ryland* (August 1905), case file no. 2423.
> *State of Iowa v. Henrietta Sears* (July 1899), case file no. 1824.
> *State of Iowa v. Charles Smith and Maggie Smith* (October 1883), case file no. 490.
> *State of Iowa v. William Spence* (September 1908), case file no. 2731.
> *State of Iowa v. Buck Timothy* (April 1894), case file no. 1415.
> *State of Iowa v. Catherine Uber* (September 1881), case file no. 246.
> *State of Iowa v. Thomas O. Waggener and Folsom Waggener* (January 1915), case files nos. 3314, 3315.
> *State of Iowa v. Al Woods* (December 1894), case file no. 1483.
> *State of Iowa v. Lizzie Woods* (October 1887), case file no. 863.
> *State of Iowa v. Clay Woodward and Emma Woodward* (January 1898), case file no. 1720.

Divorce Case Files
> *Mary A. Auerochs v. Theodore Auerochs* (January 1893), case file no. 2634.
> *Emma J. Hagan v. Andrew J. Hagan* (March 1879), case file no. 14699.
> *William H. Keller v. Naomia* [sic] *J. Keller* (April 1880), case file no. 3769.
> *Josephine Mitchell v. Frank Mitchell* (March 1886), case file no. 5129.
> *Minnie Murdoch v. Ezra Murdoch* (October 1883), case file no. 15356.
> *Josephine Robinson v. Charles Robinson* [sic] (November 1892), case file no. 2555.

Juvenile Court Case Files
> *State v. Nellie Edgington* (November 1908), case file no. 85.

Probate Files
> *In the Matter of the Estate of Martha Glaspell* (September 1898), probate file no. 4479.
> *In the Matter of the Estate of Josephine Hovey* (February 1913), probate file no. 7723.

Record Book 28.

Richardson-Sloane Special Collections Center, Davenport Public Library
City Council Papers.
City of Davenport. *Annual Reports of the Officers of the City of Davenport.* 1896–1907.
Jennie McCowen. "History of the Lend a Hand Club." Ts.
Police Department Records
> Felony Docket.
> Police Matron's Record, Books 1–3.

Scott County Tax Records.

Davenport Public Schools
School Board Minutes.

Havana, Illinois
Havana Public Library
> Public Domain Land Tract Record Sales.

Iowa City
   State Historical Society of Iowa
      Phebe Sudlow Collection.
      Henry Vollmer Clippings File.
   University of Iowa Library Archives
      Employee Card File.
Lebanon, Ohio
   Warren County Genealogical Society
      Index of Marriage Records.
      "Medicine." Ts.
   Warren County Historical Society Museum
      James Boggs, B.P., to John McCowen, 29 July 1837, ms. 920.
      Maria McCowen to John McCowen, 15 April [1846?], ms. 920.
      National Normal University Card File.
   Warren County Probate Court Archives
      John McCowen Probate File, box 244.
St. Paul, Minnesota
   Sisters of the Good Shepherd Provincial Archives
      Annals of the Convent of the Good Shepherd, Omaha, vol. 1.
      Annals of the Dubuque, Iowa, Home of the Good Shepherd, 1903–48.
      Book of Entrances and Departures, Omaha Home of the Good Shepherd, 1894–1913.
      Record of the Penitents of the Convent of the Good Shepherd, Dubuque, Iowa, 1903–25.
Washington, D.C.
   National Archives and Records Administration
      Abbie O. Craton Pension File, certificate no. 263913.

Maps

Davenport, Iowa. New York: Sanborn Map and Publishing, 1886.
Insurance Maps of Davenport, Iowa. New York: Sanborn-Perris, 1892.

Periodicals

Chicago Sunday Herald
Cigar Maker's Official Journal (Cigar Makers' International Union)
Davenport Daily Tribune
Davenport Democrat
Davenport Democrat-Gazette
Davenport Democrat and Leader
Davenport Der Demokrat
Davenport Morning Tribune
Davenport Quad-City Times
Davenport Republican
Davenport Times
Davenport Tri City Trident
Des Moines Iowa State Register
Des Moines Leader
Des Moines Weekly Leader

Dubuque Catholic Tribune
Hearst's Chicago American
Lebanon (Ohio) Western Star
Portland Oregonian
Sioux City Daily Journal
Sioux City Daily Times
Tipton (Iowa) Advertiser
Union Signal (Woman's Christian Temperance Union)
Wilton (Iowa) Review
Woman's Tribune (American Woman Suffrage Association)
Manchester (New Hampshire) Union Leader
New York Times

Published Legal Cases

Andre v. State, 5 Iowa 389.
State v. Clark, 78 Iowa 494.
State v. Evans, 27 N.C. 603.
State v. Gill et al., 129 N.W. 821.
State v. Lee, 80 Iowa 75.
State v. Marvin, 12 Iowa 499.
State v. Rice, 56 Iowa 432.
State v. Toombs, 79 Iowa 743.

City Directories

E. Coy and Co.'s Twin Cities Directory for the Year 1860. Vol. 1. Davenport: Coy, 1859.
E. H. Schmidt's Davenport City Directory, 1882–83. Davenport: Schmidt, 1882.
H. Pfabe's Davenport City Directory, 1884–85. Davenport: Pfabe, 1884.
H. Pfabe's Davenport City Directory, 1885–86. Davenport: Pfabe, 1885.
Holland's Directory and Business Record of the City of Davenport for 1884–85. Davenport: Holland, 1885.
The Manchester Directory 1881. Manchester, N.H.: Sampson, Davenport, 1880.
Morrissey and Bunn's Davenport City Directory, 1880. Davenport: Morrissey and Bunn, 1880.
Owen's Davenport City Directory for 1878. Davenport: Owen, 1878.
R. L. Polk and Co.'s Davenport City Directory, 1908. Davenport: Polk, 1908.
R. L. Polk and Co.'s Davenport City Directory, 1909. Davenport: Polk, 1909.
R. L. Polk and Co.'s Davenport City Directory, 1910. Davenport: Polk, 1910.
Rock Island City Directory, 1888–91. Omaha: Frane Orff, n.d.
Schmidt and Jacobsen's Davenport City Directory, 1881. Davenport: Schmidt and Jacobsen, 1881.
Shaffer, Bleuer, and Schlemmer's Rock Island City Directory, 1899–1900. Rock Island: Shaffer, Bleuer, and Schlemmer, 1899.
Stone's Davenport City Directory for 1888. Davenport: Stone, 1888.
Stone's Davenport City Directory for 1890–91. Davenport: Stone, 1890.
Stone's Davenport City Directory for 1892–93. Davenport: Stone, 1892.
Stone's Davenport City Directory for 1894–95. Davenport: Stone, 1894.
Stone's Davenport City Directory for 1896–97. Davenport: Stone, 1896.
Stone's Davenport City Directory for 1898–99. Davenport: Stone, 1899.
Stone's Davenport City Directory, 1902–1903. Davenport: Stone, 1902.

Bibliography

Stone's Davenport City Directory, 1906–1907. Davenport: Stone, 1906.
Stone's Rock Island City Directory, 1891–92. Quincy, Ill.: Stone, 1891.
Tri-City Directory, 1887. Davenport: Glass, 1887.
Twentieth Century Edition of the Times' Free City Directory of Davenport, Iowa. Keokuk: the Times, 1900.
Wolfe's Omaha City Directory, 1878–79. Omaha: Wolfe, 1878.

Web Sites

Ireland GenWeb Project. Sligo County Genealogy Project. Kilmacshalgan Census. http://www.rootsweb.com/~irlsli/kilmacshalgancensus1901part2.htm.
University of Virginia Geospatial and Statistical Data Center. United States Historical Census Data Browser. http://fisher.lib.virginia.edu/census.

Other Sources

Abelson, Elaine. *When Ladies Go A-Thieving: Middle-Class Shoplifters in the Victorian Department Store*. New York: Oxford University Press, 1989.
Acton, Richard. "A Remarkable Immigrant: The Story of Hans Reimer Claussen." *Palimpsest* 75 (Summer 1994): 87–100.
Adams, John R. *Edward Everett Hale*. Boston: Twayne, 1977.
Addams, Jane. *Twenty Years at Hull House*. New York: Signet, 1981.
"Additional Report Submitted by Dr. John Morris as a Minority Report." *Transactions of the Ninth Annual Meeting of the American Public Health Association* 7 (1881–83): 424–28.
Adler, Jeffrey S. "Streetwalkers, Degraded Outcasts, and Good-for-Nothing Huzzies: Women and the Dangerous Class in Antebellum St. Louis." *Journal of Social History* 25 (Summer 1992): 737–55.
Aguirre, Gertrude de. *Women in the Business World; or, Hints and Helps to Prosperity, by One of Them*. Boston: Arena, 1895.
Alcott, Louisa May. *Work: A Story of Experience*. New York: Schocken, 1977.
Allen, Robert C. *Horrible Prettiness: Burlesque and American Culture*. Chapel Hill: University of North Carolina Press, 1991.
Anderson, James Silbree. *Pioneer Courts and Lawyers of Manitowoc County, Wis*. Manitowoc: Manitowoc County Historical Society, 1997.
Andreoli, M. "Sisters of Our Lady of Charity of the Good Shepherd." In *New Catholic Encyclopedia*, 6:627. New York: McGraw Hill, 1967.
Andrews, Edmund. *Prostitution and Its Sanitary Management*. St. Louis: n.p., 1871.
Andrews, H. P., ed. *History of Audubon County, Iowa*. Indianapolis: B. P. Brown, 1915.
Arnold, Marybeth Hamilton. "'The Life of a Citizen in the Hands of a Woman': Sexual Assault in New York City, 1790 to 1820." In *Passion and Power: Sexuality in History*, edited by Kathy Peiss and Christina Simmons, 35–56. Philadelphia: Temple University Press, 1989.
Association for the Advancement of Women. *Annual Report of the Association for the Advancement of Women, 1881*. Boston: Cochrane and Sampson, 1882.
———. *Eleventh Annual Report of the Association for the Advancement of Women, 1883*. Buffalo: Peter Paul, 1884.
———. *Historical Account of the Association for the Advancement of Women, 1873–1893*. Dedham, Mass.: Transcript Steam Job Print, 1893.
———. *Report of the Fifteenth Woman's Congress, New York City, October 1887*. Fall River, Mass.: Franklin, 1888.

Bibliography

———. *Thirteenth Annual Report, 1885.* Buffalo: Peter Paul, 1886.
———. *Twelfth Annual Report of the Officers and Committees, Women's Congress, Baltimore, October 1884.* Buffalo: Peter Paul, 1885.
"Die Auswannerer." *Pennsylvania Folklife* 28, no. 4 (1979): 25–31.
Avery, Alida C. "A Plea for Purpose." In *Papers Read before the Association for the Advancement of Women, Thirteenth Annual Congress, Des Moines, October 1885,* 33–42. Buffalo: Peter Paul, 1886.
Bailey, Peter. "Parasexuality and Glamour: The Victorian Barmaid as Cultural Prototype." *Gender and History* 2 (Summer 1990): 148–72.
Baker, Mary H. "Jennie C. McCowen." *Iowa Alumnus* 22 (11 November 1924): 108.
Baker, Paula. "The Domestication of Politics: Women and American Political Society, 1780–1920." *American Historical Review* 8 (June 1984): 620–47.
Baldwin, Peter C. *Domesticating the Street: The Reform of Public Space in Hartford, 1850–1930.* Columbus: Ohio State University Press, 1999.
Baldwin, Sara Mullin, ed. *Who's Who in Davenport, 1929.* Davenport: Baldwin, 1929.
Barney, Mrs. J. K. "Police Matrons." *Lend a Hand* 2 (1887): 473–74.
Barnhart, Cornelia Mallett. "Phoebe W. Sudlow." *Palimpsest* 28 (1947): 29–30.
Barret, William L. *Prostitution in Its Relation to the Public Health.* St. Louis: n.p., 1873.
Bateman, Herman E. "Albert B. Cummins and the Davenport 'Riots' of 1907." *Arizona and the West* 18 (1976): 111–24.
Beardsley, George L. "Chartered Brothels; or, A Plea for the Regulation of Prostitution." *New Orleans Medical and Surgical Journal* 8 (September 1880): 201–48.
Bederman, Gail. *Manliness and Civilization: A Cultural History of Gender and Race in the United States, 1880–1917.* Chicago: University of Chicago Press, 1995.
Bell, Ernest A. *Fighting the Traffic in Young Girls; or, The War on the White Slave Trade.* N.p.: Ball, 1910.
Benedict, Lovina. *Woman's Work for Woman.* Des Moines: Iowa Printing, 1892.
Benson, Susan Porter. *Counter Cultures: Saleswomen, Managers, and Customers in American Department Stores, 1890–1940.* Urbana: University of Illinois Press, 1988.
Bergmann, Leola Nelson. *The Negro in Iowa.* Iowa City: State Historical Society of Iowa, 1969.
Best, Joel. *Controlling Vice: Regulating Brothel Prostitution in St. Paul, 1865–1883.* Columbus: Ohio State University Press, 1998.
Biographical History and Portrait Gallery of Scott County, Iowa. Chicago: American Biographical Publishing, 1895.
Biographical History of Shelby and Audubon Counties. Chicago: Dunbar, 1889.
Blackhawk Genealogical Society. *Index of Rock Island County, Illinois, Marriages.* Vol. 3. Rock Island: Blackhawk Genealogical Society, 1989.
Blackwell, Antoinette Brown. *The Sexes throughout Nature.* Westport, Conn.: Hyperion, 1976.
———. "Women's Industrial Position. (A Labor Symposium.) Part I." In *Papers Read before the Association for the Advancement of Women, Fourteenth Women's Congress, Louisville, Kentucky, October 1886,* 63–66. Atlantic Highlands, N.J.: Leonard and Lingle, 1887.
Blackwell, Elizabeth. *Right and Wrong Methods of Dealing with the Social Evil.* New York: Brentano, 1883.
Blair, Karen. *The Clubwoman as Feminist: True Womanhood Redefined, 1868–1914.* New York: Holmes and Meier, 1980.
Blanchard, Mary W. "Boundaries and the Victorian Body: Aesthetic Fashion in Gilded Age America." *American Historical Review* 100 (1995): 21–50.
Boles, Henry M. *Prisoners and Paupers.* New York: Putnam's, 1893.

Bibliography

Bordin, Ruth. *Woman and Temperance: The Quest for Power and Liberty, 1873–1900.* Philadelphia: Temple University Press, 1981.
Bourque, Linda Brookover. *Defining Rape.* Durham, N.C.: Duke University Press, 1989.
Bowers, Martha H., and Marlys A. Svendsen. *Davenport Architecture: Tradition and Transition.* Davenport: City of Davenport, 1982.
Boydston, Jeanne. *Home and Work: Housework, Wages, and the Ideology of Labor in the Early Republic.* New York: Oxford University Press, 1990.
Boyer, Paul. "Laura Clay." In *Notable American Women, 1607–1950,* 1:346–48. Cambridge: Harvard University Press, 1971.
Brandt, Allan. *No Magic Bullet: A Social History of Venereal Disease in the United States since 1880.* New York: Oxford University Press, 1985.
Brenzel, Barbara M. *Daughters of the State: A Social Portrait of the First Reform School for Girls in North America, 1856–1905.* Cambridge: MIT Press, 1983.
Briggs, John E. *History of Social Legislation in Iowa.* Iowa City: State Historical Society of Iowa, 1915.
Bristol, Augusta Cooper. "The Present Phase of Women's Advancement." In *Papers Read before the Association for the Advancement of Women, Thirteenth Annual Congress, Des Moines, October 1885,* 94–106. Buffalo: Peter Paul, 1886.
Bristow, Edward J. *Prostitution and Prejudice: The Jewish Fight against White Slavery, 1870–1939.* New York: Schocken, 1983.
Buck-Morss, Susan. "The Flâneur, the Sandwichman, and the Whore: The Politics of Loitering." *New German Critique* 39 (1986): 99–140.
Buhle, Mari Jo, and Paul Buhle, eds. *The Concise History of Woman Suffrage.* Urbana: University of Illinois Press, 1978.
Burnham, John C. "The Social Evil Ordinance—A Social Experiment in Nineteenth Century St. Louis." *Bulletin of the Missouri Historical Society* 27 (April 1973): 203–17.
Bushnell, Kate. *The Woman Condemned.* New York: Funk and Wagnalls, 1886.
Butler, Anne M. *Daughters of Joy, Sisters of Misery: Prostitutes in the American West, 1865–1890.* Urbana: University of Illinois Press, 1985.
——. *Gendered Justice in the American West: Women Prisoners in Men's Penitentiaries.* Urbana: University of Illinois Press, 1997.
Calhoun County. Recorder's Office. *Marriage Record.* Vol. 5, 1902–7. Salt Lake City: Genealogical Society, n.d.
Carrow, F. "Prostitution as Observed in Canton, China." *Maryland Medical Journal* 9 (1882): 202–3.
Chalfant, Rhonda. "Down at the Junction: A Study of Madam Lizzie Cook, a Prostitute in Sedalia, Missouri, 1870–1879." Master's thesis, University of Missouri, 1994.
Chapin, Augusta J. "Women's Industrial Position. (A Labor Symposium.) Part III. Woman's Work and Wages (A Synopsis)." In *Papers Read before the Association for the Advancement of Women, Fourteenth Women's Congress, Louisville, Kentucky, October 1886,* 71–72. Atlantic Highlands, N.J.: Leonard and Lingle, 1887.
Chauncey, George. *Gay New York: Gender, Urban Culture, and the Making of the Gay Male World, 1890–1940.* New York: Basic Books, 1994.
Chudacoff, Howard P. *The Age of the Bachelor: Creating an American Subculture.* Princeton: Princeton University Press, 1999.
Church, Ella Rodman. *Money Making for Ladies.* New York: Harper, 1882.
Clark, Dan Elbert. "History of Liquor Legislation in Iowa, 1878–1908." *Iowa Journal of History and Politics* 6 (1908): 503–605.

Clark, William Lloyd. *Hell at Midnight in Davenport; or, The History of a City's Shame*. Milan, Ill.: n.p., 1908.

Clarke, E. H. *Sex in Education; or, A Fair Chance for the Girls*. Boston: Osgood, 1873. Reprint, New York: Arno, 1972.

Clay, Laura. "The Right of Women to Free Competition as Workers." In *Papers Read before the Association for the Advancement of Women at Its Tenth Annual Congress, Portland, Maine, October 1882*, viii–xii. N.p., n.d.

Cleaves, Margaret Abigail. *The Autobiography of a Neurasthene*. Boston: Badger, 1910.

———. "Memorial of Delia S. Irish, M.D., of Davenport." *Transactions of the Iowa State Medical Association* 4 (1879–80): 187–90.

———. "Mental Peculiarities in Connection with Uterine Diseases." *Transactions of the Iowa State Medical Society* 4 (1879–80): 67–75.

Cohen, Patricia Cline. *The Murder of Helen Jewett: The Life and Death of a Prostitute in Nineteenth-Century New York*. New York: Knopf, 1998.

———. "Women at Large: Travel in Antebellum America." *History Today* 44 (1 December 1994): 44–50.

Combination Atlas Map of Warren County, Ohio. N.p., Everts, 1875.

Connelly, Mark Thomas. *The Response to Prostitution in the Progressive Era*. Chapel Hill: University of North Carolina Press, 1980.

Conniff, James C. G. *The Good Shepherd Story*. Peekskill, N.Y.: Sisters of the Good Shepherd, 1957.

Conway, Katherine E. *In the Footprints of the Good Shepherd, New York, 1857–1907*. New York: Convent of the Good Shepherd, 1907.

Corbin, Alain. *Women for Hire: Prostitution and Sexuality in France after 1850*. Translated by Alan Sheridan. Cambridge: Harvard University Press, 1990.

Croly, Jane C. *Thrown on Her Own Resources; or, What Girls Can Do*. New York: Crowell, 1891.

Currey, J. Seymour. *Chicago: Its History and Its Builders*. Vol. 1. Chicago: Clarke, 1912.

Dall, Caroline H. *"Woman's Right to Labor"; or, Low Wages and Hard Work*. Boston: Walker, Wise, 1860.

Davenport, City of. *Charter and Revised Ordinances of the City of Davenport, Together with Acts of the General Assembly of the State of Iowa Relating to the City*. Davenport: Day, Egbert, and Fidlar, 1875.

Dawes, Anna Laurens. "An Experiment in Police Matrons." *Lend a Hand* 4 (1889): 130.

Deacon, Desley. "Politicizing Gender." *Genders* 6 (Fall 1989): 1–19.

Degler, Carl. *At Odds: Women and the Family in America from the Revolution to the Present*. New York: Oxford University Press, 1980.

Dehey, Elinor Tong, comp. *Religious Orders of Women in the United States*. Hammond, Ind.: Conkey, 1913.

Delaney, John J. "Catholic Reformatory Agencies." *Proceedings of the National Conference of Charities and Correction* (1897): 133.

D'Emilio, John, and Estelle Freedman. *Intimate Matters: A History of Sexuality in America*. New York: Harper and Row, 1988.

Deutsch, Sarah. "Learning to Talk More Like a Man: Boston Women's Class-Bridging Organizations, 1870–1910." *American Historical Review* 97 (April 1992): 379–404.

———. *Women and the City: Gender, Space, and Power in Boston, 1870–1940*. New York: Oxford University Press, 2000.

Devoll, Sarah W. "The Results of the Employment of a Police Matron in the City of Portland,

Maine." *Proceedings of the Eighth Annual Conference of Charities and Correction, Boston 1881* (1881): 309–17.
deYoung, Mary. "Help, I'm Being Held Captive! The White Slave Fairy Tale of the Progressive Era." *Journal of American Culture* 6 (1983): 96–99.
Diffendahl, Anne P. "Prostitution in Grand Island, Nebraska, 1870–1913." *Heritage of the Great Plains* 16 (Summer 1983): 1–9.
Dodge, Grace H. "Working Girls' Societies." *Chautauquan* 9 (January 1889): 223–25.
Dougherty, Mary Agnes. "The Methodist Deaconess: A Case of Religious Feminism." *Methodist History* 21 (1983): 90–98.
Downer, Harry E. *History of Davenport and Scott County, Iowa.* 2 vols. Chicago: Clarke, 1910.
DuBois, Ellen Carol. *Woman Suffrage and Women's Rights.* New York: New York University Press, 1998.
Dugdale, Robert L. *The Jukes: A Study in Crime, Pauperism, Disease, and Heredity.* New York: Arno, 1970.
Duis, Perry R. *The Saloon: Public Drinking in Chicago and Boston, 1880–1920.* Urbana: University of Illinois Press, 1983.
Edwards, Rebecca. *Angels in the Machinery: Gender in American Party Politics from the Civil War to the Progressive Era.* New York: Oxford University Press, 1997.
Eliot, William G. *Practical Discussion of the Great Moral Questions of the Day, no. III.* St. Louis: Globe, n.d.
Encyclopedia of American Quaker Genealogy. Baltimore: Genealogical Publishing, 1994.
Espenshade, Edward B. "Urban Development at the Upper Rapids of the Mississippi." Ph.D. diss., University of Chicago, 1944.
Evans, R. J. "Prostitution, State, and Society in Imperial Germany." *Past and Present* (1976): 106–29.
Fales, Imogene C. "Women's Industrial Position. (A Labor Symposium.) Part II. The Interests of Working Women." In *Papers Read before the Association for the Advancement of Women, Fourteenth Women's Congress, Louisville, Kentucky, October 1886,* 67–70. Atlantic Highlands, N.J.: Leonard and Lingle, 1887.
Faulkner, T. A. *From the Ballroom to Hell: Facts about Dancing, a Dancing Masters Experience.* Chicago: Noble, 1894.
Fink, Leon. "From Autonomy to Abundance: Changing Beliefs about the Free Labor System in Nineteenth-Century America." In *Terms of Labor: Slavery, Serfdom, and Free Labor,* edited by Stanley Engerman, 116–36. Stanford, Calif.: Stanford University Press, 1999.
———. *Workingman's Democracy: The Knights of Labor and American Politics.* Urbana: University of Illinois Press, 1983.
Flexner, Abraham. *Prostitution in Europe.* New York: Patterson Smith, 1969.
Foner, Eric. *Free Soil, Free Labor, Free Men: The Ideology of the Republican Party before the Civil War.* New York: Oxford University Press, 1970,
Foner, Philip S. *Women in the American Labor Movement from Colonial Times to the Eve of World War I.* New York: Free Press, 1979.
Forlitti, John Edward. "The First Thirty Years of the Home of the Good Shepherd, St. Paul, Minnesota, 1868–98." Master's thesis, St. Paul Seminary, 1962.
Foucault, Michel. *Discipline and Punish: The Birth of the Prison.* Translated by Alan Sheridan. New York: Vintage, 1979.
———. *The History of Sexuality: An Introduction.* Translated by Robert Hurley. New York: Vintage, 1990.

Fraser, Nancy. "Rethinking the Public Sphere: A Contribution to the Critique of Actually Existing Democracy." *Social Text* 25–26 (1990): 56–80.

Fraser, Nancy, and Linda Gordon. "A Genealogy of *Dependency*: Tracing a Keyword of the U.S. Welfare State." *Signs* 19 (Winter 1994): 309–36.

Freedman, Estelle. "Separatism as Strategy: Female Institution Building and American Feminism, 1870–1930." *Feminist Studies* 5 (1979): 512–29.

———. *Their Sisters' Keepers: Women's Prison Reform in America, 1830–1930*. Ann Arbor: University of Michigan Press, 1981.

French, Anna Densmore. "Comparative Effect on Health of Professional, Fashionable, and Industrial Life." In *Papers Read before the Association for the Advancement of Women, Thirteenth Annual Congress, Des Moines, October 1885*, 51–61. Buffalo: Peter Paul, 1886.

Friedman, Lawrence. *Crime and Punishment in American History*. New York: Basic Books, 1993.

Fuller, Paul E. *Laura Clay and the Woman's Rights Movement*. Lexington: University Press of Kentucky, 1975.

Gallaher, Ruth A. *Legal and Political Status of Women in Iowa*. Iowa City: State Historical Society of Iowa, 1918.

Gamber, Wendy. *The Female Economy: The Millinery and Dressmaking Trades, 1860–1930*. Urbana: University of Illinois Press, 1997.

Gardner, Helen. "A Battle for a Sound Morality; or, The History of Recent Age-of-Consent Legislation in the United States." *Arena* 13 (August 1895): 353–59.

Gerrish, Frederic Henry. *The Duties of the Medical Profession Concerning Prostitution and Its Allied Vices*. Portland, Me.: Loring, Short, and Harmon, 1879.

Gihon, Albert L. "On the Protection of the Innocent and Helpless Members of the Community from Venereal Diseases and Their Consequences." *Public Health Papers and Reports* 5 (1879–80): 55–65.

Gilfoyle, Timothy. *City of Eros: New York City, Prostitution, and the Commercialization of Sex, 1790–1920*. New York: Norton, 1992.

Gilman, Sander L. "Black Bodies, White Bodies: Toward an Iconography of Female Sexuality in Late Nineteenth-Century Art, Medicine, and Literature." *Critical Inquiry* 12 (Autumn 1985): 204–38.

Gilmore, Glenda. "Gender and Jim Crow: Women and the Politics of White Supremacy in North Carolina, 1896–1920." Ph.D. diss, University of North Carolina, Chapel Hill, 1992.

———. *Gender and Jim Crow: Women and the Politics of White Supremacy in North Carolina, 1896–1920*. Chapel Hill: University of North Carolina Press, 1996.

Ginzberg, Lori D. *Women and the Work of Benevolence: Morality, Politics, and Class in the Nineteenth-Century United States*. New Haven: Yale University Press, 1990.

Ginzburg, Carlo. *Clues, Myths, and the Historical Method*. Translated by John and Anne C. Tedeschi. Baltimore: Johns Hopkins University Press, 1989.

Glickman, Lawrence B. *A Living Wage: American Workers and the Making of a Consumer Society*. Ithaca: Cornell University Press, 1997.

Goldman, Marion S. *Gold Diggers and Silver Miners: Prostitution and Social Life on the Comstock Lode*. Ann Arbor: University of Michigan Press, 1981.

Goldstein, Daniel. "Midwestern Naturalists: Academies of Science in the Mississippi Valley, 1850–1900." Ph.D. diss., Yale University, 1989.

Gordon, Linda. *Heroes of Their Own Lives: The Politics and History of Family Violence*. New York: Viking, 1988.

Gorn, Elliot. *The Manly Art: Bare-Knuckle Prize Fighting in America*. Ithaca: Cornell University Press, 1986.
Grossberg, Michael. *Governing the Hearth: Law and the Family in Nineteenth-Century America*. Chapel Hill: University of North Carolina Press, 1988.
Gugle, Sarah P. *History of the International Order of the King's Daughters and Sons*. Columbus, Ohio: International Order of the King's Daughters and Sons, 1931.
Guy, Donna J. *Sex and Danger in Buenos Aires: Prostitution, Family, and Nation in Argentina*. Lincoln: University of Nebraska Press, 1991.
Haag, Pamela. *Consent: Sexual Rights and the Transformation of American Liberalism*. Ithaca: Cornell University Press, 1999.
Haines, Richard, comp. *Genealogy of the Stokes Family*. Camden, N.J.: Sinnickson Chew, 1903.
Hale, Edward Everett. *Ten Times One Is Ten*. Boston: Little, Brown, 1917.
Hall, Emma A. "Reformation of Criminal Girls." *Proceedings of the Tenth Annual Conference of Charities* (1883): 188–99.
Halttunen, Karen. *Confidence Men and Painted Women: A Study of Middle-Class Culture in America, 1830–1870*. New Haven: Yale University Press, 1982.
Hapke, Laura. *Girls Who Went Wrong: Prostitutes in American Fiction, 1885–1917*. Bowling Green, Ohio: Bowling Green State University Press, 1989.
Hartt, Irene. *How to Make Money although a Woman*. New York: Ogilvie, 1895.
Hayden, Dolores. *The Grand Domestic Revolution: A History of Feminist Designs for American Homes, Neighborhoods, and Cities*. Cambridge: MIT Press, 1981.
Higginbotham, Evelyn Brooks. *Righteous Discontent: The Women's Movement in the Black Baptist Church, 1880–1920*. Cambridge: Harvard University Press, 1993.
Hill, Marilynn Wood. *Their Sisters' Keepers: Prostitution in New York City, 1830–1870*. Berkeley: University of California Press, 1993.
Hill, R. W. "The Children of 'Shinbone Alley.'" *Proceedings of the National Conference of Charities and Corrections* (1887): 229–39.
Hine, Darlene Clark. "Rape and the Inner Lives of Black Women: Thoughts on a Culture of Dissemblance." In *Hine Sight: Black Women and the Re-Construction of American History*, 37–47. New York: Carlson, 1994.
History of Scott County, Iowa. Chicago: Inter-State Publishing, 1882.
History of the State of Nebraska. Vol. 1. Chicago: Western Historical, 1882.
Hobbs, Mrs. J. B. "Police Matrons." *Proceedings of the National Conference of Charities and Correction, 1884* (1884): 293–94.
Hobson, Barbara Meil. *Uneasy Virtue: The Politics of Prostitution and the American Reform Tradition*. New York: Basic Books, 1987.
Horowitz, Helen Lefkowitz. *Alma Mater: Design and Experience in the Women's Colleges from Their Nineteenth-Century Beginnings to the 1930s*. New York: Knopf, 1984.
Howe, Julia Ward. "Opening Address." In *Papers Read before the Association for the Advancement of Women, Thirteenth Annual Congress, Des Moines, October 1885*, 10–11. Buffalo: Peter Paul, 1886.
———. *Reminiscences 1819–1899*. New York: Negro Universities Press, 1969.
Hoy, Suellen. "Caring for Chicago's Women and Girls: The Sisters of the Good Shepherd, 1859–1911." *Journal of Urban History* 23 (March 1997): 260–94.
Humphrey, David C. "Prostitution and Public Policy in Austin, Texas, 1870–1915." *Southwestern Historical Quarterly* 86 (1983): 473–516.
Hunter, Tera W. *To 'Joy My Freedom: Southern Black Women's Lives and Labors after the Civil War*. Cambridge: Harvard University Press, 1997.

Bibliography

Hurd, D. Hamilton. *History of Merrimack and Belknap Counties, Part I.* Philadelphia: Lewis, 1885.

Iowa, State of. *Annotated Code of the State of Iowa.* Des Moines: F. R. Conaway, 1897.

———. *Census of Iowa for the Year 1895.* Des Moines: State Printer, 1896.

———. *The Code of Iowa for 1873.* Des Moines: State Printer, 1873.

———. *Fourteenth Biennial Report of the Superintendent of Public Instruction.* Des Moines: F. M. Mills, 1870.

———. *McClain's Annotated Code and Statutes of the State of Iowa.* Chicago: Callaghan, 1888.

———. *Supplement to the Code of Iowa.* Des Moines: B. Murphy, 1902.

Iowa, State of. Bureau of Labor. *Eighth Biennial Report of the Bureau of Labor Statistics for the State of Iowa, 1897–98.* Des Moines: State Printer, 1899.

———. *Fifth Biennial Report of the Bureau of Labor Statistics, 1892–93.* Des Moines: State Printer, 1894.

———. *Second Biennial Report of the Bureau of Labor Statistics, 1886–87.* Des Moines: State Printer, 1888.

Iowa, State of. General Assembly. *Acts and Resolutions Passed at the Regular Session of the Twentieth General Assembly of the State of Iowa.* Des Moines: State Printer, 1884.

———. *Acts and Resolutions Passed at the Regular Session of the Twenty-first General Assembly of the State of Iowa.* Des Moines: State Printer, 1886.

———. *Biennial Reports of the Trustees and Superintendent of the Iowa Reform School.* In *Legislative Documents Submitted to the General Assembly of the State of Iowa.* Des Moines: State Printer, 1880, 1882, 1884.

———. *Biennial Reports of the Trustees of the Iowa Industrial School for Girls.* In *Legislative Documents Submitted to the General Assembly of the State of Iowa.* Des Moines: State Printer, 1886, 1888, 1890, 1892, 1894, 1896, 1898.

———. *Report of Pardons.* In *Legislative Documents Submitted to the Twenty-ninth General Assembly of the State of Iowa, 1902*, vol. 1. Des Moines: State Printer, 1902.

———. *Report of the Bureau of Labor.* In *Legislative Documents Submitted to the Twenty-seventh General Assembly of the State of Iowa, 1898*, vol. 3. Des Moines: State Printer, 1898.

———. *Report of the Bureau of Labor Statistics.* In *Legislative Documents Submitted to the Twenty-first General Assembly of the State of Iowa, 1886–1887*, vol. 4. Des Moines: State Printer, 1886.

———. *Report of the Joint Committee of the Seventeenth General Assembly of the State of Iowa Appointed to Visit the Hospital for the Insane at Mount Pleasant.* In *Legislative Documents Submitted to the Seventeenth General Assembly of the State of Iowa, 1878*, vol. 2. Des Moines: State Printer, 1877.

———. *Reports of the State Board of Control.* In *Legislative Documents Submitted to the General Assembly of the State of Iowa.* Des Moines: State Printer, 1900, 1901, 1904, 1906, 1907, 1909, 1911.

———. *Tenth Biennial Report of the Trustees, Superintendent, and Treasurer of the Iowa Hospital for the Insane at Mount Pleasant.* In *Legislative Documents Submitted to the Seventeenth General Assembly of the State of Iowa, 1878–79*, vol. 3. Des Moines: State Printer, 1880.

Iowa State Teachers' Association. *Proceedings of the State Teachers' Association of Iowa.* Dubuque: Iowa Normal Monthly, 1878.

"Jennie McCowen, A.M., M.D." *Iowa Medical Journal* 1 (December 1895): 531.

Jensen, Joan M. "'I'd Rather Be Dancing': Wisconsin Women Moving On." *Frontiers* 22 (2001): 1–20.

Johnson, Claudia D. "That Guilty Third Tier: Prostitution in Nineteenth-Century American Theaters." *American Quarterly* 27 (1975): 575–84.

Johnson, Hildegard Binder. "Adjustment to the United States." In *The Forty-Eighters: Political Refugees of the German Revolution of 1848*, edited by A. E. Zucker, 43–78. New York: Russell and Russell, 1950.

Jones, James B., Jr. "Municipal Vice: The Management of Prostitution in Tennessee's Urban Experience. Part I: The Experience of Nashville and Memphis, 1854–1917." *Tennessee Historical Quarterly* 50 (1991): 33–41.

Jordan, Winthrop D. *White over Black: American Attitudes toward the Negro, 1550–1812*. Baltimore: Penguin, 1968.

Juhl, Paul C. "J. P. Doremus and His Floating Photograph Gallery." *Palimpsest* 73 (Summer 1992): 62–67.

Kaposi, M. "Gefahren der Prostitution für die Bevölkerung." In *Programme of the X. International Medical Congress, Berlin 1890*, section 15, *Hygiene*, 10–22. Berlin: Verlag von August Hirschwald, 1891.

Katzman, David. *Seven Days a Week: Women and Domestic Service in Industrializing America*. New York: Oxford University Press, 1978.

Kaufman, Martin. "The Admission of Women to Nineteenth-Century Medical Societies." *Bulletin of the History of Medicine* 50 (Summer 1976): 251–60.

Kaufman, Polly Welts. *Women Teachers on the Frontier*. New Haven: Yale University Press, 1984.

Keely, Sarah P. "Reform Work for Girls." *Proceedings of the National Conference of Charities and Correction* (1892): 179–82.

Kennard, Caroline A. "Progress in Employment of Police Matrons." *Lend a Hand* 9 (1892): 180–84.

Kennedy, Susan Estabrook. *If All We Did Was to Weep at Home: A History of White Working-Class Women in America*. Bloomington: Indiana University Press, 1979.

Kerber, Linda K. *Women of the Republic: Intellect and Ideology in Revolutionary America*. Chapel Hill: University of North Carolina Press, 1980. Reprint, New York: Norton, 1986.

Kessler-Harris, Alice. *In Pursuit of Equity: Women, Men, and the Quest for Economic Citizenship in Twentieth Century America*. New York: Oxford University Press, 2001.

———. "Law and a Living: The Gendered Content of 'Free Labor.' " In *Gender, Class, Race, and Reform in the Progressive Era*, edited by Noralee Frankel and Nancy S. Dye, 87–109. Lexington: University Press of Kentucky, 1991.

———. *Out to Work: A History of Wage-Earning Women in the United States*. New York: Oxford University Press, 1982.

———. "Where Are the Organized Women Workers?" *Feminist Studies* 3 (Fall 1975): 92–110.

———. *A Woman's Wage: Historical Meanings and Social Consequences*. Lexington: University Press of Kentucky, 1990.

Kibler, M. Alison. *Rank Ladies: Gender and Cultural Hierarchy in American Vaudeville*. Chapel Hill: University of North Carolina Press, 1999.

Kunzel, Regina. *Fallen Women, Problem Girls: Unmarried Mothers and the Professionalization of Social Work, 1890–1945*. New Haven: Yale University Press, 1993.

Kwolek-Folland, Angel. "Customers and Neighbors: Women in the Economy of Lawrence, Kansas, 1870–1885." *Business and Economic History* 27 (Fall 1998): 129–39.

Langum, David J. *Crossing over the Line: Legislating Morality and the Mann Act*. Chicago: University of Chicago Press, 1994.

Lapham, Ella C. "Women in the Industrial Arts." In *Papers Read before the Association for the Advancement of Women at Its Tenth Annual Congress, Portland, Maine, October, 1882*, 8–12. N.p., n.d.

Lebsock, Suzanne. *The Free Women of Petersburg: Status and Culture in a Southern Town, 1784–1860.* New York: Norton, 1984.
Lend a Hand Club. *C.L.S.C. Program.* Davenport: Lend a Hand Club, 1888.
———. *Dime Savings Agency.* Davenport: Lend a Hand Club, n.d.
———. *Fifteenth Annual Report.* Davenport: Lend a Hand Club, 1902.
———. *Protective Circular for Women.* Davenport: Lend a Hand Club, n.d.
———. *Tenth Annual Report.* Davenport: Lend a Hand Club, 1897.
Levine, Susan. *Labor's True Woman: Carpet Weavers, Industrialization, and Labor Reform in the Gilded Age.* Philadelphia: Temple University Press, 1984.
Livermore, Mary A. *What Shall We Do with Our Daughters? Superfluous Women and Other Lectures.* Boston: Lee and Shepard, 1883.
Lofland, Lyn H. *A World of Strangers: Order and Action in American Urban Public Space.* New York: Basic Books, 1973.
Long, Mason. *Save the Girls.* Fort Wayne, Ind.: Mason Long, 1882.
Lowell, Josephine Shaw. "One Means of Preventing Pauperism." *Proceedings of the Sixth Annual Conference of Charities* (1879): 189–200.
Lynde, Mrs. W. P. "The Treatment of Erring and Criminal Women." *Proceedings of the Seventh Annual Conference of Charities* (1880): 249–51.
Lytle, H. W., and John Dillon. *From Dance Hall to White Slavery: The World's Greatest Tragedy.* N.p.: Charles C. Thompson, 1912.
Mackey, Thomas Clyde. "Red Lights Out: A Legal History of Prostitution, Disorderly Houses, and Vice Districts, 1870–1917." Ph.D. diss., Rice University, 1984.
———. *Red Lights Out: A Legal History of Prostitution, Disorderly Houses, and Vice Districts, 1870–1917.* New York: Garland, 1987.
Mahoney, Timothy R. "Down in Davenport: A Regional Perspective on Antebellum Town Economic Development." *Annals of Iowa* 50 (Summer 1990): 451–74.
The Maiden Tribute of Modern Babylon (The Report of the "Pall Mall Gazette's" Secret Commission). London: Richard Lambert, 1885.
Manson, George. *Work for Women.* New York: Putnam's, 1883.
Mark, Georgia. "The Age of Consent." *Union Signal,* 3 December 1885, 4.
———. "Morality vs. Law." *Union Signal,* 4 February 1886, 4–5.
Martin, Theodora Penny. *The Sound of Our Own Voices: Women's Study Clubs, 1860–1910.* Boston: Beacon, 1987.
McCowen, Jennie. "Heredity in Its Relation to Charity Work." *Journal of Heredity* (January 1886): 47–51.
———. "Shinbone Alley." *Journal of the Iowa Auxiliary of the American Educational Aid Association* 1 (March 1889): 9–10.
———. "Women in Iowa." *Annals of Iowa* 3, 2d ser. (October 1884): 97–113.
———. "Women Physicians in Hospitals for the Insane." In *Papers Read before the Association for the Advancement of Women, Thirteenth Annual Congress, Des Moines, October 1885,* 87–96. Buffalo: Peter Paul, 1886.
McCowen Oral School for the Deaf. *Circular of Information.* Chicago: McCowen Oral School for the Deaf, 1904.
McCulloch, Oscar. "The Tribe of Ishmael: A Study in Social Degradation." *Proceedings of the National Conference of Charities and Correction* (1888): 154–59.
McGaughey, J. B. "The Importance of the Adoption of Measures for the Prevention of Venereal Diseases." *Transactions of the Minnesota State Medical Society* (1878): 177.

Bibliography

Melosh, Barbara. *"The Physician's Hand": Work Culture and Conflict in American Nursing.* Philadelphia: Temple University Press, 1982.

Mennel, Robert M. *Thorns and Thistles: Juvenile Delinquents in the United States, 1825–1940.* Hanover, N.H.: University Press of New England, 1973.

Meyerowitz, Joanne J. *Women Adrift: Independent Wage Earners in Chicago, 1880–1930.* Chicago: University of Chicago Press, 1988.

Miller, Annie Jenness. "Artistic and Sensible Dress for Street Wear." *Arena* 6 (1892): 495–98.

Mills, Elizabeth Anne. "One Hundred Years of Fear: Rape and the Medical Profession." In *Judge, Lawyer, Victim, Thief: Women, Gender Roles, and Criminal Justice,* edited by Nicole Hahn Rafter and Elizabeth Anne Stanko, 29–62. Boston: Northeastern University Press, 1982.

"Miss P. W. Sudlow." *Iowa Normal Monthly* 12 (1889): 491–92

Mitchell, Ellen. "A Plea for Fallen Women." In *Papers Read at the Second Congress of Women, Chicago, 1874,* 1–11. Chicago: Fergus, 1874.

"The Modern Moloch." *Union Signal,* 13 August 1885, 3.

Mohr, James C. *Doctors and the Law: Medical Jurisprudence in Nineteenth-Century America.* New York: Oxford University Press, 1993.

Moldow, Gloria. *Women Doctors in Gilded-Age Washington: Race, Gender, and Professionalization.* Urbana: University of Illinois Press, 1987.

Monmouth College. *Thirty-eighth Annual Catalogue of the Officers and Students of the Monmouth College for the Academical Year Ending June 14, 1894.* Monmouth, Ill.: Clarke, 1894.

Morantz-Sanchez, Regina. *Sympathy and Science: Women Physicians in American Medicine.* New York: Oxford University Press, 1985.

Mossell, N. F. *The Work of the Afro-American Woman.* Philadelphia: Ferguson, 1908.

"Municipal Regulation in Davenport." *Philanthropist* 9 (February 1894): 5

"Municipal Regulation of Vice." *Philanthropist* 9 (February 1894): 4–5.

Murolo, Priscilla. *The Common Ground of Womanhood: Class, Gender, and Working Girls' Clubs, 1882–1928.* Urbana: University of Illinois Press, 1997.

Muscatine County, Iowa. *Marriage Record.* Vol. B, 1869–74. Salt Lake City: Genealogical Society, 1976. Microfilm.

Nasaw, David. *Going Out: The Rise and Fall of Public Amusements.* New York: Basic Books, 1993.

Nelson, Nell [pseud.]. *The White Slaves of Free America: Being an Account of the Sufferings, Privations, and Hardships of the Weary Toilers in Our Great Cities as Recently Exposed by Nell Nelson of the Chicago Times.* Chicago: Peale, 1888.

Nemeth, Charles P. "Character Evidence in Rape Trials in Nineteenth Century New York: Chastity and the Admissability of Specific Acts." *Women's Rights Law Reporter* 6 (Spring 1980): 214–25.

Nichols, Jeffrey. *Prostitution, Polygamy, and Power: Salt Lake City, 1847–1918.* Urbana: University of Illinois Press, 2002.

Nissenbaum, Stephen. *The Battle for Christmas.* New York: Knopf, 1996.

Noë, Marcia. "'A Romantic and Miraculous City' Shapes Three Midwestern Writers." *Western Illinois Regional Studies* 1 (1978): 176–98.

Noun, Louise R. *Strong-Minded Women: The Emergence of the Woman-Suffrage Movement in Iowa.* Ames: Iowa State University Press, 1969.

Novak, William J. *The People's Welfare: Law and Regulation in Nineteenth-Century America.* Chapel Hill: University of North Carolina Press, 1996.

Bibliography

Odem, Mary E. *Delinquent Daughters: Policing and Protecting Adolescent Female Sexuality in the United States, 1885–1920.* Chapel Hill: University of North Carolina Press, 1995.

———. "Delinquent Daughters: The Sexual Regulation of Female Minors in the United States, 1880–1920." Ph.D. diss., University of California, Berkeley, 1989.

———. "Single Mothers, Delinquent Daughters, and the Juvenile Court in Early Twentieth Century Los Angeles." *Journal of Social History* 25 (1991): 27–43.

Official Roster of the Soldiers of the State of Ohio in the War of the Rebellion, 1861–66. Vol. 2. Akron: Werner, 1886.

O'Grady, John. *Catholic Charities in the United States.* Washington, D.C.: National Conference of Catholic Charities, 1930.

Palmer, David D. *Three Generations: A History of Chiropractic.* Davenport, Iowa: Palmer College of Chiropractic, 1967.

Parsons, Elaine Frantz. "Risky Business: The Uncertain Boundaries of Manhood in the Midwestern Saloon." *Journal of Social History* 34 (2000): 283–307.

Pascoe, Peggy. *Relations of Rescue: The Search for Female Moral Authority in the American West, 1874–1939.* New York: Oxford University Press, 1990.

Peck, Maria Purdy. "Davenport and Its Environs." *National Magazine* (1893–94): 56–90, 167–92, 276–92.

Peiss, Kathy. " 'Charity Girls' and City Pleasures: Historical Notes on Working Class Sexuality, 1880–1920." In *Powers of Desire: The Politics of Sexuality*, edited by Anne Snitow, Christine Stansell, and Sharon Thompson, 74–87. New York: Monthly Review Press, 1986.

———. *Cheap Amusements: Working Women and Leisure in Turn-of-the-Century New York.* Philadelphia: Temple University Press, 1986.

Penny, Virginia. *The Employments of Women: A Cyclopedia of Woman's Work.* Boston: Walker, Wise, 1863.

Petrik, Paula. "Capitalists with Rooms: Prostitution in Helena, Montana, 1865–1900." *Montana: The Magazine of Western History* 31 (1981): 28–41.

Pisciotta, Alexander. "Race, Sex, and Rehabilitation: A Study of Differential Treatment in the Juvenile Reformatory, 1825–1900." *Crime and Delinquency* 29 (April 1983): 254–69.

Pivar, David J. *Purity Crusade: Sexual Morality and Social Control, 1868–1900.* Westport, Conn.: Greenwood, 1973.

Polacheck, Hilda Satt. *I Came a Stranger: The Story of a Hull-House Girl.* Urbana: University of Illinois Press, 1991.

"The Police Matron's Bill—Prisons and Station Houses." *Lend a Hand* 3 (1888): 161–67.

"Police Matrons." *Harper's Weekly* 34 (30 August 1890): 675.

Porsild, Charlene. *Gamblers and Dreamers: Women, Men, and Community in the Klondike.* Vancouver: UBC Press, 1998.

Powell, Aaron M. *State Regulation of Vice.* New York: Wood and Holbrook, 1878.

Practical Rules for the Use of the Religious of the Good Shepherd for the Direction of the Classes. St. Paul, Minn.: Convent of the Good Shepherd, 1943.

Purcell, W. L. *Them Was the Good Old Days in Davenport, Scott County, Iowa.* Davenport: Purcell, 1922.

Rabinovitz, Lauren. *For the Love of Pleasure: Women, Movies, and Culture in Turn-of-the-Century Chicago.* New Brunswick: Rutgers University Press, 1998.

Rayne, Martha L. *What Can a Woman Do; or, Her Position in the Business and Literary World.* Detroit: Dickerson, 1884.

Reeves, Winona Evans. *The Blue Book of Iowa Women.* Mexico, Mo.: Missouri Printing and Publishing, 1914.

Bibliography

Reitano, Joanne R. *The Tariff Question in the Gilded Age: The Great Debate.* University Park: Pennsylvania State University Press, 1994.

———. "Working Girls Unite." *American Quarterly* 36 (Spring 1984): 112–34.

Restad, Penne L. *Christmas in America: A History.* New York: Oxford University Press, 1995.

Rettmann, Jef. "Business, Government, and Prostitution in Spokane, Washington, 1889–1910." *Pacific Northwest Quarterly* 89 (Spring 1998): 77–83.

Reverby, Susan M. *Ordered to Care: The Dilemma of American Nursing, 1850–1945.* Cambridge: Cambridge University Press, 1987.

Richter, August. *Geschichte der Stadt Davenport und der County Scott: Nebst Seitenblicken auf das Territorium und den Staat Iowa.* Davenport: n.p., 1917.

Ripp-Schucha, Bonnie. " 'This Naughty, Naughty City': Prostitution in Eau Claire from the Frontier to the Progressive Era." *Wisconsin Magazine of History* 81 (1997): 30–54.

Roba, William. *The River and the Prairie: A History of the Quad Cities, 1812–1980.* Quad Cities: Hesperian, 1986.

———. "What Would You Do? Congressman Henry Vollmer and the Anti-War Movement, 1914–1918." Paper presented at the Fifteenth Annual Symposium of the Society for German American Studies, Washington, D.C., 26 April 1991.

Robinette, Jane. "A History of Rape Law in Iowa." University of Iowa School of Law. Photocopy.

Robinson, C. H. "The Age of Consent, So-Called." *Arena* 13 (July 1895): 211–16.

Rodgers, Daniel T. *Atlantic Crossings: Social Politics in a Progressive Age.* Cambridge: Harvard University Press, 1998.

Roediger, David R. *The Wages of Whiteness: Race and the Making of the American Working Class.* London: Verso, 1991.

Rohé, George H. "State Regulation of Prostitution, Evidence in Its Favor." *Maryland Medical Journal* 9 (1882): 83–88.

Rosen, Ruth. *The Lost Sisterhood: Prostitution in America, 1900–1918.* Baltimore: Johns Hopkins University Press, 1982.

Rosenberg, Charles. "Sexuality, Class, and Role in Nineteenth-Century America." *American Quarterly* 25 (1973): 131–53.

Ross, Steven. *Workers on the Edge: Work, Leisure, and Politics in Industrializing Cincinnati.* New York: Columbia University Press, 1985.

Rothman, David J. *Conscience and Convenience: The Asylum and Its Alternatives in Progressive America.* New York: Little, Brown, 1980.

———. *The Discovery of the Asylum: Social Order and Disorder in the New Republic.* Boston: Little, Brown, 1971.

Rotundo, E. Anthony. *American Manhood: Transformations in Masculinity from the Revolution to the Modern Era.* New York: Basic Books, 1993.

Russett, Cynthia Eagle. *Sexual Science: The Victorian Construction of Womanhood.* Cambridge: Harvard University Press, 1989.

Ryan, Mary P. *Civic Wars: Democracy and Public Life in the American City during the Nineteenth Century.* Berkeley: University of California Press, 1997.

———. *Cradle of the Middle Class: The Family in Oneida County New York, 1790–1865.* Cambridge: Cambridge University Press, 1981.

———. *Women in Public: Between Banners and Ballots, 1825–1880.* Baltimore: Johns Hopkins University Press, 1990.

Ryon, Roderick M. "Craftsmen's Union Halls, Male Bonding, and Female Industrial Labor: The Case of Baltimore, 1880–1917." *Labor History* 36 (Spring 1995): 211–31.

Sander, Kathleen Waters. *The Business of Charity: The Woman's Exchange Movement, 1832–1900*. Urbana: University of Illinois Press, 1998.

Sanger, William. *The History of Prostitution*. New York: Arno, 1972.

Schlossman, Steven L. *Love and the American Delinquent: The Theory and Practice of "Progressive" Juvenile Justice, 1825–1920*. Chicago: University of Chicago Press, 1977.

Scott, Anne Firor. *Natural Allies: Women's Associations in American History*. Urbana: University of Illinois Press, 1992.

Scott County, Iowa. Clerk of Court. *Birth Returns Microform*. Vol. 12. Scott County: Scott County Courthouse, 1990.

———. *Marriage Record Microform*. Ser. 2, vols. 10–13. Salt Lake City: Genealogical Society, 1976.

———. *Tax Records Microform*. Salt Lake City: Genealogical Society, 1989.

Scott County Iowa Genealogical Society. *Scott County, Iowa, 1850 Federal Population Census, Early Marriages (1838–1851)*. Davenport: Scott County Iowa Genealogical Society, n.d.

———. *Scott County, Iowa, Marriage Records, 1860–69*. Davenport: Scott County Iowa Genealogical Society, n.d.

Selcer, Richard F. *Hell's Half-Acre: The Life and Legend of a Red-Light District*. Fort Worth: Texas Christian University Press, 1991.

Shannon, T. W. *Self-Knowledge and Guide to Sex Instruction*. Marietta, Ohio: Mullikin, 1913.

Shumsky, Neil Larry. "Tacit Acceptance: Respectable Americans and Segregated Prostitution, 1870–1910." *Journal of Social History* 19 (1986): 665–79.

Sklar, Katherine Kish. *Florence Kelley and the Nation's Work: The Rise of Women's Political Culture, 1830–1900*. New Haven: Yale University Press, 1995.

Smith, Julia Holmes. "Need for Adjustment between Social and Business Life." In *Papers Read before the Association for the Advancement of Women, Thirteenth Annual Congress, Des Moines, October 1885*, 43–50. Buffalo: Peter Paul, 1886.

Smith-Rosenberg, Carroll. *Disorderly Conduct: Visions of Gender in Victorian America*. New York: Knopf, 1985.

Smith-Rosenberg, Carroll, and Charles Rosenberg. "The Female Animal: Medical and Biological Views of Women." In *No Other Gods: On Science and American Social Thought*, 54–70. Baltimore: Johns Hopkins University Press, 1976.

Srebnick, Amy Gilman. *The Mysterious Death of Mary Rogers: Sex and Culture in Nineteenth-Century New York*. New York: Oxford University Press, 1995.

Stanley, Amy Dru. *From Bondage to Contract: Wage Labor, Marriage, and the Market in the Age of Slave Emancipation*. Cambridge: Cambridge University Press, 1998.

Stansell, Christine. *City of Women: Sex and Class in New York, 1789–1860*. Urbana: University of Illinois, 1987.

State University of Iowa. *Bulletin of the State University of Iowa, 1869–70*. Iowa City: State University of Iowa, 1869.

———. *Catalogue of the State University at Iowa City, Iowa*. Iowa City: State University of Iowa, 1887.

———. *Twenty-second Commencement of the Law Department*. Iowa City: State University of Iowa, 1887.

Stone, Alice Richardson. *Ancestry and Descendants of Duncan Campbell Eldridge and Stephen Bawden of Scott County, Iowa*. Decorah, Iowa: Anunsen, 1986.

Stromquist, Shelton. *A Generation of Boomers: The Pattern of Railroad Labor Conflict in Nineteenth-Century America*. Urbana: University of Illinois Press, 1987.

Svendsen, Marlys A., John Pfiffner, and Martha H. Bowers. *Where the Mississippi Runs West: A Survey of Davenport History and Architecture*. Davenport: City of Davenport, 1982.

Swayze, George B. H. "The Protection of the Public against Venereal Poison." *Medical and Surgical Reporter* 14 (20 August 1880): 201–4.

Sweet, Ada. "The Ministry of Labor." In *Papers Read before the Association for the Advancement of Women, Thirteenth Annual Congress, Des Moines, October 1885*, 70–77. Buffalo: Peter Paul, 1886.

Sylvester, Stephen G. "Avenues for Ladies Only: The Soiled Doves of East Grand Forks, 1887–1915." *Minnesota History* 51 (1989): 290–300.

Szuberla, Guy. "Ladies, Gentlemen, Mashers, Snoozers, and the Breaking of Etiquette's Code." *Prospects* 15 (1990): 169–96.

Taillon, Paul Michel. "'What We Want Is Good, Sober Men': Masculinity, Respectability, and Temperance in the Railroad Brotherhoods, c. 1870–1910." *Journal of Social History* 36 (2002): 319–38.

Thersites [Floyd Dell]. "Why People Go to Brick Munro's." *Tri-City Workers' Magazine* 1 (September 1906): 1–4.

Thiry, M. "Dangers de la Prostitution." In *Programme of the X. International Medical Congress, Berlin 1890*, section 15, *Hygiene*, 1–10. Berlin: Verlag von August Hirschwald, 1891.

Thompson, Margaret Susan. "Discovering Foremothers: Sisters, Society, and the American Catholic Experience." *U.S. Catholic Historian* 5 (1986): 273–90.

Thornton, Lynne. *Women as Portrayed in Orientalist Painting*. Paris: ACR Poche Coleur, 1994.

Tipton, F. "The Negro Problem from a Medical Standpoint." *New York Medical Journal* 43 (1886): 569–72.

Tong, Benson. *Unsubmissive Women: Chinese Prostitutes in Nineteenth-Century San Francisco*. Norman: University of Oklahoma Press, 1994.

Twain, Mark. *Life on the Mississippi*. New York: Heritage, 1944.

U.S. Bureau of Labor. *Third Annual Report of the Commissioner of Labor*. Washington, D.C.: Government Printing Office, 1887.

U.S. Bureau of the Census. *Census Reports. Twelfth Census: Population*. Part 2. Washington, D.C.: U.S. Census Office, 1902.

———. *Eleventh Annual Census, Report on Manufacturing Industries in the United States*. Part 2, *Reports of Cities*. Vol. 12. Washington, D.C.: Government Printing Office, 1895.

U.S. Department of the Interior. Census Office. *Ninth Census*. Vol. 1, *The Statistics of the Population of the United States*. Washington, D.C.: Government Printing Office, 1872.

———. *Report on Crime, Pauperism, and Benevolence, Eleventh Census, 1890*. Washington, D.C.: Government Printing Office, 1895.

———. *Report on Population of the United States at the Eleventh Census, Part II*. Washington, D.C.: Government Printing Office, 1897.

———. *Report on the Social Statistics of Cities*. Part 2. Washington, D.C.: Government Printing Office, 1887.

———. *Statistics of the Population of the United States at the Tenth Census*. Washington, D.C.: Government Printing Office, 1883.

"A Wadsworth Club." *Chautauquan* 2 (October 1881): 53–54.

Wailoo, Keith. *Dying in the City of the Blues: Sickle Cell Anemia and the Politics of Race and Health*. Chapel Hill: University of North Carolina Press, 2001.

Walkowitz, Judith R. *City of Dreadful Delight: Narratives of Sexual Danger in Late-Victorian London*. Chicago: University of Chicago Press, 1992.

———. *Prostitution and Victorian Society: Women, Class, and the State*. Cambridge: Cambridge University Press, 1980.

Walsh, Mary Roth. *Doctors Wanted, No Women Need Apply: Sexual Barriers in the Medical Profession, 1853–1977*. New Haven: Yale University Press, 1977.

Wardner, Louise Rockwood. "Girls in Reformatories." *Proceedings of the Sixth Annual Conference of Charities* (1879): 178–89.

Warren, John H., Jr. *Thirty Years' Battle with Crime*. New York: Arno, 1970.

Washburn, Josie. *The First Drink, Saloon, and Dance Hall*. Omaha: Washburn, 1914.

———. *The Underworld Sewer: A Prostitute Reflects on Life in the Trade, 1871–1909*. Lincoln: University of Nebraska Press, 1997.

Watson, Irving A. *Physicians and Surgeons of America*. Concord, N.H.: Republican Press Association, 1896.

Wegars, Priscilla. " 'Inmates of Body Houses': Prostitution in Moscow, Idaho, 1885–1910." *Idaho Yesterdays* 33 (Spring 1989): 25–37.

Wells, Richard A. *Manners, Culture, and Dress of the Best American Society*. Des Moines, Iowa, and Springfield, Mass.: King, Richardson, 1890.

Willard, Frances. *Occupations for Women*. New York: Success Company, 1897.

Willard, Frances, and Mary A. Livermore, eds. *A Woman of the Century*. New York: Moulton, 1893. Reprint, Detroit: Gale Research, 1967.

Wills, J. Robert. "Olive Logan vs. the Nude Woman." *Players* 47 (October–November 1971): 36–43.

Wilson, Jennie L. *Legal Status of Women in Iowa*. Des Moines: Iowa Printing, 1894.

Wolcott, Henrietta L. T. "The Work of the World's Women." In *Papers Read before the Association for the Advancement of Women, Thirteenth Annual Congress, Des Moines, October 1885*, 12–24. Buffalo: Peter Paul, 1886.

Woman's Medical School of Northwestern University. *Woman's Medical School of Northwestern University (Woman's Medical College of Chicago): The Institution and Its Founders*. Chicago: Cutler, 1896.

Wood, Sharon E. "Savage Girls: The 1899 Riot at the Mitchellville Girls School." *Iowa Heritage Illustrated* 80 (Fall 1999): 108–21.

"Work for Women." *Chautauquan* 4 (January 1884): 219.

Wright, Albert O. "Presidential Address." *Proceedings of the National Conference of Charities and Corrections* (1896): 1–12.

Yellin, Jean Fagan. *Women and Sisters: The Antislavery Feminists in American Culture*. New Haven: Yale University Press, 1989.

Zellers, Parker R. "The Cradle of Variety: The Concert Saloon." *Educational Theatre Journal* 20 (1968): 578–85.

INDEX

Abolitionists, 8
Abortions, 12
Ackley House, 102–3, 108, 110, 112, 113, 131
Addington, Julia, 60
African American men, 180, 196
African Americans: and suffrage, 5; and Republican Party, 6; and neighborhoods, 26; and Charitable Alliance, 105; business district of, 96–97, 177, 218; and regulation of prostitution, 178–80
African American women: as slaves, 8; and respectability, 28, 117; and education, 62; and houses of ill-fame, 95; and Charitable Alliance, 105; and morals, 180; and dance halls, 233
Age hierarchies, and men's sexual satisfaction, 133, 135
Age of consent, and rape law, 4, 134–35, 136, 137, 139, 149, 150
Age of protection, 4, 133, 135
Albrecht, Henry, 135
Albrecht, Otto, 33
Alcoholic beverages: and German immigrants, 12–13, 116, 164, 227, 248, 250; and prostitution, 80, 96, 244; and drunkenness arrests, 104; and respectability, 227; and dance halls, 236, 237; and theaters, 237, 238; and masculine culture, 249. See also Prohibition; Saloons
Alcott, Louisa May, 7–8, 31
Allars, Carrie, 156, 231
Allen, Ida, 91
Allen, William, 168
American Educational Aid Association (AEAA), 104–5, 109

American Household Economics Association, 75
American Protective Association, 195
American Public Health Association, 161
American Railway Union, 46, 94
Ammerman, Ada, 132–33, 134, 136–44, 148, 150, 151, 154, 156, 187
Ammerman, Charles, 145–46
Ammerman, Frank "Kid," 156
Anthony, Susan B., 40, 44, 56
Armstrong, Rachel, 14–15, 18, 258
Arsenal Island, 10, 12
Artelle, Mary, 89, 155
Assignation houses, 172–78, 214, 221, 236, 244
Associated Charities, 105, 110, 249
Association for the Advancement of Women (AAW): and women's employment, 7, 17, 36, 38–39, 40–44; and woman's self-support, 39, 243, 255; purpose of, 42, 50, 263 (n. 29); Committee on Reform and Statistics (CRS), 43, 44–45; Woman's Congress of the AAW, 47
Atavism, 124, 180
Auerochs, Caroline, 93
Auerochs, David, 93
Auerochs, David (son), 94, 226
Auerochs, Fannie, 94, 95
Auerochs, Henry, 94, 226
Auerochs, Kate, 94
Auerochs, Louis, 94
Auerochs, Nettie, 94
Auerochs, Robert, 94
Auerochs, Theo, 94
Avery, Alida, 39

Index

Bailey, Peter, 214
Baker, J. W. H., 171
Baker, Paula, 107
Ballard, Hannah Taylor, 60
Ballard, Samuel, 265 (n. 28)
Ballard, William, 60
Barney, Mrs. J. K., 106, 107, 108, 122
Barret, William, 163
Battisfore, Cora, 23
Bauer, Miss, 70–71
Beauchaine, Leander Lawrence, 98–99, 172–73, 222
Beauchaine, Mamie Magee, 97–99, 100, 172, 220, 222–23, 225, 226, 241
Beauchaine, Marie Catherine, 223
Becker, Waldo, 240–41
Belva Lockwood club parade, 1, 4–6, 13, 245
Benedict, Lovina, 189–90, 276 (n. 8)
Benedict Home, 189, 190, 276 (nn. 8, 9)
Benevolent organizations, 34–36
Benson, Mabel, 231
Best, Joel, 160
Bickford, Lile, 45, 46, 50, 55, 63–64, 65, 68, 75–76, 77
Bijou, 232
Birdsall, Horace, 175
Black Hawk's Watch Tower, 227
Black Hills resort, 18–19, 21, 22, 91, 174
Blackwell, Antoinette Brown, 40, 41–42, 43, 125
Blackwell, Elizabeth, 158, 163
Blair, Karen, 263 (n. 29)
Blanke, W. H., 250
Boardinghouses, 22, 26, 85–88, 98, 146, 254–55
Boggs, James, 59
Boles, Henry, 126
Bone, Ambrose, 18–19, 20, 21
Boswell, Lillie, 135
Boydston, Jeanne, 37
Boyle, Victorine, 110
Bracelin, P. M., 139–40
Brennicke, Minnie, 18–20, 21, 27, 239
Bridge House, 225
Bristol, Augusta Cooper, 36, 41, 42
Brothels: and Bucktown, 6, 218, 244; and respectability, 7, 16; cigar stores as, 13, 17, 22, 23, 26, 28, 112, 134; and neighborhoods, 13, 17–18, 21, 23–26, 28, 80, 101; euphemisms for, 17; legal definition of, 21–22; one-woman enterprises, 22; in commercial district, 23, 80; folk history of, 79; and masculine culture, 134; and regulation of prostitution, 159, 163–64, 166, 173, 178, 214–18; mixed-race brothels, 179; and Benedict, 189, 190; brothel keepers as businesswomen, 218–26, 243; closing of, 222, 251–52. *See also* Prostitutes and prostitution
Brown, Alice, 70
Brown, Mary, 95
Bryan, William Jennings, 245
Bryant, Seth, 108
Bucktown: and brothels, 6, 218, 244; and Matlock, 146; and Slate House Hotel, 172–73; and saloons, 182, 213; and Smith, 183; and Himes, 192; and police matrons, 200, 201; and regulation of prostitution, 214–18, 226; and brothel keepers as businesswomen, 218–26; and theaters, 227, 228–29, 231–32, 237, 241, 254; and dance halls, 227–28, 229, 231, 232–37, 241, 254; and women's employment, 237–39; unregistered women banned from, 240, 244
Burke, Mattie, 95–97, 99, 100, 179, 221
Burmeister, Minnie, 177
Burns, Jessie, 137
Burns, Nellie, 137, 273 (n. 43)
Burtis Opera House, 24, 228, 237
Busey, Jacob, 1, 5, 6
Bushnell, Kate, 16
Butler, Josephine, 162

Campbell, Bartley, 228
Cantwell, Alonzo, 171
Carey, Henry C., 37
Carpenter, Henry, 133, 140–44, 147, 149–53, 156, 161, 177
Catholic reformatories, 186–87, 193, 195. *See also* Good Shepherd Homes
Catholics: and Young Women's Christian Associations, 34; and working girls' clubs,

35; population of, 187; and Good Shepherd Home placement, 193, 208; Beauchaine as, 223
Catt, Carrie Chapman, 43
Chamberlin, William, 1, 4, 5, 6, 151, 152, 171, 173, 247
Charitable Alliance: groups involved in, 104–5; and police matron campaign, 104, 105, 106–11, 119, 120, 122, 124, 127, 128, 130, 184, 246; name of, 105–6; and 1891–92 rape trials, 138; and police matron's hiring, 159; and suppression of prostitution, 159; and Bucktown, 213–14
Chauncey, George, 135
Chautauquan, 17
Cheney, Ednah Dow, 17, 41
Chicago, Burlington, & Quincy railroad, 10
Chicago, Milwaukee, & St. Paul railroad, 10, 175
Chicago, Rock Island, & Pacific railroad, 10, 24, 26, 94, 97, 177, 217–18
Children: child prostitutes, 90, 134, 135, 145, 150, 157, 271 (n. 7); children's jail facility, 103, 104; child-rape, 139; juvenile court system, 188, 191, 195, 197, 200, 201, 211, 212
Children's Aid Society of New York, 126
Chinese residents, 26, 196
Cigar factories, 51
Cigarmakers' International Union, 32, 33
Cigar making, 32, 250
Citizenship: and women's employment, 31, 38, 40; and free-labor discourse, 37, 38, 262 (n. 17); and motherhood, 128; and Working Woman's Lend a Hand club, 246
Citizens' League, 183, 184, 248
Civil disobedience, and Prohibition, 2–3, 12, 110, 116, 118, 181, 185
Civil War, 7, 30–31, 38, 56, 59, 74
Clarissa Cook Home for the Friendless, 48–49, 56, 57, 63, 263 (n. 3)
Clarke, E. H., 125
Clarke, Kittie, 158
Class-bridging organizations, 34, 35, 36
Claussen, Ernst, 3, 115–16
Claussen, Hans Reimer, 3

Clay, Cassius Marcellus, 38
Clay, Laura M., 30, 38, 40, 44
Clay, Mary Ann Warfield, 38
Cleaves, Margaret Abigail, 17, 61, 62, 65, 171
Cleland, John, 228
Clendenen, F. Leslie, 235, 237
Clerical work, 43, 68, 217
Cleveland, Barney, 96
Cleveland, Eliza, 96
Cleveland, Jane, 96
Coeducational institutions, 62
Colby, Clara Bewick, 44
Colville, Mary, 74–75, 80
Companionate marriage, 16, 28, 30
Concert saloons, 228–29
Contagious Diseases Acts, 162, 163
Cook, Clarissa, 49, 263 (n. 3)
Cook, Ebenezer, 49
Cook, Edna. *See* Gallagher, Jessie
Cook, Ruel, 144, 147, 149
Cooke, Martha A., 68
Cook Home. *See* Clarissa Cook Home for the Friendless
Cosgrove, Henry, 239–40, 241, 242
Coverture, 37
Craine, Clara, 76, 258
Craton, Abbie Meacham, 56–57
Craton, Lenial, 57
Craton, William, 56–57
Crawford, Jennings, 169, 170–72, 179
Creckbaum, Jennie, 19–20
Crime: and gender, 123–24; and hereditary degeneration, 124–30
Crittenton Homes, 176 (n. 8)
Croly, Jane, 47
Cross-dressing, 1, 4–5, 6, 232
Cullivan, Mary, 94, 95, 226
Cummings, May, 176
Cummins, Albert, 250, 251

Dall, Caroline H., 7, 14
Dance cultures, 233–34, 235
Dance halls: and women's employment, 214, 229, 231, 236, 240–41, 243; and Bucktown, 227–28, 229, 231, 232–37, 241, 254; and culture of treating, 234–35, 236, 237; closure of, 240, 242

307

Index

Daughters of the American Revolution, 254
Davenport Academy of Natural Science, 108, 109–10, 129
Davenport Civic Federation, 250, 251
Davenport Daily Tribune: and Belva Lockwood Club parade, 5, 6; and Kreps, 114; and women's jail facility, 119; and Ammerman, 137; and 1891–92 rape trials, 147, 149, 150
Davenport Democrat: and Prohibition, 3; and women's public roles, 4–5; and unions, 33; and regulation of prostitution, 84, 168; and May, 90; and Ammerman rape case, 137; and O'Meara, 153; and Hamerly, 154, 155; and Woods, 156; and Wilson, 172; assignation houses, 177; and Himes, 186, 191, 192; and Good Shepherd Homes, 195; and Beauchaine, 223; and Ray, 237; and Cosgrove's crusade against vice, 239–40; and Working Woman's Lend a Hand club, 245; and Peck, 248; and mulct law, 250; and McCowen Hall, 254
Davenport Democrat and Leader: and incest, 199–200; and white slavery, 237–38; and Bucktown reforms, 240, 242; and brothel closings, 251, 252; and women's employment, 256
Davenport Democrat-Gazette: and Belva Lockwood Club parade, 6; and Kreps, 113–14, 116, 118, 131; and women's jail facility, 119, 120, 122; and police matron campaign, 123
Davenport Gas Light Company, 225
Davenport Gazette, 31, 227
Davenport Ministerial Association, 235
Davenport Morning Tribune, 120
Davenport Nurses' Association (DNA), 74, 77
Davenport Republican, 191
Davenport Theater, 236
Davenport Times: and Kreps, 114, 116; and regulation of saloons, 114–16; and Ammerman, 136–38; and 1891–92 rape trials, 144, 145, 149, 150; and DeMaranville, 151; and regulation of prostitution, 168; and assignation houses, 177; and Bucktown reforms, 240

Davenport Visiting Nurses Association, 76
Davis, Annie, 133, 147, 148, 158–59, 166, 179, 190, 215
DeArmond, J. A., 140
Debs, Eugene, 245
Dell, Floyd, 234–35
DeMaranville, Adelbert, 86–87, 151, 152, 153–54, 218
Democracy, and women's dependency, 39, 40
Democratic Party: and Belva Lockwood parade, 4; and John McCowen, 59; and city government, 116, 183; and regulation of prostitution, 161; and Vollmer, 164
Department stores, 51, 53, 217
Dependency: of working women, 34, 35, 255, 256, 258; of slaves, 36–37; and industrialization, 37; and citizenship, 37, 38; women's stigmatization as dependent class, 39–40; and women's wages, 236
Der Demokrat, 249
Deutsch, Sarah, 36, 107
DeVoe, Emma Smith, 246
Devoll, Sarah, 102
Dillon, Millie, 21, 22, 91
Dime savings program, 71
Diston, May, 176
Ditzen, Henry, 198, 200
Dodge, Grace, 35, 50, 65
Dolphin, Edward, 223
Dolphin, Lee, 223
Dolphin, Mamie, 223
Dolphin, Sabina, 223
Domestic servants: and migrant women, 12; and women's employment, 32; and Working Woman's Lend a Hand club, 68; and African Americans in Midwest, 97; and mothers, 100; Kreps as, 111–12; and girls in Good Shepherd Homes, 194; population of, 217
Domestic sphere: and women's employment, 8, 15, 31, 32, 111; protection of, 9; and middle class, 28, 55; and respectability, 28, 243; and unions, 32, 37; and benevolent organizations, 34–35, 36, 38;

Index

and loss of men in Civil War, 56; and private reformatories, 210
Doremus, J. P., 12
Douglass, Frederick, 5
DuBois, Ellen, 40
Dugdale, Richard, 124–26

Economic self-sufficiency, 37
Edgar, Mrs. J. B., 110
Education: coeducational institutions, 62; and Working Woman's Lend a Hand club, 71–72, 76, 78; and nursing, 74, 76; and cooking schools, 75; and prostitution, 89, 95, 101; and hereditarian theories, 125
Edwards, Rebecca, 107
Eldridge, Annie, 77
Elite men: women's links to, 107, 108, 110; and gendered geography, 117; and dance halls, 234
Elite women: and benevolent organizations, 34, 35, 36; and women's employment, 41; and Association for the Advancement of Women, 42; and cartographies of gender, 53; and King's Daughters, 67
England, 162
Entertainment: and Davenport, 11–12, 13, 110; and regulation of prostitution, 161, 181; and mulct law, 181, 182; and Bucktown, 200, 213, 229, 242–43; parasexual entertainment, 214, 231, 236, 239, 243
Environment: and hereditary degeneration, 124–25, 127, 128; household definition of, 127; neighborhood definition of, 127, 128, 129, 130
Equal Rights Party, 2, 3–4
Etiquette, and respectability, 53–54, 207
Eugenic theories, 124

Fairchild, Ruth, 202
Fales, Imogene, 41
Falkner, Charles, 98, 99, 158, 159
Fall, Isaac, 105
Family authority: and private/public dichotomy, 103, 113, 114; and Kreps, 111, 113, 114, 118; and prostitution, 137, 145–49, 212; and Good Shepherd Homes, 188, 192, 193–94, 199, 201, 202–3; and police matrons, 188, 196; and Bucktown reforms, 240
Family intervention, 127
Family wage, 37, 38
Farm (brothel), 18, 174
Feminized culture, values of, 133
Ferd Roddewig and Sons, 225
Ficke, C. A., 248
Fifteenth Amendment, 60
Filene, Edward, 53
Fineschriber, W. H., 191
Finger, Samuel, 23
Fink, Leon, 71
Fisher, L. M., 144
Foote-Sheldon, Sarah, 109
Ford, Mary, 112
Foster, J. Ellen, 3, 42, 260 (n. 4)
Foucault, Michel, 207, 279 (n. 54)
Fowler, Abram, 84
Fowler, Clementine, 85
Fowler, Margaret Kelso, 84
Fowler, Oscar, 84, 85
Fowler, Sevilla, 84
France, 162, 163
Fraser, Nancy, 37, 107
Freedman, Estelle, 47
Free-labor discourse, 8–9, 36–37, 38, 262 (n. 17)
French, Lucius, 171
Friedman, Lawrence, 160
Friendly Visitors, 104, 110, 112, 127
Fugitive Slave Law, 248–49

Gale, Flora, 148
Gale, Florence, 147, 148, 152
Gale, Parker, 148
Gallagher, Jessie, 220–21
Galvin, Perl, 229, 231–32
Gamber, Wendy, 77
Gambling, 133, 219, 225, 226, 239, 242, 243
Ganson, Sanford, 175
Gaskey, Tom, 186, 191
Gender: and free-labor discourse, 37; and crime, 123–24; and private reformatories, 191, 211
Gender difference, 47
Gendered division of labor, 39, 41–42

309

Gendered geography: and Belva Lockwood Club parade, 6; and middle-class women, 6–7, 28, 104, 116–17; and women's changing roles, 6–7, 28, 116; and women's employment, 7, 28, 29, 53, 117, 256; and Working Woman's Lend a Hand club, 51; and urban space, 52–53, 104, 116–17, 234; and police matron campaign, 130; and regulation of prostitution, 217, 246; and dance halls, 234
Gender hierarchies, 5–6, 133, 135
Gender ideology, 16, 80
Gender roles, 245. *See also* Domestic sphere
Gender segregation, 53, 120–21
Gender transgression, 5
German-American Central Association, 248
German cultural identity, 13, 27, 227, 248
German immigrants, 12–13, 71, 116, 163, 164, 227, 248, 250
German Theater, 12, 228
Germany, 3, 162–64
Giglinger, George, 241, 242, 250
Gilmore, Glenda, 62
Ginzburg, Carlo, 13
Glaspell, Barton, 109
Glaspell, Bertha, 109
Glaspell, Martha, 108, 109
Good Shepherd Homes: and regulation of prostitution, 186–88, 276 (n. 2); and state law, 187–92; and police matrons, 188–94, 201, 202, 211, 212, 276 (n. 2), 277 (n. 18), 278 (n. 25); characteristics of girls in, 192–96, 277 (nn. 18, 19); and policing sexual conduct, 196; conditions of, 203–10, 212; girls leaving, 210–11, 279 (n. 62)
Gordon, Linda, 37, 135, 199
Gould, George, 143, 145, 146, 147, 150–51
Grand Opera House, 228
Grant, Ulysses, 38

Hadlai Heights Woman's Hospital, 75–76, 77, 78
Hagan, Andrew Jackson, 90
Hagan, Emma Jane May, 90–91, 92, 268 (n. 23)
Hagan, Minnie, 89–93, 100, 108, 192, 220–21, 222

Haikes, George, 133, 140–44, 147–51, 156
Haines, Emily, 77
Hairdressers, 19
Hale, Edward Everett, 66–67, 106
Hall, Emma A., 122–23, 124, 125, 126, 129
Hamburg, Germany, 162, 163–64
Hamerly, Bennie, 155
Hamerly, Dolly, 132, 133, 136, 138–45, 147–51, 154–56, 166–67, 187
Hamerly, John, 145, 154–56
Hamerly, Mabel, 155
Hamerly, Mary, 140, 148, 154, 155
Hamerly, Rosa, 140, 155
Hamerly, Zip, 140, 155, 221
Hampton, Lizzie, 27
Harper, Frances E. W., 42
Harris, Elisha, 125, 126
Harris, Maud, 225
Hart, Patterson, 175
Harugari, 227
Hass, Henry, 151–52, 153, 154, 160
Haughs, Nora, 179
Hawkins, William, 86
Hayden, Dolores, 75
Hebrew Ladies Society, 105
Heinrichs, Mr., 18
Heinrichs, Mrs., 18, 19–20
Heinz, Carrie, 254
Helena, Mont., 218
Hendricksen, Lizzie Huber, 85, 89
Hereditary degeneration, 123, 124–30
Herrold, Ed, 176
Hibernian Hall, 176–77, 178
Hill, Fanny, 228
Hill, R. W., 129
Hill, Sarah: appointment as police matron, 166; and regulation of prostitution, 168, 184, 215; and African Americans, 179; and Industrial School for Girls, 187; and Good Shepherd Homes, 188–98, 202, 276 (n. 2), 277 (n. 18); influence on families, 193; network for referring endangered girls, 194; records of, 195, 201–2, 215, 217; success stories of, 198, 202–3, 210; protection of girls, 199, 200–201, 202, 203, 237, 251–52; and Bucktown, 200, 201

Index

Himes, Eva, 186, 188, 189, 191–92, 195, 202, 209, 210
Himes, Mary, 186, 191–92
Hobson Vaudeville Theater, 229
Home Cooking Company, 74–75, 77, 78, 254
Homes for the friendless, 188
Hoochie-coochie, 231, 232, 234
Hotels, 22, 24, 26, 53, 227
Household labor, 37, 39–40
Household production, 30–31
House of Detention: and Ackley House arrests, 103; and Charitable Alliance, 104, 106, 119, 246; opposition to, 119–24
Housewives, 37
Hovey, W. W., 219
Howard, J. H., 95
Howard, Nettie, 110
Howe, Julia Ward, 46, 47
Hubbell, C. H., 183, 184
Huber, Charles, 222
Huber, Clara, 89, 222
Huber, Ernst, 88, 89
Huber, Kate, 85, 88–89, 93, 98, 100, 221–22, 268 (n. 15)
Huber, Lena, 88, 89
Hughes, John Joseph, 196
Hull House, 269 (n. 9)
Hurto, Elsie Mae, 148
Hutchins, E. R., 45
Hutchins, Sylvia, 96, 97

Illinois Women's Alliance, 105
Illiteracy, and prostitutes, 84, 100
Industrialization, 7, 32, 37, 117
Industrial School for Girls, Mitchellville: and Kreps, 112, 113, 118, 119, 131; and environment, 119, 127, 187; and Hamerly, 155, 156; riot of, 188; records of, 276 (n. 4)
Interracial sex, 177, 179, 196
Iowa: Prohibition law of, 2–3, 260 (n. 27); and illiteracy, 84
Iowa Bureau of Labor, 45, 46, 217
Iowa Commercial College, 24
Iowa Commission for the World's Industrial and Cotton Exposition, 44

Iowa legislature, 2–4, 22, 43, 134–35, 181, 183, 246–47, 250–51, 257
Iowa State Hospital for the Insane, 57, 61, 62, 63
Iowa State Teachers Association, 109
Iowa Supreme Court, 3, 20
Iowa Theater, 225–26, 229, 231, 232, 237, 238, 241

Jackson, Grace, 221
Jacobs, P. N., 12
Jacobsen, David, 174, 177
Jacobsen, Mrs. David, 174, 177
Jansen, J. H., 172, 173, 175
Jenness Miller, Annie, 73
Jensen, Joan, 233–34
Jews, 8–9, 34, 35, 194
John Deer Plow Works, 11
Juvenile court system, 188, 191, 195, 197, 200, 201, 211, 212

Kansas, 6
Kaposi, Moritz, 164–65, 170
Kasch, Lena, 142–43, 144
Kaufman, Polly Welts, 264–65 (n. 25)
Keely, Sarah, 128
Keller, Birdie, 220
Keller, Ella Dunning Gross, 219
Keller, Lafe, 87, 151, 219
Keller, Lyman, 84, 85, 153, 219
Keller, Naomi Josephine Fowler. *See* Mitchell, Josie
Keller, Oscar Lafayette, 84
Keller, Sevilla Clementine, 84, 86–87, 88, 218, 219
Keller, William, 84–85, 86
Keller, William (son), 84, 219
Kelley, Florence, 36, 62
Kemmerer, Theodor H., 248, 249, 250, 282 (n. 8)
Kepley, Ada H., 134
Kessler, Frank: and Beauchaine, 99; and private intervention, 113, 114, 116, 120, 127; and regulation of saloons, 114–16; and O'Meara, 114–18, 152; middle-class women, 117, 130–31; and Ammerman, 132, 140; and police conduct rules, 154;

311

and Presley, 155, 166, 167; and prostitutes, 158, 159; and regulation of prostitution, 170–71; and assignation houses, 173, 174; and Smith, 184
Kessler-Harris, Alice, 8, 37
King, Minnie, 176
King's Daughters, 67–68, 72, 74, 104, 109, 255, 258, 266 (n. 43)
Kiter, Joseph, 91–92, 93, 221
Knights of Labor, 32, 46, 71, 105
Kohlsaat, Maggie, 175–76
Krantz, Emma, 167
Krebs, Jane, 26
Kreps, Albert, 111
Kreps, Ollie, 102–3, 104, 111–14, 118–20, 122, 123, 127–31, 138, 239, 240
Kuhnen, Nicholas, 24, 32–34, 51
Kulp, John H., 171
Kunzel, Regina, 210

Labor: and free-labor discourse, 8–9, 36–37, 38, 262 (n. 17); and union wages, 31–34; household, 37, 39–40; gendered division of, 39, 41–42; women's labor associations, 46
Ladies Catholic Union, 105, 110
Ladies Christian Association, 26
Ladies Industrial Relief Society (LIRS), 104, 109, 110, 114, 127, 222
Lahrman's Hall, 227
Lamarckian genetics, 124, 127
Lapham, Ella, 41
Larrabee, William, 3
Lau, Elizabeth, 74–75
Law: and prostitution, 4, 20–22, 29, 100, 133, 238; rape law, 4, 134–36, 137, 139, 143–50, 180; local ordinances, 9, 21; and women's right to control property, 99; and separate spheres, 107; and gender and crime, 123; malfeasance law, 161, 251, 252, 257; mulct law, 181–84, 213, 222, 226–27, 229, 241, 248–51; and private reformatories, 187–92; Moon law, 282 (n. 15)
Lebsock, Suzanne, 13
Lee, Ned, 191
Leisure culture: in nineteenth century, 10; women's leisure, 37. *See also* Male leisure

Lend a Hand (journal), 67, 106
Lend a Hand club. *See* Working Woman's Lend a Hand club
Levy, Abe, 221
Lewdness, 21, 22, 232
Livermore, Mary, 56
Local ordinances: and prostitution, 9, 21
Lockwood, Belva, 1–4, 5, 6, 42, 151, 171, 247
Lofland, Lyn, 53
Lombroso, Cesare, 124
Long, Mason, 136
Love, Alfred, 5
Lowell, Josephine Shaw, 126, 127
Lynde, Mrs. W. P., 126
Lyon, Charles, 133, 140–45, 147, 149–51, 154, 156, 161, 177

Male leisure: and prostitution, 4; and women's public roles, 6; and sporting culture, 18, 91, 133, 148, 156–57, 219, 229, 234; and Bucktown, 182. *See also* Masculine culture
Malfeasance law, 161, 251, 252, 257
Mann Act. *See* White Slave Traffic Act
Manwaring, Harry "Jock," 229, 231, 232, 241, 242, 250
Marriage: and women's rights, 8; companionate marriage, 16, 28, 30; and women's employment, 31, 38
Martens, Henry, 184
Masculine culture: and saloons, 52, 133, 227, 239, 249; and sexual gratification, 133, 135–36, 137, 150, 151, 156, 157, 160, 164–65, 180, 185, 243; and brothels, 134; and politics of protection, 151
Material feminism, 75
Matlock, John, 132, 133, 140, 146, 151–54, 156–57, 160
Matlock, Lucy, 132–33, 140, 142, 144, 145–47, 150, 152, 153, 156
Matlock v. Hass (1892), 152
Maudsley, Henry, 125
May, M. E., 174, 175–76
McCowen, Elizabeth Stokes, 59
McCowen, Israel, 58, 59, 60
McCowen, Jennie: and respectability, 14–

15, 17; and gendered geography, 29; and politics, 29, 38, 60–61, 246; and Association for the Advancement of Women, 43–44; and women's employment statistics, 43–46; and women's clubs, 47; and Clarissa Cook Home for the Friendless, 48–49, 63; and Working Woman's Lend a Hand club, 50, 55, 65, 67, 68, 71, 72, 78, 254; office of, 51, 62; family background of, 57–60; medical studies of, 61–62, 265 (n. 28); and Hadlai Heights Woman's Hospital, 75; and Craine, 76; and Bickford, 77; and proximity of brothels, 80; and Charitable Alliance, 105, 106, 138; and police matron campaign, 108, 109, 110, 122–23, 217, 246; and hereditary degeneration, 128–30, 131; and police matron, 159; and regulation of prostitution, 168, 171, 172; and woman suffrage, 246, 257; death of, 257–58

McCowen, John, 57, 58–59
McCowen, Maria Taylor, 58, 59
McCowen, Mary, 58, 61, 75, 76, 265 (n. 28)
McCowen, Susan, 265 (n. 28)
McCowen Hall, 254–55
McCrum, Anna J. S., 48–49, 50, 55, 64–65, 68, 110
McCrum, William, 64
McEnnis, John, 17
McGaughey, J. B., 162
McKinley, William, 245
McPartland, John, 131, 174–75, 229, 232, 241
McPartland, Mrs. John, 174–75
Meacham, Calvin, 56
Meacham, Elvira, 56
Meacham, Emily, 56
Meacham, Laura, 56
Meacham, Lettie: and women's employment statistics, 45, 46; and Clarissa Cook Home for the Friendless, 50, 63; and respectability, 55, 65; family background of, 56–57; and migration, 64; and Working Woman's Lend a Hand club, 68; and employment opportunities, 239; and domestic service, 264 (n. 18)
Meckel, Anna, 70

Men: and Belva Lockwood parade, 1, 4–6, 245–46; and gendered geography, 6–7, 130; and free-labor discourse, 9; attitudes towards prostitutes, 16; and respectability, 28; and Civil War, 30; and unions, 32, 34; and benevolent organizations, 36; and separate spheres, 37–38, 106–7, 108; and saloons, 52, 54, 69, 71, 116; and coeducational institutions, 62; and public policy, 103–4; and Charitable Alliance, 105, 106; protection of jailed women from, 120–22, 130, 256; and hereditary degeneration, 126, 129; responsibilities of, 130, 137; and age of consent, 135; girls' charges against, 196–97. *See also* Male leisure; Masculine culture
Merrill, Claude, 18, 22
Metropolitan Hotel, 174, 175–76, 236
Meyerowitz, Joanne, 236
Middle class: and companionate marriage, 16; and domestic sphere, 28, 55; prostitution and, 79, 80; and environment, 127; and dance halls, 234
Middle-class men: and domestic sphere, 37; and saloons, 52; and sexual gratification, 135–36; and dance halls, 235
Middle-class women: and gendered geography, 6–7, 28, 104, 116–17; and employment, 7, 9, 30, 53; and benevolent organizations, 34, 112; and literary societies, 35; and woman suffrage, 40; and woman's clubs, 47; and cartographies of gender, 53; and respectability, 53, 55; and hereditary degeneration, 126–27; and urban geography, 130–31; and Working Woman's Lend a Hand club, 254
Mill, John Stuart, 34, 246
Miller, Isaias, 195
Miller, Maud, 172, 173
Mills, Mamie, 177
Minstrels, 228, 281 (n. 33)
Miscegenation law, 196
Mitchell, Ellen, 16
Mitchell, Frank, 85
Mitchell, Josie: marriages of, 84, 85, 86, 100, 267–68 (n. 11); profile of, 84–88; and boarders, 85, 86, 87, 88, 98, 146; and

Hendrickson, 85, 89; and brothels, 86, 87, 93, 153, 218–20; relatives of, 151, 226; and Matlock, 153
Mitchell, Maria, 42
Mitchellville Girls' School. *See* Industrial School for Girls, Mitchellville
Mix, George, 112
Mobility: social mobility, 36–37, 38, 72; and railroads, 49, 64; and urbanization, 53; gender barriers to travel, 60, 64; Hale on, 67
Modesty, 206–8, 212
Moline, Ill., 10–11, 19, 48, 112
Mooney, Louise, 256, 257
Moon law, 282 (n. 15)
Moore, Henrietta, 247
Morals: moral authority of benevolent organizations, 34–35; and outsider status, 38; and woman suffrage, 40, 247; and 1891–92 rape trials, 143–49, 150; and regulated prostitution, 164, 171; and African American women, 180; and Good Shepherd Homes, 203, 207; and dance halls, 233, 235, 237
Morris, John, 161–62
Morrow, Myrtle, 158
Mosher, Eliza, 42
Motherhood: language of, 34; maternal causes, 38; and prostitution, 100, 168; and hereditarian origins of crime, 124; Republican Motherhood, 124, 128
Mother Hubbard gown, 5, 6, 158
Mott, Lucretia, 38
Mulct law, 181–84, 213, 222, 226–27, 229, 241, 248–51
Munro, James "Brick," 229, 232–37, 241, 242–43, 250
Murdoch, Ezra, 91–92
Mutuality, 66, 67, 73, 255, 258

Napoleonic Wars, 162
Nathan, Charles, 231
Nathan, Mamie, 231
National American Woman Suffrage Association (NAWSA), 246
National Conference of Charities and Correction (NCCC), 122–23, 126, 128
National Women's Republican Association, 3
Neal, C. W., 248, 249, 250
Needle trades, 32
Neighborhoods: and population, 10; and brothels, 13, 17–18, 21, 23–26, 28, 101; and reputation, 17–18, 26, 112; and respectability, 18, 24–25, 27–28, 130; and women's employment, 111–12; and prostitution, 119, 124, 146; and women's jail facility, 119–20; and hereditary degeneration, 127, 128, 129, 130; and assignation houses, 178
Nelson, Nell, 105, 238
New Century Working Women's Guild, 36
Newcome House, 51
New York, N.Y., 79, 80
Nichol, Adella, 168, 171
Noon Rest, 254, 255, 258
North Carolina, 22
Nursing, 7, 57, 63, 74, 76

Occupations: and women's advancement, 7, 42; social acceptability of, 40–41. *See also* Women's employment
Odem, Mary, 211
Offerman's Island, 227
Office workers, 28
Oldendorf, Henry, 88
Olympic Theater, 228
O'Meara, Roger, 114–18, 126–27, 130–31, 152–53, 156–57
Order of the Eastern Star, 105
Orphanages, 188
Orpheon, 229, 231, 232, 241
Osborne, Sarah, 110
Outing Club, 174
Outsider status, 32, 38, 172

P. N. Jacob's Summer Garden, 12
Palace Hotel, 241
Parasexual entertainment, 214, 231, 236, 239, 243
Parent-Duchâelet, Alexandre, 162
Parents. *See* Family authority
Pascoe, Peggy, 210
Patronage, 107

Patterson, Wilson, 177
Pavilion, 229, 232–37, 241, 242, 250
Peck, Maria Purdy, 247, 248
Peck, Robert, 170, 171
Peck, W. F., 170
Peiss, Kathy, 10, 113, 234
Penny, Virginia, 7, 30, 31, 33, 41, 56
Perl Galvin's Summer Garden, 229, 231
Perry, Lou, 176, 177
Peters, Bleik, 151
Petrik, Paula, 218
Phillips, Harry, 242
Phillips, Lewis, 96
Phillips, Mary, 96
Phillips, Nannie, 96
Physicians: and child-rape cases, 139; and regulation of prostitution, 161, 164, 168–71. *See also* Scott County Medical Society
Pieceworkers, 32, 33, 73, 206
Pitts, Linsey, 96–97, 177, 218
Polacheck, Hilda, 9
Police: and cigar stores, 22; and vagrancy, 23; and neighborhoods, 26–27; and prostitution, 28, 98, 156–57, 160; and public policy, 103–4; regulation of saloons, 104, 114–16, 118; protection of jailed women from, 120–22, 130, 256; and conspiracy, 152–54, 160; and blackmail of prostitutes, 153; regulation of prostitution, 160, 161, 162, 163, 166, 173–74, 221, 248; and Mamie Magee Beauchaine, 172; and assignation houses, 174, 175; and African American prostitutes, 178, 179; and Bucktown, 200; and theaters, 228, 232; and dance halls, 237; and brothel closings, 251
Police matron campaign: and Kreps, 102–3, 104, 111–13; and private/public dichotomy, 103, 106, 113–19, 120; and public policy, 103–4, 110; and Charitable Alliance, 104, 105, 106–11, 119, 120, 122, 124, 127, 128, 130, 184, 246; and national reform campaigns, 104, 108, 122, 130; and petitions, 106, 107; and appointment of police matrons, 106–7; and respectability, 110–11, 121, 130; opposition to, 119–24, 130; and hereditary degeneration, 124–30; role of police matron, 131

Police matrons: and home protection, 4; and 1891–92 rape trials, 133, 147; and regulation of prostitution, 158–59, 166, 168, 184, 214, 215, 246; and African American prostitutes, 178, 179; and Good Shepherd Homes, 188–94, 201, 202, 211, 212, 276 (n. 2), 277 (n. 18), 278 (n. 25); and policing sexual conduct, 196–203; and Bucktown, 200, 201; and theaters, 238; and brothel closings, 251–52
Political economy, and Hall, 122, 123
Political equality, and women's employment, 47
Political parades, 6
Politics: and women's employment, 7–8, 39–42, 255; and Jennie McCowen, 29, 38, 60–61, 246; and elite women, 36; and separate spheres, 37–38, 106–7, 108; and Working Woman's Lend a Hand club, 51; and McCowen family, 57–58; and police matron appointment, 107; and Ammerman rape case, 138; and protection, 151; and regulation of prostitution, 161, 165. *See also* Public policy; Women's public roles
Poor women: and respectability, 7, 28, 53, 117; and wages, 31, 34; struggles of, 110; and gendered geography, 130; and Contagious Diseases Acts, 162; and regulation of prostitution, 164; and Good Shepherd Homes, 194–95. *See also* Poverty
Population: growth of, 9; and neighborhoods, 10; characteristics of, 11; of Catholics, 187; of prostitutes, 215, 217, 279–80 (nn. 6, 7); of domestic servants, 217
Porter, William, 174, 176, 177
Poverty: women's dependency compared with condition of paupers, 39; and prostitution, 80, 90, 96, 101, 113, 122, 184, 257; and Kreps, 111–12, 113, 118; and hereditary degeneration, 124, 125, 126; and environment, 127. *See also* Poor women
Pratt, Lucy, 80
Presley, Eva, 155–56, 166
Press: and women's employment, 14–15; and prostitutes, 16, 19, 20, 22, 26–27, 79, 81, 89–90, 92, 98, 182–83, 186; and

315

Index

unions, 33; and public policy, 103–4; and police matron campaign, 106; and Kreps, 111, 113–14, 127; and women's jail facility, 119–20, 122; and McCowen, 129; and Ammerman rape case, 136–38; and 1891–92 rape trials, 149; and Davis, 159; and assignation houses, 178; and Good Shepherd Home placement, 195; and theaters, 228; and Bucktown reforms, 241. *See also specific newspapers*

Private/public dichotomy: and police matron campaign, 103, 106, 113–19, 120; and Bucktown reforms, 240

Private reformatories, 187–92, 197, 210, 211, 276 (n. 6)

Progressive Era, 128, 161, 164, 191

Prohibition: and civil disobedience, 2–3, 12, 110, 116, 118, 181, 185; and women's public roles, 3, 4; overturning of, 3, 260 (n. 27); and politics, 151, 181; and Vollmer, 164; and anti-mulct-law protests, 249; and consent decrees, 250

Prohibition and Home Protection Party, 3, 4

Property ownership, 8, 43

Prostitute identity: and vagrancy, 7, 22–23; and reputation, 18, 19, 20–21, 22, 29; and regulation of prostitution, 168, 173; and saloons, 227; and dance halls, 236; and theaters, 238; and Bucktown, 243–44

Prostitutes and prostitution: and rape law, 4, 134–36, 137, 150; and Mother Hubbard gown, 5, 6; toleration of, 6, 9, 103, 123–24, 129, 130, 131, 154, 156–57, 159, 160, 161, 163, 212, 229, 256; and gendered geography, 6, 28; women's employment associated with, 7, 8, 9, 16, 17, 28, 29, 31, 255; and local and state jurisdiction, 9, 21; and urban migration, 12; and saloons, 13, 23, 52, 114–15, 181–82; and reputation, 15–16, 17, 20, 21, 22, 29, 86, 88, 101; and zoning, 16, 160, 243; legal definition of prostitute, 20–21, 29; arrests for, 28; and theaters, 53, 228; and respectability, 54, 130; history of, 79, 81; and poverty, 80, 90, 96, 101, 113, 122, 184, 257; and urban space, 80, 101, 103, 104, 110, 120; characteristics of prostitutes, 80–81, 99–100; profiles of prostitutes, 81, 84–99; child prostitutes, 90, 134, 135, 145, 150, 157, 271 (n. 7); and police matrons, 104; and women's jail facility, 119; and neighborhoods, 119, 124, 146; and gender and crime, 123–24; and hereditary degeneration, 126, 127, 131; recruitment of prostitutes, 134, 135, 150, 176, 177; campaigns against, 134–36; and masculine culture, 136, 156, 157, 243; and family authority, 137, 145–49, 212; and parental consent, 166–67; and assignation houses, 174, 175–76; and Good Shepherd Homes, 194, 195; and girls who left reformatories, 211; population of prostitutes, 215, 217, 279–80 (nn. 6, 7); and dance halls, 236; and red-light abatement act, 251; and brothel closings, 251–52; dangers of, 256–57. *See also* Regulation of prostitution

Protection: age of, 4, 133, 135; of domestic sphere, 9; and women's dependency, 38; jailed women protected from men, 120–22, 130, 256; and politics, 151; and toleration of prostitution, 160; and regulation of prostitution, 161, 168; police matrons' protection of girls, 199, 200–201, 202, 203, 237, 251–52

Protestant reformatories, 210

Protestants, 34, 194

Public policy: and women's employment statistics, 45; and gender difference, 47; and woman's clubs, 47; and Jennie McCowen, 61, 246; and prostitution, 81, 99, 103, 118, 128, 159–60, 180, 187, 212, 246; and police matron campaign, 103–4, 110; and Charitable Alliance, 104–11; and hereditary degeneration, 124–30; and Bucktown, 239–40. *See also* Politics; Women's public roles

Public sphere, and separate spheres, 37–38, 106–7, 108, 171

Putnam, Mary L. D., 109–10

Putnam, W. C., 174

R. G. Dun and Company, 77–78

Racial issues: and Belva Lockwood Club

316

Index

parade, 5; interracial sex, 177, 179, 196; and regulation of prostitution, 178–80

Racism: and neighborhoods, 26; and prostitution, 96; and public civility towards African Americans, 179

Railroads: and mobility, 49, 64; and women's travel, 60; and tensions with workers, 94

Railroad shops, 11

Ranney, Mark, 61–62

Rape accusations, 139, 161, 197, 198, 237, 238

Rape law: and age of consent, 4, 134–35, 136, 139, 143, 149, 150; and prostitution, 4, 134–36, 137, 150; and defense of accused men, 143–49, 150; and African American women, 180

Rape trials of 1891–92: and gender hierarchies, 133; and conspiracy, 133, 150, 151–54; and age of consent, 136, 139; and defense of accused men, 143–49; and verdicts, 149–51; consequences of, 154–57, 160

Rape victims, 200, 212

Ray, Anita, 213, 237–39, 241

Red-light abatement act, 251, 257

Reformatories for women: and environment, 127, 128; private reformatories, 187–92, 197, 210, 211, 276 (n. 6). *See also* Good Shepherd Homes; Industrial School for Girls, Mitchellville

Reforms and reformers: and women's public roles, 4; national reform campaigns, 104, 108, 122, 130; futility of prostitution reform efforts, 133; and age of consent, 135; and rape law, 150; and regulation of prostitution, 159, 163, 183, 184; and private reformatories, 189, 276 (n. 6); and children who perform in public, 195; and rape victims, 200; and dance halls, 233; and Cosgrove, 239–40, 241, 242

Regulation of prostitution: and police matrons, 158–59, 166, 168, 184, 214, 215, 246; and brothels, 159, 163, 166, 173, 178, 214–18; and Vollmer, 160–61, 164, 168, 171, 173, 178–80, 181, 184, 187, 213, 214–15, 220, 243, 248; trans-Atlantic debates on, 161, 162–65, 170; and protection of men, 161, 168; and licensing system, 166–72; and assignation houses, 172–78; and African Americans, 178–80; and municipal income, 181–84; and Smith, 183–84; and Good Shepherd Homes, 186–88, 212, 276 (n. 2); and brothel keepers as businesswomen, 218–26; and men's access to prostitution, 241; and suffrage convention, 247–48

Reimers and Fernald candy factory, 25

Republican Motherhood, 124, 128

Republican Party: and Prohibition, 4; and alliance of African Americans and Prohibitionists, 6; and free-labor discourse, 8, 36–37; and role of government in social problems, 115–16; and regulation of prostitution, 161, 184; and Smith, 183, 184; and Bucktown reforms, 242

Reputation: importance of, 7; and prostitution, 15–16, 17, 20, 21, 22, 29, 86, 88, 101; and women's employment, 16; establishment of, 17; and neighborhoods, 17–18, 26, 112; and men's sexual gratification, 137; and saloons, 227

Respectability: and gendered geography, 6, 117; and women's employment, 7, 9, 16–17, 20, 40, 53–54, 74, 256; and McCowen, 14–15, 17; respectable women vs. prostitutes, 15–16, 18, 20, 27–28, 29, 136, 145; and neighborhoods, 18, 24–25, 27–28, 130; and domestic sphere, 28, 243; and benevolent organizations, 35; and cartographies of gender, 53; and middle-class women, 53, 55; and Working Woman's Lend a Hand club, 65; and police matron campaign, 110–11, 121, 130; and Kreps, 118; and little girls, 133, 136; and regulation of prostitution, 173; and urban space, 214; and saloons, 226–27, 229; and alcoholic beverages, 227; and theaters, 228, 231, 232, 243; and dance halls, 236, 243

Retreat, 189

Revolution, The, 17

Richter, August, 3, 249

Riddle, William, 145–46

Robinson, C. H., 150
Robison, Charles, 86, 153
Rock Island, 11, 12, 48, 76, 146, 252
Rock Island & Peoria railroad, 10
Roediger, David, 8
Rollins, G. S., 247–48
Rosenkranz, Clara, 256
Rothman, David, 191
Ryan, John, 172, 173
Ryan, Mary, 53

St. James Hotel, 175
St. Louis, Mo., 161, 163, 164
St. Luke's Hospital, 76
Salmon, Lucy, 74
Saloons: and Prohibition, 2–3, 110, 164, 181; and prostitution, 13, 23, 52, 114–15, 181–82; and German culture, 13, 27; and neighborhoods, 24, 27, 111–12; and men, 52, 54, 69, 71, 116; and masculine culture, 52, 133, 227, 239, 249; police's regulation of, 104, 114–16, 118; and Vollmer, 174; and mulct law, 181–83, 248–51; and Bucktown, 182, 213; and women's employment, 200–201, 214; and presence and display of women, 214, 227, 240; and brothels, 219; and Woodward, 225, 226; wine rooms of, 227, 239, 240, 241, 248, 249; concert saloons, 228–29; and theaters, 229–32; injunctions against, 248–49; and Moon law, 282 (n. 15)
Salvation Army, 176 (n. 8)
Sanger, William, 80–81, 100–101
Santry, May, 50, 55, 65, 72, 74, 77
Santry, William, 65
Sauer, William, 65
Schestedt, Doris, 88
Schleswig-Holstein, 3, 11
Schramm, Gretchen, 256
Schwerdtfeger, Annie, 176
Scott, G. W., 251–52
Scott County, 3
Scott County Medical Society, 44, 62, 108, 168–71, 178, 184, 246
Seduction, and prostitution, 80
Seneca Falls convention of 1848, 38
Separate spheres, 37–38, 106–7, 108, 171

Separatism, and women's organizations, 47
Seraglios, 8
Sexual assault, protection of jailed women from, 122
Sexual assertiveness, and women's employment, 16
Sexual desire: and prostitution, 80, 81, 95, 100–101, 185; and African American women, 180
Sexual gratification, and masculine culture, 133, 135–36, 137, 150, 151, 156, 157, 160, 164–65, 180, 185, 243
Sexuality, African-American, 180; men's, 9, 133, 135–36, 137, 151, 156, 164–65; as economic commodity, 16, 113, 118, 214, 228–29, 256; women's, 100–101; and urban danger, 117, 130; and hereditary degeneration, 126–27; and Sisters of the Good Shepherd, 207, 212
Sexual promiscuity: and women's public roles, 5; and prostitution, 100; and saloons, 116; and hereditary degeneration, 126
Sexual relations: adult-child, 135; male-male, 135
Shaw, Anna Howard, 247
Shaw, Madame, 91
Sheldon, David, 109
Shumsky, Neil Larry, 160
Sister Magdalenes, 210
Sisters of Mercy, 90, 155, 196
Sisters of Our Lady of Charity of Refuge, 190–91
Sisters of the Good Shepherd, 186, 188, 195–96, 210, 212, 277 (n. 11)
Sklar, Kathryn Kish, 62
Slate House Hotel, 172–74, 222–23, 225, 236, 241
Slaves and slavery, 8, 36–37, 100
Smith, Julia Homes, 39, 41
Smith, Samuel F., Jr., 178, 183–84, 247–48, 275 (n. 53)
Smith, Samuel F., Sr., 183
Socialism, 12, 235
Social mobility, 36–37, 38, 72
Social policy: and gender and crime, 123–24; trans-Atlantic debates on, 161, 170

Social Purity Department, WCTU, 134–35
Social services, 107
Society of Friends, 189
Spencer, Herbert, 39
Spokane, Wa., 182–83
Standard Theater, 231, 232
Stansell, Christine, 135
Stanton, Elizabeth Cady, 40
Stapleton, Fannie, 256
Status offenses, 22–23
Stead, W. T., 132, 134, 136, 138, 145, 183
Streckfus, John, 149
Strikes, 32, 33, 94
Sudlow, Phebe, 108–9, 110
Suffrage amendment, and Iowa General Assembly, 43, 246–47
Surveillance, 207–8, 279 (n. 54)
Swain, Bertha, 95
Sweet, Ada, 38, 39
Syphilis, 156, 164, 180

Teaching: and women's employment, 41, 264–65 (n. 25); feminization of, 43; and McCowen, 57, 59, 60–61; and women's wages, 61, 69; and Bickford, 64; and Working Woman's Lend a Hand club, 68, 253
Teller, Ella, 231
Temperance movement, 4. *See also* Woman's Christian Temperance Union (WCTU)
Temple, John, 174, 175
Theaters: and prostitutes, 53, 228; and Prohibition, 110; and women's employment, 214, 228–29, 231, 232, 236, 237–41, 243; and Woodward, 225–26, 229, 231, 232, 237, 238, 241; and Bucktown, 227, 228–29, 231–32, 237, 241, 254
Thiry, Jean Hubert, 164, 170
Thomas, Richard, 18–19, 20
Thompson, Margaret A., 70, 76–77, 110
Timothy, Buck, 148
Toher, Harry, 221
Tomlin, James, 112, 123, 130
Transience, and prostitution, 81
Travel, gender barriers to, 60, 64
Tuberculosis, 180
Turkish Baths, 174, 176

Turner Hall, 13, 227, 241, 250
Turner Society, 248
Twain, Mark, 10

Union Pacific railroad, 10
Unions: and wages, 31–34; women as members of, 32, 33; and domestic sphere, 32, 37; women's labor associations, 46
U.S. Senate, 42
Universalists, 34
University of Iowa, 61, 63, 77, 109, 164, 246, 265 (n. 28)
Unmarried women, status of, 30–31
Upper Mississippi Valley, 10
Urbanization, 52–53
Urban life: in midsized cities, 9; and women's employment, 12; and etiquette, 207
Urban parks, 53
Urban space: and gendered geography, 52–53, 104, 116–17, 234; and prostitution, 80, 101, 103, 104, 110, 120; and police matron campaign, 110–11; and middle-class women, 130; and respectability, 214

Vagrancy: and prostitution, 5, 7, 90, 96, 154, 155, 195, 196, 198, 199, 202; as status offense, 22–23; and press, 79; and fines, 192; and working women in Bucktown, 240
Van Ness, Madam, 152
Venereal disease: and regulation of prostitution, 161, 164, 168, 173, 179, 180, 218; and private reformatories, 189, 197
Vice districts, 26, 27, 29
Violence: brothels associated with, 18; and regulation of prostitution, 221
Vollmer, Fred, 198
Vollmer, Henry: and regulation of prostitution, 160–61, 164, 168, 171, 173, 178–80, 181, 184, 187, 213, 214–15, 220, 243, 248; and Scott County Medical Society, 168–72, 178; and assignation houses, 173, 174
Vollmer, Jessie Peck, 164, 190, 191

Wadsworth Mottoes, 66–68
Wage-earning class, 37, 38

Index

Wailoo, Keith, 180
Walker, Belle. *See* Armstrong, Rachel
Walker, Charles, 15, 258
Wardner, Louise Rockwood, 126
Warren, John, 16
Washburn, Josie, 153, 215, 236
Washington Gardens, 12
Waterman, Charles, 113
Weaver, S. M., 20
Webb, Edward, 93, 95, 226
Webb, Emma. *See* Woodward, Emma Webb
Webb, Frank, 93
Webb, John, 93
Welcher, Mary E., 110, 113, 121, 127–28
Welcher, Thomas, 145, 148
White, W. K., 145, 150
White slavery: and women's employment, 8–9, 105, 237–38, 239; and prostitution, 257
White Slave Traffic Act, 8, 257
Whitty, Mike, 86
Wiley, John, 84
Wiley, John (son), 84, 85
Wiley, Margaret Fowler, 84, 85
Wilkinson, George, 18
Willard, Frances, 42, 130, 134
Williams, Gus, 228
Wilson, Grace, 172, 173
Wittig, Emilie, 76, 80
Wittig, Emma, 70
Wittig, Meta, 76, 80, 239
Woman-run businesses, 25–26, 28, 41–42, 50, 72, 74–75, 218–26, 243
Woman's Christian Temperance Union (WCTU): and Prohibition and Home Protection Party, 3, 4; and women's public role, 4; and prostitution, 16; membership of, 42; and police matrons, 104; and Charitable Alliance, 105, 130; and separate spheres, 107; and child prostitutes, 134; and suppression of prostitution, 159; and private reformatories, 189
Woman's clubs, and working women, 46–47, 65
Woman's Congress of the AAW, 47
Woman's Exchange, 73–74, 255
Woman's Rights Convention, 257
Woman's rights movement, 38

Woman's self-support: and respectability, 16, 28; and Alcott, 31; and Women's Educational and Industrial Union, 35–36; and Association for the Advancement of Women, 39, 243, 255; and woman-owned businesses, 41; barriers to, 42; and McCowen, 43, 44; and woman's clubs, 47; and woman's work for woman, 49; and Working Woman's Lend a Hand club, 66, 70, 77, 243, 255; and Charitable Alliance, 109; and Good Shepherd Homes, 205, 206
Woman suffrage movement: and Lockwood, 4; and black suffrage, 5; and German immigration, 12; and women's natural rights, 40; and Fifteenth Amendment, 60; and politics, 103; and woman's self-support, 243; and McCowen, 246; success of, 257, 258
"Woman's work for women," 49
Women professionals: and gendered geography, 28; and benevolent organizations, 35; and Association for the Advancement of Women, 42; and Working Woman's Lend a Hand club, 68; and woman suffrage, 247
Women's Alliance. *See* Charitable Alliance
Women's Educational and Industrial Union (WEIU), 35–36
Women's employment: prostitution associated with, 7, 8, 9, 16, 17, 28, 29, 31, 255; and respectability, 7, 9, 16–17, 20, 40, 53–54, 74, 256; and Association for the Advancement of Women, 7, 17, 36, 38–39, 40–44; and gendered geography, 7, 28, 53, 117, 256; political meaning of, 7–8, 39–42, 255; and white slavery, 8–9, 105, 237–38, 239; and urban life, 12; and Civil War, 30; and citizenship, 31, 38, 40; and isolation, 32, 34, 40, 41; and benevolent organizations, 34–36; and opportunity, 40–41; statistics on, 43–46; expansion of, 44; and woman's work for women, 49; casual market for, 65; and education, 71; and theaters, 214, 228–29, 231, 232, 236, 237–39, 237–41, 243; and prostitutes as percentage of workforce, 217, 280 (n. 7)

320

Women's independence: and women's wages, 31, 38–39; and Association for the Advancement of Women, 36; and democracy, 40

Women's leisure, and household labor, 37

Women's organizations: benevolent organizations, 34–36; and separatism, 47; and suppression of prostitution, 159; and regulation of prostitution, 162, 171, 172, 248; and mulct law, 253; and McCowen Hall, 254

Women's Prison Association, 120

Women's public roles: and Prohibition, 3, 4; and men's cross-dressing, 4–5, 6; and gender hierarchies, 6; and women's employment, 9; and respectability, 28; and prostitution, 81; and regulation of prostitution, 171, 172. *See also* Politics; Public policy

Women's Relief Corps of the Grand Army of the Republic, 38, 59

Women's wages: and women's employment, 8, 16, 17, 28, 40, 69, 256; and women's independence, 31, 38–39; and union wages, 31–34; and woman-owned businesses, 41; discrepancy in relation to men, 45–46, 236, 237; and teaching, 61, 69; and Working Woman's Lend a Hand club, 71, 237

Wood, Della, 133, 144, 147–48, 152, 154, 211

Woodhull, Victoria, 5

Woodruff, George, 91

Woods, Al, 177

Woods, Anna, 140, 148

Woods, Mamie, 132, 133, 136–44, 147–48, 150, 151, 154–56, 187

Woodward, Emma Webb: profile of, 93–95; and boarders, 98, 146; marriages of, 100; arrest of, 158; and brothels, 224–25, 238; and Iowa Theater, 225–26, 229, 231, 232, 237, 238, 241

Woodward, Henry Clay, 224–26, 229, 231, 232, 237, 238, 241

Woodward, William G., 23

Working-class men: and saloons, 52; and sexual gratification, 136; and dance halls, 235

Working-class women: and respectability, 7, 28, 53, 117; and benevolent organizations, 35; and women's employment, 40; and gendered geography, 130; and assignation houses, 174, 176; and dance halls, 234, 235; and Bucktown, 240, 241

Working girls' clubs, 35, 36, 46, 50, 70, 71, 255, 257

Working Woman's Lend a Hand club: organizers of, 50, 54–56, 64, 65; purpose of, 50–51, 77, 78, 254, 255; club rooms of, 51–54, 69–70, 77, 80, 253–54; and Wadsworth Mottoes, 66–68; members of, 68–70, 253; programs of, 70–77, 78, 237, 239, 253; and location of prostitutes, 80; and Ackley House arrests, 103; and Charitable Alliance, 105, 109, 110; and Bucktown, 213–14, 254; and mock election of 1900, 245–46; and woman suffrage, 246, 247–48; building of, 257–58

Wulf, Fred, 25

York, Jennie, 235

Young, Mrs. J. B., 110

Young Women's Christian Associations (YWCAs), 34–35, 36, 38, 42, 46, 71, 255, 257, 258

Youth culture, 10, 234

Zakrzewska, Marie, 42

Zoning, and prostitution, 16, 160, 243

Gender and American Culture

The Freedom of the Streets: Work, Citizenship, and Sexuality in a Gilded Age City, by Sharon E. Wood (2005).

Home on the Rails: Women, the Railroad, and the Rise of Public Domesticity, by Amy G. Richter (2005).

Worrying the Line: Black Women Writers, Lineage, and Literary Tradition, by Cheryl A. Wall (2005).

From Welfare to Workfare: The Unintended Consequences of Liberal Reform, 1945–1965, by Jennifer Mittelstadt (2005).

Choice and Coercion: Birth Control, Sterilization, and Abortion in Public Health and Welfare, by Johanna Schoen (2005).

Closer to Freedom: Enslaved Women and Everyday Resistance in the Plantation South, by Stephanie M. H. Camp (2004).

Masterful Women: Slaveholding Widows from the American Revolution through the Civil War, by Kirsten E. Wood (2004).

Manliness and Its Discontents: The Black Middle Class and the Transformation of Masculinity, 1900–1930, by Martin Summers (2004).

Citizen, Mother, Worker: Debating Public Responsibility for Child Care after the Second World War, by Emilie Stoltzfus (2003).

Women and the Historical Enterprise in America: Gender, Race, and the Politics of Memory, 1880–1945, by Julie Des Jardins (2003).

Free Hearts and Free Homes: Gender and American Antislavery Politics, by Michael D. Pierson (2003).

Ella Baker and the Black Freedom Movement: A Radical Democratic Vision, by Barbara Ransby (2003).

Signatures of Citizenship: Petitioning, Antislavery, and Women's Political Identity, by Susan Zaeske (2003).

Love on the Rocks: Men, Women, and Alcohol in Post–World War II America, by Lori Rotskoff (2002).

The Veiled Garvey: The Life and Times of Amy Jacques Garvey, by Ula Yvette Taylor (2002).

Working Cures: Health, Healing, and Power on Southern Slave Plantations, by Sharla Fett (2002).

Southern History across the Color Line, by Nell Irvin Painter (2002).

The Artistry of Anger: Black and White Women's Literature in America, 1820–1860, by Linda M. Grasso (2002).

Too Much to Ask: Black Women in the Era of Integration, by Elizabeth Higginbotham (2001).

Imagining Medea: Rhodessa Jones and Theater for Incarcerated Women, by Rena Fraden (2001).

Painting Professionals: Women Artists and the Development of Modern American Art, 1870–1920, by Kirsten Swinth (2001).

Remaking Respectability: African American Women in Interwar Detroit, by Victoria W. Wolcott (2001).

Ida B. Wells-Barnett and American Reform, 1880–1930, by Patricia A. Schechter (2001).

Taking Haiti: Military Occupation and the Culture of U.S. Imperialism, 1915–1940, by Mary A. Renda (2001).

Before Jim Crow: The Politics of Race in Postemancipation Virginia, by Jane Dailey (2000).

Captain Ahab Had a Wife: New England Women and the Whalefishery, 1720–1870, by Lisa Norling (2000).

Civilizing Capitalism: The National Consumers' League, Women's Activism, and Labor Standards in the New Deal Era, by Landon R. Y. Storrs (2000).

Rank Ladies: Gender and Cultural Hierarchy in American Vaudeville, by M. Alison Kibler (1999).

Strangers and Pilgrims: Female Preaching in America, 1740–1845, by Catherine A. Brekus (1998).

Sex and Citizenship in Antebellum America, by Nancy Isenberg (1998).

Yours in Sisterhood: Ms. Magazine and the Promise of Popular Feminism, by Amy Erdman Farrell (1998).

We Mean to Be Counted: White Women and Politics in Antebellum Virginia, by Elizabeth R. Varon (1998).

Women Against the Good War: Conscientious Objection and Gender on the American Home Front, 1941–1947, by Rachel Waltner Goossen (1997).

Toward an Intellectual History of Women: Essays by Linda K. Kerber (1997).

Gender and Jim Crow: Women and the Politics of White Supremacy in North Carolina, 1896–1920, by Glenda Elizabeth Gilmore (1996).

Delinquent Daughters: Protecting and Policing Adolescent Female Sexuality in the United States, 1885–1920, by Mary E. Odem (1995).

U.S. History as Women's History: New Feminist Essays, edited by Linda K. Kerber, Alice Kessler-Harris, and Kathryn Kish Sklar (1995).

Common Sense and a Little Fire: Women and Working-Class Politics in the United States, 1900–1965, by Annelise Orleck (1995).

How Am I to Be Heard?: Letters of Lillian Smith, edited by Margaret Rose Gladney (1993).

Entitled to Power: Farm Women and Technology, 1913–1963, by Katherine Jellison (1993).

Revising Life: Sylvia Plath's Ariel Poems, by Susan R. Van Dyne (1993).

Made From This Earth: American Women and Nature, by Vera Norwood (1993).

Unruly Women: The Politics of Social and Sexual Control in the Old South, by Victoria E. Bynum (1992).

The Work of Self-Representation: Lyric Poetry in Colonial New England, by Ivy Schweitzer (1991).

Labor and Desire: Women's Revolutionary Fiction in Depression America, by Paula Rabinowitz (1991).

Community of Suffering and Struggle: Women, Men, and the Labor Movement in Minneapolis, 1915–1945, by Elizabeth Faue (1991).

All That Hollywood Allows: Re-reading Gender in 1950s Melodrama, by Jackie Byars (1991).

Doing Literary Business: American Women Writers in the Nineteenth Century, by Susan Coultrap-McQuin (1990).

Ladies, Women, and Wenches: Choice and Constraint in Antebellum Charleston and Boston, by Jane H. Pease and William H. Pease (1990).

The Secret Eye: The Journal of Ella Gertrude Clanton Thomas, 1848–1889, edited by Virginia Ingraham Burr, with an introduction by Nell Irvin Painter (1990).

Second Stories: The Politics of Language, Form, and Gender in Early American Fictions, by Cynthia S. Jordan (1989).

Within the Plantation Household: Black and White Women of the Old South, by Elizabeth Fox-Genovese (1988).

The Limits of Sisterhood: The Beecher Sisters on Women's Rights and Woman's Sphere, by Jeanne Boydston, Mary Kelley, and Anne Margolis (1988).

www.ingramcontent.com/pod-product-compliance
Lightning Source LLC
Chambersburg PA
CBHW030106010526
44116CB00005B/117